People and Places of Nature and Culture

Also by Rod Giblett

The Body of Nature and Culture
Forrestdale: People and Place
Health Recovery: The Taoist Tai Chi™ *Way*
Landscapes of Culture and Nature
Postmodern Wetlands: Culture, History, Ecology
Sublime Communication Technologies

Cultural Studies of Natures, Landscapes and Environments

Series Editors: Rod Giblett, Warwick Mules and Emily Potter

Coming out of Cultural Studies, this series examines nature as the largely forgotten other of culture. It also considers landscapes and the environment, as well as the political, economic, semiotic, philosophical and psychological dimensions of all three terms. Firmly placed in the tradition of cultural studies of nature and landscape begun by Raymond Williams and continued by Alexander Wilson and others, it will publish interdisciplinary work that draws on established approaches within Cultural Studies, as well as developing new ones. It will make a unique and vital contribution not only to academic enquiry but also to new ways of thinking, being and living with the earth. The series will be of interest to a wide range of theorists and practitioners who are seeking directions out of, and solutions to, our current environmental and cultural malaise.

People and Places of Nature and Culture

Rod Giblett

intellect Bristol, UK / Chicago, USA

Dedicated to David McKie

First published in the UK in 2011 by
Intellect, The Mill, Parnall Road, Fishponds, Bristol, BS16 3JG, UK

First published in the USA in 2011 by
Intellect, The University of Chicago Press, 1427 E. 60th Street,
Chicago, IL 60637, USA

Copyright © 2011 Intellect Ltd

All rights reserved. No part of this publication may be reproduced, stored in a retrieval system, or transmitted, in any form or by any means, electronic, mechanical, photocopying, recording, or otherwise, without written permission.

A catalogue record for this book is available from the
British Library.

Cover designer: Holly Rose
Copy-editor: Michael Eckhardt
Typesetting: Mac Style, Beverley, E. Yorkshire

ISBN 978-1-84150-401-8

Contents

Acknowledgments	7
Preface: From Sustainability to Symbiosis	9
PART I: Cultural Nature	13
Chapter 1: The Nature of Natures and the Cultures of Natures	19
Chapter 2: Is the Public Sphere to the Biosphere as Culture is to Nature (as Male is to Female)?	39
PART II: Landscape Aesthetics	57
Chapter 3: Nature's Fairest Forms: Aesthetics of Nature	61
Chapter 4: Pleasing Prospects Revista'd: The Gentleman's Park Estate	77
PART III: Colonial Country	95
Chapter 5: Home in the Wilds: Wild(er)ness as a Cultural Category	99
Chapter 6: Riding Roughshod Over It: Mateship Against the Bush	117
PART IV: National Parklands	135
Chapter 7: Nature Sanctuarized: 'Our' National Parks as Modern Cathedrals	139
Chapter 8: Sites and Rights of Enjoyment: Nature and Native Title in National Parks	157

PART V: Industrial Land Use	177
Chapter 9: Eating Earth: Mining and Gluttony	181
Chapter 10: Kings in Kimberley Watercourses and Wetlands: Sadism and Pastoralism	199
PART VI: Land Symbiotics	217
Chapter 11: 'We are the Land Ourselves': Aboriginal Country is a Cultural Landscape	211
Chapter 12: Home is Here: Livelihood, Bioregion and Symbiosis	237
References	259
Index	275

Acknowledgments

The dedication of this book to David McKie is a small token of gratitude for his support and efforts on my behalf during the most difficult and trying period of my life. I would also like to give a special thanks to Anne Brewster and Jon Stratton for their friendship and support during this period. David is a leading postmodern ecologist and a pioneering proponent of a green Cultural Studies, as he demonstrated in the book he wrote with Tom Jagtenberg, *Eco-Impacts and the Greening of Postmodernity* (Sage, 1997). Major intellectual and political debts are also owed to four other postmodern ecologists: Felix Guattari, Michel Serres, Raymond Williams and Alexander Wilson.

This book has had a long period of gestation all through the Nineties and Noughties amounting to twenty-one years. Publication thus marks its coming of age and the achievement of its majority (and hopefully adulthood). During this period a large number of people have contributed advice, comments and suggestions for which I am immensely grateful. Naturally (or culturally) I am responsible for what follows. Various chapters have also been presented and/or published previously. The first part of Chapter 2 was presented as a paper at the Cultural Studies Association of Australia Conference at Fremantle, Australia in December 1996 and was later published in *Continuum* 11: 3 (1997: 74–84). I would like to acknowledge the assistance of Geoff Craig and Wendy Parkins in suggesting readings for this chapter and an anonymous referee for *Continuum* for his/her helpful comments and suggestions on the version presented at the CSAA Conference, especially for pointing out the pertinence of Hannah Arendt's *Human Condition*. An earlier and longer version of the remainder of this chapter was published as a review article entitled 'Going Green' in *Continuum* 11: 2 (1997: 128–139).

I gratefully acknowledge Zoë Sofoulis' work as the basis for Chapter 9. Without Zoë's generous sharing of her ideas and her writings, this chapter would not have been possible, nor would I have read Melanie Klein's work when I did without her advocacy of it. I would also like to thank her for her helpful comments on earlier versions. Furthermore, I would also like to acknowledge the stimulating comments of the 'Moving the Boundaries' seminar series in Fremantle at which a longer and earlier version of this chapter was presented. A shorter version was presented at, and published under the title of 'Terraphagy and the Politics of Mining' in the proceedings of the Third International Conference on Environmental

Issues and Waste Management in Energy and Mineral Production, Perth, Western Australia, August 1994.

Early versions of Chapters 3, 7 and 10 were presented as work-in-progress research seminars to staff and postgraduate students in the School of Communication and Cultural Studies at Curtin University of Technology. I am grateful for the opportunity to present my work. I am also grateful to Peter Hutchinson of the National Native Title Tribunal for his helpful comments on Chapter 7. Chapter 10 was first published in *Span 36: 2* (1993: 541–559), and then reprinted in Hugh Webb's and my co-edited collection, *Western Australian Wetlands: The Kimberley and South-West* (Perth, Western Australia: Black Swan Press/Wetlands Conservation Society, 1996). Much of Chapter 11 was presented in a plenary session of the International Australian Studies Association conference on 'Country' held at the University of Queensland, Ipswich Campus in July 2000. I am grateful to the organisers for their invitation to attend, especially Leigh Dale. I am grateful to Hugh Webb for reading Chapter 11 in its entirety and for his re-assuring endorsement that 'I would not change a word'. The first two sections of Chapter 12 were presented as a paper at the Habitus 2000 Conference at Curtin University of Technology in September 2000 and published in the proceedings. The third section of Chapter 3 was presented at the 'Imaging Nature' Conference on Cradle Mountain in Tasmania in June 2004. I am grateful to Libby Lester for giving me the opportunity to do so.

Early versions of some other parts of this book were presented at Curtin University of Technology, both in the School of Communication and Cultural Studies and in the Research Institute for Cultural Heritage, and at Edith Cowan University, both in the School of Communications and Multimedia (now Arts) and in the Centre for Ecosystem Management. I am grateful to all those colleagues and students who made critical comments over the past twenty or so years, especially Catherine Beche-Mathison for pointing out the difficulties with understanding an earlier presentation of the 'two paradigms' in Figure 2. I hope I have now clearly presented this set of distinctions.

David McKie, John Kinsella, Ian Saunders and Warwick Mules all read the manuscript and made valuable comments and suggestions for which I am grateful, as I am for the continued friendship and support of my current colleagues in the School of Communications and Arts at Edith Cowan University. An anonymous referee for Intellect Books made a number of helpful comments and suggestions to which I have responded and for which I am grateful. I am also grateful for some financial support from the Centre for Research, Entertainment, Arts, Technology, Education and Communications (CREATEC) at ECU that assisted with marketing and publicity.

Preface: From Sustainability to Symbiosis

Developing a better relationship between humans and the earth, people and place, culture and nature is vital for trying to achieve environmental sustainability in the age of climate change and national disasters. Yet the concept of the environment not only implies separation between humans and the earth, but also a relationship of mastery over, and enslaving of, the earth. By the earth I mean ambiguously both soil and the planet. To be more precise, I am referring to the planet as (partly) soil and as (wholly) living (not a lump of dead matter orbiting in space). A master-slave relationship between humans and the earth is hardly sustainable, especially if sustainability is defined simply as 'enough for all forever', and if 'all' includes all creatures of the earth, not just humans. The slave, by definition, does not have enough. Enslavement takes those who had enough and makes them the property of those who had enough, but end up with more by virtue (or more precisely, vice) of having slaves – who ends up with less than enough. Rather than environmental sustainability, a more intimate and reciprocal relationship of mutuality with the earth means providing enough for all, including humans and other creatures on the earth, and the earth itself, forever. Social justice entails mutuality with the earth, and vice versa, where the social is the community of all beings. Mutuality with the earth involves what this book calls bio- and psycho-symbiotic livelihoods in bioregional home-habitats of the living earth.

One of the most powerful ways in which mastery over the earth is exercised is via the discourses of nature. I define discourses as institutionalized ways of seeing, saying and doing. Discourses of nature include: 'the environment' that separates a subject from its environs, and produces a master-slave relationship between them; natural history that objectifies nature in taxonomic grids, and sets up a subject-object relationship between natural historian and nature; resource extraction that sadistically takes good things from nature in the form of commodities and returns bad things to it in pollutants and wastes; scientific ecology that colonizes nature and relegates the machinations of the earth-household to a secluded feminine sphere; political economy that treats nature as a common source of free goods; nature aesthetics (beauty, picturesqueness and sublimity) that aestheticizes nature in the surface of landscape and that valourizes the sense of sight and denigrates the others; monumentalism and sanctuarism that preserve bits of nature in national parks or wilderness zones, and exploit the rest; and resource extraction that commodifies nature wherever it can everywhere.

The main priority of sanctuarism is the preservation of species and ecosystems. Whilst this is certainly important in the face of declining biodiversity and degraded habitats in the age of climate change and hyper-capitalism, a richer appreciation of the world we human beings live in is necessary to make the earth a more habitable place for all living beings. Mutuality with the earth involves what I call bio- and psycho-symbiotic livelihoods in bioregional home-habitats of the living earth. This is a much more intimate and mutually beneficial relationship with the earth than 'environmental sustainability'. In *People and Places of Nature and Culture* I propose what Oelschlaeger (1991: 160 and 474) and others call 'sacrality' as the counter and complement to sanctuarism, and argue for a shift in emphasis from the latter to the former. Sacrality and mutuality embrace a broader sense of local and global space and place imbued with *significance* whose boundary is the ecosphere rather than just the biosphere. *Significance* is Julia Kristeva's (1984: 17) term for embodied, nonsensical and playful processes of cultural production. The ecosphere includes bioregions and home-habitats, as well as cities and communications in the electromagnetosphere (or 'spectrum') and orbital extra-terrestrial space (see Giblett 2008b).

One of the central ways in which humans relate to the earth is through work. Work is the means by which human life is sustained by the earth. In *People and Places of Nature and Culture* I argue that the concepts and categories of 'the environment', natural history, scientific ecology, landscape aesthetics and their associated practices in conservation landscapes and industrial land-use work-over (if not overwork) nature (defined simply as a collective noun for land, living beings, air, water, energy and planetary motion). By contrast, Australian Aboriginal Country, conservation counter-aesthetics and symbiotic livelihoods in a bioregional home-habitat work (with) the earth as living being. Instead of nature aesthetics and conservation landscapes that privilege some sites over others, and the sense of sight over the others, *People and Places of Nature and Culture* advocates a conservation counter-aesthetics that appreciates and values all places and senses. Instead of modern, scientific ecology and political economy separated from each other on either side of the nature/culture divide, the book proposes a participatory, postmodern political ecology that promotes mutuality in the earth-household of the ecosphere. Instead of institutionalised ways of seeing, saying and doing in relation to nature, it calls for a way of being and living exemplified in Aboriginal Country (and as addressed in Chapter 11 of this book).

Nature is a problematic term, and a number of competing definitions and discourses of it struggle for hegemony. Nature has been split between the first nature of indigenous cultures and the second nature of 'agri-urban' cultures. Whilst the latter constructs a subject-object distinction and relationship between people and the earth, the former is predicated on an inter-subjective, even mutually abjective, relationship. 'Abject' is Julia Kristeva's (1982: 1–2) term for the mediating category between subject and object that makes both possible. The subject-object relationship is evident in natural history, modern scientific ecology, nature aesthetics and landscape gardening, as well as in nature conservation in national parks and wilderness areas, and nature exploitation in industrial land-use. Abjects are to be found in Aboriginal Country and in bioregional and symbiotic livelihood.

Preface: From Sustainability to Symbiosis

This split between first and second nature is gendered; nature has a gendered construction. Not only has nature been feminized, but it has been feminized in two contradictory ways: first, as the life-giving and death-dealing Great Mother, or Great Goddess, associated with the swamps; and, secondly, as the benign and malign Mother Earth or Mother Nature affiliated with the fields. Culture likewise has been split between matrifocal and gylanic cultures in which the sexes were equal, and patriarchal and hierarchical cultures in which men are dominant. Culture is defined simply as a collective noun for arts and crafts (including horticultural, hunting, gathering, building dwellings, culinary, decorative and other domestic arts, and crafts), language and writing (as both trace and inscription), ritual and exchange. Both of these splits between matrifocal and gylanic cultures and between the Great Mother and Mother Earth have been mapped over each other. Split culture equates with split nature: matrifocal and gylanic cultures are associated with the Great Mother, or Great Goddess, whereas hierarchical and patriarchal cultures are aligned with the Mother Earth or Mother Nature. Split culture and nature cut across and deconstruct a simplistic distinction and unresolved binary opposition between culture and nature.

The benign and malign Mother Earth or Mother Nature is also affiliated and aligned with the European landscape aesthetic in which the surface of the land is an object of visual consumption and pleasure, and the depths of the land are either an object of exploitation in production or an abject of repression, as has occurred with wetlands as I argue in *Postmodern Wetlands: Culture, History, Ecology* (Giblett 1996). The European landscape aesthetic, in turn, produced the ways in which Europeans and their settler Diasporas in Australia and the United States saw and shaped the land through the perceptions and practices of the gentleman's park (and suburban enclave) estate, national parks and wilderness, mining and pastoralism, and the 'Bush' of Australian mateship. The seven central chapters (4–10) of *People and Places of Nature and Culture* critique these culturally constructed, consumed and/or conserved 'natural' landscapes for their will to mastery over the earth.

Mastery over the earth culminates in industrial land-use. In order to promote eco-mental health, in Chapters 9 and 10 I undertake an ecological psychoanalysis of the investments of desire and capital, yields of pleasure and profit, and relations of power and work in the mining and pastoral industries. I argue for a move away from an emphasis on resource-exploitation, or greed and gluttony, to a relationship of gratitude for generosity, of respect for, reciprocity with, and restoration of the earth. In more psychoanalytic terms, these two chapters critique the oral and anal sadism of industrial land use in the mining and pastoral industries, and promote eco-mental health.

The final chapter of *People and Places of Nature and Culture* also uses psychoanalytic terms to celebrate a desire for, and the pleasures of, dialogue and mutuality with the living earth in bio- and psycho-symbiosis in bioregional home-habitats of the living earth. The psychoanalytic ecology, participatory ecology and postmodern ecology developed throughout the book address the personal, political, corporeal, cultural and historical dimensions – the psychodynamics, economics, semiotics and symbiotics – of our relationship with the living earth at the local, regional and global levels and at the micro- and macro-scales. These ecologies are developed, illustrated and elaborated by reference to a wide range of British, American and Australian people, and places of nature and culture.[1]

Postmodern Wetlands: Culture, History, Ecology focussed, as the title and subtitle suggest, on a specific landform and on issues surrounding it. *People and Places of Nature and Culture*, by contrast, focuses on a range of landscapes and issues surrounding them. Although the scope of the book is broad and its range extensive, it has clear spatial, temporal and conceptual parameters. The geographical trajectory traced here is from the European centre to the colonial periphery, from home to the unhomely, from the pastoral landscape of the gentleman's park estate at home and abroad in the pastoralist industry in the colonies and latterly in the entry statements of the enclave estates (both impacting fatally on the indigenous wetlands and woodlands of so-called 'postcolonial' societies) to the 'primitive wilderness' of indigenous peoples (and their conjuncture and clash).

A similar historical story is told beginning with the Ancient Greek idea of nature as living organism and the modern European concept/metaphor of nature as dead machine, through modern European landscape aesthetics of the sublime in vertiginous forms and the picturesque in the 'pleasing prospects' of the gentleman's park estate, through their exploratory and colonising Diasporas that saw and/or shaped the land in accordance with the European model, to the settler and industrial landscapes of national parks, wilderness, Australian bush, mining and pastoralism. Not only space (or more precisely three-dimensional, Euclidean space), but also time (or more precisely linear, chronological time) have been mastered through the enclosure and colonisation of pre-history, of the past, and foreclosure and colonisation of the future as implied by the double spatial and temporal meaning of 'prospect'. History has colonized pre- and pro-history.

A countervailing conceptual and temporal circle is traced in *People and Places of Nature and Culture* from nature as living organism, through nature as dead matter, back to the living earth; from the discourses (scientific and aesthetic) and economics (agricultural and industrial capitalist) of mastery to the practices of mutuality; from oral and anal sadism to bio- and psycho-symbiosis; from the cultural construction and discourse of nature as a way of seeing, saying and doing to Aboriginal Country as a way of being; from the rural, colonial, national and industrial to the indigenous, bioregional and eco-spherical; from European city to Aboriginal Country; from history to pre-history; from timeline to time-circle; from Mother Nature to the Great Goddess; from sanctuarism to sacrality; from cultural nature to living earth; from landscape to land symbiotics; from mastery to mutuality; from sustainability to symbiosis.

Forrestdale, 1989–2010

Note

1. The 'Asian wisdom traditions' pertinent to this topic are excluded from consideration herein not only for reasons of space but also because I discuss Taoist ecology and the Taoist body of the earth elsewhere (see Giblett 2008a: Chapters 10 and 11).

Part I

Cultural Nature

'Nature' (with scare quotes) is a cultural category for Paul Hirst and Penny Woolley (1982: 160). As a cultural category, nature (with or without scare quotes) has a history and a politics. Chapter 1 begins by tracing the history of the cultural category of nature and critiquing its politics. Cicero (first century BCE) drew the distinction between the first nature of the natural world and the second nature of the human world of herding, tilling, mining, forging and building. Second nature works over first nature. Yet second nature is cultural, a 'culture of nature'. And first nature in Cicero's terms is partly the first 'culture of nature' of first peoples. Yet rather than one 'culture of nature' as Alexander Wilson (1992) seemed to imply or suggest in the title of his classic study, *The Culture of Nature*, a number of cultures of nature struggle for hegemony, including the third culture of nature of modernity and industrial technologies, and the fourth culture of nature of hypermodernity and communication technologies.

The Renaissance (c.1400–1600CE) was pivotal for the transition from second to third nature and culture. During this period mercantile capitalism developed the view of nature as machine, as dead matter, in contrast with the ancient Greeks (c.700–300BCE) for whom nature (*phusis*) is living organism. The view of nature as machine became dominant in modernity (c.1600CE–). If nature was machine then natural history was mechanical engineering that theorized its workings, taxonomized its parts and took it apart to find out how it works. Mercantile technology put the machine of nature back together and made it work faster and more productively. Natural history objectified nature in what Michel Foucault calls 'the discourse of nature'. It also set up a subject position for the natural historian to exercize power over nature by producing scientific knowledge about it. Yet rather than natural history being the one and only discourse of nature as Foucault suggests, a number of competing discourses of nature, such as scientific ecology and landscape aesthetics, operate in a network of power/knowledge relations and vie for hegemony through various nefarious alliances of class, gender and ethnic interests over others.

Industrial capitalism (c.1750–) inherited the view of nature as machine, but then went on to make the machine of nature work even faster and more productively for its own ends. Nature was explored, colonized and exploited by capitalists and imperialists alike in cahoots with each other. These processes were tied up with and underpinned by the feminisation of nature. Yet whereas traditional societies had valued nature as female in reverential rites, industrial capitalism denigrated nature as female in misogynist terms. Feminisation of nature per se is not so much a problem politically and culturally as *how* nature is feminized: whether it is as the matrifocal and implacable, life-giving and death-dealing Great Goddess of the slimy swamps, or as the benign and malignant Mother Earth of patriarchal agriculture and industrial capitalism.

Patriarchal masculinity split feminized nature into virgin land ready for penetration by agriculture and mining associated with Mother Earth, or Mother Nature, and cloacal swamps, fascinating and horrific, affiliated with the Great Goddess or Great Mother. Patriarchal capitalism sexualized the machinery of nature in the virgin land of what I have called the 'pastoro-technical idyll of organic community' (see Giblett 2008b: 22). It also applied the machines of industrial capitalism to draining and filling the cloacal swamps to make them into virgin land. This chapter concludes by deconstructing and decolonising these views and practices by *pre*–historicising them. All of them do not apply in and to the figure of the Great Goddess, or Great Mother, of Old Europe (*c.* 6500–3500BCE) and of the cloacal swamps, fascinating and fertile.

The modern view mathematized nature by seeing mathematics as the master code not only of nature, but also of the relationship between culture and nature. Nature was opposed in binary terms to culture, with culture as the prime term (or 1) and nature as lack (or 0). Postmodern ecology deconstructs the binary opposition between culture and nature by demonstrating that this hierarchical, value-laden distinction is predicated on the demonisation and repression of nature as culture's 'other'. In *Postmodern Wetlands* (Giblett 1996) I applied Jacques Derrida's deconstruction to the cultural construction of wetlands as places of disease and death, horror and melancholy. Yet as wetlands have also been colonized and destroyed by mapping, enclosure, filling and draining, deconstruction needs to be complemented with decolonisation.

It is all very well to deconstruct the culture/nature binary by demonstrating that it is a hierarchical taxonomy as Derrida did in *Of Grammatology* (albeit in a limited compass around the incest taboo), but nature also needs to be decolonized. In *People and Places of Nature and Culture* I deconstruct and decolonize the discourses of nature as well as the hierarchical taxonomies that privilege culture over nature, city over country, drylands over wetlands, mountains over marshes, rivers over swamps, surface over depth.

Yet more than just deconstruction and decolonisation of discourses and hierarchical taxonomies of nature and ecological psychoanalysis of industrial land uses are needed in order to make the shift from mastery to mutuality. Arguing for an extension of an ethics and practice of land-care beyond the conservation of special places, *People and Places of Nature and Culture* maintains that earth-care should embrace the whole ecosphere, including the electromagnetosphere necessary for radio, television and telephone communication, as well as extraterrestrial space where the satellites orbit. The shift argued for here is from the sanctuarism of national parks and wilderness to the sacrality of Aboriginal Country and the living earth.

To this end, this book (and Chapter 2 in particular) develops a participatory, postmodern, political ecology drawing on the work of the French theorists and thinkers Michel de Certeau, Michel Foucault, Felix Guattari, Luce Irigaray, Julia Kristeva, Jean-François Lyotard, Michel Serres and Paul Virilio. 'A postmodern ecology' is 'post' modern scientific ecology confined to the biosphere. 'A participatory ecology' is concerned with the interaction of the public and private spheres with the biosphere. 'A postmodern, political ecology' does not consign nature to the sequestered workings of a feminized private sphere, nor does it reveal the secrets of nature and bring them into the full light of day in scientific knowledge. Rather it deconstructs and decolonizes these enlightenment metaphors of the striptease of truth by developing the holistic concept of the ecosphere. Embracing the public, private, bio- and other -ospheres (atmosphere, hydrosphere, lithosphere, etc.), the ecosphere is the social, political, biological and economic earth-household in which all human beings live and depend upon for our livelihood and very life. It also embraces the electromagnetosphere and the geo-stationary orbitosphere, both of which are required for the techosphere of modern communication.

A participatory, postmodern, political ecology has a number of other features, such as: deconstructing and decolonising the hierarchical privileging of the *polis* over the *oikos*, of the masculine public sphere over the feminized private sphere and biosphere; decolonising nature, including colonized regions of the human body; thinking critically about a communal sense of cultural and natural heritage; revaluing the spiritual interactions of human cultures with natural environments and earthly entities; and diagnosing the ecological symptoms in all discourses and theories (even when ecology is absent or ostensibly so). Its primary aim is earthly mutuality in the interactions between the public and private spheres and the bio- and other -ospheres that give and sustain life on this planet earth.

Chapter 1

The Nature of Natures and the Cultures of Natures

When advertisers for an enclave estate in Perth, Western Australia, use a photograph showing a Norfolk Island pine (whose native soil is 5000 kilometres away) behind a house under construction and caption it with 'nature and home building in harmony', one cannot help agreeing with Raymond Williams (1976: 184; see also 1972: 146–164), the 'father' of both cultural studies and ecocriticism, that 'nature' is perhaps the most complex word in the English language. One cannot also help acknowledging with David Arnold (1996) the problem of nature and wondering with Kate Soper (1995) what is nature? Perhaps no other word in the English language has had to bear so much cultural, political and downright ideological baggage; perhaps no other word in the language has had to serve so many purposes from marketing mass-produced beer as 'naturally brewed' to referring to packaged honey as natural, one of which is obviously agricultural and industrial rather than natural, and the other of which is seemingly so obviously natural that it seems highly redundant to refer to 'natural honey'. The concept of 'natural honey' raises the question of what would be unnatural or synthetic honey? Honey produced by exotic bees rather than indigneous ones? Both beer and honey have been processed, and therefore human agency has been brought to bear on ingredients that may or may not be considered to be natural. Wheat, barley and honeybees are not indigenous or native to Australia – nor Norfolk Island pines for that matter to Western Australia.[1]

Second Nature

These exotic species are what Cicero in the first century, before the common era, called 'second nature'. By this he meant nature worked over and manipulated by humans, especially, in these cases, transported. For Cicero, second nature involved cultivation and agriculture, settlements and cities, weaving and sewing, mining and metallurgy. Agriculture is nature made over into second nature which occurs not only 'in the cultivation of the soil', as Cicero (1972: 184–185) put it, but also 'in the building of houses, in the weaving and sewing of our clothes and in the working of bronze and iron', all the means by which 'we seek with our human hands to create a second nature in the natural world'. They are also the means by which 'we' create a second culture in the natural world. Second nature (and culture) involves permanent dwellings, agriculture, mining of minerals and forging them into metals. These are all cultural activities that involve working over the natural world in what I call the 'cultures of natures', following and extending Wilson (1992). Second nature (and culture) is nature worked over, not simply worked like first nature (and culture), though for Cicero first nature is unworked. Second nature is a kind of living machine.

Cicero's distinction smacks of the doctrine of *terra nullius* applied most famously to Australia by Captain James Cook that denies the work of Aboriginal hunter-gatherers and nomads in working nature and in producing first nature. By placing second nature *in* the natural world, and by not making a distinction between nature and first nature, he equates hunter-gatherers and nomads with nature and so denies their work in shaping and using the land. There is a pre-human natural world to acknowledge and respect but there is also a first nature (and culture, the culture of first peoples) that is and was worked by Aboriginal people that also needs to be acknowledged and respected.

The means by which 'we' create a human world *in* the natural world are also the means by which 'we' create second nature (and culture) *on* first nature and culture. Second nature is nature worked over by patriarchal culture and made into second culture. Rather than the opposition between culture and nature (which is arguably patriarchal, colonialist and capitalist as I will try to show in Chapter 2), the crucial distinction for understanding the relationship between human beings and the earth, and achieving earthly mutuality between them, is that between the cultures of first, or worked, nature and the cultures of second, or worked-over, nature.

Yet, increasingly, human beings are living in a world dominated by communication technologies, a development that took place a long time after Cicero and that was not envisaged by him. To account for the role of communication technologies in today's world McKenzie Wark has developed the idea of 'third nature'. He argues that:

> [...] from the telegraph to telecommunications, a new geography has been overlayed on top of naure and second nature. The development of third nature overlaps the development of second nature [...] Second nature [...] is progressively overlayed with a third nature of information flows, creating an information landscape which almost totally covers the old territories. (1994: 120)

To do so, third nature (and culture) has exploited the resources of nature in, and extended the boundaries of the earth-household into, the electromagnetic spectrum and orbital extraterrestrial space. But it has done so in precisely the same terms of domination and mastery that characterized second nature (and culture), a topic I discuss in *Sublime Communication Technologies* (Giblett 2008b). First, nature (and culture) works nature; second, nature (and culture) works over nature; and third, nature (and culture) overworks nature. The development of third nature (and culture) from second nature (and culture) is one of degree rather than kind. Each of these natures and cultures entail a distinct 'culture of nature', so rather than just one 'culture of nature' there is a number of competing 'cultures of natures'.

History of Nature

Yet the rise of modernity is equally, if not more, crucial for plotting the history of nature than the development of communication technologies. Indeed, the latter is largely the product and development of the former as I argue in *Sublime Communication Technologies*, rather than a complete break. Instead of third nature (and culture) being nature overworked by communication technologies, it is nature overworked by modern mercantile, and later industrial, capitalism. The third nature (and culture) of modernity involves the development of science (especially natural history), mercantile capitalism, privatized agriculture, mass cities and later industrial technologies. In contrast with Wark, communication technologies constitute fourth, hypermodern nature (and culture). They extended the boundaries of the human world into the electromagnetosphere and orbital extraterrestrial space, created a communication network in the natural world and enabled the greater exploitation of terrestrial natural resources. Hypermodern fourth nature (and culture) hyperworks nature in speeded up, real-time communication. Hypermodern nature is also 'the new nature' of the 'feral future' in which some species 'win' and prosper in human-modified environments, whilst others 'lose' and become extinct (see Low 1999 and 2002; see Chapter 12 for a critique of the rhetoric of 'winners' and 'losers').

The major shift from first and second to third modern nature (and culture) is from nature as living organism to nature as dead machine. More recently, a fifth postmodern nature (and culture) ('post' modern third and hypermodern fourth nature [and culture]) has returned to and promoted first nature as living:

Figure 1: Five Cultures Of Nature

Culture of Nature	*Of, Characterized By*
First	First, Aboriginal Peoples; Living Organism; Worked Nature; Hunting, Gathering, 'Fire-stick Farming', Dwelling; Immediate Nature
Second	Herding, Tilling; Over-worked, Mediated Nature; Agriculture, Pastoralism, Mining, Architecture; Living Machine; Mercantile Capitalism
Third	Engineering, Industry; Worked-over, Modern, Represented Nature; Dead Machine; Industrial Capitalism
Fourth	Communication Technologies; Hyper-worked, Hyper-modern Nature; Colonisation and Commodification of the Electromagnetosphere and of Orbital, Extra-Terrestrial Space
Fifth	Postmodern Nature; Bio- and Psycho-Symbiotic Livelihoods in Bioregional Home-Habitats of the Living Earth

Postmodern nature is practiced by all those wildlife officers who juggle the competing interests of humans and other species, and try to ensure the survival of endangered, threatened, endemic and local ones (see Low 1999 and 2002). As part of its cultural history the category of nature has lived, died and been reborn. The concept of nature was invented in Ancient Greece as an organism (see Lloyd 1992: especially 20–21; and Collingwood 1945: 31 and 95), lived for fifteen hundred years, began dying over the last couple of hundred years, according to Carolyn Merchant (1980) in *The Death of Nature* and Bill McKibben (1990) in *The End of Nature,* and for Rupert Sheldrake in *The Rebirth of Nature* (1991) was reborn recently. The nature that was born, lived, died and was reborn, was the first nature (and culture) of first peoples and the second nature (and culture) of pre-modernity as Cicero construed it. The death of nature as living organism occurred with the transition to third nature (and culture).

By arguing that 'we are at the end of nature', McKibben does not mean 'we' are at 'the end of the world' (1990: 7). By 'nature' (his scare quotes) he means 'a certain set of human ideas about the world and our place in it'. The end of nature would be the end of that set of ideas. Yet 35 pages later he defines 'nature' (his scare quotes again) as 'the separate and wild province, the world apart from man [sic] to which he adapted, under whose rules he was born and died' (McKibben 1990: 43–44). These two definitions confuse concept and referent, and ignore the history of nature. They collapse the unmediated natural world and immediate first nature into mediated second culture of nature. There will always be 'a world apart from man' however much human beings change the climate through global warming and destroy that aspect of the natural world.

The death of nature for Merchant is much more specifically located historically. For her:

> [...] the new mechanical order and its associated values of power and control [...] mandate[d] the death of nature [...] The removal of animistic, organic assumptions about the cosmos constituted the death of nature – the most far-reaching effect of the Scientific Revolution of the seventeenth century. (Merchant 1980: 190 and 193)

Merchant then goes on to discuss a number of mechanistic thinkers, including Francis Bacon and René Descartes.

The scientific revolution of the seventeenth century not only troped nature as machine but also invented natural history. The beginning of the death of nature coincided with the birth of natural history: nature as living agent and vital organism began to die, or was killed outright, when nature began to be studied as dead matter and inert object. The birth of natural history occurred in roughly 1657 according to George Seddon (1997: 10), appealing to Michel Foucault, though for the latter 'this date of birth is not, of course, absolutely definitive; it is there only to symbolize a landmark' (Foucault 1970: 128). Indeed, so uncertain was Foucault about locating this landmark that he later revised the date of birth backwards some two hundred years by arguing that 'the sciences of nature [...] were born, to some extent, at the end of the Middle Ages, from the practices of investigation' (1977: 226).

For Collingwood (1945: 5 and 95), too, writing 30 years before Foucault and Merchant, 'nature as machine' is an important modern invention that he associates with the so-called Renaissance and with 'the denial that the world of nature is an organism', an assertion that it is 'devoid of both intelligence and of life', and the development of the trope of the natural world as dead machine. The rebirth of the arts and sciences in the Renaissance coincided with, and constituted, both the death of nature as organism and the birth of mercantile capitalism.

With the rise of modernity nature was produced as an object of discourse (especially in, by and initially for natural history) and the subject (in two senses) of science. Natural history, the first modern discourse of nature, produced nature as an object of scientific investigation and set up the subject position of the natural historian who investigated nature as object scientifically through observation. The discourse of nature produced a subject-object relationship with nature, both the first nature (and culture) of first peoples and the natural world. The development of what Foucault calls the 'discourse of nature' involved observation and representation ('seeing linking spontaneously with saying' in his terms) (1970: 157–162 and 135). The discourse of nature was an institutionalized way of seeing and saying the natural world, and the first nature of first peoples.

In the discourse of nature, Foucault argues, nature 'is posited only through the grid of denominations without [which] [...] it would remain mute and invisible' (1970: 160). Nature became visible and was made to speak in the discourse of nature through, and by, the denominative grid of taxonomy. The visibility of nature was also reproduced in landscape, a piece of land either viewed aesthetically or painted aesthetically. Nature was dragged dumb and inarticulate from what could be called the mutosphere into the semiosphere, and made or taught to speak like some sort of wild child. Until the seventeenth century signs in European culture, for Foucault, were 'part of things themselves [as they still are for Aboriginal Australians as we shall see in Chapter 11], whereas in the seventeenth century they became modes of representation' (1970: 129). The concept of nature from then on in European culture and its settler Diasporas represents nature (air, land, water, living beings, and so on), whereas previously the sign of nature was part of the thing itself. The former implies a highly mediated relationship between concept and referent, whereas the latter entails an immediate relationship between sign and thing. First nature (and culture) is immediate nature, second nature (and culture) is mediated nature, third nature (and culture) is represented nature, and the natural world is 'unmediated nature'.

The concept/referent of nature was killed in the grid of denominations and in what Foucualt later called 'a certain grid of explicit or implicit interrogations' just as at about the same time the grid of private property was killing the commons in the enclosure movement, the grid of drains was killing wetlands and the grid plan town of the colonial settlement was killing Aboriginal lands (see Giblett 1996). The discourse of nature killed nature as living subject and produced nature as dead object. It also produced the natural historian as the subject with the power to exercize mastery over, and gain scientific knowledge from and of, nature as object. What Foucault calls 'the positions of the subject' are constructed and defined by what he goes on to call 'the situation that if is possible for him [sic] to occupy in relation to the various domains or groups of objects' (1972: 52; see also 54–55). These positions and situations include questioning, listening, seeing and observing. All of these situate the subject in what Foucault calls 'an optimal perceptual distance' from the object. The natural historian is constructed as living subject at the expense and on the basis of nature as dead object. Nature died so that the scientist might live. Nature in this sense was shortlived; it was cut down in the bloom of its youth at fifteen-hundred-years-old before it reached maturity and the age of majority. Nature was thereafter always going to remain in the minority.

Yet, ironically or inevitably, the birth of the discourse of nature and the simultaneous death of nature led to the proliferation of discourses of nature. The dead body of nature was discoursed upon by long-lost relatives who had not wanted anything to do with it when it was alive. Nature is like a long-lost wealthy aunt who dies without leaving a will and whose relatives dispute her inheritance endlessly and talk about her not having talked, or listened, to her for years. The discourse of nature – natural history – killed nature, but produced a proliferation of the discourses of nature. There is now no single and homogeneous discourse of nature but a number of competing and heterogeneous discourses of nature.

The discourses of nature include: 'the environment' that separates a subject and its environs, and produces a master-slave relationship between them;[2] the scientific objectification of nature and the subject-object relationship between them; the aestheticisation of nature in landscape, especially in monumental and sublime landscapes, such as mountains, forests, geysers and waterfalls, and in pleasing prospects and pastoral landscapes, such as gentlemen's parks and enclave estates, or either as in landscape writing; nature feminized in the virgin lands of wilderness (see Kolodny 1975 and 1984); nature misogynized in swamps (see Giblett 1996: especially Chapters 2, 4, 6 and 8); nature enclosed in private property; nature preserved in sanctuaries, such as national parks and zoos; and nature commodified by industrial capitalism in producer resources and consumer 'goods', and signified as an object of consumption in advertising and tourism. The body of nature was killed, but the aesthetic surfaces that represented nature were multiplied and the discursive construction of nature proliferated.

Landscape writing that aestheticises the static surfaces of nature can be contrasted with nature writing that celebrates its dynamic depths. I define 'nature writing' as the creative, written tracing of the bodily and sensory enjoyment of both the processes and places of nature. Nature writing defined in these terms is thus much more than simply the writing of place or the expression of a sense of place. It is the celebration of the flows of life and energy in and between a body, a place and their natural processes. The work of Henry David Thoreau is exemplary in this regard (as I have shown previously – see Giblett 1996: Chapter 10; and 2009: Chapter 1), whereas the work of William Wordsworth is a prime example of landscape writing (as I will show in Chapters 3 and 4). I define 'landscape writing' as the creative, written inscription of the visual appreciation for the surfaces of nature in the aesthetic modes of the sublime, picturesque and beautiful.

The birth of nature writing is usually placed in 1788–1789 with the publication of Gilbert White's *The Natural History of Selborne* (White 1987). White's book was one of Thoreau's favourites according to one of his biographers (Richardson 1986: 309). Two prominent anthologies of nature writing, *The Oxford Book of Nature Writing* and *The Norton Book of Nature Writing*, both begin with selections from White's book (see Finch and Elder 1990;

and Mabey 1995).³ Thoreau's work figures prominently in both anthologies, whilst none of Wordsworth's work is included in either. Landscape writing also features in Thoreau's work (see Giblett 2008a: 58–60). Both landscape writing and nature writing can be found in the work of most nature writers (and landscape writers).

For nature writing to be born, natural history had to be born too and nature had to die. Why there was a gap of 300 years between the contemporaneous birth of natural history and the death of nature, and the birth of nature writing is another question. Perhaps nature writing marks the end of the death of nature and the beginning of the rebirth of nature. The long period of gestation was perhaps a life-and-death struggle. Nature writing is the bastard child of the illicit union between literature and natural history. As a bastard, nature writing is disowned by both its parents of literature and natural history, but it has been immensely popular. White's book is 'reputedly the fourth most published book in the English language' after the Bible, Bunyan's *Pilgrim's Progress* and the works of Shakespeare. Although it is the child of both literature and natural history, and so of dubious bourgeois parentage on both sides (especially when it inherits and reproduces the European landscape aesthetic), nature writing is a bastard who crosses the great divide between the two cultures of the humanities and the sciences and delivers a plague on both their houses (especially when it promotes earthly mutuality, and psychoanalytic and postmodern ecology).

This process of the discursive proliferation of nature was evident in the heyday of natural history in the late nineteenth century when, as Tom Griffiths puts it:

> [...] the popularisation of natural history [...] was inseparable from frontier experience, intimations of war, hunting prowess, evolutionary morals, social status and manly pursuits. Natural history became an outdoor school of character formation. (1996: 21)⁴

Natural history, not nature, became an outdoor school to which only men, especially the 'coming man' of settler modernity, were admitted: natural history was masculinized just as nature was feminized. One was not possible without the other. In fact, the two were married either *de facto* or legally; the masculine discourse of natural history was married to feminized nature (see Schiebinger 1993). Yet this was also the period when perhaps the marriage was breaking down as the masculine discourse of the frontier hero in the wilderness was estranged, if not divorced, from the feminized culture of the cities (as we shall see later in Chapter 5). Ultimately, however, there was no conflict between the two, as the masculine natural historian and wilderness hero, and nature feminized as benign and culture feminized as effete, were part of the same patriarchal paradigm.

The discourses of nature police and regulate the ecosphere (or attempt to) in an analogous way to the discourses of sexuality as Foucault argued in the first volume of his *History of Sexuality* (1981). Rather than sexuality being repressed in the nineteenth century (the old orthodoxy), Foucault argued that there was a proliferation of discourses of sexuality that policed and regulated (or at least attempted to) the sexual lives of populations. Similarly, rather than nature being simply repressed or merely exploited under patriarchal capitalism, there has been a proliferation of the discourses of nature that police and regulate the lives of populations (and not just human populations). Just as the discourses of sexuality loudly proclaim that which was supposedly speechless, so the discourses of nature speak about the mute operations of nature. And just as the discourses of sexuality were founded on speaking the speechless, so the discourses of nature speak the mute. Everywhere nature is spoken about and for, but nowhere is nature allowed to speak for itself. Lots of talk about 'the environment', even 'our environment', but little talk about our interconnectedness with the earth, about the ecosphere.

Within both contemporary 'high' and 'popular culture' nature has been overworked, represented and commodified from theme parks to nature documentaries, from gardens to zoos, from shopping malls to ecotourism, from landscape painting to literature, from pastoralist cattle kingdoms to suburban gardens, from enclave estates to the intimate charm of the petit bourgeois lounge room with its bric-a-brac and exotic curios from other places. Nature is now not only a source of resource commodities, but also a signifier in the service of profit. Nature, as Andrew Ross has argued cogently:

> [...] which was once assigned the lowest possible value in the account books of industrialization, is now fetching the highest market prices. Once the source simply of raw materials to be extracted and transformed into commodities, nature is now a valuable origin of exchange value in its own right. In the age of environmental accounting, nature enters the market [...] for its own sake, as a desirable signifier. (1994: 8)

A signifier, moreover, floating free like currency disconnected from the referent of the gold standard and within a paradigm of polysemic and multiaccentual signifieds. As a result, nature has become the site of struggle between competing (class, gender, ethnic and overlapping and intersecting ecological) interests over what and how it shall mean. Nature is not an unproblematic and universal category.

Nature nowadays is an abstract concept, collective noun, cultural construction, rhetorical figure and sign in search of a referent. Nature can be defined as much by what it is not as by what it is as Donna Haraway has done cogently:

> [...] nature is not a physical place to which one can go, nor a treasure to fence or bank, nor an essence to be saved or violated. Nature is not hidden and so does not need to be unveiled. Nature is not a text to be read in the codes of mathematics and biomedicine. It is not the 'other' who suffers origin, replenishment and service. Neither mother, nurse, nor slave, nature is not matrix, resource, or tool for the reproduction of man. Nature is, however, a *topos*, a place, in the sense of a rhetorician's place or topic for consideration of common themes; nature is, strictly, a commonplace [...] nature is the place to rebuild public culture. Nature is also a *trópos*, a trope. It is figure, construction, artefact, movement, displacement. Nature cannot pre-exist its construction [...] Nature is a topic of public discourse on which much turns, even the earth [...] nature for us is *made*, as both fiction

and fact [...] nature is made, but not entirely by humans: it is a co-construction among humans and non-humans [and the non–human]. (1992: 296–297)

Nature is tropical figure and topical place. Yet the topes of nature are not troped equitably. Different *topoi* are troped in different ways with some being valorized at the expense or the detriment of others. There is a politics of the tropes of topes, a politics of *trópoi* of *topois* as I have shown elsewhere in relation to wetlands (see Giblett 1996: especially 167).

Alternatively, and even oppositionally, monstrous counter tropes may deconstruct and decolonize the concept/metaphor of nature by setting up noise or interference in the communication channel about nature. For instance, Luce Irigaray refers to nature as 'that glass enclosure, that spangled sepulchre' (1985: 228). Nature is here troped as fragile and transparent private property enclosed from the robust and opaque global commons, and as a tomb decorated like a planetarium in which the necrophiliac (even necrophagic) rites of patriarchal capitalism are performed on the dead body of once living land and water.

Discourses of nature serve hegemonic class, gender and ethnic interests. A number of competing definitions of nature are currently in circulation, some of which see it as deadwood, as a passive object to be exploited, while others see it as a living tree, as mystical force to be revered. It is this oxymoronic troping of nature as dead tree, as passive force *and* as living wood, as mystical agency, that characterizes our hypermodern moment. Besides the discourses and tropes – and growing out of them and feeding back into them – there are opposing ways of life in relation to the natural environment.

The Gendered Construction of Nature

The concept/referent of nature has a gender politics (to which Foucault was blind as he was blind to the gender politics of sexuality). Nature has been feminized, and culture masculinized, in western and other cultures. Culture has been construed and troped in masculine terms and nature in feminine ones in the western patriarchal tradition. Horkheimer and Adorno made the most cogent and concise critique along these lines when they argued that:

> [...] woman became the embodiment of the biological function, the image of nature, the subjugation of which constituted that civilization's title to fame. For millennia men dreamed of acquiring absolute mastery over nature, of converting the cosmos into one immense hunting ground. It was to this that the idea of man was geared in a male-dominated society. This was the significance of reason, his prouded boast. (1972: 248)

As a result, Simone de Beauvoir argued, 'man seeks in woman the Other as Nature [...] Nature is a vein of gross material in which the soul is imprisoned [...] the dark chaos from whence life wells up' (1972: 248). In the patriarchal tradition, 'life' (whatever that is and however it could be separated from nature other than as culture) is valorized over nature.

Nature is ore, the soul is gold (the ore is to be mined for gold); nature is prison, the soul a prisoner (the prison doors are to be opened to let the prisoner fly free); nature is secluded, inchoate, whereas 'life' or culture is open, purposive; nature is receptive, 'life' or culture projective; nature is feminized in these terms in a misogynist manner, whereas 'life' or culture is masculinized in the patriarchal paradigm. Ascribing life to culture and denying it to nature meant the death of nature.

Life and death can thus be added to the list of qualities assigned to the culture/nature divide by patriarchal culture (see Giblett 1996: 43–44):

Activity	Passivity
Culture	Nature
LIFE	DEATH
Father	Mother
Head	Heart
Man/Maculine	Woman/Feminine
Reason	Emotion
Action	Speech
Doing	Becoming
River	Swamp
Flow	Stagnation
Sublime	Slime
Duration of consciousness and infinite spatiality	Eternity and infinite temporality

How ridiculous, however, to ascribe life to culture when patriarchal culture is a lumber room of the junk of old traditions culminating in the dead matter of the commodity; how absurd to turn the womb of new life into the tomb of death and consign the once living body of nature to the dustbin of (natural) history.

In the face of the patriarchal move to essentialize the culture/nature binary (woman is nature and vice versa, man is culture), a politics of resistance and restoration would historicize it (nature has been constructed historically as woman). Such a politics could even *pre*–historicize it by making the crucial distinction between the agricultural, neolithic and patriarchal Earth Mother or Mother Nature and the palaeolithic, 'pre-patriarchal', matrifocal Great Goddess or Great Mother who is 'not just benevolent and fertile [but] also death-dealing and the destroyer' (Sjöö and Mor 1991: xix).

Following feminist archaeologists such as Marija Gimbutas (1982, 1989, 1991), and feminist scholars such as Barbara Mor, Max Oelschlaeger (1991: Chapter 1, especially 17–18, 27; and n.71: 364) has argued that what preceded the culture/nature split in Palaeolithic times in the past, and what refuses it in indigenous cultures/country in the present, for example, in Aboriginal Country (see Webb 1996: 61–75; and Chapter 11 of this book) is the Great Goddess or Mother. The Great Mother or Goddess is something beyond

The Nature of Natures and the Cultures of Natures

or before agricultural, pastoral and mining country. The Great Goddess or Mother is, in a word, 'swamp' (see Giblett 1996). Michel Serres has answered the question 'what is nature?' with the terse reply: 'the city's or culture's hell' (1995: 73). The city's hell is more precisely the swamp and the slum is the city's swamp as I have argued elsewhere (see Giblett 1996: especially Chapters 3, 4 and 6; and Giblett 2009: Chapter 3). The patriarchal and sublime city is quite distinct from, and antithetical to, this pre-agricultural (and later pre-industrial) Aboriginal country, to the swamp primeval, to primal slime, and absolutely dependent, if not parasitical, on agricultural, pastoral and mining country.

I have tried to plot the contrast and contest between these terms in tabular form. The table charts the conceptual space and trajectory of this book in which I argue *for* and advance the claims of the left paradigm *against* the right – and for a paradigm shift, a shift in thinking, being, living, and meaning-making, from the right to the left. I use the term 'paradigm' in both Thomas Kuhn's sense of a theoretical framework that gives meaning, and in Ferdinand de Saussure's sense of the vertical axis of language (or semiosis) from which terms are chosen along the horizontal (or syntagmatic) axis in putting words (or signs) together to make meaning. I also argue for a shift from the '-isms', the discourses and ideologies of the right, to the '-ities'. the intuitions and performances of the left; from monumentalism, parasitism and sanctuarism to monstrosity, mutuality and sacrality.[5] In general, the table charts the transiton from (and distinction between) nature (and culture) split between the first (and fifth) nature (and culture) of the life-giving and death-dealing Great Mother or Great Goddess associated with the swamps, and the second (third and fourth) nature (and culture) of the benign and malign Mother Earth or Mother Nature affiliated and aligned with the fields. It also charts culture split between matrifocal and gylanic cultures in which the sexes were equal, and patriarchal and hierarchical ones in which men are dominant. The former and latter terms of these splits are both equated: the nature of Great Mother or Great Goddess is associated with matrifocal and gylanic cultures, and Mother Earth or Mother Nature with patriarchal and hierarchical cultures.

The table deconstructs the culture/nature binary by *pre*–historicising it. It does not set up a new binary opposition as the relationship between the terms is not one of lack and supplement, zero and one. Rather the relationship is one of historical supersession and prehistorical persistence. The right column is inscribed on the left and the left is traced in the right. The left is the secret of the right. For example, slime is the secret of the sublime as couched in Zoë Sofoulis' parenthetical portmanteau 's(ub)lime' (see Giblett 1996: especially Chapter 2). There is a relationship of dependence, if not parasitism, of the right on the left, and of domination of the right over the left. I do not seek to invert this order (which would reproduce the hierarchial power structure of the right paradigm) but to advance the claims of the left, partly by critiquing the right and partly by advocating the left. The two sides are the obverse of each other (+1 and −1), not a binary opposition (0 and +1), but the Yin and Yang of our hypermodern condition not yet brought into postmodern complementarity and sustainability of earthly mutuality and social justice, especially for Aboriginal peoples of the world:

Figure 2: Two Laws, Two Paradigms, Five Natures, Five Cultures – One World.

Category	Paradigm	
	Left, Intuitions, '–Ities'	*Right, Ideologies, '–Isms'*
RULE	Matrifocal	Patriarchal → Filiarchal[6]
SOCIAL STRUCTURE	Gylany	Hierarchy
ORIGINARY PERIOD	Palaeolithic	Neolithic
TIME/SPACE (CHRONOTOPE)	Infinite temporality, eternity	Infinite spatiality, linearity
CHRONOTROPE (FIGURE OF TIME)	Cycle, circle	Straight line, arrow
MOTHER FIGURE	Great Goddess, Great Mother	Earth Mother, Mother Nature
MODUS OPERANDI	Life-giving, death-dealing	Benign, malignant
RULING PRINCIPLE	Body of the Mother	Law of the Father → Sons
FETISH	Uterus	Phallus
REPRESENTATIVE PLACE	Swamp	City
PHILOSOPHY	Slime	Sublime
PSYCHOLOGY	Uncanny	Sublimation[7]
TRANSFORMATION	Solid into Liquid	Solid into Gas
ELEMENT	Water	Air
HUMOUR	Phlegmatic, sanguinous	Melancholic, choleric[8]
FORM	Monstrous[9]	Monumental
EXPRESSION	Grotesque[10]	Surmountainous[11]
STRATUM (BODILY, EARTHLY)	Lower	Upper
RULING PASSION[12]	Horror	Terror
QUAKING ZONE	Native	Feral
SELF-OTHER (SMALL 'o')	Abject, 'I-You'[13]	Subject-Object, 'I-It'[14]
(PSYCHO)DYNAMICS	Generosity, gratitude	Greed, gluttony
ORALITY AND ANALITY[15]	Satisfaction	Sadism
GUEST–HOST[16]	Symbiosis	Parasitism
RELATIONSHIP	Mutuality	Mastery
MODALITY	Dialogue	Discourse
WAY	Intuitive ways of being, living and sensing	Institutionalized ways of seeing, saying and doing
-LOGIC	Dialogic	Monologic
MEANING-MAKING	Semiosis, *Significance*	Semiotic, Signification
-ACCENTUALITY	Multi-accentuality[17]	Uni–accentuality
OTHER (BIG 'O')	Impassible abject	Impossible object
PRODUCT	'Slimy bads'	'Shiny goods'
PROCESS	Performance	Production
EXCHANGE	Gift, Offering	Commodity, Money
BODY PART/PLACE	Cloaca	Capital
BODY AS/OF	Earth	Machine[18]
HUMAN BODY	Performing actions	Engaged in events[19]
BODY TECHNIQUE	Active rest[20]	Passive speed[21]
TEMPO	Slow	Fast

Category	Paradigm	
	Left, Intuitions, '–Ities'	Right, Ideologies, '–Isms'
MIND REGION	Id	Super-ego
SACRED INTERIOR SPACE[22]	Womb	Tomb
HABITATION (LIVING PLACE/ SPACE)	Bioregional home-habitat	'Intimate charm', grid-plan town, 'Elysiums for gentlemen'[23]
SPATIAL ORIENTATION	Lying low	Standing high
TEMPORAL ORIENTATION	Means	Ends
DIMENSION	Depths	Surfaces, heights
POSITION	Supine	Erect
WRITING[24]	Trace, nature	Inscription, landscape
KNOWLEDGE	Intuitive, corporeal	Ideological, intellectual
POWER[25]	Tactic	Strategy
POLITICS	Left, Radical	Right, Reactionary
RELATION TO THE REPRESSED	Return to the Repressed	Surmounting the Repressed
DOMINANT SENSES[26]	Smell, Taste, Touch	Sight, Hearing
LANGUAGE[27]	Magic, mimetic, mystery, wisdom	Communication, transportation of messages, information
MEDIA	Immediacy	Mediated
PROXIMITY[28]	Auratic weave of time and space	Phony spell of the commodity
REPRESENTATIVE LAND TYPE	Wetland (swamp, marsh, bog, fen, slough, lagoon, shallow estuary and lake, etc.)	Dryland (gentleman's park estate, enclave estate, shopping mall, city, suburb, etc.)
'AESTHETICS', SENSORY APPRECIATION, ENJOYMENT	Exquisite[29] living spaces, places, processes and lifeful beings	Beautiful forms, picturesque landscapes, pleasing prospects, dead products, lifeless things
COUNTRY	Aboriginal	Agricultural, Pastoral, Mining and Urban
REPRESENTATIVE LAND-USE TECHNOLOGIES	Hunting, gathering 'Fire-stick Farming', Dwelling, Craft	Herding, tilling Agricultural, Pastoralist, Mining, Architectural, Engineering, Manufacturing, Transportation, Communication
TECHNOLOGICAL DEVICE	Tool, complement	Prosthesis, supplement[30]
NATURE (OF WORK)	First, Fifth, Worked	Second, Worked–over → Third, Overworked → Fourth, Hyperworked
LAND RIGHTS	'Native Title'	Crown Land, Private Property
'OWNERSHIP'	Commons (owned by none, shared by all)	Enclosure (owned by one, shared with none)
COLONIAL TO NATIONAL	Heath, 'Wilderness', Scrub,	'England's Green and Pleasant

Category	Paradigm	
	Left, Intuitions, '–Ities'	*Right, Ideologies, '–Isms'*
LANDSCAPE	Desert	Land', 'Bush', National Parks, National Monuments, Nature Reserves
ECOLOGY	Premodern, Postmodern, Political, Psychoanalyitc, Feminist	Modern, Scientific
ECONOMY	Communal, Euthenics[31], Oikonomia	Political, Commercial, Chrematistics[32]
SOCIO-ECONOMIC SPHERE[33]	Popular, marketplace	Official, market
SACRED EXTERIOR SPACE	Sacrality	Sanctuarism
SACRED PRACTICE	Spirituality	Religion
CULTURE OF NATURE	Aboriginal; First, Fifth	Agri–urban; Second, Third, Fourth
PLANET PLACE	(The) Earth	The environment
LIFE IS	Local	Global
-WORLD	On-world	Off-world
HOME IS	Here, now, present	There, then, past, future

'My Mother Would Lodge Me'

I will try to illustrate and elaborate some of the major aspects of this set of distinctions, especially those pertinent to the topics of *People and Places of Nature and Culture* (and not elaborated elsewhere), with a reading of a passage from Charlotte Brontë's novel *Jane Eyre*, first published in 1847. This is the scene on the heath of Chapter 28. The heath-scene can be read as an allegory of the country and the city, though reference to this passage from *Jane Eyre* is curiously absent from Raymond Williams' *The Country and the City* (1973), the foundational text of ecocriticism. This absence is interesting as the passage does support his distinction between 'unmediated nature' and 'working agriculture' both found in the country.

The scene enacts the complicity between agricultural mother nature and patriarchal father law. Yet, as an encounter too with 'unmediated nature', it can also be read as an allegory of something beyond, or before, agricultural country: the Great Goddess. The passage on the heath can thus be read as Jane's attempt to act out a primitivist regression to an infantile state of dependence on (her) mother (nature) without realising that there are two mother figures: the benign and malignant Earth Mother of the agricultural and patriarchal fields, and the implacable matrifocal Great Goddess or Mother of the heath who is both life-giving and death-dealing. Jane returns to the Great Goddess on the heath only to repudiate it/her and re-affirm her own petty-bourgeois individualist independence, or in other words, her subjugation to the law of the Father and dependence on Mother Earth.

Chapter 28 of *Jane Eyre* begins at the crossroads of Whitcross, the white cross, the empty place or blank space, the intersection of lines of flight. Jane is at a crossroads herself for this is the point in the novel at which she has left Rochester after discovering that he is married to the mad woman in the attic. As a result, she finds herself an outcast from (patriarchal) society, faced with a choice – to go on or to go back; to go on being outcast or to return into the patriarchal (and pastoral) fold. On the heath she finds that 'not a tie holds me to human society at this moment'. What is outside human society, or more precisely patriarchal society, what precedes and refuses it, is matriarchal, or more preferably matrifocal, society centred on the Great Goddess. By going outside patriarchal society she finds the Great Goddess for, as Jane says, 'I have no relative but the universal mother, Nature: I will seek her breast and ask repose'. But Jane has not distinguished between the benign and malignant Mother Nature of agriculture and the implacable Great Goddess of the heath outside and prior to agriculture.

Jane's striking into the heath is no mere elitist pastoral return to nature indulged in by the jaded middle and upper classes, no facile picnic in the country, no day-tripping tourist excursion into a picturesque landscape, but, as in the occasional explorer's expedition into the wild(er)ness within and without, a return to the Great Goddess, even a return to a womb-like space in the heath:

> I struck straight into the heath; I held on to a hollow I saw deeply furrowing the brown moorside; I waded kneedeep in its dark growth; I turned with its turnings, and finding a moss-blackened granite crag in a hidden angle, I sat down under it. High banks of moor were about me; the crag protected my head: the sky was over that. Some time passed before I felt tranquil even here: I had a vague dread that wild cattle might be near, or that some sportsman or poacher might discover me. If a gust of wind swept the waste, I looked up, fearing it was the rush of a bull; if a plover whistled, I imagined it a man. Finding my apprehension unfounded, however, and calmed by the deep silence that reigned as evening declined at nightfall, I took confidence. As yet I had no thought: I had only listened, watched, dreaded; now I regained the faculty of reflection. What was I to do? Where to go?

Jane finds a safe and secure place away from men, or more precisely male hunters, and from agriculture, from the law of the Father and the agriculture of Mother Earth, in the strong and wild nature of the Great Goddess who she appreciates sensually, especially and initially via the sense of touch, that most immediate and intimate of senses:

> I touched the heath: it was dry, and yet warm with the heat of the summer day. I looked at the sky; it was pure; a kindly star twinkled just above the chasm ridge. The dew fell, but with propitious softness; no breeze whispered. Nature seemed to me benign and good; I thought she loved me, outcast as I was; and I, who from man could only anticipate mistrust, rejection, insult, clung to her with filial fondness. Tonight, at least, I would be her guest, as I was her child: my mother would lodge me without money and without price.

The Great Goddess becomes, or is her mother, who encloses her, folds her into herself, invaginates her, enwombs her rather than entombs her, and watches over her as she sleeps in a metaphor of re-birthing:

> Beside the crag the heath was very deep: when I lay down my feet were buried in it; rising high on each side, it left only a narrow space for the night-air to invade. I folded my shawl double, and spread it over me for a coverlet; a low, mossy swell was my pillow. Thus lodged, I was not, at least at the commencement of the night, cold. My rest might have been blissful enough, only a sad heart broke it. It plained of its gaping wounds, its inward bleeding, its riven chords. It trembled for Mr Rochester and his doom; it bemoaned him with bitter pity; it demanded him with ceaseless longing; and, impotent as a bird with both wings broken, it still quivered its shattered pinions in vain attempts to seek him.

Despite the care of the Great Goddess, she accepts the patriarchal construction of herself as castrated creature, as lack, who desires the phallus (of the law) and the phallic man embodied and personified in Rochester.

Her sad heart is patriarchal to the core, which leads her to repudiate the ministrations of the Great Goddess and to return to the realm of patriarchal society, to the law of the Father of the city, or at least of urban civilisation, and to the Mother Earth of agriculture:

> But next day, Want came to me, pale and bare. Long after the little birds had left their nests; long after bees had come in the sweet prime of day to gather the heath honey before the dew was dried – when the long morning shadows were curtailed, and the sun filled earth and sky – I got up and looked around me. What a still, hot perfect day! What a golden desert this spreading moor! Everywhere sunshine. I wished I could live in it and on it. I saw a lizard run over the crag; I saw a bee busy among the sweet bilberries. I would fain at the moment have become bee or lizard, that I might have found fitting nutriment, permanent shelter here. But I was a human being, and had a human being's wants: I must not linger where there was nothing to supply them.

This assertion of want gives rise to a Romantic death-wish so that she might 'mingle in peace with the soil of this wilderness' in an oceanic feeling of oneness. But she resolves that 'life, however, was yet in my possession' though life is construed in terms of the law of the Father, of patriarchal culture *à la* de Beauvoir and the Protestant work ethic with 'all its requirements, and pains, and responsibilities'. The heath, the wilderness, the womb of the Great Goddess ends up being seen as the place of want, if not of death, the womb as tomb (see Giblett 1996: 147), the place of new life as a place of death, the topos of life troped as death.

As a result, Jane turns her back on the Great Goddess, and returns to the law of the Father and the agriculture of Mother Earth by retracing her steps to Whitcross, then by following a road away from the sun until she hears, significantly, a church bell, emblematic of patriarchal culture, beckoning her back. She rejects the immediate touch of the Great Goddess in close proximity on the heath for the mediated sound of Mother Earth and Father Law in the far distance. She then sees the symbols of patriarchal civilisation and religion, of the law of the Father and of the Mother Earth of agriculture:

> I turned in the direction of the sound, and there, amongst the romantic hills, whose changes and aspects I had ceased to note an hour ago, I saw a hamlet and a spire. All the valley at my right hand was full of pasture fields, and cornfields, and wood; a glittering stream ran zigzag through the varied shades of green, the mellowing grain, the sombre woodland, the clear and sunny lea [...] Human life and human labour were near. I must struggle on: strive to live and bend to toil like the rest.

Here is the agriculture of romanticized country, of Mother Earth and the law of the Father rather than the heath of the Great Goddess. The closest pictorial analogue I have come across is Frederic Edwin Church's *West Rock, New Haven* (painted two years after the publication of *Jane Eyre*) with its agricultural foreground, forested midground and white spire in the background (reproduced in Johns, Sayers, Kornhauser with Ellis 1998: 145). This is England's 'green and pleasant' land, transposed (or transplanted) in the painting to New England; it is nature worked over by culture into agriculture and architecture, into landscape and townscape, into second nature, all of which can be contrasted with the heath, of first nature and of the Great Goddess. Jane rejects the latter for the former, repudiates the/her Great Goddess and re-affirms the triumph of culture over nature. In the process she becomes complicit with patriarchal society and its cultural heritage of the destructive distinction between culture and nature rather than affirming and celebrating her sensory engagement with the/her Great Goddess on and in the heath.

Notes

1. Honeybees (*Apis mellifera*) have recently been described as 'one of the planet's most successful animals' and as 'perhaps Australia's most widespread exotic invader'. See (Low 1999: 184).
2. I discuss 'the environment' in Giblett (2008a: 115–116).
3. For historical and literary surveys of nature writing, see Brooks (1980) and Stewart (1995). For how to do it, see Murray (1995).
4. A similar argument has also been made by Pratt (1992: especially 15–37).
5. I am grateful to Kevin Ballantine for the '-ism/-ity' distinction.
6. For the post-pastoral transition from patriarchy to filiarchy (the rule of the sons), see Chapter 9.
7. I discuss the sublime, sublimation, slime and the uncanny in Giblett (1996: Chapter 2).
8. I discuss the elements and the humours in Giblett (1996: Chapter 7; and 2009: coda to Chapter 5).
9. I discuss the monstrous in Giblett (1996: Chapter 8; and 2008a: Chapter 5).
10. I discuss the grotesque lower bodily and earthly strata in Giblett (1996: Chapter 6; and 2008a: Chapter 4).

11. I discuss the surmountainous in Giblett (1996: Chapter 2).
12. I discuss horror and terror in Giblett (1996: Chapter 2).
13. For 'I-You', see Buber (1970).
14. For 'I-It', see Buber (1970).
15. I discuss the psycho-dynamics of generosity, gratitude, greed and gluttony, and the orality and anality of sadism and satisfaction, in Chapters 9 and 10.
16. I discuss symbiosis and parasitism in Chapter 12.
17. I discuss Voloshinov's concept of the multi-accentuality of signs in Giblett (2008b: Chapter 1).
18. I discuss the earth as body, the body as earth and the body as machine in Giblett (2008a).
19. I make and discuss this distinction in Giblett (2008a).
20. I discuss Marcel Mauss' body techniques, including those of 'active rest', in Giblett (2008a: 11–16 and 165).
21. I discuss the body techniques of passive speed in Giblett (2008b).
22. I discuss the womb and the tomb in Giblett (1996: Chapter 6).
23. 'Elysiums for gentlemen' (see Carter 1989: Chapter 7) are the grid-plan town and modern, colonial city. As Elysium is the home of the blessed *after* death, the grid-plan city is necropolis, the city of the dead. 'Intimate charm' (see Carter 1989: Chapter 9; and Leach 1993: Chapter 3) is the defining feature of the modern interior spaces of the private home (exemplified in the windows of the display homes) and the display windows of the department store, the temples of industrial capitalist consumption (the private made public, privately, family-owned companies making an idealised private space public). For the 'completeness' of the petty-bourgeois interior in which every surface is covered, bourgeois existence as 'the regime of private affairs'and the petty-bourgeois interior as the battlefield over which 'the attack of commodity capital has advanced victoriously' to such an extent that 'nothing human can flourish there again', see Benjamin (1979b: 188; 1979c: 48–49, 100–101; 1996b: 446–447, 484–485; and 1999: 30).
24. I discuss writing as trace and as inscription in Giblett (1996: Chapter 3; 2008b: Chapter 4; and 2008a: Chapter 7).
25. I discuss Michel de Certeau's distinction between tactic and strategy in Giblett (2008a: 115–117).
26. I discuss the senses in Giblett (2009: coda to Chapter 5).
27. For Walter Benjamin's distinction between language as magic and mimesis, and language as communication and semiotic, see Steiner (2010: 47); for communication as transportation, see Giblett (2008b: Chapters 1–3).
28. I discuss Walter Benjamin's concepts of the aura and of the phony spell of the commodity in Giblett (2008b: Chapter 4).
29. I discuss Rebecca Solnit's concept/metaphor of the exquisite in Giblett (2009: Chapter 7).
30. I make and discuss the distinction between complementary tool and supplementary prosthesis in Giblett (2008b: Chapter 6).
31. 'Euthenics' is Ellen Swallow's term for 'the science of controllable environment' enacting 'principles of ecology of earth and home' (see Gottlieb 1993: 216–217), and for 'a science that could educate a population to live in harmony with its environment' (see Clarke 1973: 198) whose features are both natural and artificial, 'produced by humans' (see Gottlieb 1993: 216).
32. 'Chrematistics' is defined by Daly and J. Cobb Jr. (1994: 138) as 'the branch of political economy relating to the manipulation of property and wealth so as to maximize short-term monetary exchange value to the owner. Oikonomia, by contrast, is the management of the household so as to increase its use value to all members of the household over the long run'.
33. I discuss Mikhail Bakhtin's distinction between the official and popular sphere, and between the market and marketplace, in Giblett (2008a: 56–58).

Chapter 2

Is the Public Sphere to the Biosphere as Culture is to Nature (as Male is to Female)?

The short answer to the question posed by the title of this chapter is yes and no. The question and this answer are important for a participatory, postmodern political ecology as they concern not only the relationship between culture and nature, but also how the relationship has developed historically, especially in modernity, and how the primary terms of the question have been gendered as masculine and feminine respectively. This move deconstructs and decolonizes the culture/nature binary and reconstructs a political ecology. The primary aim of a participatory, postmodern political ecology is earthly mutuality in the interactions between the public and private spheres and the biosphere and other spheres (such as the atmosphere, hydrosphere and lithosphere) that give and sustain life on this planet.

I give a longer answer to the question posed in the chapter title by critiquing Jürgen Habermas's (1989: 5 and 27) definition of the bourgeois public sphere as the sphere of private property (land-)owning men 'come together' as a public. Already couched within this definition is a relationship with the earth, or at least parts of it in private ownership. This 'coming together' is based on the distinction between the public and the private, and the exclusion of women (and some men) from the public sphere and their confinement in the private sphere. As John Thompson has succinctly, if not bluntly put it, 'the exclusion of women was constitutive of the public sphere' (1995: 73), just as the exclusion of first nature was constitutive of second, third and fourth culture.

The constitution of the public sphere was impossible without the exclusion of women; the constitution of second, third and fourth culture without the exclusion of first nature. Yet the public and private spheres rest on the biosphere (plus the lithosphere, hydrosphere, atmosphere, electromagnetosphere, extra–terrestrial orbitosphere, etc. – collectively, the '-ospheres' for short), or 'nature' in a number of senses. The public and private spheres and the -ospheres are included in, and are parts of, the ecosphere, the earthly household sphere. Every human and every human and other activity is a part of this sphere. Whether this household is a home or a hotel room, and whether we human beings are living in a mutually beneficical relationship in (and with) it, is another matter.

Polis and *Oikos*

In *Knowledge and Human Interests* Habermas theorizes nature along Marxian lines by distinguishing between nature-in-itself preceding human history, subjective bodily nature and objective environmental nature (see Whitebook 1979: 47; and McCarthy 1984: 113). Never (to my knowledge) has he theorized the public sphere in its relation to 'nature' in all three senses, collectively the '-ospheres'. This chapter not only aims to fill that gap (for its own sake), but also to advance a critical ecological understanding of the interrelationship between culture and nature, and between the public and private spheres and the -ospheres. I argue that the Ancient Greek public sphere was a masculine space of discourse and power and that the modern masculine spheres of the nation-state and civil society always appropriate and exploit, depend upon yet exclude, the -ospheres and the private sphere of domestic labour. These latter two spheres have been gendered as feminine spaces of the commons or free goods, unaccounted for literally in patriarchal bourgeois political economy. The masculine public sphere of the nation-state and bourgeois civil society is roughly to the -ospheres and the feminine private sphere as culture is to nature. This is my yes and no answer.

I present this answer as a rough heuristic device as civil society, defined by Habermas as the 'realm of commodity exchange and social labour governed by its own laws', belongs strictly to the private sphere according to Habermas (1989: 3 and 30). Similarly Thompson has defined civil society 'as a sphere of private individuals, organizations and classes which are regulated by civil law and [are] formally distinct from the state' (1995: 121). Civil society thus includes both transnational corporations (TNCs) and non-government organizations (NGOs). These are unlikely bedfellows with many NGOs resisting the domination of many TNCs, especially in their hegemonic alliance with the nation-state. Yet both are children of the same parents, and both need to acknowledge and deconstruct their common parentage. Earlier Thompson traced how civil society 'emerged as a domain of privatized economic relations which were established under the aegis of public authority' (1995: 69).

Yet rather than privatized economic relations simply existing under the protection and patronage of public authority, civil society in the form of transnational corporations has made incursions from the private sphere into the public sphere to such an extent that it may have subsumed it. At one point Habermas even sees the modern public sphere as 'specifically a part of "civil society"' (1989: 3). Civil society has subsumed, or has attempted to subsume, the bourgeois public sphere, perhaps most markedly and more recently in globalized, transnational corporate capitalism. Consequently, civil society as an aspect of culture does not equate with, and is not restricted to, the private sphere. Nevertheless, like the public sphere, it is gendered as a masculine sphere of competition and rivalry. It is also a site of struggle between TNCs and NGOs with the latter trying to wrest some vestiges of a viable public sphere (and civil civil society) from the uncivil clutches of the former.

The masculine public sphere is not only the sphere of private property (land-)owning men that comes together as a public just for the heck of it and to have a yack, but also to exercize political power as the *polis*, the sphere of public authority (Habermas 1989: 18 and 30). The *polis* is distinguished from the *oikos*, both the feminine private sphere of the domestic household and the -ospheres, or the '*oikos*', in the modern metaphorical and ecological sense of the earth-household. Modern European philosophy, science and culture took up the Ancient Greek distinction between the public sphere (*polis*) and private sphere (*oikos*), but it did not take up the Ancient Greek view of nature as living being as organism. Rather it took up the Renaissance view of nature as machine, as dead matter, and posed, if not opposed, it to culture as living (see Horigan 1988). The birth of natural history and the death of nature gave life to (third) culture (as discussed in Chapter 1). Natural history was a living, cultural practice exercized by the discursive subject on the dead object (or body) of nature (see Schiebinger 1993). Culture was enlivened insofar as nature was dead; culture was necrophagic on the dead body of nature. The nature aesthetics of landscape painting, architecure and gardening also transformed 'dead' nature into living culture (as will be discussed in Chapters 3 and 4).

In drawing the distinction between *polis* and oikos, Hannah Arendt argues that 'according to Greek thought, the human capacity for political organization is not only different from but stands in direct opposition to that natural association whose centre is the home (*oikia*) and the family' (1958: 24). Habermas elaborates this distinction by arguing that:

> [...] in the fully developed Greek city-state the sphere of the *polis*, which was common to the free citizen, was strictly separated from the sphere of the *oikos*; in the sphere of the *oikos*, each individual is in his [sic] own realm. (1989: 3)

The free citizen was a property-owning man in the public sphere of the *polis* and an individual in his own realm of the private sphere of the *oikos,* a king in the castle of his own house.

Following on from Nancy Fraser's (cited by Eley 1992: 308) critique of the gender-blindness of Habermas' model, not only are these spheres gendered as he himself perhaps unwittingly intimates in his use of the masculine possessive pronoun, but also, as he goes on to argue:

> [...] status in *polis* was [...] based upon status as the unlimited master of an *oikos*. The reproduction of life, the labor [sic] of slaves, and the service of the women went on under the aegis of the master's domination; birth and death took place in its shadow; and the realm of necessity and transitoriness remained immersed in the obscurity of the private sphere. In contrast to it stood, in Greek self-interpretation, the public sphere as a realm of freedom and permanence. Only in the light of the public sphere did that which exist become revealed, did everything become visible to all [...] Just as the wants of life and the procurement of its necessities were shamefully hidden inside the *oikos*, so the *polis* provided an open field for honourable distinction. (Habermas 1989: 3–4)

Habermas's metaphors of darkness and light, of hiding and showing, of the striptease of truth as Derrida puts it, are symptomatic of his Enlightenment intellectual lineage.

The masculine public sphere is an accessible and open place of life and light, whereas the feminine private sphere of the household and the -ospheres are confined and closed spaces steeped in death and darkness (as are the -ospheres in the Enlightenment[2]). Along similar lines Lyotard calls the *oikos* the secluded:

[…] in the final analysis, *oikeion* is everything that is not *öffentlich* [public]. And the opposition between the *oikeion* and the *politikon* exactly matches up to that between the secluded (the *Zurückgezogene* [the withdrawn] or the *Abgeshiedene* [the secluded]) on one side and the *Öffentliche* on the other. The political is the public sphere, while the *oikeion* is the space we call 'private' […] It is the shadowy space of all that escapes the light of public speech. (1993: 101–102)

The *oikos* is also the shadowy space that the light of public speech requires in order to constitute itself. It is the dark and shamefully hidden, the obscene, there for reason to penetrate and enlighten. It also includes the secluded and shadowy spaces of the -ospheres, with their dark and hidden processes of biochemical and geological transformation that the public sphere depends upon and does not enquire too closely into – if at all. By metaphorical extension, *oikos* was later used as the basis for ecology by modern scientists, such as Haeckel in 1866. Scientific ecology extended the bounds of the household out to include the earth-household, but by doing so the earth was treated as a feminized domestic sphere, as a source of common free goods. Nature as machine was, and still is, consigned to the dark and secluded machinations of the feminized (earth) household. Nature is constituted as a set of micro-phenomena composed of events and processes that the scientist-mechanic tinkers with and fine-tunes with little or no control over the macro-life of the ecosphere.

Deconstructing and decolonising Habermas's elaboration of the *polis/oikos* distinction I want to argue that the feminine private sphere takes place not only under the aegis of the master's domination as if he wittingly condoned it or allowed it, as if he knew about it but turned a blind eye towards it, nor only in the shadow of the master's domination as if it were its dark underside, but also as its necessary other on which the master's public sphere is dependent, if not parasitic. It also resists his domination and enlightenment. The *polis* and the *oikos* are thus distinguishable on the basis of the power differential that operates between and accrues to them. Arendt argues that 'the *polis* was distinguished from the household in that it knew only "equals", whereas the household was the centre of the strictest inequality' (1958: 32). The *polis* knew only 'equality' between land-owning men, whereas the *oikos* was the centre of the strictest inequality between men and women. Yet the *polis* and the *oikos* were not equal spheres that co-existed in blissful harmony. The *polis* gained power over the *oikos* in what Arendt sees as a zero-sum game: 'historically, it is very likely that the rise of the city-state and the public realm occurred at the expense of the private realm of family and household' (1958: 29).

Unlike Habermas, Arendt acknowledges the dependency of the *polis* upon the *oikos*. The *oikos* is the sphere of necessity, whereas the *polis* is the sphere of freedom. The former is the condition of possibility for the latter as she goes on to argue: 'if there was a relationship between these two spheres, it was a matter of course that the mastering of the necessities of life in the household was the condition for freedom of the *polis*' (Arendt 1958: 30–31). The *oikos* was the excluded 'other' that the *polis* required for its existence, maintenance and sustenance. The *oikos* performs the function of the demonized other that the *polis* needed in order to constitute itself as selfsame as Arendt goes on to argue: 'as far as the members of the *polis* are concerned, household life exists for the sake of the "good life" in the *polis*' (1958: 37). Household life, by implication for this view, is not the good life. The good life is elsewhere, the bane of modernity, not here at home, a counter to which I discuss in the final chapter by arguing that home is here and life is local.

Extending the historical account into recent times Arendt relates that:

> [...] the emergence of the social realm, which is neither private nor public, strictly speaking, is a relatively new phenomenon whose origin coincided with the emergence of the modern age and which found its political form in the nation-state. (1958: 28)

She also notes that: 'the word "social" is Roman in origin and has no equivalent in Greek language or thought' (Arendt 1958: 23). Thus, Habermas points out that with the *polis* and *oikos* 'we are dealing here with categories of Greek origin transmitted to us bearing a Roman stamp' (1989: 3). That stamp means that for us in the modern world, as Arendt suggests, 'the social and the political realms are much less distinct' (1958: 33). Yet collectively the two realms exercize power over the household as she goes on to suggest: 'with the rise of society, that is the rise of the "household" (*oikia*) or of economic activities to the public realm, housekeeping and all matters pertaining formerly to the private sphere of the family have become a collective concern' (Arendt 1958: 33) in what she earlier called 'a gigantic, nation-wide administration of housekeeping' (Arendt 1958: 28). Perhaps this shift constitutes the acquisition of power by civil society at the expense of, and over, the *oikos* in both senses, and the *polis*.

The social realm of civil society has successfully inveigled itself between the public sphere and the private sphere, and now mediates the two and their relationship to the -ospheres. By contrast, the bourgeois public sphere in its heyday mediated (and ameliorated the worst excesses of) the relationship between public political authority and private personal relations. Between the realm of public authority and the state, Thompson argues that:

> [...] on the one hand, and the private realm of civil society and personal relations, on the other, there emerged a new sphere of 'the public': a bourgeois public sphere which consisted of private individuals who came together to debate among themselves the regulation of civil society and the conduct of the state. (1995: 69–70)

In order to do so effectively they needed reliable information, so the definition of the public sphere needs to be broadened to include communication and 'the media'. Edward Herman and Robert McChesney have done so by defining the public sphere as 'all the places and forums where issues of importance to a political community are discussed and debated, and where information is presented that is essential to citizen participation in community life' (1997: 3; see also 136). And all life for that matter, including the community of plants and animals, by all citizens of the earth in a participatory ecology. This larger community of living beings is the biosphere. The biosphere is also situated within an even larger context of non-living things. This larger context of living beings and non-living things is the ecosphere.

Yet the 'coming together' to debate and discuss issues of common concern in the bourgeois public sphere was short-lived. According to Thompson, for Habermas, 'in the specific form in which it existed in the eighteenth century, the bourgeois public sphere did not last for long' (Thompson 1995: 71). A major contributing factor to the decline of the bourgeois public sphere was that 'the periodical press became part of a range of media institutions which were increasingly organized as large-scale commercial concerns'. With this decline came a massive shift in power. Whereas the tyranny of the state had been constrained by the bourgeois public sphere, now the excesses of civil society had to be regulated – but by what? The state? This shift is starkly contrasted by Thompson who argues that:

> [...] for the early liberal thinkers, the main threat to individual liberty and freedom of expression was a threat that stemmed from the state: the rights of the individual had to be protected against the excessive use of state power [...] With the transformation of media organizations into large-scale commercial organizations, the freedom of expression was increasingly confronted by a new threat, a threat stemming not from excessive use of state power, but rather from the unhindered growth of media organizations *qua* commercial concerns. (1995: 74)

Perhaps the only bulwark against this ever-present threat is a 'reinvented publicness' with its deliberative, rather than special interest, democracy (see Thompson 1995: Chapter 8). Deliberative democracy should also have its participatory ecology. The ecosphere is the context not only for all living beings and non-living things but also includes the semiosphere where issues of importance to a political community should be discussed and debated, and where information is presented that is essential to citizen participation in community life, including communities of plants and animals. The ecosphere is global in scope and outcome and local in application and provenance. It should be the touchstone and context for stemming the power of all large-scale commercial organizations.

The Spheres

In the chart opposite (see Figure 3) I have attempted to plot the music, and noise, of the various spheres and hemispheres as they rotate amongst and around each other, and as they have changed and developed historically. Domination and regulation, exploitation and dependence are exercized from the left-hand column across to the right; opposition and resistance from right to left. It is thus a hierarchical arrangement, though I have not represented it as such spatially. Reading this arrangement from top to bottom down the rows is a process of both finer conceptual elaboration and gross historical shift across long durations, not one I would think could specified with any great temporal precision. I have plotted the difficulty of locating civil society, or the social, within exclusively the public or private spheres but embracing aspects of both, or more precisely as colonising aspects of both spheres. I have broadly characterized this chart as:

Is the Public Sphere to the Biosphere as Culture is to Nature (as Male is to Female)?

Figure 3: The Spheres: From Ancient Greeks Through Modern Ecologists and Modern Bourgeoisie to Postmodern Ecologists.

Duration	Sphere		
	Public Sphere	*Private Sphere*	*-Ospheres*
1. ANCIENT GREEKS/ MODERN ECOLOGISTS	Masculine Land Property-owning men *Polis* Public authority Politics	Feminine Domestic labour *Oikos* 'Home economics'	<u>Feminine Commons Free goods 'Oikos' Ecology</u>[3]
2. MODERN BOURGEOISIE	Nation-State	Bourgeois public sphere Periodical press, Coffee houses	Bourgeois private sphere Conjugal family, 'Intimate charm'	
		Civil society (commodity exchange, social labour) The social Commercial economy TNCs, NGOs		
	Third Culture Political economy Chrematistics Semiosphere		Third Nature Great economy Oikonomia Mutosphere
3. POST-MODERN ECOLOGISTS	Fifth Culture of Nature Participatory, Political ecology Earth-home economics Euthenics Earthly mutuality Bio- and psycho-symbiosis ECOSPHERE		

Economically and historically, as this chart suggests, there was a shift in modernity away from the household as the site of both production and consumption to the market as a site of production, to the household as a site of consumption (only) and to a commercial economy. As a result, Thompson concludes,

> [...] the 'private' realm thus comprised both the expanding domain of economic relations and the intimate sphere of personal relations which became increasingly disengaged from economic activity and anchored in the institution of the conjugal family. (1995: 69)

Modern economics, Habermas argues, was thus:

> [...] no longer oriented to the *oikos*; the market had replaced the household, and it became 'commercial economics' [...] the forerunner of political economy was part of 'police-science' [...] This shows how closely connected the private sphere of civil society was to the organs of the public authority. (1989: 20)

Not only that but this also shows how the public sphere and civil society gave rise to commercial economy.

And to reproduction of their gendering in modernity. In a feminist reconsideration of the public and private spheres Joan Landes argues that they were not merely connected but that the former protected and regulated the latter. For her, Habermas locates:

> [...] the *specificity* of the modern public sphere in the civic task of a society engaged in critical public debate to protect a commercial economy [...] [H]e deems the bourgeois public sphere to be the site for the political regulation of civil society. (1995: 95)

This commercial economy is sanctioned by public authority and dependent not only on the social labour of commodity production in the sphere of civil society, but also on the labour of reproduction (in a number of senses) in the private domestic sphere and in the -ospheres. As a result, women were, as Geoff Eley puts it, 'essentially confined within the household' (1992: 310) and deemed to be 'close to nature' so 'the very inception of the public sphere was itself shaped by [and made possible] a new exclusionary ideology directed at women' (1992: 311). And at nature I would add, not because there is any necessary or essential connection between women and nature, but because they were made to perform similar economic and ideological functions of the commons enclosed as private property, as a source of free goods. I have represented this ideology in my chart by having nature embracing partially the feminine private sphere, or having the latter confined partially to the former.

The distinction between nature (both the -ospheres and partially the domestic private sphere), and culture (both the public sphere of political authority and the private sphere of civil society), was aligned in the Enlightenment, as Keith Baker (1992: 199) puts it, with the distinction between male and female. The result was, as Nancy Fraser suggests, that 'the bourgeois conception of the public sphere [...] was a masculinist ideological notion that functioned to legitimate an emergent form of class rule' (1992: 116) over, I would add, both other classes and nature. This function has progressively been taken over by civil society in the form of TNCs, which has extended its reach, its class rule and its masculinist ideology to the point where it encompasses the globe and the ecosphere. A process, which began in the era of colonialism and achieved efficiency in imperialism has reached its height in 'globalisation' for, as the editors of a special issue of *The Ecologist* on globalisation put it, 'while the global economy is not new, the scale and circumstances in which globalisation is occurring has enabled capital to pursue a much more aggressive class politics' (1996: 123–124).

The vehicles for this class politics of the commercial economy of capitalism are transnational corporations which are, for Tom Athanisiou:

> [...] the dominant institutions of the age [...] Corporations have become planetary in their operations and outlook, but the political apparatus – the state – remains national in its orientation, and is declining in power to the point where 'economic transnationalism' is 'hollowing out the state'. (1996: 193, 48 and 195)

Civil society in the form of TNCs may have successfully subsumed the public sphere of political authority beneath its drive to maximize profits by minimising costs. In order to attract investment, the United Kingdom recently advertised that its wage rates were competitive with some 'Third World' countries. Lenin thought that imperialism was the highest stage of capitalism, but globalism is an even higher stage in which transnational corporations have replaced nation-states as the engines of capitalism and colonisation.

The bourgeois conception of the public sphere, civil society and the global economy served also to legitimate, and was dependent upon, an emergent form of class rule over the earth and its resources. This is the conquest of nature, or perhaps more precisely as Fred Alford puts it, 'the scientific conquest of nature' (1985: 17). This conquest was made possible by the culture/nature and subject/object distinctions as Donna Haraway has cogently argued: 'the damaging distinction between [...] nature and culture' (1978: 22) (or perhaps more precisely, the distinction between them in which culture damages nature) is a version of 'the philosophy of science that exploits the rupture between subject and object to justify the double ideology of firm scientific objectivity and mere personal subjectivity' (1978: 5). This rupture and double ideology are implicated with what she sees as 'the basically capitalist ideology of culture against nature'. On this scenario, the philosophy of science participated in the agri-cultural culture/nature split, and capitalism pitted culture against nature in such a way that the former would inevitably win and the latter lose.

Feminist historians of science such as Carolyn Merchant have moreover shown how the capitalist ideology of culture against nature is also patriarchal as it gendered an active, aggressive and masculinized culture against a passive, supine and feminized nature (1980: 143). In sum, and in short, the damaging distinction between culture and nature is agricultural, patriarchal, capitalist and colonialist. Under patriarchy, a gendered construction and hierarchisation of reality operates. This hierarchisation goes beyond abstractions such as culture and nature, and beyond landscapes; mountains, seas and rivers tend to be masculinized in patriarchy, whereas bogs, swamps, fields and parks tend to be feminized (albeit split between the beautiful virgin and the fascinating femme fatale). It goes to the level of fundamental corporeal and cultural categories, to the gendered construction of reality, especially to psycho(eco)logical gendering (the sublime, the subject and consciousness as masculine and the slimy, the abject and the unconscious as feminine).[4]

The conquest and colonisation of nature gave rise, in turn, to what Alfred Crosby (1986) calls ecological imperialism, or to what John MacKenzie (1988) calls simply the empire of nature, our most prized, but least visible colony. This natural imperialism, though, is neither confined spatially to the former European colonies nor restricted temporally to the nineteenth century and before (as both Crosby and Mackenzie suggest), but is ongoing everywhere today under the aegis of 'globalisation', or neo-colonialism. Indeed, modernity is arguably colonisation of nature 'at home', in Europe, whereas colonialism is modernity away from 'home', in the colonies. Globalisation is colonisation of nature everywhere (see Giblett 1997: especially 136; and 1996: especially Chapter 3). Postmodern ecology decolonizes nature. Capitalists, colonists and scientists have colonized nature; they do not want their empire of nature to be decolonized.

Participatory Political Ecology

In the era of so-called postcolonialism, it is necessary to ask the question: what process of decolonisation has been carried out in relation to the colonisation of nature? Very little, if at all, is the answer. Decolonisation will not be fully achieved until nature is decolonized; both objective environmental nature and subjective bodily nature. This decolonisation could be achieved through what could be called participatory, political ecology. It deconstructs and decolonizes: the hierarchical privileging of the *polis* over the *oikos*, of the masculine public sphere over the feminized private sphere and the -ospheres; the reproduction of this binary opposition by NGOs even in privileging the *oikos* over the *polis*; and the economic exploitation of the -ospheres by TNCs. It also reconstructs economy in relation to ecology on the basis of earthly mutuality and bio- and psycho-symbiosis in bioregional home-habitats.

Part of that reconstruction has to take place around labour as the rule of nature is mediated though labour. For Habermas:

> [...] although we must presuppose nature as existing in itself, 'we ourselves have access to nature only within the historical dimension disclosed by labour processes'. Accordingly 'objective environmental nature' refers not to nature-in-itself but to a nature that is 'constituted as *objective nature for us* only in being mediated by the subjective nature of man [*sic*] through processes of social labour'. (cited by McCarthy 1984: 114)

Yet this objective environmental nature is also constituted as subjective bodily nature for us, and constitutes our subjective bodily nature, through the processes of domestic labour and the -ospheres. These latter include what Hutchinson calls the 'interfaces [and exchanges] between the liquid, the solid and the gaseous states of matter' (1970: 3), the music of the -ospheres revolving in what Wendell Berry calls 'the great economy' (1987).

The social processes of labour through which nature is mediated to us are not only physical acts of work, but also technological tools by which we human beings manipulate nature. It is these tools which provide the limit case for Habermas of our access to and knowledge of nature. As Joel Whitebook puts it, Habermas is complicit with the class rule of the earth as he 'condemns nature to being exclusively an object of domination', (Whitebrook 1979: 45; see also 55) and so 'nature can only be known as an object of possible technical control'. Yet modern human beings can know environmental and bodily nature not only through the social process of labour in civil society, but also through the domestic processes of labour in the house, and through the ecological processes at work in the earth-household and the processes in our own bodies, including multi-sensory engagement and enjoyment.

Not only, as Tom Jagtenberg and David McKie argue, is 'all communication [...] biospheric in its action' (1997: 2), but also all our actions are in communication with the -ospheres. A truism of the 1960s was that 'we are what we eat' but, as Jagtenberg and McKie point out, 'what we eat also shapes the planet' (1997: 204). What hypermodern human beings eat also shapes us, our bodies and our health. Ecologically (as a land and society organism as Aldo Leopold [1991: 217] put it), we are what we eat; corporeally we, and environmentally the earth, are becoming what we have eaten, or what is left behind after we have eaten. The result is what Verena Conley, following and translating Michel Serres, calls a plaque: 'a great many humans form a "plaque", a formation that *disturbs* [the] functioning [of physical communality] [...] *plaques* of physical *scoria* of humans [...] are encrusted upon and overlap the globe' (Conley 1997: 65).

These plaques of humanity are reshaping the globe, like plate tectonics. They are also superseding any simplistic notion of an individual subject acting alone in relation to nature, as well as problematising a hard and fast divide between nature and culture. Plate tectonics are natural, but plaque tectonics are a cultural reconstruction of nature. They are the urban landscape on the surface of the earth. They are patriarchal culture married to mother nature, a sleazy father law groping the fertile female body of the earth. Serres argues that:

> [...] on Planet Earth, henceforth, action comes not so much from man [*sic*] as an individual or subject, the ancient warrior of philosophy and old-style historical consciousness [...] no, the decisive actions are now, massively, those of enormous and dense plates of humanity. (1995: 16)

This plaque, this excrescence on the face, or more precisely in the mouth (which cannot be spat out because it sticks so much, though it may be sloughed off) of the earth, these plates of humanity are not just cities but megalopolises: New York, Philadelphia, Washington; Europe as city; Newcastle, Sydney, Wollongong; Yanchep, Perth, Mandurah. Cities are not merely malignant cancers on and in the body of the earth, but also artificially constructed benign comfort zones for their residents. Cities are the child of the marriage between patriachal culture, the Law of the Father, and the benign and malignant Mother Nature.

A participatory, political ecology would thus be an urban ecology, or part of what Paul Virilio calls 'grey ecology', which 'opens itself up to the cosmos, to culture. Here no mastery is possible' (2009: 25). Here mutuality is possible. He has asked 'would it not be appropriate to set up a grey ecology alongside the green? An ecology of those "archipelagos of cities", intelligent and interconnected, that will soon reshape Europe and the world' (Virilio 1998: 59). If they have not already done so, and not only the terrestrial world, but also the extra-terrestrial world where the satellites orbit (see Giblett 2008b: Chapter 9). Cities are interconnected into networked islands and bunkered enclaves not only by trade and transportation, but also by telecommunications and transmissions. Virilio's grey ecology includes an urban ecology, 'an ecology that would be concerned not only with the air and noise pollution of the big cities but, first and foremost, the sudden eruption of the "world-city", totally dependent on telecommunications, that is being put in place at the end of the millennium' (1998: 59). And still being put in place in the beginning of this one. Telecommunications makes trade and transportation today possible. It also includes an ecology of the body, as ecology for Virilio 'no longer deals with water, flora, wildlife only. It deals with the body itself as well' (1998: 47).

Nevertheless, as Robert Frodeman argues, 'we are in symbiotic relation to the oxygen-producing plants of the world' (1992: 319) – whether we human beings like it or not. As Conley also argues, 'we are always, *a priori*, in an ecological rapport with the world and nature' (1997: 18), though this 'rapport' operates on a biological and political continuum from the mutually beneficial to the downright destructive, from the commensal to the parasitic. The latter operates especially so in the era of 'western development' wherein, for Michel de Certeau:

> [...] 'nature' only figures an object of labour and the terrain of socio-economic struggles. It has no value other than the negative one of peasant 'resistance' to be overcome, of a biological limit always to be transcended, or of traditionalist anchorings to be rejected. (1984: 232)

Or of a slave to be enslaved and exploited. Instead of living in mutually beneficial and bio- and psycho-symbiosis with the planet rooted in the earth, parasitic citizens, pieces of plaque, tend to live what Chesnaux (cited by Jagtenberg and McKie 1997: 8–9) calls 'off-ground,' off-planet, off-world, in the extra-terrestrial world of modern cities. Parasitic citizens even become, in Michel Serres' telling image, astronauts floating in space (as depicted on the cover of *People and Places of Nature and Culture*) connected by an umbilical cord to the 'mother ship' (1995:

120 and 122) (I discuss Serres's image of the astronaut floating in space in greater detail in the final chapter below). Parasitic citizens try to live away from home without the earth instead of living at home with the earth. Hypermodern human beings are Locke's and Kant's children. For Locke, 'negation of nature is the way to happiness' (cited in Jagtenberg and McKie 1997: 14), and for Kant the sublime is the faculty by which 'we' (hypermodern urban people) calculate ourselves as independent of nature (cited by Giblett 1996: 35). Insofar as hypermoderns calculate ourselves as independent of nature, we have inculcated the sublime.

A participatory, political ecology deconstructs and decolonizes the hierarchical distinction in Ancient Greek thought and practice between *polis* and *oikos*, and in modern bourgeois patriarchy between culture and nature, male and female, and decolonizes the conquest of the earth, the colony of nature. Its primary aim is earthly mutuality. This participatory, political ecology is associated with the third type of 'generalized ecology' that Felix Guattari envisages: 'ecology should abandon its connotative link with images of a small minority of nature lovers or accredited experts; for the ecology I propose here questions the whole of subjectivity and capitalist power formations' (1989: 140). Including the whole of corporeality, I would add, for capitalism is corporeal. The body of capital is an orally and anally sadistic monster that consumes good things from the earth and produces goods and bads. The body of the earth is inscribed with and by the body of capital.

Part of the questioning that Guattari proposes must entail a thorough interrogation of the subject's interpellation as bodily being in relation to spaces and places, and in relation to the history of the colonial expropriation and resource exploitation of indigenes' lands. Generalized ecology for Guattari is not just a matter of 'the environment', but also of human psyche and society as:

> [...] we cannot conceive of solutions to the poisoning of the atmosphere and to global warming due to the greenhouse effect, or to the problem of population control without a mutation of mentality, without promoting a new art of living in society [...]. (1995: 20)

Here, society is not conceptualized as something separate from nature or 'the environment', but as integral and interdependent with it. A mutation of mentality involves diagnosing the symptoms of psychogeopathology, engaging in a talking cure of their causes and preventing their manifestation in the first place by promoting eco-mental health through earthly mutuality and psycho-symbiosis (see Chapters 9, 10 and 12).

Guattari's third ecology is a critical meta-discourse of nature that functions analogously to Foucault's meta-discourse of sexuality. It demonstrates that the discourses of nature have concealed precisely what it is they were ostensibly designed to reveal: the interconnectedness of subjectivity and corporeality, economy and ecology, power and the planet. It extends the biopolitics of human bodies to the body of the earth. It shows the ways in which investments of desire, yields of pleasure and relations of power have been enacted in and over not only the human body, but also the earth-body. It also enables resistance to the capitalist colonisation of both bodies by promoting eco-health through symbiosis and earthly mutuality. It is a different way of talking and being in relation to the living earth; a participatory, postmodern political ecology.

The key features of a participatory, postmodern political ecology include: decolonising nature, including colonized regions of the human body; thinking critically about a communal sense of cultural and natural heritage, envisaged by Paul Virilio, which would be 'tied to re-establishment of *memory* built on topical spaces, local experience, and shared discourses' (cited in Conley 1997: 87); revaluing the spiritual interactions of human cultures with natural environments and earthly entities; diagnosing the ecological symptoms in all theory, even when ecology is absent or ostensibly excluded as 'there is an ecological dimension in all theory' (Conley 1997: 123) just as there is with gender; engaging with and enjoying the natural world in multi-sensory ways and celebrating this enjoyment in creative practice; and deconstructing (and decolonising) the nature/culture binary more extensively than Derrida did (see Giblett 1996: especially Chapters 3 and 5).

Deconstruction and decolonisation of the culture and nature binary includes deconstruction and decolonisation of the 'two cultures' of the hard and life sciences on the one hand, and the social and human sciences on the other. The 'two cultures' divide reproduces the nature/culture split in epistemological and institutional terms. In this split nature is assigned to, and colonized by, the hard and life sciences on the one hand as its exclusive object, whereas culture is assigned to the social and human sciences on the other as its object. A participatory, political ecology deconstructs and decolonizes the disciplinary binarism that privileges the hard and life sciences over the soft social sciences and humanities. It produces an interdisciplinary dialogue on ecology, the interactions of species, including humans, with their environments, built and non-built.

A participatory, political ecology overcomes what Jagtenberg and McKie call the 'well-established divide between scientific considerations of ecosystems, which *include* everything but people, and social theoretic considerations of communities which *exclude* everything but people' (1997: 163). The humanities have established themselves on the latter side of this divide, as Conley suggests, with their pre-occupation with hardware, software and wetware (humans) (1997: 2) (what about non–human wetware? other animal species? plants? habitats? ecosystems? geology?). They have also had a fetishistic fascination with commodities (ignoring or repressing the natural world which supplies the raw materials for their production in the first place) and a superstructural fixation on ideology, institutions and political economy (occluding the earthly foundation to the economic base). As Michael Jacob has put it succinctly, 'all economic activity is founded on environmental wealth' (1989: 33). In terms of the Marxian base/superstructure model, the economic base rests on the earth; the economic base has an earthly foundation. If the foundation is put under too much pressure and starts to crumble, the house will fall.

The humanities and social sciences have been complicit with the scientific colonisation and capitalist exploitation of the natural world and with the split between the 'two cultures' of the sciences and the humanities. Between them, Conley (1993: 84) (following Ilya Prigogine and Isabelle Stengers), earlier called for a new alliance. The excluded third term between the sciences and the humanities is ecology, so Jagtenberg and McKie propose that 'sociology and communication and cultural studies might [...] integrate traditional social perspectives with ecology as the fourth dimension' (1997: 258, xiii, 46–50) of social space (to add to class, gender and ethnicity). However, ecology, or in plainer, less abstract and more Anglo-Saxon terms, a global sense of living place, is not some sort of afterthought or supplementary category to add to the cultural studies mantra of class, gender and ethnicity (or 'race'), but is pivotally and vitally necessary for, and to, these categories. Rather than ecology being what Conley called 'the last and least term in a socio-economic series of race, class, gender and ecology' (1993: 77), it would be a fully articulated term of disciplinary space within the academy as it should be fully articulated culturally.

'Society', communication and culture are already integrated into class, gender, ethnicity and ecology in what Michel Serres calls 'the natural contract' (1995) which, Conley argues, is 'the very precondition to all other contracts' (1997: 18), including employment contracts. The natural contract is also the very stuff of human and other life on this fair and green, groaning and suffering planet earth. Greening the humanities and the modern condition is an urgent intellectual and political task whose aim is to establish a symbiotic, mutually beneficial relationship with the earth. Such a dual project is aligned strongly with the 1960s and the radical politics of feminism and decolonisation. For all three, the personal is political. Humans are biological beings but whether we are ecological and decolonized selves is another question. A transdisciplinary environmental studies would develop those selves and decolonize the empire of nature (including ourselves).

With the decline of the public sphere of the nation-state, particularly in its capacity to regulate the private sphere of globalized, transnational corporate capitalism, we hypermoderns should be neither nostalgic for the good old days when the bourgeois public sphere could ostensibly control the worst excesses of civil society, nor utopian about 'the market' and its capacity to pursue so-called 'environmentally sustainable development' (an oxymoron). Civil society in the form of TNCs may have successfully brought about the demise of the public sphere as a fully functioning, separately operating entity and regulatory force, but it is still dependent on the domestic private sphere and the -ospheres for the production of its commodities and for the reproduction of its producers and consumers – a fact which civil society in the form of NGOs is constantly reminding it. It could only bring about the demise of these spheres at the cost of itself, living beings and the earth as a living entity. Participatory, political ecology reinstates the -ospheres as the source of all wealth, as the foundation of the economic base, in an economy regulated by the public sphere and the capacity of the -ospheres to provide commodities, to absorb wastes and to go on functioning as a living organism – otherwise we human beings are dead meat.

Notes

1. The title of this chapter alludes to and elaborates on that of Ortner (1974).
2. In Giblett (1996) I argue that there is no (movement or process of) enlightenment without a corresponding and concomitant 'endarkenment', whether it is of the 'dark continent' of Africa or female sexuality, or of the 'black waters' of swamps and marshes.
3. See Clarke (1973: 40–41; and 167–169). Swallow, for Clarke, was not only 'the woman who founded ecology' as his sub-title proclaims, but also the woman for whom 'home economics […] was home ecology'.
4. I elaborate this hierarchisation in Giblett (1996).

Part II

Landscape Aesthetics

What constitutes nature and how our relationship to it is worked out is invariably couched in aesthetic terms. In any discussion of nature, aesthetics usually raises its ugly head! What is valued in nature is usually what pleases aesthetically. Conversely, what displeases aesthetically is not usually valued culturally. Wetlands are a case in point, as they are both aesthetically displeasing and culturally devalued. In *Postmodern Wetlands: Culture, History, Ecology* I discussed these aspects of a particular landscape, or more precisely, of the wetlandscape (see Giblett 1996). I considered wetlands as an impassable abject, the obverse of the impossible object of the sublime, and I gave a critique of the will to fill wetlands. In *People and Places of Nature and Culture* I discuss nature, landscape and country in general and give a critique of the will to master nature in and by the categories of aesthetics and landscape themselves. These categories are not ideologically neutral, nor are they culturally universal but have colonized lands and cultures.

In both books landscape figures prominently as one of the central devices and means by which Europeans and their settler Diasporas understand and relate to land. In *Postmodern Wetlands* I critiqued the way in which the European landscape aesthetics of the sublime, the picturesque and the beautiful denigrated wetlands. In *People and Places of Nature and Culture* I critique the European landscape aesthetics of the sublime, the picturesque and the beautiful for its hierarchical taxonomy of landscapes in which, for instance, mountains are privileged over marshes, fields over fens. The European landscape aesthetic was part of the explorer's and settler's cultural baggage that they took with them and either found or recreated in the colonies with devastating consequences. Yet the Aboriginal inhabitants and owners of colonial land had lived symbiotically with it for tens of millennia before.

Chapter 3 critiques the aesthetics of nature for the way it valourizes some landscapes, landforms and objects in, or associated with, them (sublime mountains, pleasingly picturesque prospects, beautiful small things) to the detriment of others (dismal swamps, melancholic marshes, despondent sloughs). The discourses of nature and of the public and private spheres contributed to the development of landscape aesthetics in eighteenth-century Europe. Conservationists inherited this landscape aesthetic and in some instances have struggled against it to produce a conservationist aesthetics that values all land whether or not it is aesthetically pleasing. Yet, given that aesthetics was for Hegel (2004: 43) concerned with only the senses of sight and hearing, and that aesthetics enshrines and reproduces the sadistic subject-object distinction, this chapter concludes with a call for a conservation counter-aesthetics that values all the senses, deconstructs the masterly distinction between subject and object, and decolonises the lands colonised by landscape aesthetics.

The European landscape aesthetic produced the ways in which Europeans and their Diasporas have seen and shaped the land through the percepts and practices of the gentleman's park estate and the tourist's package, national parks and wilderness, mining and pastoralism and the 'Bush' of Australian mateship. Particularly nefarious and insidious in both capitalist and conservationist circles has been the Romantic aesthetic of the organicist built and natural landscapes with its pastoro-technical idyll of harmony between various features of the landscape, and between house and garden in city and country. The reproduction of the landscape of the gentleman's park in the suburban enclave estate, especially in the artificial ponds, tree-lined avenues and pleasing prospects of its entry statements, has had a fatal impact on the indigenous woodlands and wetlands of Australia. Through clearing and filling, shaping and planting an alien landscape has destroyed unique local floral and fauna.

Chapter 4 critiques the landscape aesthetics and the class and gender politics of the gentleman's park. It also critiques the cultural politics of the gentleman's park as early explorers and settlers in Australia sought and found it in land modified by Aboriginal people. Yet explorers and settlers did not recognize or acknowledge, let alone respect, the work of Aboriginal people in producing the kind of land they sought. Nor did this land give rise to any sense of solidarity between the two hunting cultures for here was a land shaped for hunting. Where settlers did not find the gentleman's park, they tried to recreate it with devastating effects on Aboriginal people and on indigenous flora and fauna. Both finding and recreating the Australian gentleman's park dispossessed Aboriginal people.

Chapter 3

Nature's Fairest Forms: Aesthetics of Nature

Why are swamps dismal? Marshes melancholic? Sloughs despondent? Moors dreary? Tarns sullen? Why are parklands picturesque and prospects pleasing? Why are small, well-formed, smooth and enclosed scenes and surfaces beautiful? Why is the experience of big, massive and ruggedly formed objects sublime and terrifying? Why are the abject, smelly and formless depths of slime uncanny and horrifying? These questions pose a problematic of the aesthetics of nature for the modern European cultural tradition and its settler Diasporas. Yet they are not of merely historical or theoretical interest as they have wider cultural pertinence and practical consequences for the conservation of ecosystems and for the way humans live in the ecosphere. The aesthetics of nature in landscape painting, gardening and writing, and in visual representations in tourism promotion, nature documentaries, televisual lifestyle shows, coffee table books and geographic magazines are all big business.

Nature Aesthetics and Landscape

Yet nature has not really been regarded as a proper object for aesthetics. The idea of the aesthetics of nature is a historical misnomer in European philosophical terms, though it has been a commercial success in the modern culture industries. This official disregard for the aesthetics of nature can be traced back to at least the eighteenth century. Theodor Adorno (1984) argues that beginning with Friedrich Schelling, the principal philosopher of Romanticism, aesthetics has shown an almost exclusive concern with works of art, not with nature. There is an historical irony here in that the Romantics are usually considered to have been more concerned with nature than with art, but they valued and valorised art over nature.

Adorno goes on to contrast what he calls this post-Kantian neglect of 'the beautiful in nature' with Kant's 'perspicacious analyses' (1984: 91) of it in *The Critique of Judgment*. Although Kant theorized some aspects of the aesthetics of nature, he was primarily concerned in *The Critique of Judgment* with that in nature which evokes or produces the experience or the state of the sublime. Thus, the aesthetics of nature does not merely involve the beautiful as Adorno suggests, but also the sublime, not to forget the picturesque, all three of which could occur in relation to landscape considered as painting, or as writing, or as gardening, or as viewing an actual piece of land.

In answering the question 'why was natural beauty dropped from the agenda of aesthetics?' Adorno answers his own question by stating that 'the reason is not that it was truly sublated in a higher realm, as Hegel would have us believe. Rather, the concept of natural beauty was simply repressed'. This raises another question: why? Because, as he goes on to argue, 'art and aesthetics after Kant have tacitly incorporated what in traditional aesthetics used to belong to nature'. Post-Kantian aesthetics represses the concept of natural beauty because the former was founded on the incorporation of the latter. Nature was made into art; cultural transformation of nature into art occurred in early nineteenth-century Europe (see Woodring 1989). Just as sex was transformed into discourse at about the same time as Foucault argued, so was nature transformed into art. This process of incorporation subl(im)ated nature (and natural beauty) into the realm of aesthetics, part of the proliferation of the discourses of nature, but this process was founded on the repression and oppression of nature.

A countervailing transformation of what Tim Bonyhady calls 'art into nature' (2000: 358) began in the 1960s, only to be obstructed more recently. He goes on to argue that 'if the gap between art and nature narrowed dramatically in the 1970s and 1980s, it reopened wide through the 1990s' (Bonyhady 2000: 366). The 'environmental aesthetic' retrieved from the nineteenth century and espoused by Bonyhady seeks to reclose the gap in the 2000s, but it uncritically reproduces the official aesthetic modes of the sublime, the picturesque and the beautiful. By constract, a conservation counter-aesthetics critiques not only the class and gender politics of all three and the category of the aesthetic itself, but also the privileging of the aesthetic senses of sight and hearing over the others. It promotes a full bodily interaction with land, even an erotic ecology.

Arguably all sublimation involves a corresponding and concomitant process of repression. The two processes of subl(im)ation and repression, as I have argued elsewhere following Zoë Sofoulis, go together (see Giblett 1996: especially Chapter 2). One is not possible without the other. They are two sides of the same coin as it were, or more precisely are two complementary processes, which mirror each other, which go in opposite directions as it were. Whereas sublimation raises up what might otherwise descend into the merely beautiful into the ethereal realms of the aesthetic, repression pushes back what is further below, what wants to come to consciousness.

As a result of this dual process of sublimation and repression, nature was split between the sublimated and aestheticized on the one hand, and the repressed and demonized on the other. Some aspects of nature were sublimated, or more precisely seen as the site for the experience of the sublime, such as the mountainous, whilst others were repressed, such as the slimy and swampy. As a consequence, the mountainous has been seen as the height of the sublime, whereas the swampy has been the depths of the slimy (see Giblett 1996: especially Chapter 1). This hierarchical privileging can be mapped spatially, as well as corporeally and metaphysically, as I have attempted to do elsewhere (see 'A Psychogeocorpography of Modernity' in Giblett 1996: Figure 1, Chapter 2).

The three official, or philosophically legitimated, aesthetic modes of the beautiful, picturesque and sublime are those in which the senses of sight and hearing can achieve expression and satisfaction. Yet Freud formulated a fourth modality that is not necessarily aesthetic, but even counter-aesthetic. This is the uncanny, which is related closely to the sense of smell and is the obverse and repressed of the sublime as I have also argued elsewhere following Sofoulis (see Giblett 1996: especially Chapter 2). Nature was thus not totally sublimated, nor was it simply repressed, but split in two. Nature per se was not a proper object for aesthetics because nature was split into the aesthetically pleasing (the beautiful, the picturesque), the aesthetically discomfiting (the sublime) and the aesthetically displeasing, or simply the unaesthetic or even counter-aesthetic (the slimy, the swampy and the uncanny). The aesthetically pleasing and discomfiting in nature can be discussed and contrasted as instances of landscape aesthetics, whereas the aesthetically displeasing and the counter-aesthetic are not instances of anything, or are instances of nothing (and nothingness).

This split can be illustrated by reference to landscape writing (as distinct from nature writing) in two seventeenth-century English 'country house' or 'estate' poems and one nineteenth-century Romantic picturesque poem. For Andrew Marvell, 'Nature's glories' can be found in:

[…] fragrant gardens, shady woods,
Deep meadows, and transparent floods. (Fowler 1994: 283)

Similarly, for William Wordsworth:

With exultation, at my feet I saw
Lake, islands, promontories, gleaming bays,
A universe of Nature's fairest forms.

Nature's glories and fairest forms can be contrasted with what Charles Cotton calls:

[…] nature's shames and ills –
Black heaths, wild rocks, bleak crags, and naked hills,
And the whole prospects so inform, and rude. (Fowler 1994: 375)

Nature's 'shames and ills' differ from nature's glories in both prospect and form. Nature's 'shames and ills' are displeasing prospects, whereas nature's glories are 'pleasing prospects' (see Williams 1973: title of Chapter 12; and the following chapter of *People and Places of Nature and Culture*). Nature's glories, or the beautiful and picturesque, are what Wordsworth called 'nature's fairest forms', lying supine at his feet over which he stands in mastery, whereas nature's 'shames and ills', the slimy and uncanny, are 'inform' (both informal and inside form) rather than formless (lacking form or too big for form to contain), a feature of the sublime for Kant (1952: 90).

It is easy to highlight the normativity of this hierarchial, value-laden distinction simply by inverting it in carnivalesque and parodic play as Raymond Briggs does in *Fungus the Bogeyman*, ostensibly a 'children's book'. In the upside-down, topsy-turvy world of

Bogeydom 'landscapes [displayed in the National Bogey Gallery] show ditches, dead trees, sewer outflows and black stagnant lakes' (1977: unp). I hazard a guess that no national art gallery in the right-side-up world houses such 'landscapes'. They house paintings depicting dismal swamps or the black waters of wetlands, but only as the setting or backdrop for, say, the story of Evangeline, or of the runaway slave, or the noble savage. Not only do the Bogey 'landscapes' *not* constitute landscapes in subject-matter and tone, but also they do not constitute a nation's view of itself and of its national territory suitable for displaying in one of its monuments to itself.

Nature may not have been a proper object for aesthetics in the sense of the formal, theoretical study of aesthetic experience, but nature has been an object for aesthetic practice and experience in landscape painting, gardening and writing since the sixteenth century, landscape photography since the nineteenth century and landscape cinematography since the early twentieth century. The aesthetics of landscape and the ideology of country split nature into an aestheticized and passive object of contemplation on the one hand, and an agricultural and compliant slave for manipulation by the active agency of the landlords in accordance with their design on the other.

Although Raymond Williams had second thoughts later in his life and preferred the concept of livelibood (as we shall in the final chapter), the crucial distinction for him is not between culture and nature, but between the country and the city, and within the country between 'unmediated nature' ('a physical awareness of trees, birds, the moving shapes of land' [though this already smacks of the natural historian's abstraction of species from their habitats and ecosystems, and the explorer's doctrine of *terra nullius* that denies the work of indigenes in shaping the country and nature]) and 'working agriculture' ('in which much of the nature is in fact being produced') (Williams 1973: 118 and 119). Or perhaps more precisely, re-produced. The country was constructed in the service of a bourgeois, and burgeoning, agrarian and industrial capitalism. Indeed, Williams shows how the strongest feeling for the aesthetic and other pleasures of nature in the country were evinced precisely when that capitalism was making its strongest and most irreversible inroads into re-shaping the countryside (1973: 118). At the same moment, and indeed in the same breath and stroke of the brush and pen, as nature was being aestheticized, nature was also being exploited economically by hand, tool and machine. The former was a compensatory and disavowing device for the latter.

Although agrarian capitalism was not responsible for the invention of nature, it was complicit with the scientificisation of nature and it did heighten and extend a process instituted by agriculture. Williams states, 'The real invention of the landlords [was] to make Nature move to an arranged design' (1973: 124). The category of country was constructed by an emergent landed gentry and entrepreneurial capitalist class as a means of securing and maintaining its hegemony through the control of land as its resource base. Country was a cultural construction of nature which, as Ann Bermingham argues, 'becomes a key concept linking the cultural representation of social institutions and apparatuses with the economics of the enclosed landscape' (1986: 1). Williams' history attests to the rise of this ideology of nature, this capitalist construction of the categories of landscape and nature, which was simultaneous and concomitant with the capitalist exploitation of the land. For Williams, 'a working country is hardly ever a landscape. The very idea of landscape implies separation and observation' (1973: 120). Landscape is an aesthetic category, a visual experience for the roaming eye/I which/who occasionally stops to take in the pleasing, picturesque prospect from a static viewpoint as we will see in the next chapter.

Barbara Bender argues that 'landscape was originally coined in the emergent capitalist world of western Europe by aesthetes, antiquarians and landed gentry – all men' (1993: 1–2). Or more to the point, all masculinist. Landscape itself is a capitalist and masculinist category that explorers, colonists, anthropologists and tourists have imposed on non-capitalist cultures and lands. Recent studies of the anthropology of landscape have thus universalized a capitalist masculinist category to all cultures (see, for example, Hirsch and O'Hanlon 1995). The complicity of anthropology with imperialism and patriarchy stands revealed. Colonisation and imperialism takes place culturally through the imposition of categories; they are categorical. Neither imperialism nor its avatar in tourism is possible without landscape. Landscape art, J. M. Coetzee argues, is 'by and large a traveller's [and tourist's?] art intended for the consumption of vicarious travellers: it is closely connected with the imperial eye – the eye that by seeing names and dominates – and the imperial calling' (1988b: 174). Landscape is the visible surface of the land that allows the eye the power to wander and to name, or more precisely to rename as the places had Aboriginal names.

Landscape is the visible and renamable surface of the land. It is not the invisible and mute depths of the land that working country is dependent upon. Landscape, for Denis Cosgrove, is 'the surface of the physical earth, the surface upon which humans live, which they transform and which they frequently seek to transcend' (1993: 282). Landscape renders the land as a surface of inscription for aesthetics, grid-plan towns, drains and railways, and not as what he calls 'the elemental depths of the inorganic world below'. Yet the depths below are more organically productive than the surface above; the depths of the wetland are more organically productive than the surface of the dryland. Landscape reduces land to surface, to virtually two dimensions of length and breadth, either in the prospect of the land lying supine beneath one, or in the painting of the landscape standing erect before one. Landscape is the surface of inscription and production that denies and represses the depths of the land.

With landscape the surface of the land is set up against the self. The notion of landscape, as Veronica Brady puts it glossing Judith Wright, 'implies a division between the self and the land' (Brady 1998: 433). The land becomes a surface against which the self poses itself, and a screen (psychological, cinematic and televisual) onto which it projects its fears and desires. Landscape separates subject and object. Landscape is a phenomenological and psychological category of the distinction between subject and object. For Eric Hirsch, 'one concomitant of the process of ever-increasing intervention in nature was the simultaneous generation of new ideas of separation, such as that between subject and object' (1995: 6–7), especially between 'the experience of a viewing "subject" and the countryside as a desirable "object" to behold', and own. Landscape and landscape aesthetics entail separation between subject and object in the very act of seeming to join them together.

Landscape is a not a category of the object itself; landscape is not a category of the land, but a category of human visual land perception. As Wolfgang Sachs puts it, 'The landscape is the construct of a society that no longer has an unmediated relationship with the soil' (1992: 154). The concept of landscape encodes, measures and reproduces our alienation from nature. Landscape measures our distance from land. Landscape is capitalist – and by no means universal.

This distinction between subject and object is embedded in the English word 'landscape' whose genealogy has been traced by John Barrell, who relates how the term was:

> [...] introduced [into England and English] from the Dutch in the sixteenth century to describe a pictorial representation of the countryside [...] Later the word came to include within its meaning both this sense [...] and another, more loose [sense] of a piece of countryside *considered as a visual phenomenon* [...] [Nevertheless b]oth these senses [...] had this in common, that they referred to a tract of land, or its representation in painting, which lay in prospect – that it is to say, which could be seen all at one glance, from a fixed point of view [...] But later still [in the mid-eighteenth century], a more general meaning attached to the word, so that one could now talk of *the* landscape of a place [...] And so we can trace these stages of the word 'landscape': from first denoting only a picture of rural scenery, it comes to denote also a piece of scenery apprehended in a picture, in prospect, and finally it denotes as well land 'considered with regard to its natural configuration'. This extension of the second meaning into the third is, clearly, a most important one. It implies a change in attitude to land something like this: in the first place, a particular piece of land, under the eye is considered pictorially; in the second place, *the whole of natural scenery is considered as having, somehow, a pictorial character* [...] The words 'landscape', 'scene', and, to a lesser extent 'prospect', [...] demanded, in short, that the land be thought of *as itself composed into the formal patterns which previously a landscape-painter would have been thought of as himself* [sic] *imposing on it*. (1972: 1–3; my emphases)

Land not composed into formal patterns was not, by definition, landscape. Such land by and large was some sort of wetland, and wetlandscape was an impossibility, a contradiction in terms (see Giblett 1996: especially Chapter 1).

Wordsworthy Country Landscapes

William Wordsworth's *Guide to the Lakes*, first published in 1810 (which then went through five editions to 1835 and was his only bestseller), and both versions (1805–1806 and 1850) of *The Prelude* represent the pinnacle of a Romanticist construction of landscape and are an exemplar of landscape writing (as distinct from nature writing and as discussed in Chapter 1).[1] Wordsworth's guidebook categorizes an aesthetic taxonomy of English landscapes almost as systematically as any botanist classifying the flora of a region. In this value-laden and hierarchical taxonomy mountains are the supreme, sublime landscape, whereas tarns are the most abject and worthless. Furthermore, the latter are masculinized and the latter feminized. In this section I deconstruct this taxonomy and its gender politics. I argue for an appreciation of all land irrespective of whether or not it conforms to the dictates of the Romanticist landscape aesthetic.

In *The Guide* Wordsworth begins his 'Description of the Scenery of the Lakes' by setting up 'a Model of the Alpine country' which for him is 'the sublime and beautiful region' (1906: 21) par excellence against which he will measure all other regions. He uses this model for the Lake country beginning, naturally, with its mountains not only because of some sort of affinity with the Alps, but also because 'they who have studied the appearance of Nature feel [...] the superiority, in point of visual interest, of mountainous over other countries' (1906: 29). Indeed, in the later version of *The Prelude* Wordsworth was to re-iterate that Nature has 'her Alpine throne' (1850, VI: 431). The superiority of mountains over other types of country comes down to a matter of sight, appearance and feeling. With mountains the eye is able to range over vertical surfaces standing up regally (even phallically) in front of the viewer rather than having to roam over horizontal surfaces (such as plains) lying supine at the feet of the viewer.

Mountains, or perhaps more precisely their forms, are also superior to other country because they evoke the feeling of the sublime. In the *Guide to the Lakes* Wordsworth harps on 'mountains of sublime form' (1906: 16), on 'a sublime combination of mountain forms' (1906: 17) and on 'the sublime forms of nature in mountainous districts' (1906: 156n). The sublime is superior to the beautiful because the former is primary, even originary, and the latter secondary and derivative:

> [...] sublimity is the result of Nature's first great dealings with the superficies of the earth; but the general tendency of her subsequent operations is towards the production of beauty; by a multiplicity of symmetrical parts uniting in a consistent whole. (1906: 35)

The sublime concerns the rude fashioning of surfaces, and not depths, in the upthrust of mountains, whereas the beautiful is epitomized by the feminized lake in which mechanical parts are united into an 'organic' or pastoro-technical whole. The sublime is a Bachelor Machine for a Bachelor Birth, a mountainous or monstrous birth that sees, as Wordsworth did, the mountains as the birthplace of life rather than the primal slime of the intertidal zone.[2]

In Wordsworth's taxonomy of nature aesthetics the eternal mountainous is productive of the sublime, whereas the temporal lacustrine evokes the beautiful. The feeling of the beautiful is evoked in the lacustrine landscape where the benign beneficence of nature flows.

By ascribing the beautiful to the natural Wordsworth ascribed to it what was in fact cultural. For him these were natural sentiments, whereas the sublime is a cultural construction, albeit high cultural. In the famous letter Wordsworth wrote to the *Morning Post* (and reprinted now with *The Guide*) protesting at the construction of the Kendal and Windermere railway, he maintains that some scenes are naturally beautiful, whereas an appreciation of others require the addition of 'culture', especially those evocative of the sublime:

> [...] a vivid perception of romantic scenery [though Wordsworth rated this in his *Guide* proper 'a poor and mean word' (1906: 149)] is neither inherent in mankind, nor a necessary consequence of even a comprehensive education. It is benignly [rather than divinely] ordained [by whom? one wonders] that green fields, clear blue skies, running streams of pure water, rich groves and woods, orchards, and all the ordinary varieties of [English?] rural nature, should find an easy way to the affections of all [English?] men [*sic*]. (1906: 150–151)

By contrast, it is divinely (or malignantly depending on the way in which you look at it) ordained that dismal swamps, dreary marshes, smelly fens, slimy tarns and all the uncanny varieties of wetlands should never find a way into the affections of cultured Europeans and their settler Diasporas. Yet it is the benign constructions of European rural landscapes that have proved malignant, like a cancer, wherever they have been imposed on the neo-Europes of Australia, Canada, New Zealand and the United States, to the detriment of Aboriginal people and indigenous fauna, flora and ecosystems.

Rather than the delights (or horrors) of the slimy and the swampy, Wordsworth wants to educate his readers into the frisson and terrors of the sublime and the mountainous. He goes on in the *Guide* to maintain that:

> But a taste beyond this [for the ordinary varieties of rural nature] [...] is not to be implanted all at once; it must be gradually developed both in nations and individuals. Rocks and mountains, torrents and wide-spread waters, and all those features of nature which go to the composition of such scenes as this part of England is distinguished for [and which evoke the sublime, I would add], cannot, in their finer relations to the human mind, be comprehended, or even very imperfectly conceived, without processes of culture or opportunities of observation in some degree habitual. (1906: 150–151; see also 157)

The purpose of Wordsworth's *Guide* proper is designed to be such a 'process of culture' leading, as he put it, 'to habits of more exact and considerable observation' (1906: 22). The rural and the pastoral are beautiful, which for Wordsworth is natural, whereas the massive and mountainous are sublime, which for him is cultural. Yet the former is just as much cultural as the latter. The English pastoral landscape is hardly beautiful universally, and indeed the beautiful itself is hardly universal but is the product of a particular time and place, of the European aesthetic tradition.

For Wordsworth, the lake is also unlike the marsh or swamp in that it can be seen all at once from one given point in prospect, whereas the swamp and marsh are constricting and its aspects can only be taken in, if at all, from a number of different viewpoints. The lake also affords the long view of distant and intriguing bays, which provoke curiosity as to their contents, whereas the swamp and marsh are by definition so full of trees, or sedges, that no such view is afforded the viewer, and so no such curiosity is aroused in him or her. Indeed, there is no sense of edge or shore with the swamp or marsh unlike the deep-bottomed lake with their '*boundary-line* [...] gracefully or boldly indented' (1906: 34). The lake is feminized as a graceful or curvaceous figure.

Yet Wordsworth later noted approvingly 'a new habit of pleasure [...] arising out of the perception of the fine gradations by which in Nature one thing passes away into another, and the boundaries that constitute individuality disappear in one instance only to be revived elsewhere under a more alluring form' (1906: 73). The lake is not only feminized as a graceful or curvaceous figure but also as a seductive form. Important here for Wordsworth is the maintenance of form: without form there is no aesthetics. Things in nature can be gradated as long as in passing from one instance into another boundaries do not disappear altogether (such as into a dismal swamp or slough of despond where there are no clear boundaries between land and water) never to return in any form whatsoever – alluring or not.

Objects can be gradated into other objects as long it is into a more alluring form and not simply into a stale reminder of something it is not. Wordsworth goes on to bemoan the fact that where 'the opposite shores are out of sight of each other, like those of the American and Asiatic lakes, then unfortunately the traveller is reminded of a nobler object [that is, mountains]; he [*sic*] has the blankness of a sea-prospect without the grandeur and accompanying sense of power' (1906: 34), without, in other words, the feeling of the sublime. With these 'American and Asiatic lakes' the traveller has a horizontal prospect of these lakes but not a sense of the vertical tumults of mountainous seas, which evoke the sublime. Indeed, for William Gilpin, writing a few years earlier than Wordsworth, 'nothing can be more sublime than the ocean' (1794: 43). If seas were mountainous they could evoke the sublime. Sea-like mountains return the analogy to its source and double the feeling of the sublime. For Wordsworth, the mountains of the Lakes district were 'lifting themselves in ridges like the waves of a tumultuous sea' (1906: 27). Hence, they possessed 'magnitude and grandeur' and so could evoke the sublime.

Seas could be mountainous, and mountains tumultuous like seas: the parallelism of analogy is acceptable but not rivalry in size. Largeness is the domain of mountains, not lakes. Mountains should be large but not lakes in Wordsworth's view. Largeness is the domain of the sublime, and the mountainous, where smallness is the province of the beautiful, and the lacustrine. Sublimity, a feeling of pleasure bordering on pain, is associated with objects gigantic, massive and mountainous, including seas, whereas beauty is a sense of pleasure evoked by small objects (see Giblett 1996: especially Chapter 2). The sublime is evoked by looking up at monumental, formless, phallic and patriarchal objects towering above and terrifying one; the beautiful involves looking down at small, well-formed, feminine objects lying before one; the picturesque entails looking out across femininized pleasing prospects lying supine before one; and the uncanny is evoked by what one cannot see but one can smell or feel behind or beneath and horrifying one, the maternal, the abject and the slimy.

Conservation Counter-Aesthetics

Rather than relating to the land as landscape and so as a visual experience, to relate to the land as working country, not just country worked by humans, and to experience the land through all five senses would be to engage in part in a conservation aesthetics. Or perhaps more precisely, it would be to engage in a conservation counter-aesthetics given the problematic nature of aesthetics in general, and of the aesthetics of nature in particular, especially with their valorisation of the sublime, the beautiful and the picturesque and of the senses of sight and hearing, and their denigration of the slimy and the uncanny and of the senses of taste, touch and smell. Rather than appealing to aesthetics, and so predominantly to the sense of sight, a conservation counter-aesthetics appreciates all the senses.

Rather than valorising the landscapes of nature or the beautiful in nature, or the experience of the sublime gained from some aspects of nature, Aldo Leopold in the 1940s developed a conservation or land aesthetics for all environments which would go hand in hand with a conservation or land ethic. In fact, without a conservation and land aesthetic, a conservation and land ethic could be an unpleasurable set of dicta and rules. Without an appreciation for, and without the pleasures gained from, the colours and shapes and life and smells and touch (and sights and sounds) of a piece of land, a locality, a bioregion, a species, conservation is a conversion religion of denial and loss. Without a conservation counter-aesthetics the conservationist is a conservation ascetic.

A conservation counter-aesthetics does not necessarily entail an appreciation for 'natural beauty,' whatever that is. Indeed, for Adorno, 'natural beauty is defined by its undefinability' (1984: 107). Yet despite its indefinability, Adorno was able to pinpoint earlier that 'the essence of what appreciation of natural beauty is [...] focuses exclusively on nature as appearance, never on nature as the stuff of work and material reproduction of life' (1984: 97). And not just human life, but all life. A conservation counter-aesthetics focuses precisely on nature as the stuff of work and material reproduction of life. Leopold's conservation aesthetics was in fact forged on and in relation to the piece of degraded farmland in Wisconsin he and his family worked and rehabilitated. He described and celebrated this place and these processes in his nature writing. With the conservation counter-aesthetics there is no hard and fast divide between nature as aesthetic object and nature as work object and subject, even abject. On the contrary, they are intimately interconnected.

This difference has profound implications for the positioning of the subject, or more precisely for the subject who focuses on nature as appearance and who is the agent of landscape aesthetics. For Adorno, 'delight in nature is tied up with the notion of the subject as being-for-itself and potentially infinite. The subject projects itself on nature, gaining a sense of nearness to nature by virtue of its isolation' (1984: 96). In fact, the subject gains such a sense of nearness to nature to the degree it is isolated or alienated from it. Aesthetics of nature, especially the sublime, is a solitary experience. Earlier Adorno argued that 'over long periods of time, the appreciation of natural beauty amalgamated itself with the suffering of the lone subject in an instrumentalized and mutilated world, bearing the marks of melancholia and world-weariness' (1984: 93–94). Melancholia is not to be found so much today in the 'dreary marsh' or 'slough of despond' as it was found to be in modernity, but in the mechanized and mutilated world of hypermodernity. A conservation counter-aesthetics delights not so much in a hypostatized and reified nature, but in a dynamic and processual environment or better bioregion. As a result the subject becomes implicated with the biological processes of the world, albeit mutilated but not annihilated, and ceases to be alone.

A conservation counter-aesthetics throws into relief a touristic aesthetics of nature. If anybody bears in Adorno's elitist and hypercritical terms 'the marks of melancholia and world-weariness' in 'the instrumentalized and mutilated world' of modernity it is the mass-packaged tourist. The touristic packaging and marketing of nature is for Adorno a process of neutralization:

> [...] integrated in the commercial world (as 'tourist industry,' for example) and devoid of its critical sting, the immediate appreciation of nature has become neutralized. As nature becomes synonymous with national parks and wildlife preserves, its beauty is purely tokenistic. Natural beauty is an ideological notion because it offers mediateness in the guise of immediacy. (1984: 101)

It offers, in other words and in terms of the two paradigms organising this book, second, third and fourth nature in the guise of first nature; offers worked-over, over-worked and hyper-worked nature in the guise of merely worked nature. A conservation counter-aesthetics, by contrast, offers the opportunity of immediacy with fifth nature by regarding its 'object' less as an object whose appearance is to be appreciated and more as agent whose processes are to be participated in, or as a subject with which to enter into intersubjective dialogue and exchange, even ultimately as an abject with which to deconstruct and decolonize the subject-object distinction altogether. For Leopold, conservation aesthetics involves 'the perception of the natural processes by which the land and the living things upon it [and above it, below it, in it and dependent on it] have achieved their characteristic form (evolution) and by which they maintain their existence (ecology)' (1949: 173). Nature writing is the creative expression and celebration of these processes, as exemplified in Leopold's own writing very much in the Thoreauvian tradition.

Conservation counter-aesthetics' appreciation in nature writing and other media for a piece of land is diachronic and synchronic, historical and structural rather than merely sensory, and certainly not exclusively visual. The recent invention of ecotourism can enact a conservation counter-aesthetic rather than an aesthetics of nature if it refuses the tokenistic beauty, and even the sublime mountainous of the national park and nature reserve, and enters into the biological processes of these and other areas, especially wild(er)ness, which would then be not just or even an aesthetic category, but a conservation bodily category and experience.

Wordsworth bemoaned the scenery habit in his contemporaries, but the habitués of scenery were the early tourists for whom he specifically wrote his guide (the first part is called 'Directions and Information for the Tourist'). The purpose of the *Guide* is to tutor the tourist in the European landscape aesthetic. Subsequent tourists inherited and reproduce this aesthetic. The categories of the sublime and the picturesque, for John Sears, 'shaped the way tourists viewed the landscape' (1989: 10). Or perhaps more precisely, these categories shaped the way tour operators and tourists constructed the land, or some aspects of it, into landscape, into the sublime or picturesque. There is, as Malcolm Andrews puts, 'a peculair circularity in the tourist's experience' (1989: vii; see also 55–56) with him or her seeking the picturesque scenes in reality he or she has seen in pictures, and the tourism industry cashing in at both ends of the process.

The tourist is an avatar of the picturesque, and the guide book the tourist's holy writ, as Barthes argued in the 1950s that:

> The *Blue Guide* hardly knows the existence of scenery except under the guise of the picturesque. The picturesque is found any time the ground is uneven. We find again this bourgeois promoting of the mountains, this old Alpine myth. Only mountains, gorges, defiles and torrents can have access to the pantheon of travel. (1973: 74)

Why? Because only they had access to the pantheon of aesthetics. The tourist is the product and reproducer of the European landscape aesthetic.

Yet the tourist is not only a traveller in space but also a time-traveller. The tourist travels to exotic places, and exotic times. The past is another country as J. P. Hartley says as the opening gambit of his novel *The Go-Between*. The tourist is not only an avatar of the picturesque, but also a connoisseur of periodisation. Space and time are married in the aesthetics of the sublime, picturesque and beautiful places associated with the periodisation of past times. The tourist's journey is a journey in time and space which enacts his or her superiority over other places, peoples and pasts. Space and time are measured in class terms and figure class difference. Colonialism not only colonized space in terms of territory, but also time in terms of the future and the past.

Present 'un(der)developed' societies are constituted as premodern and therefore as the past of modern societies, so time is mapped on to space and space is used to figure time. A journey to another country is thus not only a journey in space, but also in time. The travelling anthropolgist Claude Lévi-Strauss related in *Tristes Tropiques*: 'Instead of covering vast distances one has moved back imperceptibly in time' (1974: 85). The tourist re-enacts spatially the nineteenth-century theory of temporal social stages. A journey in space becomes a journey in time and in the social hierarchy. The tourist travels back in time and down the social hierarchy in order to mark his or her distance socially and temporally from the 'primitive' – whether it is a group of people or an area of land.

The tourist marks his or her class superiority over 'primitive' people and places by positioning 'them' in the past, whereas 'we' are in the present. Many travellers in America during the nineteenth century, as Henry Nash Smith argues, figured their journey through America from 'civilisation' across the frontier, into the wilderness beyond, as a journey back through the social from the 'civilized' to the 'primitive' to recreate western civilisation again in new lands (1950: 218–220). The tourist re-enacts this journey and this theory of social stages. The tourist descends into another place and time to ascend the social hierarchy and lord it over the local and the 'primitive', and then returns 'home' to ascend socially for having done so by displaying the trophies (souvenirs, photographs, etc.) of their triumphal tour.

Commenting on Lévi-Strauss' journey recounted in *Tristes Tropiques* Michel de Certeau argues cogently that 'the Bororos of Brazil sink slowly into their collective death, and Lévi-Strauss takes his seat in the French Academy […] the intellectuals are still borne on the backs of the people' (de Certeau 1984: 25). The tourist descends into the lower realms of the social hierarchy and heightens his or her sense of superiority to the degree by which he or she opens up a gap between him or herself and the local. He or she later returns home to ascend to a higher social position by virtue of the cultural and symbol capital he or she has accumulated by travelling to exotic locations and times. The tourist journey becomes imbued with greater significance than a mere journey in the present. A tourist journey in his or her own country can also be a journey back in time to a pre-modern, or pre-industrial, or early industrial, landscape, steeped in nostalgia manufactured by the cultural heritage industry.

The tourist transcends space and time; the tourist has what Dean MacCannell calls 'a transcendent consciousness' (1976); the tourist does not have an immanent consciousness grounded in a particular time and local place; the tourist is not a local. For the tourist as 'the representative consciousness of modernity', in MacCannell's terms, life is elsewhere – in time and space, in other places and in the past, not here and now. A conservation counter-aesthetics, by contrast, values local history, local knowledge and a sense of local place. It appreciates local lands, flora, fauna and folk not as another marketing opportunity for the tourist industry, but as the very stuff of life for locals themselves. It celebrates the cyclical, rather than the linear, model of time; it is immersed in the now-time.

A conservation counter-aesthetics also deconstructs and decolonizes the privileging of certain sights and scenes as more aesthetically pleasing than others, and of the senses of sight and hearing as the sole seats and sites of pleasure. For Adorno, the 'essential indeterminacy of natural beauty manifests itself in the fact that *any* fragment of nature […] can become beautiful' (1984: 104). But the point is that not just *any* fragment of nature does and has become beautiful, whereas the fundamental tenet of a conservation counter-aesthetics is that all fragments of nature are aesthetically pleasing, or rather, given that aesthetics has only been concerned with the senses of hearing and sight, sensually pleasing or even just challenging.

Adorno's tenet derives to some extent from William Gilpin who maintained that 'there are few parts of nature which do not yield a picturesque eye some amusement' (1794: 54).

Picturesqueness is not in the land, is not a quality of the land itself but is in the eye of the beholder for whom some parts of nature are more likely to give 'amusement' than others. Gilpin suggested earlier that 'we' pursue like a hunter 'this great object' of the picturesque through 'the scenery of nature. We seek it among *all* the ingredients of landscape – trees – rocks – broken-grounds – woods – rivers – lakes – plains – valleys – mountains – and distances' (1794: 42). And *not* in fens, marshes and swamps as a rule, which are certainly not counted among the ingredients of landscape, and hardly even the scenery of nature; they are more the *ob*scenery of nature (see Giblett 1996: especially Chapter 4). Picturesque landscape for J. M. Coetzee 'is, in effect, landscape reconstituted in the eye of the imagination according to acquired principles of composition' (1988a: 40 and 1). Landscape, as he puts it bluntly, is 'picturesque when it composes itself' (Coetzee 1988a: 39). This cryptic statement implies the question: composes itself into what? Into a picture, of course, is the tautological reply with its foreground, mid-ground and background and framing devices. By implication, landscape is not picturesque when it does not compose itself, when it is uncomposed or agitated, discordant (the musical metaphor of 'composed'), *deshabille* (the vestamentary metaphor), or even decomposed (the organic metaphor) like a swamp.

William Morris expressed similar sentiments to Gilpin and Adorno when he maintained that 'surely there is no square mile of earth's inhabitable surface that is not beautiful in its own way, if we men [sic] will only abstain from wilfully destroying that beauty' (1914: 170). Yet certain sorts of inhabitable surfaces (for whom? for what?) and wild scenes have been regarded as more aesthetically pleasing than others. And what of earth's uninhabitable surfaces and depths? A conservation counter-aesthetics subsumes the aesthetics of nature beneath the economy of nature (ecology) rather than the Wordsworthian obverse: whatever is (useful) in nature is (or should be) valuable. But a conservation counter-aesthetics does not merely privilege economy of nature (ecology) to the detriment or exclusion of aesthetics. Rather it regards as valuable everything in nature.

Notes

1. The *Guide* (Wordsworth 1906) is herafter cited in parentheses by year and page number, and *The Prelude* (Wordsworth 1972 and 1984) is hereafter cited by the year of the two different versions, book number and line number.
2. For Bachelor, or Celibate, Machines see Giblett (1996: 29, 50 n.7; 2008a: 95–99; and 2008b: 35 and 167–168). See also Theweleit (1987: especially 330n) and de Certeau (1984: 150–153; and 1986: 156–167).

Chapter 4

Pleasing Prospects Revista'd: The Gentleman's Park Estate

The distinction between aesthetic landscape and working country is simultaneously blurred and maintained, mystified and displayed in the gentleman's park estate. It is both working country and aesthetic landscape; indeed, the landscape is produced and maintained by working the country, by the workers who shape the country into parklandscape. The latter would not be possible without the former. Yet the signs of the latter are obscured in and by the former – deliberately so – until they only persist as traces: traces of the labour and labourer who made the parklandscape. Sole authorship of the parklandscape is ascribed to the gentleman owner who inscribes himself on the surface of the land in reforming it in accordance with the dictates of the European parklandscape aesthetic. Whereas the European landscape aesthetic embraces the sublime, the picturesque and the beautiful, the European parklandscape aesthetic is largely reduced and confined to the picturesque.

The ideal of the gentleman's park was sought and, if it was not found, recreated wherever possible in the European colonies by their settler Diasporas. When it was found, it was thought to have been created by nature or God, and not by the labour of Aboriginal people. Labour was obscured, mystified and ascribed to nature or God just as the labour of the gardener in the European gentleman's park estate was obscured, mystified and ascribed to the owner. The ideal of the gentleman's park estate was not only found or recreated in large pastoralist holdings in Australia. It was the product of an organic desideratum of harmony between house and garden that was sought and recreated in the suburbs. This pastoro-technical idyll was founded on the ideal of organic harmony between house and garden.

When this entailed wholesale clearing of native bushland in the colonies and its replacement with exotic plants (weeds) rather than preservation or restoration of a native garden of local species, it had, in Alan Moorehead's terms, a 'fatal impact' (1966) on indigenous flora and fauna. The invasion of Australia was not just a military operation involving naval ships, armed soldiers and settlers, but also a biological usurpation using alien plants, animals and diseases. European explorers and settlers not only wrested ownership of land from Aboriginal owners and conducted genocide by gun and disease. They also introduced alien species of flora and fauna and modified the landscape in both country and city. Clearing bushland to produce a clean slate for the suburb perpetuates the idyll of the gentleman's park estate. The suburb is ideally a picturesque parkland with houses situated harmoniously in gardens. The picturesque reigns supreme as the dominant landscape aesthetic not only at home in the suburbs, but also away from home – the picturesque rules okay?

Wordsworthy Country Houses

The ideal pursued in the gentleman's park estate with its country house is to display private property and obscure, at the same time, the work that makes the country an object of both aesthetic appreciation and legal ownership, of private production and consumption. Rather than the (master of the) house (being seen to) own(ing) the country, the country will own the house. Power is mystified by being obscured. Private property (the gentleman's estate) and peasant labour are naturalized in and by the parklandscape. The relations of private property should be inverted so that the house belongs to the country.

Such sentiments were voiced by Wordsworth in his *Guide to the Lakes*, where he is concerned not only to taxonomize the landscape of lakes and mountains and to give directions about how it should be appreciated (as we saw in the previous chapter), but also to provide advice about constructing the landscape of houses in parks, and the relationship between them: 'your house will belong to the country and not the country be an appendage to your house' (1906: 139; see also 141). The relations of private property are ostensibly reversed in the relationship between country and house – instead of the gentleman owning the country with his house as the visible marker and enforcer of that ownership, the country supposedly owns the house, taking it into itself as its own, and even growing out of it.

Houses, for Wordsworth, should not only grow out of the ground on which, and the grounds in which, they are set, but should also even be a part of 'Nature':

> [...] hence buildings, which in their very form call to mind the processes of Nature, do thus, clothed in part with a vegetable garb, appear to be received into the bosom of the living principle of things, as its acts and exists among the woods and fields; and, by their colour and their shape, affectingly direct the thoughts to that tranquil course of Nature and simplicity, along which the humble-minded inhabitants have, through so many generations, been led. (1906: 63)

Such houses embosomed within 'the living principle of things' or 'Nature', or more precisely agricultural 'Mother Nature', are contrasted for Wordsworth with 'many grand mansions' that 'breathe out death and desolation' (1906: 145).

The benign processes of nature (insofar as they are still active in the working country of fields and woods) are the aspects with which the buildings should be in harmony rather than with the elemental forces of nature of the sublime active in the landscape of mountains and the mountainous seascape of oceans. For Wordsworth, 'the best of all graces which a country can have [are] flourishing fields and happy-looking houses' (1906: 142). The worst of all disgraces a country can have are, by contrast, dreary moors, dismal swamps, living wetlands, unhappy-looking houses, and even sublime mountains, for these are the heights and depths of the power of nature manifested raw and crude in the landscape rather than cooked and refined in the country. Country is quite clearly an agricultural construct that conjoins flourishing fields and anthropomorphized 'happy-looking houses' couched in the pathetic fallacy.

Yet this embosoming of buildings in the 'living principle of things' is an appearance; it is an artifice as contrived as the harmonious organic desideratum that underpins it. For Wordsworth, 'the rule is simple; with respect to grounds – work, where you can, in the spirit of Nature, with an invisible hand of art' (1906: 74). The art of landscaping (and landscape painting and writing) is ideally the invisible handmaiden of 'Nature' by which the landscaper works in harmony with feminized, virginal nature. For Wordsworth:

> Laying out grounds, as it is called, may be considered as a liberal art [...] and its object [is] [...] to move the affections under the control of good sense; [...] but speaking with more precision, it is to assist Nature in moving the affections [...] No liberal art aims merely at the gratification of an individual or a class; [...] the true servants of the Arts pay homage to the human kind as impersonated in unwarped and enlightened minds. (1906: 144)

Wordsworth had a universalising democratic and French revolutionary desire to see nature *not* moving to the arranged design of the agrarian capitalists, but to see the invisible hand of art working in harmony with nature. Ultimately and ideally, the relationship between house and landscape should be organic, with both working and growing in harmony with the other. Work is naturalized, made organic. This invocation of harmony and the shift it entails from biological to musical metaphor is never remarked upon, nor is the appropriateness of the musical to the biological considered. It is a given, a norm, an unexamined assumption. Wordsworth states categorically that 'the principle is that the house must harmonize with the surrounding landscape' (1906: 78). Yet this harmony is predicated on what he calls 'the snugness and privacy of the ancient houses' (1906: 74), and the private sphere more generally, enclosing and privatising the commons of the biosphere and other -ospheres. The intimate charm of the bourgeois private sphere is operational in both the city and the country, in and out of doors.

The model of autochthonous, organic harmony that Wordsworth draws on and wishes to extend to all houses is that of the 'humble cottages':

> [...] these humble dwellings remind the contemplative spectator of a production of Nature, and may (using a strong expression) rather be said to have grown than to have been erected; – to have risen, by an instinct of their own, out of the native rock – so little is there in them of formality, such is their wildness and beauty. (1906: 62)

The ideal cottage is ostensibly natural but it is culturally an instance of the pastoro-technical idyll in which the built features of the landscape (house and park, house-in-park as an organic whole) should conform to a pastoral and organic ideal. The romantic pastoro-technical idyll was later inverted in high modernity and in modernism to produce the utopia of the techno-pastoral ideal, the machine that operated 'organically' (see Berman 1983: especially

164–171). For the architect and city planner le Corbusier, city housing was 'a machine for living' that created within itself an artificial (albeit sterile) sense of organic wholeness, whereas for Wordsworth a country cottage was a living machine that grew out of its organic and non-organic context. Despite the inversion, both are an ideal of the private sphere privatising and enclosing the commons of the biosphere, initially the lithosphere, and to a large extent the terrestrial hydrosphere (rivers and wetlands). Both are instances of the modern enclosure of the commons, as is the gentleman's park estate.

Commanding Prospects

A phenomenology of the picturesque landscape in the gentleman's park estate is traced in Jane Austen's *Pride and Prejudice*, published three years after Wordsworth's *Guide to the Lakes*. In Chapter 43 (Chapter 1, Volume 3) Elizabeth Bennet approaches Pemberley House through Pemberley Woods, enters the house to view its interior and its grounds and then takes a walk through the gardens. Like Jane Eyre at Whitcross (as we saw in Chapter 1), this is a crucial scene in the novel as Elizabeth has rejected (for the moment) Darcy's proposal of marriage. Her appreciation of the house and woods is crucial in changing her prejudice against Darcy's pride. How could a man of such good taste be a brute and a cad?! Good taste is an index of good character that belies the aestheticsation of landscape, the class acquisition of land and the labour of the gardener.

Like *Jane Eyre*, *Pride and Prejudice* enacts a class and gender politics of the landscape via an allegory, in this case of the gentleman's park estate. It shows how the picturesque mode dominates the European parklandscape aesthetic to the point that they are conflated. It also shows how the labour of the gardener is obscured and mystified in the aesthetic taste of the gentleman 'working' in 'harmony' with nature. House and garden form an 'organic' whole. The siting of the house not only reproduces class domination over other classes and the land, but also the domination of men over women, and of a masculinized house and estate over feminized landscape and nature. The house is located in a position of mastery, both military and masculine, over the surrounding country. The house has a commanding prospect rather than merely a pleasing prospect.

To achieve that position the visitor has to enter the estate from below and ascend to the top of a 'considerable eminence'[1] to be placed in a characteristically superior position to look down on and master the landscape from above. According to John Barrell, the character's point of view, 'like the painter's viewpoint, had to be on rising ground' (1972: 11). This 'high viewpoint […] creates a space between the landscape and the observer'. The viewer is a strangely passive subject who finds themselves, as if they had been lost previously. To the viewer, Pemberley Wood first appears (rather than the viewer catching sight of the woods). The viewers find themselves in a position to look across a valley and then their eye is caught by Pemberley House (rather than the viewer catching sight of the house). The viewer's gaze is lost in the landscape unless it is caught by the house. Instead of the hunter's gaze taking the land captive to act in it and kill its animal inhabitants, the house actively catches the viewer's passive gaze.

The house captures the viewer's gaze like the hunter's prey and stops it wandering over the landscape. Although the house is set in the landscape, the latter plays second fiddle to the former. Pemberley House 'was a large, handsome, stone building, standing well on rising ground, and backed by a ridge of high woody hills; – and in front, a stream of some natural importance was swelled into greater, but without any artificial appearance'. The stream of some, but not great, natural importance is swelled into greater, though not artificial, importance. But what is this greater importance, greater than the natural but not unnatural like the artificial? It is a mediating category between the two that modifies and improves upon, but does not deny or obscure, nature.

For want of better terms this mediating category could be called the 'naturalized cultural', or the 'cultured natural' landscape; the cultural made to seem natural and the natural worked over by the cultural, not sufficiently to obliterate all traces of the natural and to produce the artificial, but not the natural left in its untended, untamed, untutored or wild state either. The artificial, the natural and the naturalized cultural are distinguished from each other with the last category valourized over the first two. Indeed, the nameless stream (though it probably also takes its name from, or is given its name by, the house) in front of the house seems to issue from the large, handsome, stone house standing well on rising ground as its source. The house not only commands the prospect of the landscape visually, but also seems to produce the water that gives the land life. Water is made to seem to spring from the patriarchal, phallic house not from the matrifocal earth and its water sources.

The naturalized culture of the stream is reinforced by the reference to the fact that its 'banks were neither formal, nor falsely adorned'. Presumably they were also neither informal nor unadorned. They conformed to the design aesthetic dictates for early English landscape gardens of the nineteenth century. The landscape of Pemberley House is a product of the cult of nature, a culturally 'natural' culture of nature. The land of the gentleman's estate is an aesthetic commodity, land worked into landscape using the tools and techniques of agriculture, if not of industrial capitalism. The estate is an index not only of aesthetic taste but also of agricultural acumen and technological know-how managed by the gentleman and deployed by his landscape gardeners.

The development of industrial technology and its agricultural application was a crucial watershed in changing the face (and body) of the land as Williams argues:

> [...] when men could produce their own nature, both by the physical means of improvement (earth-moving with new machines; draining and irrigation; pumping water to elevated sites) and by the understanding of the physical laws of light and thence of artificial viewpoints and perspectives, there was bound to be a change from the limited and conventionally symbolic and iconographic decoration of the land under immediate view. (1973: 122–123)

Yet it was not just 'men' in a general, generic sense, but a specific class of the gender who called themselves 'the Improvers', or what Williams calls the agrarian capitalists, who produced (their own) nature from their own point of view, as Williams goes on to argue: 'for what was being done, by this new class, with new capital, new equipment and new skills to hire, was indeed a disposition of "Nature" to their own point of view' (1973: 123).

Yet their capitalist point of view not only encompassed the land from an agricultural point of view, but also included the landscape from an aesthetic point of view. The picturesque, as Simon Ryan argues, 'was closely connected with the transformation of the English countryside by the landed aristocracy [...] if the land was picturesque it was ripe for transformation into wealth' (1996: 72 and 57). The picturesque is a machine for transforming pleasure into profit, for making the aesthetically pleasurable into the financially profitable. This applies just as much to gentleman's park estate as to the developer's enclave estate.

The agrarian capitalists dispositioned Nature by improvements both in 'working agriculture' and in 'artificial landscapes'. Austen reinforces both in her novels in general as Williams (1973: 115) suggests, and in *Pride and Prejudice* in particular as we are seeing. Both impulses are capitalist for, in working agriculture, as Williams puts it, 'the land is being organized for production' whilst in the worked, aestheticized landscape the land is being 'organized for consumption' (1973: 124). The aim of the agrarian capitalists was 'to arrange and rearrange nature according to a point of view', 'to make Nature move to an arranged design', as Williams (1973: 123–124) goes on to argue in both the worked and consumed aesthetic landscape and the working and producing agricultural land.

This desire underpinned and drove late eighteenth- and early nineteenth-century landscape gardening. Humphry Repton, the coiner of the term 'landscape gardening' and the first person to call themselves a 'landscape gardener', aimed, in the words of John Martin Robinson, 'to produce something that combined utility and elegance, those two great rallying cries of late eighteenth century designers' (1980: unp.). Utility is a euphemism for profit as Repton (1980: 95) himself acknowledges, and elegance boils down to beauty. Repton also did not mystify profit as he recognizes that it is produced by 'labourious exertion'. Similarly he did not valourize the beauty of landscape gardening in high aesthetic terms but saw it as 'pleasurable recreation'. Repton argues that landscape gardening involves the mediation of these two contradictory imperatives, and not their union.

Austen, too, combined the agricultural and the aesthetic in the desideratum of organic harmony in her first novel, *Sense and Sensibiltiy*, when she has Edward Ferrars state in Chapter 18 of Volume 1 that:

> 'I have no knowledge in the picturesque, and I shall offend you by my ignorance and want of taste if we come to particulars. I shall call hills steep, which ought to be bold; surfaces strange and uncouth, which ought to be irregular and rugged; and distant objects out of sight, which ought only to be indistinct through the soft medium of a hazy atmosphere'.

Edward roundly rejects the rhetoric of the picturesque in favour of the practical, though he does not eschew the aesthetic, nor the organic:

> 'I call it a very fne country – the hills are steep, the woods seem full of fine timber and the valley looks comfortable and snug – with rich meadows and several neat farm houses scattered here and there. It exactly answers my idea of a fine country, because it unites beauty with utility – and I dare say it is a picturesque one too'.

Beauty united with utility is the desideratum, and whether or not fine country is picturesque is secondary. Likewise Marianne Dashwood concedes that 'admiration of landscape scenery is become a mere jargon'. Edward is neither a philistine nor an improver as he likes 'a fine prospect, but not on picturesque principles'. A fine prospect must be likeable on practical principles.

The producing land pleases the bank balance and the consumed landscape pleases the eye, as does the stream in Pemberley Woods in *Pride and Prejudice* for 'Elizabeth was delighted. She had never seen a place for which nature had done more, or where natural beauty had been so little counteracted by an awkward taste'. Nature alone was not sufficient; nature left alone was not adequate, despite its or her bounty and beauty. Nature was all very well and good in its place, but however beneficent it or she was, nature always needed to be supplemented (rather than complemented) and manipulated by cultured, dexterous taste. Nature lacks, culture supplies. Not only Elizabeth but also her companions, the Gardiners, 'were all of them warm in their admiration; and at that moment she felt, that to be mistress of Pemberley might be something!' 'Pemberley', a synecdoche for the woods, the grounds, the park, the garden and the house, and indeed ultimately its 'master', is reduced to an object of ownership, to private property though Elizabeth would never be able to own it, to be master, only to be mistress, of it.

Elizabeth and the Gardiners are admitted to the house and they follow the dutiful housekeeper 'into the dining-parlour. It was a large, well-proportioned room, handsomely fitted up' in keeping with, and metonymic of, the handsomeness of the house and its owner. Yet rather than the small, interior view of the domestic sphere, Elizabeth is more interested in the larger, exterior view of the landscape – the prospect – as she, 'after slightly surveying it, went to a window to enjoy its prospect'. Pemberley House was not alone in having a prospect, preferably a pleasing one, if not a commanding one. Even the humble and 'defective' Barton Cottage is described in Chapter 6 of Volume 1 of *Sense and Sensibility* as having an extensive prospect that 'commanded the whole of the valley, and reached into the country beyond'.

Not only houses and cottages, but also, as Williams puts it, 'castles and fortified villages had long commanded "prospects" of the country below them' (1973: 121; see also 125). From their superior position the viewer has a prospect in front of which s/he is set up (the literal meaning of the word as Barrell [1972: 23] points out) and over which s/he looks (s/he is literally an 'overseer'). The prospect makes the land into landscape, makes, as Barrell puts it, 'the land [into] something out there, something to be looked at from a distance' (ibid.). In the prospect the observer appreciates the play of sunlight and the colours produced by different objects and their surfaces. The country is inferior, the house superior; the country is a threat, or at least a potential source of threat, the house a possible military command post against peasant uprising; a position of mastery over recalcitrant nature.

The 'prospect' that Elizabeth enjoys is one of the 'pleasing prospects' Williams discusses in Chapter 12 of *The Country and the City* of that title with its 'characteristic eighteenth century [...] double meaning [divided into] practical [and] aesthetic' (1973: 121; see also Andrews 1989: 21). The term also has a double spatial and temporal meaning: it implies both the landscape and the future lying before one, which could either be pleasing or displeasing. The latter applies to Edwin Clayhanger in Arnold Bennett's novel as 'the prospect stretching far in front of him made him feel sick' (1910: 114). No doubt a spatial prospect could make one feel sick too if it were sufficiently ugly or dismal. As Malcolm Andrews points out, 'Prospect means literally a "looking forward"' (1989: 63). Even the literal meaning is ambiguous as one could be looking forward over land lying before one or to an event in the future stretching before one. Either way, the prospect serves to position the subject in a position of mastery in space and time.

Rather than the spatial sense of the term, Austen uses the temporal one occasionally in *Sense and Sensibilty*, intermittently in *Mansfield Park* and repeatedly in *Emma*. Yet even in *Emma* the spatial sense is used to figure the temporal, such as in Chapter 45 (Volume 3, Chapter 9) when one character's prospects are described as closing whilst another's are opening. Prospects both spatial and temporal should preferably be opening rather than closing. The future and the landscape before one should be clear and open in extent, not confined and limiting in constraint.

This connotation of confinement arises out of some witty and revealing repartee around the double meaning of 'prospect' in Chapter 10 of Austen's *Mansfield Park*. After Henry Crawford slights Julia Bertram he says to her that "'[...] your prospects, however, are too fair to justify want of spirits. You have a very smiling scene before you'". Julia replies:

> 'Do you mean literally or figuratively? Literally I conclude. Yes, certainly the sun shines and the park looks very cheerful. But unluckily that iron gate, that ha-ha, give me a feeling of restraint and hardship. I cannot get out, as the starling said'.

Julia feels trapped and imprisoned by her prospects. She uses the constraining physical features of the gentleman's park estate to figure that sense of restraint. The iron gate is a symbol of private property keeping the unwanted and uninvited out and protecting the privileged within. The ha-ha, a concealed ditch for keeping sheep in and for giving an uninterrupted aesthetic view of the parklandscape without the ugly intrusion of fences, whilst obscuring the fact that it is private property and working agriculture, symbolizes a sense of her own powerlessness and construction as a feminine woman, and as an aesthetic object caught in a cage like a bird.

Austen was thus no mere booster of prospects. Her view of prospects became more sophisticated during the course of her novel-writing career. Elizabeth Bennet's approach to, and tour of, Pemberley House (and later gardens) can be compared and contrasted with Emma Woodhouse's view of Donwell Abbey in *Emma* published three years after *Pride and Prejudice*:

> [...] she viewed the respectable size and style of the building, its suitable, becoming characteristic situation, low and sheltered – its ample gardens stretching down to meadows washed by a stream, of which the Abbey, with all the old neglect of prospect, had scarcely a sight – and its abundance of timber in rows and avenues which neither fashion nor extravagance had rooted up. (Volume 3, Chapter 6)

The fashion and extravagance of rooting up avenues of trees to which Austen's narrator alludes seems to be the slavish following of the fashion for prospects and the extravagance for improvement, especially rooting up avenues just to make a prospect.

Although such an avenue may obstruct a prospect, it may also provide 'delicious shade' and may lead:

> [...] to nothing; nothing but a view at the end over a low stone wall with high pillars, which seem intended, in their erection, to give the appearance of an approach to the house, which had never been there. Disputable, however, as might be the taste of such a termination, it was in itself a charming walk, and the view which closed it extremely pretty.

The pretty view is then described in some detail with the conclusion that 'it was a sweet view – sweet to the eye and the mind. English verdure, English culture, English comfort, seen under a sun bright, without being oppressive'. A pretty view, in doubtful taste of England's 'green and pleasant land', is preferable to an opening prospect in fashionable extravagance of rooted-up avenues.

Cutting down avenues of trees seems to have perplexed, if not distressed, Austen and been at the heart of her views about prospects and improvements. In Chapter Six of *Mansfield Park*, published a year after *Pride and Prejudice* and two years before *Emma*, the estates of Compton and Sotherton are compared and the merits of 'improvement' debated. The owner of Compton has engaged an 'improver' and has had the grounds 'improved'. Rushworth, the owner of Sotherton, is contemplating doing the same as he claims that cutting down an avenue at Compton 'opens the prospect amazingly' and he wants to follow suit at Sotherton. He asserts that if Humphry Repton, or 'anybody of that sort', were to be engaged to 'improve' Sotherton, they would 'certainly have the avenue at Sotherton down'.

As these pronouncements mispresent Repton's views, either Rushworth is displaying his ignorance of Repton's work (and Austen is exposing him for doing so) or Austen is being unjust to Repton as John Dixon Hunt has argued that 'many of her descriptions and discussions of landscaping parallel Repton's ideas' (Hunt 1992: 163). Hunt goes on to argue that Elizabeth Bennet's 'education' in *Pride and Prejudice* 'involves very Reptonian emphases' and that 'the very Reptonian landscape of Pemberley Woods is not only 'a typically Reptonian landscape' but also that her approach 'takes her through the picturesque features'. Similarly the description of Donwell Abbey in *Emma* is described by Hunt as 'a very Reptonian landscape' (1992: 164).

Fanny Price, the heroine of *Mansfield Park*, protests against Rushworth's ecological injustice by quoting Cowper: 'Ye fallen avenues, once more I mourn your fate unmerited'. Her bookish, tree-hugging sentiments are largely ignored. Edmund Bertram lends her some support in spatial terms by praising the house, but suggesting that 'it is ill placed. It stands in one of the lowest spots of the park; in that respect, unfavourable for improvement'. It thus stands in a spot unfavourable for the construction and enjoyment of a pleasing or commanding prospect. The spatial poetics of the gentleman's park estate and landscape gardening operates for Austen in a geographical hierarchy. The house situated with a commanding prospect, like Barton Cottage, over a valley below and the country beyond, or situated with a pleasing one, like Pemberley House, atop a considerable eminence is privileged over one located in a low situation, like Donwell Abbey, with an old neglect of prospect, or, like Sotherton, that does not lend itself to improvement by the construction of a prospect and destruction of an avenue. Prospects should be pleasing, if not commanding, but they should be appropriately situated for Austen, in keeping with the location and history of the house. Imposing a prospect for the sake of fashion is mere slavishness to fleeting, contemporary taste; destroying an avenue to do so, an extravagance, a wanton and distasteful display of power and wealth.

The prospect situates the subject in a position of mastery over the visible extent of the surface of the earth, and over time stretching out into the foreseeable future. But it also encloses and constrains as we have seen. The mastered prospect (both spatial and temporal) masters the master and mistress of the house and estate. Whereas landscape (both aesthetically and agriculturally) colonizes the surface of the earth, the pleasing prospect went one step further to colonize both this and the foreseeable future. By doing so it also colonized the commons and Aboriginal uses of the land in the past and attempted to foreclose their reintroduction in the future. Enclosure of the commons and foreclosure of the future went hand in hand.

This position of mastery over space and time, or at least over the surface and the future of places (as mastery over space and time only came with the communication technologies of the railway, telegraph, photograph, cinema, car and radio [see Giblett 2008b]), is not only marked geographically, but also by gender. On the one hand, subtending the practical, are the military, the agricultural, the masculine; and on the other hand, subtending the aesthetic, are the beautiful and the feminine. Both the practical and the aesthetic are exercized against the Neolithic Mother Earth who is made to produce agricultural commodities by industrial capitalism, and who is rendered an object of consumption in landscape aesthetics (painting, writing, and gardening). Both sets of categories are visual, both rely on and valourize the sense of sight, and both are objectifying.

There is an aesthetics of time just as much as there is of space. Or more precisely, the aesthetics of space is used to figure the aesthetics of time. Just as much as a pleasing prospect can stretch away hopefully before one into the future, so can a pleasing retrospect stretch away nostalgically behind one into the past (or conversely a displeasing prospect despairingly into the future or despondently into the past). Just as the beautiful is near and close at hand, so the temporality of the present moment can be beautiful in its finery and smallness. Just as the sublime can loom large and terrifying above one, so can the eternity of an immense event threaten to crush and destroy one. Just as the uncanny lurks behind one unseen and invisible, horrifying and monstrous, so can one be returned to something repressed in the past. The aesthetics of the sublime, the picturesque and the beautiful positions the viewing subject in time and space, whereas the counter-aesthetics of the slimy and the uncanny upsets and overwhelms the embodied subject and returns it to the abject, to the fluid process of time and space.

Furthermore, the aesthetic is a sublimation of the practical, of the oral by the visual. Wordsworth in his *Guide* bemoans 'the craving for prospect' and even 'the thirst for prospect' as 'immoderate, particularly in new settlers' (1906: 74–75). Either way, prospect is the sublimated satisfaction of an oral desire for solid sustenance and liquid refreshment. The desire for a water view, that stock-in-trade of the suburban ideal especially in Australia, the driest continent on earth after Antarctica, enacts a sublimatory landscape aesthetics. The aesthetic sublimates the oral into the visual, the desire for food and water from the Great Mother into the desire for viewing pleasing prospects.

Yet unlike Jane Eyre in that eponymous novel, Elizabeth Bennet in *Pride and Prejudice* is not concerned with the land as the possible source of sustenance, but with the landscape as aesthetic object. She has sublimated production into consumption. She views the prospect primarily in aesthetic terms rather than in practical ones. The landscape is an object of sight, an aesthetic object. Land as landscape is object. Land as landscape is made up of objects which take different positions in relation to the viewer as the subject for whom positions to view the landscape are set up in the process. Landscape produces the subject of sight. Landscape sets up a subject-object relationship with the land, never an inter-subjective, let alone mutually abjective, relationship. A subject-object relationship implies mastery, or in Elizabeth's case, possible 'mistressy': '"And of this place," thought she, 'I might have been mistress!"'

After their tour of the interior of Pemberley House, Elizabeth and the Gardiners are 'consigned over' like a parcel to a nameless gardener to conduct a tour of the exterior. Presumably he accompanies them on their walk during which not only is his work in shaping the land into landscape rendered invisible, but also his presence is unacknowledged. He is silent as he has no reported speech. The picturesque and the practical do not meet in the work and words of the gardener whose practical work makes the picturesque possible. The picturesque landscape renders invisible the practical working of the land and makes mute the practical worker of the land. The picturesque landscape makes the land speak about wealth, power, privilege and prestige and makes it visible in picturesque ways, but silences the landscape worker and makes him invisible. Nature is mute.

After Elizabeth and the Gardiners leave the house they unexpectedly encounter D'Arcy. In the novel he does not emerge dripping from the water as in the famous wet shirt scene of the BBC television series with Colin Firth as D'Arcy, but is simply coming from the stable having just arrived home. After an exchange of embarrassed pleasantries (as Elizabeth and the Gardiners did not expect the owner to be home and he did not expect visitors) they walk across the inevitable lawn towards the equally inevitable river. As they approach the river, 'they had now entered a beautiful walk by the side of the water, and every step was bringing forward a nobler fall of ground, or a finer reach of the woods to which they were approaching'. The walker in the landscape is the active agent of the appearance of objects. The pedestrian viewer creates out of nothing like the God of Genesis, brings objects into view with the power of his or her gaze to name them, yet at the same time kills them by objectifying them in discourse. Without the approach of the walker and the activity of his or her gaze, the objects would remain invisible. The objects present themselves for viewing like so many obedient, jostling servants, like so many foot soldiers on parade.

Besides the narrow view in which objects could only present themselves in groups, the grounds also afforded the wider view when:

> [...] they entered the woods, and bidding adieu to the river for a while, ascended some of the higher grounds; whence, in spots where the opening of the trees gave the eye power to wander, were many charming views of the valley, the opposite hills, with the long range of woods overspreading many, and occasionally part of the stream.

Viewing spots on the walk give the eye power to wander in the dialectic of activity and passivity that characterizes the grammar of the landscape. The landscape is at once a passive object to be viewed but also, at other times, active agent, giving the eye of the viewer power to reconstitute land as object of the gaze. The top of an eminence is the ideal position for giving the eye the power to wander 'over a wide tract of country' as is it does for Marianne Dashwood in Chapter 6 of Volume 3 of *Sense and Sensibility*.

Yet this activity ascribed to the landscape is only a secondary agency given to it by the designer of the landscape who contrived, in the first place, the views that give the eye of the viewer power to wander. It enables the observer, as Barrell puts it, 'to see the landscape, not as something in which he [sic] is involved, and which is all around him, but as something detached from him, *over there*: his eye may wander over the view, but his own position is fixed' (1972: 21). The stationary eye wandering over a prospect from a fixed position and high viewpoint is redolent with military and hunting connotations. It produces, as Barrell goes on to argue, 'an impression of the order of [the eye's] progress over the objects in the landscape, rather than of those objects themselves'. As a result for Barrell 'the features of a landscape [...] are made passive under the eye' (1972: 22).

In this scene from *Pride and Prejudice*, as Williams argues of Austen's novels in general, 'the land is seen primarily as an index of revenue and position; its visible order and control are a valued product, while the process of working it is hardly seen at all' (1973: 115), if at all! The annual incomes of Austen's landed gentry are produced by the earthly foundation to the economic base, but this relationship is figured in indexical, not ecological, terms.

Money equals land. Land has value only insofar as it can be equated with monetary value. It has no value in its own right, only as a source of monetary value, as the site of production. Austen's novels are the culmination of a tradition which Williams calls 'a rural [though hardly even that in the sense of agricultural as it is a country] landscape [is] emptied of rural labour and of labourers; a sylvan and watery prospect' (1973: 125). The pleasing prospect is wooded and watery, timbered and riverine, not marshy or swampy; it is dryland not wetland.

The pleasing prospect and picturesque landscape is not what Williams calls 'an unmediated nature: a direct and physical awareness of trees, birds, the moving shapes of land' (1973: 3), nor is it 'working agriculture in which much of the nature is in fact being produced' (1973: 118). It is mediated nature, nature produced as an object for aesthetic consumption. Elizabeth is only aware of the wood, not of trees, let alone birds; she cannot see the trees for the wood! In and over the landscape nothing moves except the eye of the viewer. The land does not move; the land is passive; the land is rendered motionless and timeless, locked into pleasing prospects and pleasant shapes as it is also in the moving pictures of television, such as in the BBC series of *Pride and Prejudice*, which reduces the novel to romance fiction and neglects its class and landscape politics.

Indeed, landscape reduces nature to object; the discourse of landscape produces nature as aesthetic object of consumption for landscape aestheticist and colonist, just as the discourse of natural history produced nature as dead object for scientific investigation, and the discourse of industrial capitalism produces nature as source of agricultural and mining production, and sink for its wastes. Nature ceases to be agent and subject, or living organism, and becomes dead matter, or commodity. The drive is, as Barrell puts it, 'to control nature in order not to be controlled by it' (1972: 24). Control or be controlled is the Hobson's choice of the mastery of nature for capitalist, landscape aestheticist and colonist.

The Australian Gentleman's Park is Aboriginal Country

When Europeans came to Australia they found parts of it that conformed to their ideas (and ideals) of the gentleman's park so they could conveniently overlook the fact that it was already Aboriginal Country. For the early explorers and settlers, as Alan Moorehead put it in the 1960s with remarkable insight:

> [...] there was a strong tendency to fit the natural phenomena into preconceived European ideas. Open bush country was described as parkland [...] Where the landscape simply would not conform to European standards it was described as dull and uninteresting and was ignored. (1966: 152)

Or where it would not, as Moorehead acknowledges later, 'the country was [...] forced to conform to the European pattern' (1966: 168). European ideas, patterns and standards of the landscape reigned supreme in both viewing and working the land in order to create the view and produce wealth.

The irony for Tom Griffiths was that 'Europeans thought they had discovered a genuine wilderness but found instead a "park" unwittingly prepared for them' (1996: 14). Griffiths goes on to argue that 'colonists described the land as like a "gentleman's park", and that the term "park" had its origins in twelfth-century Britain as a description of aristocratic reserves for hunting' (1996: 15). Yet both wilderness and park were aristocratic hunting preserves, the latter more homely, less unhomely than the former. The fact that Australia was seen to possess the latter rather than the former, at least initially, was a sign of God's providence, and that colonisation was divinely ordained, if not predestined. Here was a land that God had prepared for settlement so who was a mere mortal settler to refuse His beneficence?

Yet, rather than seeing this land as the product of another culture, of Aboriginal culture and its practices of hunting, gathering and 'fire-stick farming', explorers initially, and settlers later, saw it as the product of nature. For Captain James Cook, according to Judith Wright, 'Aborigines had nothing at all to with the state of the country as he found it. In his journal he asserted that, "We see this Country in the pure state of Nature. The Industry of man has had nothing to do with any part of it and yet we find all such things as Nature hath bestowed upon it in a flourishing state"' (Wright 1991: 143). Cook erased Aboriginal culture from the country with a stroke of his pen in the doctrine of *terra nullius* in order to try to create *ex nihilo*, like God, a *tabula rasa* on which European culture could then rewrite the history of the country. Nature was constructed in Latinate philosophical, legal and theological terms.

This view occluded the relationship between Aboriginal people and their country, and made it into a figure of speech, an ironic play on words. For the early settler, Elizabeth Macarthur, 'the greater part of the country is like an English park, and the trees give it the appearance of a wilderness or shrubbery, commonly attached to the habitations of people of fortune'. Deborah Bird Rose concludes bluntly after quoting Macarthur that 'Aboriginal people had created these nourishing terrains through their knowledge of the country, their fire-stick farming, their organization of sanctuaries, and their rituals of well-being' (1996: 72; see also Smith 1985: 248). Nourishing terrains give sustenance. They do not sublimate the oral and alimental into landscape aesthetics.

Early settlers were people of fortune whose fortune was there for the taking and who could not believe their good fortune. Settlers enjoyed the good fortune afforded to them by James Cook in the doctrine of *terra nullius* that denied the work of Aboriginal people in creating the country, and by Aboriginal people creating a landscape that happened to look in places like a gentleman's park. As Tim Bonyhady puts it after discussing the sentiments of Macarthur and like-minded contemporaries, 'at least some of Australia's "parks" were an Aboriginal creation' (2000: 79).

If the land was a gentleman's park, then the landowner was, *ipso facto*, a gentleman, if not a lord, and the land a servant, if not a serf. Many settlers from lowly class positions found themselves elevated quickly up the social scale by taking advantage of the good fortune passed on to them by Cook and afforded them by Aboriginal people. Tom Griffiths argues that 'tens of thousands of years of systematic Aboriginal burning cultivated a squatter's dream' (2002: 236), and fulfilled a wish-fulfilling fantasy of good fortune from good pastures. As a result, and as Herb Wharton puts it, 'the graziers ruled like feudal lords' (Sabbioni, Schaffer and Smith 1998: 100). If the settler was the lord of an estate, then the original occupants and owners were serfs. The land and its traditional owners were constituted as peasant resistance to be overcome. The land and its traditional owners were also, like peasants, immiserated. For Lisa Bellear:

> Aboriginal Country
> Is seeping
> In misery
> In death. (Sabbioni, Schaffer and Smith 1998: 27)

It may have been fortuitously ironic that a land thought to have been wilderness was in fact (at least in part) a gentleman's park. This similarity did not lead to any fellow feeling or solidarity with Aboriginal people as it did not with the fact that both cultures were hunter cultures (or at least one had been before it became agricultural and hunting became an aristocratic privilege and recreational pursuit, and the hunting preserve alienated and sublimated into the gentleman's park estate).

On top of the fortuitous irony it was doubly and cruelly ironic that this land was in fact (a different factuality constituted by a different culture) also the product of a hunter culture like the settler's own. The land was already conforming to the British model. As Simon Ryan argues, 'the way in which Australian areas are seen as resembling gentleman's parks can be understood [...] as a way of establishing the land as "naturally" suited to a reproduction of Britain's land-owning and, therefore, social system' (1996: 9–10; see also 74–76).

It was not as if settlers simply imposed an alien land system holus-bolus and willy-nilly onto the land, but they found a land that looked familiar, that conformed superficially and visually (at least in places near the coast) to the dictates of the European landscape aesthetic of pleasing prospects in the gentleman's park estate. Where it didn't conform, the places where it did gave a warrant for trying to make those that didn't do so. They then imposed on both, and their unique biota, an alien agricultural and legal system. The one was imposed on the others to the point that it was impossible to differentiate what was there originally on settlement and what was a product of settlement. History was blurred and the past and future subsumed to the present of colonisation as the land (and its history) was blurred by settlement. Colonisation colonized time and space, or at least the past and place.

The 'gentleman's park' (whether in England or Australia), with its pleasing prospects devoid of understorey, was originally designed (and produced) to make the hunter's prey visible. The irony for George Seddon is that 'the park-like woodlands of Australia, also seen as natural, were equally anthropogenic and equally the product of a hunting culture' (1997: 66; see also Ryan 1996: 82). This cruel irony of the two cultures having hunting in common is founded upon and doubles the initial fortuitous irony of the land conforming in places to the pattern of the gentleman's park. This double irony places the victim in a double bind; a position of powerlessness from which it is impossible to escape except by making a counter meta-statement about the system of the double bind and irony itself. The whole land rights movement has been making that statement, not least in their use of the word 'wilderness'.

Note

1. This location is nicely parodied by Vladimir Nabokov in *Ada* when he has Van Veen describe Ardis Hall as being located on the 'considerable eminence of old novels' with a nice play on the double meaning of 'eminence'.

Part III

Colonial Country

Wildernesss is generally regarded as some sort of pristine natural place largely free from human or industrial modification. The former denies the ownership and work of Aboriginal peoples, whilst the latter, in its official manifestation in the Australian National Wilderness Inventory, by using geographical information systems to plot wilderness value as remote from industrial society, overlooks the role of telecommunications and information technology in mapping what is ostensibly remote from it. Chapter 5 critiques the history and politics of wilderness as a construct of settler societies that project a premodern past onto the hypermodern present. It argues that wilderness, like nature, is a polysemic sign in search of a referent and that wilderness, like landscape, entails a disjunction between subject and object. The chapter concludes by arguing for postmodern wilderness that acknowledges wildness within as well as without.

Australian bush, too, is a construct of a settler society that, like American wilderness, was the crucible in which national identity was forged and later solidified in national parks for both nations. Chapter 6 goes on to critique the history and politics of the bush as a construct of a settler society that projected the solidarity of masculinized mateship onto the screen of a feminized landscape split between a fascinating and horrifying preternatural land, obdurate and uncompliant on the one hand, and a benign agricultural and pastoral landscape either found ready and waiting or created by clearing on the other. This chapter traces a genealogy of the Australian landscape from recent films through prominent visitors such as D. H. Lawrence and Anthony Trollope, to the nationalist writers and painters of the *Bulletin* and Heidelberg schools in Australia who portrayed it largely as either heaven or hell, both of which are projections.

Chapter 5

Home in the Wilds: Wild(er)ness as a Cultural Category

The concept of wilderness is central to conservation discourse about preservation of pristine (or near pristine areas) of the natural environment. Yet it has not always had these connotations but has changed remarkably over time. Like the concept of nature (as we saw in the first chapter), wilderness has a human, cultural history. In medieval and Renaissance English 'wilderness' meant 'place of wild deer', or more precisely 'wild-deer-ness', whereas in more recent times it has come to acquire associations of a place of untouched nature. Untouched by what or whom though is often unclear and herein lie many of the problems associated with the concept. If wilderness is an area untouched by human hands then, as Marx said in a slightly different context, the only place where this sort of nature could be said to exist anywhere is a coral reef in Australia in the process of formation. Yet European explorers and settlers regarded much of Australia as untouched by human hands. The doctrine of *terra nullius* enshrined this perception as what constituted modification of nature for them was agriculture and pastoralism, but it is now known that Aboriginal people modified the land for over 50,000 years.

Wilderness is a Construct of Settler Societies

To regard areas touched by Aboriginal hands as untouched by human hands and to attempt to conserve them as 'wilderness' is a gross act of racism and colonisation. Much criticism has been levelled at the concept of wilderness and at the American and Australian Wilderness Societies when it is defined in these terms. The view of wilderness as uninhabited land goes back to the definitions of Bob Marshall, Founder of the American Wilderness Society, in the 1930s. Marshall defined wilderness in 1930 as a 'region which contains no permanent inhabitants, possesses no possibility of conveyance by any mechanical means, and is sufficiently spacious that a person crossing it must have the experience of sleeping out' (cited by Gottlieb 1993: 16). Wilderness is the modern construction of a premodern, uninhabited landscape as if no one existed before modern 'Man'.

Marshall hardly changed his mind in seven years on the score of the question of inhabitation. In 1937 he designated wilderness as places 'in which there shall be no roads or other provision for motorized transportation, no commercial timber cutting, and no occupancy under special use permit for hotels, stores, resorts, summer homes, organization camps, hunting and fishing lodges or similar uses' (cited by Gottlieb 1993: 17–18). And not evidently for Aboriginal inhabitants either. Yet there was no warrant, not even a biblical one, for seeing wilderness as uninhabited, as one Biblical scholar attests: 'I find little evidence for the view that *the* wilderness is a generic term denoting uninhabited land as such in contrast to inhabited areas' (Funk 1959: 209).

From questions of human inhabitation attempts at definition of wilderness (though there is no pre-existing wilderness prior to its definition) shifted to human modification and the role of technology. Wilderness was defined in the 1970s by William Godfrey-Smith as 'any reasonably large tract of the Earth, together with its plant and animal communities, which is substantially unmodified by humans and in particular by human technology' (1979: 310). One cannot help asking: which human technology? 'Fire-stick farming'? Or just modern industrial technology? Wilderness has been redefined as areas untouched by industrial technology (so they must be roadless areas). This is what has become known as the American definition and it is enshrined in the United States 1964 Wilderness Act, though this Act also defines wilderness as 'land unmodified by human action' with 'no permanent inhabitants'.

More recent revisionist attempts at definition, especially within the policy arena and in Australia with the development of the National Wilderness Inventory, have defined wilderness on, or in terms of, a continuum from a highly modified industrial urban environment at one end of the spectrum and wilderness at the other end, where wilderness is defined in terms of the 'two essential attributes' (Lesslie and Maslen 1995: 3) of 'remoteness and naturalness' (Lesslie and Maslen 1995: 4), though both these attributes raise the question of remote from what? And natural in what or whose terms? The latter question is answered in terms of both visible landscape and invisible biophysical features. The former question is answered with the qualification, 'remote from and undisturbed by the influence of modern technological society' (ibid.). Modern transportation and its infrastructure are referred to here (including 'aircraft landing grounds' but not jet trails or flight paths across the sky) and not communication technologies. Modern communication technologies, such as telecommunication satellites and their use in mobile telephony and in Geographical Positioning Systems, mean that every place on earth is subject to the influence of modern technological society – including the National Wilderness Inventory itself and the places it is studying by using this technology.

Yet the *National Wilderness Inventory Handbook* does not acknowledge this influence as it does not recognize the profoundly ironical and self-deconstructive role Geographical Information Systems played in the formulation of the inventory in the first place. Modern information technologies were used to record data about areas supposedly remote from access or uninfluenced by modern technological society (and perhaps in some very remote and inaccessible areas some were brought under the influence of that society for the first time). This lack of self-reflexivity about its own methodology and use of information technologies is a massive blind spot that discredits its whole enterprise of mapping high wilderness value in terms of remoteness from modern technology society. The only influences of modern technological society considered are those which can be mapped superficially and represented cadastrally. The inventory reduces the three dimsensions of space, including height and depth, to two dimensions of length and breadth. Wilderness becomes a surface phenomenon, though ironically extra-terrestrial space from the 1960s was seen as the final frontier to cross, conquer and colonize, just like its terrestrial counterpart for 100 years previously. The inventory is complicit with the colonial and neo-colonial practice of mapping, its reduction of land and the depths of the earth to surface, and its synchronic frame-freezing of one moment in time.[1]

Like the explorer's and settler's use of the gun and the camera, the *Handbook* does not acknowledge the mediated nature of the wilderness experience, and of the wilderness inventory. Wilderness is hypostatized into a positivist object with which the individualist subject has an unmediated relationship. Yet despite these drawbacks, the inventory has produced some interesting results in its maps of some areas. For example, Aboriginal-owned land in Western Australia has a higher wilderness value than land in conservation and nature reserves. This irony puts paid to any criticism that Aboriginal cannot look after their country.

Remoteness from access and settlement defines wilderness largely in relation to what it is not rather than in terms of what it is. Similar difficulties afflict definitions of wilderness in terms of absence of human inhabitation, though historically for settler societies this has not troubled the consciences of many. Wilderness in the United States, for example, has a long and vexatious history in relation to what it is *not*. What is not wilderness could be regarded as civilization, though that is to regard Aboriginal people as uncivilized or barbarian. What is not wilderness, however, could be regarded as urban civilizations, either ancient, imperial civilization or modern, industrial, capitalist civilization. For both sorts of civilizations, and especially in the United States, there was 'a no-man's land' between the two – the frontier.

In a famous paper called 'The Significance of the Frontier in American History', first published in 1893, Frederick Jackson Turner (1961: 37–62) noted the official closing of the frontier in 1890 with the census of that year, and hence the passing of wilderness as an area beyond or outside the frontier. Wilderness would from then on be within or inside the frontier and it would therefore change its status as being no longer in contradistinction to modern, industrial, capitalist civilization but a part of that civilization as all wilderness now is, as there are no areas of the earth's surface uninfluenced by modern communication technologies. As Turner saw, but perhaps without the same sense of opprobrium which now attaches to the terms, the closing of the frontier, or as he also put it, 'winning a wilderness', marked the triumph of 'the colonization of the Great West', or the wilderness.[2]

Yet there is no one single, homogeneous frontier. In settler societies there are agricultural, pastoral, mining and trading frontiers across cultures, time and space. English colonization employed a farming frontier in North America, Turner argues (1961: 45), whereas the French used a trading frontier. What of other settler societies such as Australia and South Africa? Despite their differences, all settler societies employed the gun; all valorized the sense of sight and the use of visual technologies such as the telescope, the sextant, the theodolite, the camera; and all consumed voraciously the landscape and the land – and the land as landscape.

All these aspects are present in J. M. Coetzee's stunning fictionalized account of pioneer South Africa in which the explorer Jacobus Coetzee 'inhabited the past again, meditating upon my life as tamer of the wild. I meditated upon the acres of new ground I had eaten up with my eyes' (1974: 82). The eyes become an instrument of visual sadism troped in oral terms that devour the landscape. Yet in extending out beyond the gazing eye to master and masticate the landscape, the body loses a sense of its boundaries between itself and wilderness. The wild is boundless; the tamed is bound. Jacobus Coetzee goes on to relate that:

> [...] in the wild I lose my sense of boundaries. This is a consequence of space and solitude. The operation of space is thus: the five senses stretch out from the body they inhabit, but four stretch into a vacuum. The ear cannot hear, the nose cannot smell, the tongue cannot taste, the skin cannot feel. (Coetzee 1974: 84)

The body is reduced to one organ (the eye) and the five senses are reduced to sight. For Coetzee, in the wild:

> [...] only the eyes have power. The eyes are free, they reach out to the horizon all around. Nothing is hidden from the eyes. As the other senses grow numb or dumb my eyes flex and extend themselves. I become a spherical reflecting eye moving through the wilderness and ingesting it. Destroyer of the wilderness, I move through the land cutting a devouring path from horizon to horizon. There is nothing from which my eye turns, I am all that I see. Such loneliness! Not a stone, not a bush, not a wretched provident ant that is not comprehended in this travelling sphere. What is there that is not me? I am a transparent sac with a black core full of images and a gun. (1974: 84)

The tamer of the wild is reduced to an eye and a gun, an ocular weapon. The gun is no longer not only a prosthesis for killing, but the body is a prosthesis for the gun to get around, the eye a prosthesis for the gun to be aimed, and the rest of the body a quadraped to carry, hold and fire the gun.[3]

The wild is reduced to an object of sight as are the objects in it. These objects can in theory be counted and be subjected to the mathematical, enumerative imperative and to capitalist accounting. But to be counted the wild has to be killed as the living wild is too mobile, too protean, too vital to be counted. The wild is one; the tamer of the wild divides the one into the many to conquer it, but in the process proliferates its parts into countless infinity:

> We cannot count the wild. The wild is one because it is boundless. We can count fig trees, we can count sheep because the orchard and the farm are bounded. The essence of orchard tree and farm sheep is number. Our commerce with the wild is a tireless enterprise of turning it into orchard and farm. When we cannot fence it and count it we reduce it to number by other means. Every wild creature I kill crosses the boundary between

wilderness and number. I have presided over the becoming number of two thousand creatures, omitting the innumerable insects that expired beneath my feet. I am a hunter, a domesticator of the wilderness, a hero of enumeration. He who does not understand number, does not understand death. (Coetzee 1974: 85)

The explorer and the settler are slaves to linear time, of the arrow of time on its progressivist trajectory out of a primitive past of landscape and people, through a narrow defile of the cramped present into the terror of an unknown but supposedly glorious future, trapped in the prison of modern, mechanically measured time; the time of the watch, of imperial, linear history, of the time it takes to pull the trigger and see the target keel over, or not, and of the time it takes to travel from point A to point B, from settlement to settlement or from settlement to some unknown, unexplored place or point.[4]

What of English colonization of Australia? Was there a frontier and a wilderness in Australia? If so, what sort of frontier? There is some dispute amongst historians about whether Australia actually had a frontier and what was the nature and function of that frontier if it had one. Henry Reynolds has made a living by arguing that it had a frontier in such books as *The Other Side of the Frontier* (1982) and *Frontier* (1987), as the titles suggest. Paul Carter has countered in the most interesting and provocative book written about Australia that 'the rhetorical significance of the frontier [...] empties the beyond of any cultural significance even before it is subdued' (1989: 158). Yet that is precisely the point of the frontier. It enables the beyond to be emptied of cultural significance for the settler so that the beyond could be imbued with some sort of significance and so be subdued semiotically and exploited more readily. Without being imbued with significance it could never be subdued. It would remain mute and inarticulate.

Rather than being emptied of cultural significance, the myth of the frontier, as Carter argues later, 'was a necessary myth to make the artificially silent land speak' (1989: 165–166). The myth of the frontier made the mute land speak in predetermined ways; it brought dumb nature into articulate culture. Nature, which had belonged to what could be called the mutosphere, was brought into the cultural semiosphere (see Figure 3, Chapter 2). The myth of the frontier gave speech to the wild land just as the wild child was made to speak. It produced a discourse with a subject and an object; it translated the language of the other into the discourse of the same.

Wilderness is Not Home

Just as mute wilderness was antithetical to the cultural semiosphere, it was also antithetical to home, to the private sphere. In European societies and their settler Diasporas wilderness, as Carter goes on to argue, is 'the antithesis of home', it is 'places where space failed to congregate into picturesque forms, where nature failed to speak' (1989: 289–290). Wilderness was the place where nature was inchoate and inarticulate, like the wild children and wild men found in it. Wilderness was the place where nature was not composed into the picturesque. It was the place where nature was either transcended into the sublime, or decomposed into the slimy and swampy. Wilderness was split beween the sublime (where and when it was valourized, especially in Ansel Adams' wilderness photography of white, snow-clad mountains), and the slime (where and when it was denigrated in the black waters of swamps). Either way, wilderness was antithetical to the picturesque, to the pleasing prospects of the gentleman's park estate, to landscape and to the aesthetics of the beautiful and picturesque. In its swampy downside it was unaesthetic, or anti-aesthetic, or even anaesthetic. Wilderness was both the antithesis of home and the picturesque. It was the unhomely, or in Freud's terms, the uncanny.[5]

Yet the wilderness and home did not co-exist in blissful mutual definition and respect. The wilderness was constituted as the place ripe for exploration and as the site ready for settlement. By placing a home in the unhomely, in the wilds, the wilds were tamed. Rider Haggard's narrator of *King Solomon's Mines*, taking the offshore view from a passing ship, relates how:

> [...] there is the deepest green of the bush, growing as God planted it, and the other greens of the mealie gardens and the sugar patches, while here and there a white house, smiling out at the placid sea, puts a finish and gives an air of homeliness to the scene. For, to my mind, however beautiful a view may be, it requires the presence of man to make it complete, but perhaps that is because I have lived so much in the wilderness, and therefore know the value of civilisation, though to be sure it drives away the game. (1989: 35–36)

Haggard perpetuates the Wordsworthy myth of happy-looking, homely country houses albeit displaced into an unhomely, colonial setting of wilderness in which the wildness is tamed by the home and the homely. A 'home in the wilds' was a cliché of colonial writing. Australia was no exception as James Macarthur bemoaned the disheartening toil of 'forming a home amidst the wilds' (cited by Bonyhady 2000: 85). Similarly, in D. H. Lawrence's novel *Kangaroo*, set in Australia, 'the chimneys were faintly smoking, there was a haze of smoke and a sense of home, home in the wilds' (1950: 89).

Yet the taming of the wilderness was never neat. The frontier in Australia was never a line on a map encroaching ever westwards from the East as one might imagine the American frontier (though, like Australia, it also had an early western outpost). Following Jan Critchett, Tom Griffiths has argued that in Australia 'the frontier was local, shifting and inescapable. It was not a linear frontier, and the enemy was not on the other side of neutral ground; the disputed area was "the very land each settler lived upon"' (1996: 109). As an island continent, the points of invasion of Australia were coastal then working inland, and the frontier was not just a singular agricultural frontier, but also a pastoral and mining frontier as Reynolds points out.

The frontiers of agriculture and pastoralism still exist in the Australian mind, and in the Australian landscape if a recent map produced by a rural realtor is anything to go by. This map shows the extent of pastoralism and agriculture across the continent. Although the wilderness was conquered by the frontier with the forces of an invading and colonising industrial, capitalist civilization behind it, the droving, pastoralist settlers on horses were the cavalry in this war, their sheep and cattle the infantry. Pastoralism, as Stephen Pyne puts it, 'often resembled war [...] carried out by other means' (1997: 99).[6] Aboriginal people in Australia certainly saw cattle and sheep as invaders, infantry and destroyers of their land (as we shall see in Chapter 10). Sheep and cattle were 'the shock troops' not only of 'empire' as Tom Griffiths (2002: 228) puts it coyly (or more precisely of the white invasion of Aboriginal country), but also of what Mulligan and Hill call 'the war on the wilderness' (2001: 16, 27 and 29). Settlers on horseback were the cavalry.

In Aboriginal terms, sheep and cattle turned cared-for-country into wilderness. Aboriginal people use 'wilderness' to refer to spoilt country, country damaged by agriculture, mining, pastoralism and cities as distinct from country that is cared for. Wilderness for them is not country remote from agricultural, mining, pastoral and other industries, but that country itself used by those industries. On this view, and as Deborah Rose puts it in a landmark essay:

> [...] country is becoming a 'wilderness' – man-made and cattle [as well as sheep, wheat, barley, mining, and city]-made wilderness where nothing grows, where life is absent, where all the care, intelligence and respect that generations of Aboriginal people have put into the country have been eradicated in a matter of a few short years. (1988: 386)

Wilderness is here not home, not 'country that is cared for' as Rose (1988: 386) calls it, but the alien landscape produced by the white settlers. The settler's home in the wilds is the Aboriginal person's unhome. Instead of accepting the construction of their land as wilderness, as unhomely, pristine nature, Aboriginal people have fought fire with fire and constructed clapped-out cattle, sheep and buffalo country, mined and farmed country and cities as wilderness, as uncared-for-country. A linguistic decolonisation is taking place here with the concept of wilderness, just as it did with the concept of country.

Rather than a category of land, or even land use, wild(er)ness is thus an idea, a state of mind (see Oelschlaeger 1991; and Nash 1982), a conjunction between subject and object (like the sublime), a sign in search of a referent (like nature), though, of course, for the wilderness experience to occur there has to be certain sorts of lands, lands variously unoccupied by humans or unmodified by humans or by modern industrial technology, or even land occupied and worked by Aboriginal owners and/or inhabitants. Wilderness, on the one hand, like landscape, involves a disjunction between subject and object; wilderness, on the other hand, like the sublime, involves a conjunction between subject and object. Wilderness operates in the interstices of this paradox.

Yet the experience of wilderness was not just any sort of experience, for the wilderness experience has been primarily a visual experience (as Coetzee's narrative shows). Recent revisionist definitions of wilderness aestheticize the unaesthetic or anaesthetic. Certain sights and sounds are valourized, often in distinction with what they are not: the sight (and often sounds) of no roads, no cities, no farms, no cars, for some, no people; as distinct from what they are: the sight, sounds, and sometimes smells, taste and touch of mountains, forests, deserts, trees, flowers, birds, insects, other animals, even wetlands and Aboriginal inhabitants.

Wilderness, as Andrew Ross has argued, has been regarded primarily as:

[...] a place where the sublimity of an unpeopled landscape (its indigenous inhabitants having long since been evicted) erases all of the legacies of social difference borne by visiting nature trekkers, and allows them to transcend those social identities that are judged to be restrictive and irrelevant in the face of unmediated Nature. (1994: 103)

Unlike the tourist who travels back in time and down the social hierarchy to primitive peoples and places, and so marks his or her temporal and social difference from them, the trekker travels to wilderness to transcend time and the social hierarchy in the sublimity of an infinitely spatial 'Nature' in which cultural difference and historical time is frozen. For Tom Griffiths, 'Wilderness zones [as he calls them] are a form of historic park [...] They offer the feel of the past, commemorate and mourn what we have lost' (1996: 261 and 263). Wilderness zones are a mournful monument to the world hypermodern human beings have lost. Wilderness zones are a heritage theme park.

In settler societies such as the United States and Australia prior to the late nineteenth century, wilderness, in the terms of Jay Appleton (1975: 95–106), and generalising broadly, was a *hazard*, a *threat* and an *impediment* to travel, whereas settlement was a *refuge* from the dangers of the wilderness, with the frontier as the dividing line and boundary between them. As Paul Carter points out, 'however far back the frontier is pushed, there is always something threatening on the other side' (1989: 158). There is always something out there in the outback, as there was and still is in Australia, something 'out there' that might come (in here) and get you.

The frontier, whether it is the frontier of settlement, or the mining frontier, or the pastoral (cattle or sheep) frontier, defined civilisation and wilderness against each other. Yet they were not in balance or harmony. The frontier indicated the extent of the incursions of modern industrial capitalism into the wilderness. Wilderness, as nature writers such as Henry David Thoreau saw, was the raw material (and not just the source of raw materials) for modern industrial civilisation. In the nineteenth century, Elizabeth Mankin Kornhauser argues that 'the wilderness, which had been feared and loathed in the eighteenth century, was now viewed as America's most distinctive feature – a symbol of the nation's potential as well as the country's history' (1998: 73). In the twentieth century, in settler societies, wilderness is a hazard, threat and impediment to be overcome and a retreat in which to seek refuge from the dangers of settlement in the different dangers of the wilderness.

The frontier experience, and the wilderness experience which accompanied and then replaced it, was imbued from the very beginning with masculinist notions of mastery. The frontier experience for Robert Gottlieb was 'strongly associated with images of mastery over the natural environment' (1993: 212). The wilderness experience, which superseded it, was imbued with similar images. It produced nature as sublime, particularly in the early conservationist movement. For William Cronon, 'the modern environmental movement is itself a grandchild of romanticism and post-frontier ideology' (1996b: 72). The Sierra Club in particular, Gottleib goes on to point out, had 'a male perspective on the natural environment as rugged, adventuresome and monumental, rather than diverse, interactive and holistic' (1993: 213). It subscribed to the patriarchal paradigm rather than the matrifocal one (see Figure 2, Chapter 1).

Despite the differences in position between the founder of the Sierra Club, John Muir, and the then President of the United States, Theodore Roosevelt, over the damming of the Hetch Hetchy valley, both shared a ruggedly masculinist idea of wilderness. Theodore Roosevelt, Gottleib goes on to argue, was 'the foremost champion of the masculine definition of the wilderness experience. During the Progressive Era [1880s to 1920s], Roosevelt, through his writings and actions, became the embodiment of this highly gendered concept of wilderness' (1993: 213). Like the myth of the Wild West that it superseded, wilderness-going re-enacted the masculine myth of what Richard Slotkin calls, following William Carlos Williams, 'regeneration through violence' (Slotkin 1973) and 'regeneration through regression to the primitive' (Slotkin 1992: 36, 38, 44, 167–168, 318 and 843). Like the tourist, the wilderness trekker is a time traveller to the past and a regresser to the primitive. The wilderness trekker, in addition, returns via the uncanny to the repressed and then seeks to transcend it through sublimation.[7]

Not only was wilderness masculinised, but nature was also masculinized by association with wilderness. Wilderness reinforced the distinction between the private sphere and the -ospheres. As Robert Gottlieb puts it:

> [...] the early protectionist and conservationist approaches derived largely from the nostalgia regarding the passing of the frontier and the response to urban and industrial forces that transformed the frontier and restructured work, family and community as well. (1993: 212)

He goes on to argue that 'the outdoors, or Nature, increasingly separated from concepts of home, work and community, was [...] situated as a male preserve, with the preservation of Nature and the conservation of resources distinctive male goals' (Gottlieb 1993: 215). The concept and experience of wilderness masculinized nature and feminized culture.

Post-bellum culture in the United States brought about what Tony Bennett calls 'the feminisation of culture', whilst 'nature [...] was itself being increasingly recodified as a masculinized domain' (1998: 151). Or more precisely, wilderness, just like natural history before it (as we saw in Chapter 1), recodifed nature as a masculinized domain. As natural history became effete, cultured and feminized, wilderness concomitantly and correspondingly came to the rescue to remasculinize the mastery of nature. The horrors and the deprivations of the Civil War and post-war reconstruction prompted a displacement of the drive to mastery, the will to power from the intractable enemy with which one was locked in mortal combat to the conquerable primitive landscape. As culture became increasingly commercialized physically, and threatening spiritually, men sought refuge in culture's and industrial civilisation's other, in physically challenging and spiritually refreshing wilderness. The unhomely, rather than the home, became a haven in a heartless world for masculinist men, whereas the home was a haven for feminized women (and men).

Culture was abandoned to the feminine and to the private sphere, rendering any complicity between masculinity and it null and void. Nature was effectively split between a source of industrial resource commodities for production and aesthetic landscape experience for consumption (leisure and recreation) with no possibility of rapprochement between them, let alone mutuality, just as it had been with the gentleman's park. Wilderness inherited the European landscape aesthetic, particularly the sublime.

The American frontier officially closed in 1890, though the frontier mythology persisted into the obsession of the 1940s with the frontiers of science, and of the 1960s with the frontiers or extra-terrestrial space.[8] But what does it mean to say that the frontier closed? It implies that there was no longer anywhere else worth settling. All the land that could have been subjected to agriculture and pastoralism had been. There was still a boundary between pastoral land and the desert that the mining frontier crossed. But this boundary was not a frontier for pastoralists and settlers. What was beyond was not wilderness defined by a frontier, but wastelands defined by pastoralism and settlement, and destroyed by nuclear bombing. In this sense, Tom Griffiths argues, 'the Australian frontier could never be said to have "closed" as America's was said to have been in 1890. The Never-Never never ended: the American dream was the Australian nightmare' (1997: 10; and 2002: 224). But the American nightmare of nuclear bombing in the deserts of Nevada and on the Marshall Islands also became Australia's nightmare in the deserts of Maralinga and on the Montebello islands.[9] The pastoral and mining frontiers in Australia have never been closed. Both stay open, limited by Aboriginal land rights and royalty negotiations, conservation values and pressure for conservation, as well as the former limited by rainfall and feed and the latter by yields and demand, and both by commodity prices.

The frontier was always not only spatial and temporal, but also a cultural divide between peoples, with space used to figure time. The pastoral and mining frontiers may never be closed in Australia, but the cultural frontier between the European invaders and Australian indigenes has been since the 1970s. Tim Flannery argues that 'explorers cannot exist without a frontier, and the frontier of Australian exploration has almost always been between two cultures [...] The principal frontier – between Aboriginal and European Australia – closed in 1977' (1998: 12). This was the year in which W. J. Peasley removed 'the last of the nomads' from the western Gibson Desert. As a result, Flannery argues, 'the frontier between autonomous Aboriginal and European cultures had vanished, just 189 years after it opened in Sydney Cove' (1998: 372).

Yet the frontier opens with exploration rather than with settlement as Flannery argued initially. The Australian European/Aboriginal frontier had been opened some 182 years before 1788 as the very first entry in his anthology shows and with the first recorded contact. In 1606 Willem Jansz landed from the *Duyfken* in the Gulf of Carpenteria and 'some savage, cruel, black barbarians [...] slew some of our sailors' (Flannery 1998: 17). The Australian frontier between autonomous Aboriginal and European cultures had remained open for 371 years of bloodshed, 'battles', massacres, and the assimilationism of the 'stolen generation'. The American frontier opened in 1492 with Columbus' 'discovery' and was closed in 1890, according to Turner, after the lapse of 398 years (and a similar history of genocide), and so achieved the dubious distinction of being open 27 years longer than the Australian frontier.

The American frontier was re-opened in 2000 with population levels in some places falling 'to the point where they would qualify for the old definition of "frontier" – [less than] 6 people to every 2.6 square kilometres' (Eccleston 2002: 24). The census of 1890 marked for Turner the closing of the frontier; the census of 2000 marked its re-opening. Just as the opening and closing of the frontier was marked by the dispossession of Amerindigenes, and mass exterminiation of them and their livelihoods located on the prairie and based on the buffalo, so the re-opening of the frontier is marked by the repossession by Amerindigenes of their lands and the resurgence of the buffalo. The land is reverting to a Buffalo Commons. Places where towns once stood, such as Merchison in South Dakota, are returning to 'wilderness'.

Wildness is the Bog in our Brain and our Bowels

With the closing of the American frontier, wilderness had ceased to exist outside the nation, and was thereafter internalized within the national boundaries in isolated pockets and within the national psyche in outdoor experience, in wilderness trekking. In order for the American nation to maintain its self-definition in contradistinction to wilderness, the wilderness out of which the nation had been forged, conservationists such as John Muir and Aldo Leopold argued that America needed to preserve vestiges of that wilderness (experience) within itself. For them, wilderness became a refuge (albeit aestheticized), a sanctuary from the hazards of the city.

These historical shifts can be traced somewhat in Henry David Thoreau's *The Maine Woods*, published posthumously three years after his death and one hundred years to the year before the American Wilderness Act of 1964. Wilderness for him was an omnibus category that was by turns aesthetic in evoking the sublime in mountains or portraying the picturesque in scenery, or anti-aesthetic in provoking horror in swamps. For Thoreau, the wilderness was associated with 'the glorious river and lake scenery' (1988: 2) that he encountered in the back blocks of Maine. Wild for him approximated to unsettled (Thoreau 1988: 3), or more precisely to the unsett*lered* and to the nomadic indigene. Thoreau referred to wilderness not only as unsettled but also to 'the unnamed and unincorporated wilderness' (1988: 8), as if it were not yet consumed by and digested into the body of modern industrial capitalist civilization. He also referred to 'the grim, untrodden wilderness' (Thoreau 1988: 12) that raises the question of grim for, and untrodden by, whom or what?

Similarly his reference to 'a wholly uninhabited wilderness' (Thoreau 1988: 19) raises the question of uninhabited by whom or what? He did later, however, refer to the woods as 'not an empty chamber [...] but an inhabited house' (Thoreau 1988: 248) (and so not uncanny, but again inhabited by whom?). Possibly he is drawing a distinction between wilderness uninhabited by whites and woods as inhabited by whites, or at least by spirits for he testified that, 'I believe that the woods were not tenantless, but chokeful of honest spirits as good as myself any day' (Thoreau 1988: 248). The woods were homely for Thoreau unlike the unhomely forest or swamp wilderness for his contemporaries. He also concedes that 'it is difficult to conceive of a region uninhabited by man' (Thoreau 1988: 94). Thoreau was not in the front line of conquest and therefore saw a battlefield from which the vanquished had been banished, though the scars of the battle had healed to such an extent that he could refer to 'that pleasant wilderness [...] showing no traces of man' (1988: 39 and 43), at least from the long view as Thoreau was forever picking up arrow heads so it did show traces of North Amerindigenes.

For Thoreau, wilderness was placed in contradistinction to 'civilization', though whose or which civilization is another question. In the Maine Woods he heard 'some utterly uncivilized, big throated owl hoot [...] loud and dismally in the drear and boughy wilderness' (Thoreau 1988: 49). 'Dismal' and 'dreary' were terms often reserved for swamps and marshes in nineteenth-century, Anglo-American culture, so wilderness could be swamplike for Thoreau – if not actually a swamp.[10] For Thoreau, swamps and wilderness were ambiguous places, both pleasant and dismal, 'stern, yet gentle wilderness' (1988: 53) as he put it. In the Maine wilderness 'Nature was here something savage and awful, though beautiful' (Thoreau 1988: 94). Wilderness for him was not only grim and dreary but also 'serene and placid', terms that he uses to describe a wild stream, a good place to go to but also a good place to leave to go home. For Thoreau, 'it was a relief to get back to our smooth, but still varied landscape' (1988: 210).

Whereas wilderness was uncanny or unhomely for his contemporaries, for Thoreau it was rough, a feature evoking the sublime for Edmund Burke, whereas European civilization was smooth, a feature of the beautiful for Burke (1958: 114). Wilderness was 'other' in both time and space for, according to Thoreau: 'this was primeval, untamed, and forever untameable *Nature*, or whatever else men call it' (1988: 93). Wilderness is historically positioned retrospectively before modern industrial capitalism; wilderness is represented as pre-industrial. The explorer and the settler of the wilderness travel back in time into a primitive past; the wilderness trekker regresses to the primitive as we have seen. Wilderness was not only unnamed but also unnameable, outside and beyond language and its drive to name things, beyond the discourse of natural history that produced the subject of the naturalist and the object of nature, but by doing so killed nature to give birth and life to the naturalist. By calling nature and wilderness into 'life' or language, one was simultaneously pronouncing their death sentence as everything which lives must die as Thoreau affirmed.

Home in the Wilds: Wild(er)ness as a Cultural Category

Yet Thoreau also saw that in nature the dead is reborn and that wilderness had its own language, such as in what he called 'the voice of the loon, loud and distinct', which was 'a very wild sound, quite in keeping with the place'. This sound not only gave 'voice to its wildness', but also 'gave expression to the wilderness' (Thoreau 1988: 306–307). The language of the wilderness is a language foreign to human ears, though Thoreau sensed affinity between the voice of the loon and the language of his own body when breathing heavily through his nose half-awake late at night, 'as if its language were but a dialect of my own, after all' (1988: 307). The language of the wilderness has affinities with the language of the human body coalescing in wild(er)ness.

Wilderness for Thoreau was primarily forest. Wilderness was also wet, what he called 'the dark, damp wilderness' (Thoreau 1988: 298). The forest, he directs his readers, is 'even more grim and wild than you had anticipated, a damp and intricate wilderness, in the spring everywhere wet and miry' (Thoreau 1988: 107). In fact, the wilderness is the complete antithesis of the familiar, and the familial, the domestic, and the domesticated. Thoreau proclaims that:

> [...] here was no man's garden, but the unhandseled [unhandled or unused] globe. It was not lawn [that bane of suburbia], nor pasture, nor mead [those necessaries of pastoralism], nor woodland [for the sport of hunting], nor lea [grass land or untilled land], nor arable [those requirements for agriculture], nor waste land [to be denigrated]. (1988: 97)

In addition, open plain was definitely not wilderness for Thoreau (1988: 136).

Wilderness and forest were thus synonymous for Thoreau; 'the luxuriant and fungus-like forest' the same as 'the damp and shaggy wilderness' (1988: 139), though he does insist that 'these are not the artificial forests of an English king, – a royal preserve merely' (1988: 108). Later, he draws a distinction between the primitive or wild forest and the tame forest (Thoreau 1988: 205). Wilderness for Thoreau is 'other', what he calls 'the fresh and natural surface of the planet Earth [...] It was Matter, vast, terrific – not his Mother Earth' (1988: 97). Wilderness was not the Mother Earth of agriculture but the Great Goddess or Great Mother. Wilderness, for Thoreau, was not the benign and malignant Mother Earth of tilled fields, patriarchy, agriculture and neolithic times, but the implacable Great Mother or Goddess of the swamps, of matrifocal cultures and palaeolithic times. In the wilderness, for Thoreau, 'there was clearly felt the presence of a force not bound to be kind to man' (1988: 97), though it could be merciful (1988: 386). The combination of the merciless and merciful distinguishes the Great Goddess or Mother from the benign and malignant Mother Earth.

Thoreau saw the wilderness as 'no-man's land' (1988: 110) in the military sense as the unoccupied zone between two warring parties, though it was never literally no-man's land in the sense of being unowned but many peoples' land. Yet it was more precisely the frontier that was 'no-man's land' between the withdrawing indigenes who had left their mark on the land and whose traces could still be found, and the advancing armies of settlers, sheep and cattle making their mark on the land in trails and towns. This invasion consumed and transformed the wilderness. Thoreau saw wilderness as 'necessary for a resource and background' and as 'the raw material of our civilization' (1988: 210–211) as did Aldo Leopold (1949: 108) nearly one hundred years later. For both writers this was more a statement of evidential historical fact rather than something to bemoan, and certainly not something to crow about.

Yet for both writers, wilderness was not only a physical resource but also spiritual source. Thoreau refers to 'the beautiful but mystical lore of the wilderness' (1988: 314). To destroy wilderness completely would also mean destroying 'our' civilization because it would mean destroying the very thing which not only gave 'our' civilization definition as Leopold (1949: 201) called it (though he saw this as 'the human enterprise' in a racist and ahistorical gesture), but also destroying what for him supplied the physical and spiritual raw materials of that civilization. Wilderness is premodern, cold, raw material to modern, industrial, thermodynamic, cooked commodities. Raw wilderness, as Leopold put it, supplied the timber, coal and oil to power the machines that cooked the minerals and the food to feed the mechanical monster of modern industrial capitalism (1949: 201).

Wilderness is a human artefact, or more precisely a European settler aesthetic and land-use artefact to which various, often contradictory, meanings have been ascribed. To refer then to 'the howling wilderness', as many did in the nineteenth century, from Charles Kingsley referring to the Fens to Governor Denison talking about three quarters of Australia, is to slip into a conjunction of terms as clichéd but as telling as 'dismal swamps'. Just as all swamps were dismal so all wilderness was howling in nineteenth-century Anglophone settler societies, though Henry Lawson described 'a blasted, barren wilderness that doesn't even howl. If it howled it would be a relief' (1976: 122). When it did for one Australian explorer in 1874 it showed that howling wilderness was being figured as an oral-sadistic monster as he referred to 'the jaws of that howling wilderness' (Flannery 1998: 312).

Thoreau wrote in his *Journal* that 'the wilderness, in the eyes of our forefathers, was a vast and howling place or *space*, where a man might roam naked of house and most other defence, exposed to wild beasts and wilder men' (1962, *XII*: 182). The wilderness as howling can be traced back to the Authorized (or King James) Version, and many subsequent ones, of the Bible (see Deuteronomy 32: 10). Yet for the agnostic, if not atheist, Thoreau 'generally speaking, a howling wilderness does not howl: it is the imagination of the traveller that does the howling' (1988: 300). Howling wild(er)ness is a state of the imagination triggered by the sights and sounds (and even smells, taste and touch) of a site. It is a pre-touristic experience of nature. It is the antithesis of home for the explorer and the settler and so the home of the primitive; both 'primitive' landscape and people. For Thoreau, what 'to the white man [is] a drear and howling wilderness [is to] the Indian a home, adapted to his nature, and cheerful as the smile of the Great Spirit' (1988: 260). Wilderness is also home for many Australian Aboriginal people as we shall see in Chapter 11.

Thoreau made a distinction and saw a conjunction between wilderness and wildness, between lands beyond the frontier and a state of the imagination. Writing in his *Journal* Thoreau maintained that:

> [...] it is in vain to dream of a wildness distant from ourselves. There is none such. It is the bog in our brain and bowels, the primitive vigor of Nature in us, that inspires that dream. I shall never find in the wilds of Labrador any greater wildness than in some recess in Concord, i.e. than I import into it. (1962, IX : 43)

Wild(er)ness for Thoreau was produced out of the conjunction between observer and observed, in the relation between subject and object, unlike the disjunction between landowner and landscape, prospector and prospect. It was not a quality of the object itself nor was it a scientific category or object, but a relation between subject and object, even a mutual abjection between them.

Wild(er)ness is a phenomenological category. Thoreau wrote later in his *Journal* that:

> I know the thing that really concerns me is not there, but in my relation to that [...] I think that the man of science makes this mistake, and the mass of mankind along with him: that you should coolly give your chief attention to the phenomenon which excites you as something independent on [*sic*] you, and not as it is related to you. The important fact is its effect on me [...] the point of interest is somewhere between me and them (i.e. the objects). (1962, X: 164–165)

Similarly, the interest in wilderness lies somewhere between a western conservationist or tourist and land unmodified by modern industrial technology. It does not lie in the land itself (if that were possible), nor between an Aboriginal inhabitant and his or her domain. For Thoreau, 'what we call wildness is a civilization other than our own' (1962, XI: 450). Writing in his most famous essay, 'Walking' (and probably the most famous essay in nature writing), for Thoreau, 'in Wildness is the preservation of the world [...] Give me a wildness whose glance no civilisation can endure [...] Life consists with wildness. The most alive is the wildest' (1982: 609–611).

For Thoreau, wilderness is landscape not changed or shaped by human labour. Arguably there are only a few, if any, landscapes not shaped or affected by human intervention in some way. Thoreau's view is ultimately a racist view of wilderness, the kind of view which gave rise to the doctrine, or legal fiction, of *terra nullius* in Australia only recently overturned in the so-called 'Mabo decision', which recognizes legally native title. Thoreau's view overlooks the way in which Aboriginal peoples have shaped the landscape through the soft and small technologies of burning and tilling, gathering and hunting. Thoreau's concept of wilderness harks back to a premodern wilderness that he construed as prior to human intervention.

A critical postmodern concept of wilderness would also hark back to the 'premodern', and distinguish within it between the pre-human and the pre-capitalist, thus acknowledging the ways in which Aboriginal peoples have shaped the land and the terrible depredations and degradation wrought by industrial capitalist technology on them and their lands. A critical postmodern concept of wilderness would also recognize that it is itself the product of an industrial society. Postmodern wilderness is the other of the hypermodern city, but not its other to denigrate as with the modern wasteland of the wetland, or to valourize over the city as urban conservationists are wont to do. Rather, postmodern wilderness and hypermodern city need to learn to live in mutually beneficial symbiosis.

Notes

1. I discuss maps and mapping in Giblett (1996: Chapter 3) and the crossing, conquering and colonisation of the frontier of orbital extra-terrestrial space in Giblett (2008b).
2. For a survey of the mammoth American literature on the frontier, see Opie (1986: 7–25).
3. Coetzee goes on to give a long meditation on the gun drawing on which I discuss the gun and the camera (and the camera as gun) in Giblett (2008a: 118–121; and 2008b: 67–73).
4. I discusss the prison of measured time in Giblett (2008a: especially Chapter 8).
5. I discuss the sublime, slime and the uncanny in Giblett (1996: Chapter 2) and American landscape and wilderness photography in Giblett (2009: Chapter 6).
6. For further discussion of pastoralism, see Chapter 10.
7. I discuss the uncanny as the return *to* the repressed in Giblett (1996: Chapter 2).
8. I discuss both frontiers in Giblett (2008b: 187–190).
9. I discuss the landscapes of nuclear bomb-testing in Giblett (2009: Chapter 6).
10. I discuss Thoreau as patron 'saint' of swamps in Giblett (1996: 229–239).

Chapter 6

Riding Roughshod Over It: Mateship Against the Bush

In a famous pronouncement about the bush in Australian feature films Ross Gibson relates how:

> Mad Max fights for hegemony over it. Picnickers are subsumed into it, never to return. The man from Snowy River spurs his small and weedy beast in a race to master it. It maps out the sorrow of the stoic shearer's wife who sees cause to lament that on Sunday, Jack Thompson is too far away. (1993: 209)

To Gibson's list no doubt one could add some other instances from Australian films: bronzed diggers bound for Gallipoli run for athletic supremacy through it; an erstwhile perving cameraman seeks the dark secrets of ground zero, and his father, in it; Aboriginal people sing songs and tell stories lovingly of it whilst in exile from the kingdom; and 'whities' project their fears of entrapment in the 'dead heart' of the 'red centre' onto it.

The Australian landscape is so pervasive in Australian film that it wouldn't be going too far to suggest that it is one of the quintessential features of Australian film, and of what has been constituted as 'Australian national cinema'. Indeed, for Gibson, 'the majority of Australian features have been about landscape' (cited by O'Regan 1996: 209).[1] Australian landscape is perhaps the feature that makes Australian cinema into a distinctively national, if not nationalist, cinema. Gibson goes further to suggest that 'the landscape cinema asserts an Australian difference' (1993: 216). The landscape is for him 'the leitmotif and ubiquitous central character' of many Australian films (Gibson 1993: 209). It is perhaps not only the biggest star of Australian film but also the lowest paid – unless the return it generates in tourism is taken into account.

The connection here between tourism and what has been called the 'AFC' (Australian Film Commission) genre is not coincidental or accidental. Susan Dermody and Elizabeth Jacka argue in their discussion of Fred Schepsi's film, *Chant of Jimmie Blacksmith*, based on Thomas Kenneally's novel, that the film represents what they call 'a kind of beatific bush tourism' (Dermody and Jacka 1988: 119). But, they go on to point out, 'there is something a little too close to a patronising fetishism in our late desire to admire and aesthetically claim the landscape'. Or more precisely, in the desire of film-makers to *re*claim it aesthetically, especially after it already been claimed and aestheticized by explorers, settlers, writers and painters before the film-makers got in on the act.

By making the Australian landscape the biggest star of their films, film-makers not only reclaimed it but also entered it into the star system and sublimated it into the realm of heavenly bodies as an industrial commodity disconnected from the body of the earth. In the mid-80s Bruce Clunies-Ross claimed that 'the hinterland, or wild Australia, is the source of the most pervasive images. Even in many of the films made in the last decade, when metropolitan conceptions of Australia have been prominent, the starring role has been taken by the great Australian landscape' (1986: 225). But which Australian landscape is the great one? As John Barnes argues, 'there is not one homogeneous Australian landscape [...] not one quintessentially Australian landscape' (1986: 93). Rather, there are a plurality of heterogeneous Australian landscapes, ecosystems and habitats: rain-, jarrah, karri, tingle, etc. forests; banksia, sheoak, mallee, wattle, etc. woodlands; melaleuca swamps, samphire marshes, mangrove mudflats; pindan and beach sand-dunes; granite and limestone hills, and mountains, and so on.

The Bush

Like the man from Snowy River who rides roughshod over the Australian landscape, some film theorists write roughshod over it. For Tom O'Regan, for instance, 'Australian cinema is not dominated by rural and outback stories' and 'there are more city and town stories' (1996: 210). Without calling a division and doing a head count (as the resolution to this debate will not be achieved by quantitative research methods), many Australian films are set in both locales (the *Mad Max* trilogy to take one prominent example) and concern the relationship between the two. Although white Australia has been predominantly urban in its places of residence, it has looked to (and filmed, photographed, painted, waxed lyrical, and written reams of poetry and prose about) the landscape outside the cities ('the bush'), as a source of cultural (especially nationalist) mythology,[2] and continues to do so as frequent references to 'the bush' in the news media attest, such as recent stories regarding banks closing branches or telcos reducing services in 'the bush'. Rather than the city or the country, it is more the interplay and relationship between 'the city and the country' that has been important than any sort of exclusive allegiance to one or the other in Australian film, literature and painting.

Australian national, if not also cultural, identity is tied up with the Australian landscape. Gibson suggests that 'the idea of the intractability of Australian nature is essential to the national ethos' (1993: 211; see also Williams 1996: 4–105). In fact, the national ethos, or more precisely the dominant white, Anglo-Celtic and masculine ethos of the Australian nation, is constructed in relation to, if not conflict, with Australian nature. The drive was to conquer nature and tame the Great South Land (see Lines 1991), for the spoilers to gain the spoils (see Bolton 1993), but the result was that the battle and the land was only half won (see Blainey 1983). The formation of this national ethos can be traced back, as Gibson does, to the earliest European explorers, such as William Dampier, and their bleak descriptions of the (for them) intractable Australian landscape. No doubt the birth of the nation can be found here; no doubt the nation was forged in this crucible.

Yet this fascination with the Australian landscape in Australian film, literature, painting and photography is found not only in the conflict and interrelationship between the city and the country, but also in the difference between various landscapes in the country. The Australian country landscape is not just the dun-coloured bush, but also the smooth park-like estates, the rolling pastoral downs, the sweeping plains of golden grain, the rugged mountain ranges (and not so much the dismal swamps, the disappointing lakes, the dreary marshes).

A number of Australian country landscapes are portrayed in Peter Weir's 1975 film *Picnic at Hanging Rock*, based on Joan Lindsay's (1967) novel.[2] The film is set in some highly codified spaces: the cold, neoclassical architecture and carefully tended gardens of Appleyard College (even the name is indicative of an enclosed European garden landscape); Lake View (again indicative of a European landscape aesthetic of the gentleman's park estate, the pleasing prospect and the picturesque); the golden countryside of grain fields, and the green and lush bush of the picnic ground shot in impressionist colours and tones; and finally the dark and gloomy rock louring over and ultimately consuming three of the school girls.

The different landscapes of this film can be read allegorically as characters that act out a drama of the colonial history of the land. These filmic landscapes are a character, even the central character as Gibson suggests, in this and other Australian films. Appleyard College, its buildings and grounds represent a starchy European culture foisted onto an alien, nationalistic, Australian landscape represented in turn by the golden fields and rolling countryside around the college. There is a strict line of demarcation between the two marked by the walls, hedgerows and lawns of the college. This is the line between a little bit of transplanted Europe and the vastness of Australia. Yet Australia is composed of three landscapes in this film. The 'great Australian landscape' is polysemic.

First, there is the golden summers of rolling countryside, the landscape of agriculture and pastoralism as painted by the Heidelberg School in impressionist mood; secondly, there is the landscape of the bush of the picnic grounds at the base of the rock, partly a Europeanized landscape because it is a picnic ground and a park (or park-like) landscape, and partly the landscape of the green and sombre Australian bush also as painted by the Heidelberg School with a vague kind of threat posed by its ants, birds, and heat; and third, and finally, the rock itself, which stands in for preternatural nature, nature before the coming of the Europeans, nature outside culture, wild, untamed nature, nature feminized as threat, not the benign and virginal nature of the bush or the fields, but Aboriginal Nature, the Great Goddess or Mother. The rock is horrific and monstrous even overshadowing the film itself. John Carroll waxes lyrical that 'the film of *Picnic at Hanging Rock* is visually dull compared with the uncanny and mysterious, wild beauty of the rock itself' (1982: 223). Uncanny indeed.

In the final chapter of the novel, not published until 1987 (twenty years after the rest of the novel and twelve years after Peter Weir's film), the girls are met by an old Aboriginal woman who leads them into the rock in a kind of reversal of birth, and not a mere regression to the primitive as for the masculine wilderness trekker. High up on the rock the girls find 'the monolith – a single outcrop of stone something like a monstrous egg, rising smoothly out of the rocks ahead above a precipitous drop to the plain' (Lindsay 1987: 23). The monolith is feminized in matrifocal, not misogynist, terms. The monstrous monolith is not a masculinist monument but a feminist fertility 'symbol' (see Figure 2, Chapter 1). The point of view over the plain is neither a pleasing nor commanding prospect but a horrifying, vertiginous drop.

The Australian landscape seen through masculine European eyes enacts a fear of, and fascination with, the Great Mother, and a desire for and a fantasy of a young, virginal nature. These sorts of sentiments of the Australian landscape and this kind of tension between the two are expressed in D. H. Lawrence's 1923 novel *Kangaroo*, set, as the title suggests, in Australia. It was described by the Jindyworobaks of the 1930s as 'a superb piece of natural description' (Elliott 1979: 229) though conceding that Lawrence 'did not feel at home in the bush' as it was an unhomely place for him, as he shows in *Kangaroo*:

> And they ran on bridges over two arms of water from the sea, and they saw what looked like a long lake with wooded shores and bungalows: a bit like Lake Como, but oh, so unlike. That curious sombreness of Australia, the sense of oldness, with the forms all worn down low and blunt, squat. The squat-seeming earth. (Lawrence 1950: 86)

The landscape is at first measured against the European norm and found to be different. It is then described in terms of the intractable old Great Mother (she is even figured in terms of the squat figurines depicting her).

The Great Mother Earth is contrasted with the lithe, virginal bush (she is even figured as a young Aboriginal woman in statuesque pose in a static tableau, which may say more about the fact that the scene is being viewed from a train than anything profound about the landscape itself):

> And then they ran at last into real country, rather rocky, dark old rocks, and sombre bush with its different pale-stemmed, dull-leaved gum-trees standing graceful, and various healthy-looking undergrowth, and great spiky things like yuccas. As they turned south they saw tree-ferns standing on one knobbly leg among the gums, and among the rocks ordinary ferns and small bushes spreading in glades and up sharp hill-slopes. It was virgin bush, and as if unvisited, lost, sombre, with plenty of space, yet spreading grey for miles and miles, in a hollow towards the West. Far in the West, the sky having suddenly cleared, they saw the magical range of the Blue Mountains. And all this hoary space of bush between. (Lawrence 1950: 86–87)

The Australian landscape for Lawrence is split between the hoary old Great Mother Earth and the young virgin bush.

The Australian landscape could be beautiful for Lawrence, and even more:

> The strange, as it were, *invisible* beauty of Australia, which is undeniably there, but which seems to lurk just beyond the range of our white vision. You feel you can't *see* – as if your

eyes hadn't the vision in them to correspond with the outside landscape. For the landscape is so unimpressive, like a face with little or no features, a dark face. It is so aboriginal, out of our ken, and it hangs back so aloof [...] And yet when you don't have the feeling of ugliness or monotony, in landscape or in nigger you get a sense of subtle, remote, *formless* beauty more poignant than anything ever experienced before. (1950: 87)

In other words, or in one word, you can experience the sublime. Yet perhaps this was the minority view of a sophisticated European (albeit of working-class origins) of the 1930s, one not shared by the majority of Australians, who saw the landscape in more prosaic terms.

With the rise of Australian nationalism, and its articulation in the 1890s, the national ethos in relation to nature becomes fully fledged and moderates into ambivalence, if not grudging respect and even love. A number of nationalist writers and painters could be pointed to here but one writer who articulated these sentiments explicitly in 1903 was 'Tom Collins' (Joseph Furphy) in *Such is life*:

[...] before midday I was out on the [...] track [...] Here and there the marks of the wagon were still identifiable, where the long team and heavy load has cut off corners of the winding track. Presently the heavy wheel-marks diverged to the right, and disappeared in the all-pervading scrub. Then the faint track became suddenly fainter, where half the scanty traffic branched off to the left, in the direction of Lindsay's paddock.

The technology of transportation marks a mark on, and leaves traces, in the scrub. This sense of a European presence in the landscape transforms unhomely wilderness into the homely, however tenuous. The paddock carves out private property in the unowned scrub.

This middle landscape of track and paddock in the scrub, mediating between the 'civilisation' of the former and the 'wilderness' of the latter, is the crucible of Australian national identity. For Collins, 'it is not in our cities or townships, it is not in our agricultural or mining areas that the Australian attains full consciousness of his own nationality; it is in places like this, and as clearly here as at the centre of the continent'. It is in the Australian pastoralist landscape located in the scrub that Australian nationalism is forged. The scrub for Collins does not conform to the dictates of the beautiful and the sublime: 'to me the monotonous variety of this interminable scrub has a charm of its own; so grave, so subdued, self-centred; so alien to the genial appeal of more winsome landscape, or the assertive grandeur of mountain and gorge'.

Part of the distinctiveness of the Australian pastoralist landscape, mediating between track and paddock on the one hand and scrub on the other, lies in the fact that it contains indigenous flora and fauna. Scrub is woodland of indigenous flora that contains indigenous fauna and Aboriginal people:

To me this wayward diversity of spontaneous plant life bespeaks an unconfined, ungauged potentiality of resource; it unveils an ideographic prophecy, painted by Nature in the

Impressionist mood, to be deciphered aright only by those willing to discern through the crudeness of dawn a promise of majestic day. Eucalypt, conifer, mimosa; tree; shrub, heath, in endless diversity and exuberance, yet sheltering little of animal life beyond half-specialized and belated types, anachronistic even to the Aboriginal savage.

Australian scrub may not conform to the dictates of the European sublime and beautiful but it does (or can be made to) conform to the Impressionist picturesque, especially when it contains tracks and paddock, sheep and cattle, settlers and houses – the stock-in-trade of the Heidelberg School of Australian Impressionist painters.

This is a benign, feminized landscape for Collins:

Faithfully and lovingly interpreted, what is the latent meaning of it all? Our virgin continent! How long has she tarried the bridal day! [...] she has waited in serene loneliness [...] waited, ageless, tireless, acquiescent, her history a blank.

Not only is the stock reference made to the Australian landscape as virginal, awaiting the penetration of phallic and heroic explorers, pastoralists, squatters, settlers and city fathers, but also a fairly typical reference is made to 'this recordless land' whose 'history is a blank'. Such sentiments were satirized later in the 1920s by writers such as the paired 'M. Barnard Eldershaw' who have one of their characters intone pompously that 'Australia of itself is nothing [...] The country is a *tabula rasa* – a blank sheet' (cited by Falkiner 1992: 51). It was a philosophic blank slate for the European imagination. On this blank slate the Australian nation thought that it could write its own story irrespective of the people who already lived in it and the environmental constraints and limitations it posed.

The landscape as a *tabula rasa* also served a psychological function as, in Gibson's words, it 'becomes the projective screen for a persistent national neurosis deriving from the fear and fascination of a preternatural continent' (1993: 212). In fact, it becomes the flat screen for the projection of desires, fears and fantasies about nature. The cinema screen replicates that projective screen by providing a technological analogue to it and reproducing the space for those desires, fears and phantasies to be played out.[3] Australian national desires, fears and fantasies about nature are now played out on the cinema screen as well as on the landscape itself in mining, pastoralism, agriculture, forestry and cities.

It is the pastoral landscape rather than the urban or agricultural landscape and certainly not some untamed, wilderness beyond the frontier that Tom Collins sees as the source of Australian national identity and as the crucible of Australian nationalism – and nation. What Collins is talking about can be summed up in two words: the bush. What is 'the bush'? There is no single, definitive answer to this question, but a number of commentators have hazarded a guess. Anthony Trollope first visited Australia in 1871, recorded his impressions and published them two years later. An astute observer, he was aware of some of the contradictions that befall the notion of 'the bush'. He advised that:

> [...] readers who desire to understand anything of Australian life should become acquainted with the technical meaning of the word bush. The bush is the gum-tree forest, with which so great a part of Australia is covered, that folk who follow a country life are invariably said to live in the bush. Squatters who look after their own runs always live in the bush, even though their sheep are pastured on the plains. (Trollope 1987, I: 149)

Bush not was only synonymous with the country but was also associated for Collins with the track through, and the paddock in, the scrub. Bush is pastoralized scrub.

By contrast, for Marcus Clarke scrub was an oral-sadistic monster, whereas the bush was merely melancholic. He related how 'that awesome scrub, silent and impenetrable [...] swallowed up its victims noiselessly' (Clarke 1993b: 53). It was 'a strange, dangerous, fascinating, horrible, wonderful place' (Clarke 1993b: 54). Scrub was an uncanny place, fearful and fascinating at the same time, that could consume the victim painfully. Henry Lawson similarly described 'the long, long, agony of scrub [...] with here and there a natural clearing, which seemed even more dismal than the funereal "timber" itself [...] plains like dead seas [...] scrub indescribably dismal – everything damp, dark, and unspeakably dreary' (1976: 139). As swamps were dismal in nineteenth-century Anglophone culture, so was scrub. One, however, got 'used to weird and dismal, as one living alone in the bush must necessarily be' (Lawson 1976: 109). After all, what could one expect for these were 'God-forsaken scrubs' (Lawson 1976: 241).

The difference between the bush and scrub (undifferentiated without an article definite or not) could be accounted for in terms of occupation, transportation and land use. The bush is the frontier; scrub is wilderness. Trollope argues later that:

> [...] woodland country in Australia – and it must be remembered that the lands occupied are mostly woodland – is either bush or scrub. Woods which are open, and passable – passable at any rate for men on horseback – are called bush. When the undergrowth becomes thick and matted so as to be impregnable without an axe, it is scrub. (1987: II: 22)

And when it is impassable to men on horseback, it is scrub too. 'The bush' was an amalgam of different non-urban landscapes of trees and plains, of frontier and forest (but not of settled agriculture nor of un-settlable wetlands). As John Barnes puts it succinctly, 'The bush [was] any landscape with trees and any area *sparsely* settled' (1986: 97; my emphasis). In other words, the bush was not any area unsettled, or any area un-settlable, such as scrub or wilderness.

Bush may be passable in terms of transportation and pregnable in terms of occupation (the military and sexual metaphors are a dead giveaway), but it was not necessarily pleasurable in terms of aesthetics. When he was in south-western Australia travelling between Albany and Perth, Trollope complains that 'the bush in these parts never develops itself into scenery, never for a moment becomes interesting. There are no mountains, no hills that affect the eye, no vistas through the trees tempting the foot to wander' (1987, II: 296). The bush does not necessarily compose itself into the picturesque and sometimes, as in this case, it never does. Writing of this region George Seddon argues that 'that balance of foreground, middle ground and background, with composed masses to the right and to the left that make up our inherited sense of the picturesque, hardly work in banksia woodland or jarrah forest or indeed in much of Australia' (1997: 136).

Even when the bush is composed into the picturesque prospect of the park-like it can become monotonous, that stock response that Trollope inevitably trots out:

> The fault of all Australian scenery is its monotony. The eye after awhile becomes fatigued with a landscape which at first charmed with its park-like aspect. One never gets out of the trees, and then it rarely happens that water lends its aid to improve the view. As a rule it must be acknowledged that a land of forests is not a land of beauty [...] every lover of nature is a lover of trees. But unceasing trees [...] become a bore, and the traveller begins to remember with regret the open charms of some cultivated plain. (1987, II: 22–23)

A land of forests is not a land of beauty because forests are too big to be beautiful and the beautiful too small to be a forest. But what is more interesting and noteworthy here is the fact that the land is supposed to conform to the dictates of the European landscape aesthetic. The land is ascribed agency and given life, but this agency and life is supposed to mean that land and water improve the view for the jaded traveller. How anthropocentric, or more precisely andocentric, or just plain Eurocentric, can you get?!

Even when the landscape was picturesque and fulfilled aesthetic requirements, and so was not boring to watch, it was boring to travel through and failed to fulfil the transportational requirement of teleology as Trollope related:

> There arose at last a feeling that go where one might through the forest, one was never going anywhere. It was all picturesque – for there was rocky ground here and there and hills in the distance, and the trees were not too close for the making of pretty vistas through them – but it was all the same. One might ride on, to the right or to the left, or might turn back, and there was ever the same view [...] One seems to ride forever and to come to nothing, and to relinquish at last the very idea of an object. (1987, I: 191-192)

One therefore loses at last the very idea of being a subject until one became lost and abject, and ceases to be one against the many. As one early bushman put it, 'one wants somebody to sympathize with so desperately in the bush' (Landor 1998: 261). Almost anybody would do but preferably somebody to sympathize with, and to have sympathy with one.

Mateship

In order to provide that sympathy of fellow-feeling with one, as well as to produce and maintain a bulwark against the threat of the bush and the fear of the loss of individual and collective identity it posed, the mythology of mateship was developed. The bush is the crucible of Australian national identity because it is here that mateship, that linchpin of Australian national identity, was forged. Henry Lawson reflected on:

The mateship born of barren lands,
Of toil and thirst and danger. (1976: 374)

Mateship was born of barren wilderness; mateship was born of an infertile mother; mateship was a Bachelor Birth from a Bachelor Machine because it denied and repressed the role of the Great Mother Earth in giving new life and because it gave birth to mateship without her.

Mateship was born of masculine solidarity against the bush. Flora Eldershaw and Marjorie Barnard reflected singly, jointly (as M. Barnard Eldershaw) and somewhat critically on the phenomenon of Australian mateship in the 1930s, 40s and 50s. Mateship for them is 'the solidarity of men against the bush' (Barnard Eldershaw 1939: 52), or elsewhere for Eldershaw (1952: 217), against nature. Mateship is the formation of patriarchal, or perhaps more precisely filiarchal, solidarity; the brotherhood of white men, of southern sons, of the 'coming man' of colonial modernity against the threats posed by the feminized black bush and its (or 'her') black people.

The solidarity of mateship against the bush was also soldierly and military, as the title of Rob Linn's 1999 book, *Battling the Land: 200 Years of Rural Australia*, indicates.[4] The 'Aussie Battler' is a fighter for survival not only against big government and squatters with large runs, but also against 'the bush'. Often the social and class struggle against the former was displaced into the struggle for survival against, and mastery over, the latter. Flora Eldershaw and Marjorie Barnard advise that 'the pioneer must take the offensive against the land [...] Defeat may be final but victory never is' (Barnard Eldershaw 1939: 223). The pioneer must take arms against the sea of troubles posed by the bush for, by not opposing them, they will end him. For them, 'the bush is like the sea, it has no paths, always the same, unchanging, the silence made visible' (Barnard Eldershaw 1939: 13; see also 53 and 61). Unlike wilderness that made the mute land speak, the bush made silence visible. The bush could be represented in painting but wilderness could never be – it could only be gestured towards. The wilderness could be represented in writing but the bush could never be – it could only be defined.

The bush was thus largely a visual category, whereas wilderness was primarily a verbal one. It was difficult to depict wilderness in painting. The closest most painters could come was to paint a picture of 'a home in the woods' (not the wilds) as Thomas Cole did in 1847, or of settlers 'journeying through the wilderness' as Frederic Edwin Church did in 1846. It was easier to depict the bush in painting as Eugene von Guérard did in 1855 and 1857 with his picturesque prospects from one hill or mount across a plain or a swamp to another hill or mount, and as the Heidelberg School did with pleasing prospects of pastoral landscapes with their figures of people or cattle in the bush.

Yet mateship is not just passive male bonding amongst men to produce the ties of hom(m)oerotic friendship but also active masculine colonisation of the feminized bush. Eldershaw argues that 'men must assert themselves against the lonely immensities and scrawl something in the monotone' (1952: 217). The metaphor of inscription on the land is used to trope the masculine relationship to the landscape, just as the track for Collins marked and left traces in the scrub. Part of the fear of the bush was that it would inscribe men, leave its mark on them before they would be able to leave their mark on it. It was case of write or be written on; leave your mark on the land with fence, or road, or railway, or town, or lot, or be marked by the land, permanently scarred for life physically and mentally.

Yet mateship was not only solidarity *against* the bush; it could also be solidarity *with* the bush. Tim Flannery argues that 'the development of Australian "mateship" and the sense of "a fair go" strongly parallel the Aboriginal sense of reciprocal obligation and also provide refuge (this time in social solidarity) from natural catastrophe' (1997: 56). Mates may have had a sense of reciprocal obligation with the bush like the original inhabitants and owners, but not with them as Tim Rowse points out that 'there is a gross lack of reciprocity in "wild Australia", for property is being stolen under duress' (1996: 105). The land, not the land-owners, were the partners which were given grudging respect and with which they entered into some sort of exchange, however mutually unbeneficial and parasitic.

There is thus a difference between the mateship, on the one hand, of the pastoral drover, shepherd and the tree-felling bush worker in solidarity with each other and, to some extent, *with* the bush; and, on the other, the solidarity of the industrial farm worker and mill worker (or perhaps more precisely the mill itself) with each other and *against* the bush. The mateship of the manual bush worker could represent a sense of sacrality towards the bush and satisfaction from it, whereas the machinery of the mill enacts mastery over the bush and oral sadism against it. In Katherine Susannah Prichard's 1926 novel *Working Bullocks* Deb 'wondered how the men dared put the long sharp–toothed perpendicular saw [...] through the body of a log' (1980: 180). It appalled her when 'the saw [...] sets its cruel teeth in the raw wood' (ibid.). Worse was to follow when 'the steam-driven saws ate through the wood' (ibid) and the wood let out screams and moans (Prichard 1980: 180, 182 and 184). The result for the bodies of the logs was 'dismemberment, that tearing of their living flesh' (Prichard 1980: 177).

The fear of the machines turning on the mill workers gripped them and invaded their fantasies. Deb 'did not wonder that Charley Johansen had "the horrors" when he was drunk [and] fancied the saws were chasing him with their bright shark's teeth'. Stone-cold sober, 'Deb had a horror of machines and the way they ate up everything before them [...] like great devouring monsters' (Prichard 1980: 183 and 187). Industrial machines are figured as oral-sadistic monsters (a subject to which I return in Chapter 9). Prichard contrasts 'all that inhuman machinery' in 'the dark interior of the mill' (1980: 177 and 183) – a possible allusion to Blake's 'dark satanic mills' – with 'the natural gait of work in the bush' and the life of the trees themselves that she personalizes:

In the forest the fallers, bullock-drivers and men at the bush landings treated great trees respectfully. They watched trees and logs as though they were animated and at any moment might be expected to crush a man out of existence. In the bush, men were reverent of a great tree. They gathered to utter oaths of admiration, standing off to appraise his stature, do him homage, before bringing him down. They celebrated his measurements and magnificence with yarns, legends of great trees, at crib time, smoking and gossiping dreamily. But in the mills there was no time for rites to appease dead trees. (1980: 183–184)

There was no time for any sort of rites, for the mill was subject to the work discipline of industrial capitalism exercised by machines and the mechanical measurement of time by the clock.

The City or the Bush?

Although Barnard and Eldershaw developed the critical concept of mateship as solidarity *against* the bush, they were aware, like Prichard, that it also could imply solidarity *with* the bush, though there was also the solidarity of the bush against the city:

> [...] bush is the name given to the shaggy pelt of the country, timber and scrub, and it is much more. It is the inland of Australia in its parts or totality, it is the country. It carries with it a whole complex of ideas, a code word, into which is written down a loyalty to and affinity with a strange and often difficult country, a decoy word in its insignificance, an endearment in its belittlement, a domestication of the vast [...] It is everything outside the towns, where men earn their living on and from the earth even if there is not a tree in sight. (Barnard and Eldershaw 1939: 125)

The bush made the unhomely homely, tamed the wilderness, placed a home in the wilds and made the silent land speak. Whatever else the bush was, or still is, it is in the country and not in the city. For Trollope 'nearly every place beyond the influences of big towns is called "bush" – even though there should not be a tree to be seen around' (1987, I: 186). The city defined itself against the bush; the city defended itself against the bush.

Even though Australia is, and always has been, a highly urbanized nation (as distinct from country or continent), it, as a nation, has sought its identity in what it is not; in the bush outside, initially, and later within its own boundaries, as the United States did with the frontier and wilderness. The bush is the other against which, and in relation to which, Australia has constructed itself as a nation. Yet this other is not the other without but the other within, within its own boundaries. Part of the fascination with, and fear of, the bush lies in what it is not; in its otherness. It is not city, it is even anti-city, as Ian Burn suggests when he argues that 'the bush had a cultural meaning in this country prior to the landscape acquiring a specific form [...] [by] referring generally to unsettled or sparsely settled areas, a kind of "anti-city"' (1992: 26; see also Spearitt and Stephen 1992). Just as the wilderness was the antithesis of home, so the bush was the antithesis of the city.

The bush was not only unsettled or sparsely settled areas; it was also not other sorts of landscape, not mountains and gorges (as Collins suggests); nor is it swamps and marshes. The bush and the Australian landscape is, in Australian films in particular, quite specific as it has been in Australian landscape painting. As Tim Bonyhady puts it, 'for most colonial landscape painters [and indeed for colonial landscape writers and their successors – the landscape film makers], the Australian wilderness was made up of mountain ranges and forests, waterfalls and lakes' (1985: 63). For most of them it was *not* made up of swamps, marshes, bogs or sloughs, or if it was it was from a distance in picturesque prospects as in some of Eugene von Guérard's paintings. Only rarely, as in H. J. Johnstone's 'Evening Shadows, Backwater of the Murray, Kent Town', does a painting take the close up point of view in a swamp and show its Aboriginal owners, albeit romanticized as 'noble savages'.

The city made the bush what it is; the city brought the bush into being. Richard White argues that 'the city dweller's image of the bush [was of] a sunlit landscape of faded blue hills, cloudless skies and noble gum trees, peopled by idealized shearers and drovers' (1981: 85). This image was encapsulated in Dorothea McKellar's jingoistic creed, 'I Love a Sunburnt Country', that every school child (including myself) in the country (nation) in the 1950s learnt by heart. It is also found in Henry Handel Richardson's *Ultima Thule*, published in 1929, with its reference to 'its dun and arid landscape', 'inimitable blue distances and gentian-blue skies', 'the scanty, ragged foliage; the unearthly stillness of the bush', 'the long red roads, running inflexible as ruled lines towards a steadily receding horizon', 'the blue in the green of the new leafage', 'the scent of aromatic foliage' (cited by Barnes 1986: 88).

Richardson perpetuates what Henry Lawson enumerated some 35 years before her as some popular Australian mistakes:

1. An Australian mirage does not look like water; it looks too dry and dusty.
2. A plain is not necessarily a wide, open space covered with waving grass or green sward; [...] it is either a desert or a stretch of level country covered with wretched scrub.
3. A river is not a broad, shining stream with green banks and tall, dense eucalypti walls; it is more often a string of muddy water-holes – 'a chain of dry water-holes', someone said.
4. There are no 'mountains' out West; only ridges on the floors of hell.
5. There are no forests; only mongrel scrubs.
6. Australian poetical writers invariably get the coastal scenery mixed up with that of 'Out Back'.
7. An Australian western homestead is not an old-fashioned, gable-ended, brick-and-shingle building with avenues and parks; and the squatter doesn't live there either. A western station, at best, is a collection of slab and gavlanized-iron sheets and humpies, and is the hottest, driest, dustiest, and most God-forsaken hole you could think of; the manager lives there – when compelled to do so [...]

8. An Australian lake is not a lake; it is either a sheet of brackish water or a patch of dry sand [...]
9. In conclusion. We wish to Heaven that Australian writers would leave off trying to make a paradise out of the Out Back Hell [...] (Lawson 1976: 128–130)

Both Richardson's and Lawson's view are representations of the Australian landscape. Both are equally valid or invalid. Both are constructions and projections. Both fall on either side of a bifurcated view of the Australian bush (as I will show below).

Richardson's landscape is by and large the literary version of the landscape paintings of the Heidelberg School. Both depict, like Collins, the pastoral landscape as the national landscape. By and large it is the painted pastoral landscape (especially Hans Heysen's paintings and those of the Heidelberg School) that has become *the* Australian national landscape. Ian Burn has suggested that 'the image of the Australian bush produced in the late nineteenth century by the artists of the Heidelberg School has mediated the relations to the bush of most people growing up in Australia during the past fifty or so years' (1980: 83). The paintings of the Heidelberg School have mediated nature and the bush for generations of white Australians. There is no unmediated bush just as there is no unmediated wilderness as we saw in the previous chapter.

Yet it is not as if the painters of the Heidelberg School had an unmediated relationship with nature and the bush, and that the viewer of the paintings alone has a mediated relationship with them. The bush for them was mediated by class and gender politics. Burn goes on to argue that 'the Heidelberg painters taught us to see our bush environment in a new way, but at the same time distorted our comprehension of that environment. The pictures allude to a reality of the bush, but embody the illusions of a class "way of seeing"' (1980: 98). And a gendered way of seeing, I would add. Pastoral discourse and the pastoralist mode are masculine (as I will show in Chapter 10). The landscapes of the Heidelberg School were pastoral, if not pastoralist. The bush of the Heidelberg School was neither unmediated nature nor working country. The bush of the Heidelberg School, Burn argues furthermore, is 'not seen through a lived or worked experience' (1980: 83). Like the pleasing prospects of the gentleman's park in England, the pleasing prospects of the Heidelberg School in Australia hid the labour of those who made them possible, both the Aboriginal owners and the invading settlers.

Like the enclosed commons of England, the paintings of the Heidelberg School hid the acts of dispossession and the relations of private property that produced the landscape. For Burn 'the bush landscape as depicted by Roberts and McCubbin conveys no sense of itself as landed property' (1980: 84). These landscapes hid not only history and ownership but also labour and the labourer, as did pleasing prospects. Burn goes on to argue that 'the people in the pictures [of the Heidelberg School] are city folk and the incidents narrated are part of the social relationship to the bush of an urban class' (1980: 85). And so not part of the social relationship to the bush of the rural classes, the landowners, the squatters, the drovers and the labourers.

Like the people in their pictures, the painters of the Heidelberg School were 'city folk', yet according to Burn they were not an alienated urban intelligentsia: 'the bush pictures of Roberts and McCubbin [...] are a projection from the city, but not of values of an *alienated* urban intelligentsia' (1980: 88). Their pictures were projections of the values of a nostalgic and organic country intelligentsia. Based in Melbourne, they were unlike their contemporaries, the *Bulletin* writers, based in Sydney. What Richard White calls 'the new intelligentsia' of the 1890s in Australia, 'projected on to their image of the bush their alienation from their urban environment: they sought an escape from what the city represented' (1981: 102). They chose 'the bush as an imaginative refuge'. Yet there is a difference between the painters of the Heidelberg School and the writers of the *Bulletin* School, and amongst the writers of that school.

The Heidelberg School produced images of the pastoral landscape as rural Arcady, whereas the *Bulletin* School, especially Lawson, produced images of the bush as rural melancholy. Ian Burn asks:

> [...] what is the relationship of the bush image of the Heidelberg painters to the image of the bush produced by writers like Lawson, Paterson, Furphy, and others associated with the *Bulletin*? The painters' perception of the bush *seems* contradictory to the perception of the writers. The latter's vision is not a rural Arcady, but more an environment of material hardship which brings out ideal and admirable qualities in people. (1980: 88)

Yet all the *Bulletin* writers cannot be lumped together like this, as Paterson was a writer of rural Arcady. There is a distinction to be drawn, as Lawson does, between his melancholia of the bush and the Arcadia of Paterson.

Weird Melancholy

If the dominant tone of the Heidelberg School is golden, the dominant mood of some of the *Bulletin* writers is melancholy. Without the bush, the silent land remained invisible and the invisible induced melancholy, that stock-in-trade epithet of Marcus Clarke for whom the 'dominant note of Australian scenery' was 'Weird Melancholy' (1993a: 45–46). Writing 40 years before Clarke, Baron Charles von Hügel remarked that 'everything breathes a melancholy grandeur in which every word fades into silence [...]' (1994: 250). Wilderness made the mute land speak, but when the melancholy grandeur of the land made every word fade into silence, the bush made silence visible, rendered the mute land into picturesque prospects.

Like all depictions of the bush, and other Australian landscapes for that matter, the weird melancholy of the bush is a projection. Michael Wilding has even asked whether 'that classic description [of Clarke's is] yet another drug-induced perception, and the "weird melancholy" something perceived, if not produced, with the aid of hashish?' (1986: 144). Similarly, did

Lawson perceive, if not reproduce, 'weird melancholy' with the aid of alcohol? Lawson describes 'how I had brought the atmosphere of weird melancholy from the heart of the Bush' (1976: 60). Lawson ascribes to the heart of 'the Bush' what he should have ascribed to his second-generation settler culture and its psyche, and possibly his own psychopathology. Weird melancholy was not found in the bush but in the heart of the writer. Melancholy rises up out of the uncanny return to the repressed of the slimy, not out of the bush.[5]

Clarke's own description acknowledges this, as this famous passage falls into two distinct parts; the first of which bemoans 'Weird Melancholy'; the second of which celebrates it, and the grotesque and the monstrous features of the bush. In this second part Clarke has even been seen by Mulligan and Hill as what they call an 'ecological pioneer' (Mulligan and Hill 2001: 30–31). In terms of the two paradigms that underpin and organize *People and Places of Nature and Culture* (see Figure 2, Chapter 1), Clarke both celebrates and denigrates the left-hand paradigm and shows how melancholy arises out of repressing the left. It thus seems simplistic to place Clarke amongst the writers who see the bush just as hell, as David Tacey does (1995: 111). For him, the bush bears traces of the grotesque and monstrous Great Mother who gives birth to new life out of her fertile womb.

Yet the heart of the bush for Lawson is not the womb of the Great Mother, but the breast of a wet nurse, a surrogate mother: 'the grand Australian bush – the nurse and tutor of eccentric minds, the home of the weird, and of much that is different from things in other lands' (1976: 111). The bush is not mother, not homely home, not England, not the mother country, but the unhomely, the uncanny, the wet nurse to which unloved children have been farmed out and the tutor (not the parent) who teaches them. Unlike Collins, for Lawson, bush and scrub were not synonymous. Bush was the uncanny and scrub was the repressed.

The bush is not the womb of new life but the home, for Lawson, of the living dead: 'The living death in the lonely bush […]' (1976: 190). Lawson perpetuates a mythology that M. Barnard Eldershaw located in sixteenth and early seventeenth-century Europe when 'Australia [was] the Land of the Dead, the last ghostly home of the monsters driven from the known world' (Barnard Eldershaw 1939: 24). How ironic, then, that some Aboriginal people saw some white explorers and settler as their deceased ancestors returning from the dead. This obsession with death and the monstrous produces melancholia. Julia Kristeva argues that 'the death drive ushers in a melancholic subject' (1995: 31). In melancholia, I have argued elsewhere, following Freud and others, the subject experiences itself as lost (see Giblett 1996: 177). Similarly, the traveller in Australia may get lost or lose himself or herself in the bush and then try to find himself, driven by death in what he perceives is a dead landscape.

Living death is not only the fate of the white inhabitants, but it is also accentuated by the dead landscape of white, ring-barked trees. Lawson describes how, 'after Nyngan, the bush grew darker and drearier, and the plains more like ghastly oceans; and here and there the "dominant note of Australian scenery" was accentuated, as it were, by naked, white, ring-barked trees standing in the water and haunting the ghostly surroundings' (1976: 141). Not only ring-barked trees, but any tree of the bush in moonlight could be ghostly for Lawson:

'there's no timber in the world so ghostly as the Australian Bush moonlight' (1976: 290). The bush by day or night with trees ringbarked or not could all be weirdly melancholic.

Nor only the bush when it is dry could be weirdly melancholy but also when it is wet. For Lawson, 'the "break-up-of-the-drought" is as aggressively, resentfully, weirdly melancholy as anything else in the Bush [...] the dark, dismal, dripping, rotting, scrubby gullies' (1976: 42). If the dry bush represents the living dead coming out of a barren womb, the wet bush is the decomposing tomb. For Lawson, the bush, wet or dry, by day or night, with trees ringbarked or not, was not the fertile womb and regenerating tomb of living earth. No wonder he drank himself into an early grave!

Two major traditions of Australian settler landscapes compete against each other. They can be couched in what John Carroll calls 'two extremes, either the illusion of cosy and mysteriously redemptive Bush exorcized of threat, or the intimidating vision of an unthinkable desert land that is pure horror' (cited by Tacey 1995: 111). On the side of the bush as heaven (or Arcadia), Tacey places Paterson, Kingsley, Prichard and the Heidelberg School (and Richardson I would add) (1995: 111). On the side of the bush as hell, he places Lawson, Lawrence, White and Nolan (and Baynton [1995], I would add, but not Clarke as he does). The point is not which side is right or wrong but that the bush is both or neither, because both are projections of biblical and European landscapes. Neither side is the view of Aboriginal Australians (to which I turn in Chapters 9, 10 and 11) who are largely absent from the work of both sides except as trope or romanticized noble savage set in Arcadia, such as in John Glover's paintings.

Notes

1. Gibson originally said that 'in so many ways these films [referred to in the opening paragraph of this chapter] are *about* the Australian landscape' (1993: 209).
2. I discuss Australian landscape and wilderness photography in Giblett (2009: Chapter 7).
3. For a more extensive reading of the film, see Schaffer (1988: 53–57).
4. I discuss cinema in Giblett (2008b: Chapter 5).
5. I discuss this book, as well as the militaristic metaphors and psycho-ecology of farming, in Giblett (2009: Chapter 8).
6. See Giblett (1996: especially Figure 1, 'A Psychogeocorpography of Modernity' 26).

Part IV

National Parklands

National parks are commonly regarded today as conservation landscapes, but the initial impetus to set them aside was monumentalist and sanctuarist rather than conservationist. The monument commemorated a significant moment in time and the sanctuary set aside a special place in space. They were products of the patriarchal paradigm. By setting aside monumental, usually mountainous and forested, landscapes, national parks were the inheritors and perpetrators of a romantic landscape aesthetic, especially of the sublime. The first national parks in the United States had spectacular natural features such as peaks, canyons, waterfalls or geysers, or various combinations thereof. The first national parks were parklands, not parkwaters; drylands, not wetlands. It took 60 years for a national park to be declared in a wetland.

These national parklandscapes were imbued with nationalist significance. The United States sought, found and maintained a sense of national identity in privileged national landscapes. The impetus to create national parks was nationalist as they legitimated the nation's claim to the national territory. National parks nationalized special places by carving out and enclosing national space within global space. The national parks also nationalized time by demarcating and inscribing national history within global history. The national parks were a kind of nationalist graffiti marked in rocky landscapes. They made their mark in time and space. The ruinous landscapes of national parks were often likened to cathedrals. They gave a sense of history and longevity to a new nation. By nationalising time and space, national parks dispossessed Aboriginal people from their lands and from their past and future.

Chapter 7 deconstructs the monumentalism and sanctuarism in the writings of John Muir, father of the American national parks, or at least of the idea for them. It also critiques the gender politics of Muir's contradictory ideas of nature divided between a stern and sublime Father God in the mountains and a soft and smiling Mother Goddess in the swamps. Although early in his career Muir had a close encounter with the latter which converted him to nature-worship, for the remainder of his life he preferred and privileged the former over the latter. Although nature for Muir was imbued with a romantic, aesthetic theology, it was always alive, never mere dead matter. Muir was both sanctuarist in his views about national parks and sacralist in his views about nature.

Chapter 8 goes on to trace critically this history of the first national parks and of the national park idea. It argues for inhabitation of national parks by Aboriginal peoples and for recognition of 'native title' in national parks. It concludes that as national parks were recreational sanctuaries outside the cities of industrial capitalism they were the product of them. They were the 'good deed for the day' of industrial capitalism that preserved a remnant of what it was elsewhere destroying wholesale for consumption by the jaded, day-tripping city-dweller or holidaying tourist. National parks *are* industrial capitalist landscapes.

Chapter 7

Nature Sanctuarized: 'Our' National Parks as Modern Cathedrals

John Muir was, and still is, a monumental figure in the American conservation movement, if not its patriarch. He has been described as 'the spiritual father of American environmentalism' (Worster 1993: 189), as 'the father of our [United States'] national parks and forest reservations' (Tilden 1970: 537), and as 'a patriarch of the National Park system' (Mitchell 1994: 52). The father of the idea for national parks is generally recognized as George Catlin who is credited with proposing it in 1832 (as we shall see in the next chapter). In this chapter I consider Muir's ideas about national parks and the gender politics of his paradoxical views of nature. For Muir, nature in general is sacralised, yet his views on where and how nature is sacralised depend on the aspect or site under discussion. For Muir, nature in mountains and forests was aestheticized and sublimated, especially if such areas were 'set aside' and preserved in the sanctuaries or 'modern cathedrals' of national parks, whereas nature for him could also be inhabited, invigorated and enlivened by all living things, including rock and stone, and even human beings (but not Aboriginal peoples).

Under Muir's leadership the American conservation movement has largely been concerned with conserving sanctuaries, those special places for plants and animals and those aesthetic landscapes for taking refuge from the depredations of modern urban industrial capitalism. American conservationism has often been more precisely 'sanctuarism', concerned with giving sanctuary and preserving sanctuaries rather than with caring for the ecosphere as a whole. Certainly those special places need to be conserved – humans need sanctuaries and sanctuaries are needed for plants and animals. In the famous John Muir–Gifford Pinchot struggle over the damming of Hetch Hetchy valley in Yosemite National Park, and of its descendants I am on Muir's and his childrens' side every time.

The American conservation movement arose in the aftermath of what Stephanie Coontz calls 'the apogee of the private sphere' (cited by Flichy 1995: 67) – (1870–1890) – in which 'refuge' and 'sanctuary' were repeatedly and routinely applied to the home. By taking these terms from the private sphere and applying them to the biosphere, the latter was privatized. Even public lands were construed in private terms. The commons, owned by none and shared by all, were colonized in public lands such as national parks, and enclosed in private terms such as 'refuge' and 'sanctuary'.

This care for special places needs to be extended to the earth household as a whole, as a special space with special places. Deconstructing Muir's work with its romantic aesthetic of the sublime as a naturalistic theology, and valuing his work on nature as living being, is one step to doing so. It is also part of a pro-active political ecology that promotes and exercizes earthly mutuality – and not a reactionary sanctuarism constantly trying to save endangered species or special places threatened with destruction. Rather than always fighting rear-guard actions, political ecologists are the avant-garde.

Muir sublimated mountains and forests into a patriarchal God, not so much in what Murray Bookchin calls his 'inverted Calvinism' (1991: il; for Muir's Calvinist upbringing, see Fox 1981: 28–30) (as the relationship between God and nature is not merely turned upside down) as his naturalistic Calvinism, or perhaps more precisely naturalistic Campbellism.[1] Instead of 'the natural world as a path to a knowledge of God' (Grove 1995: 15), as in Calvinism, the natural world for Muir was a manifestation of God. Although he is often regarded as a pantheist, Michael Zimmerman argues that 'Muir may have been a *panentheist*, one who regards nature as a manifestation of but not exhaustive of the divine' (1994: 385, n.48). Muir's God was incarnated in His son of the elected, and even predestined,[2] elements and features of mountains and forests such as geysers and glaciers especially, but also in rock and stone, wood and water, plants and animals, and even human beings (though again not Aboriginal peoples).

Yet when Muir celebrates living nature not just in forests and mountains, but also in glaciers and swamps, at work destroying and creating life, nature is thereby enlivened or invigorated in 'panentheism' (see Sheldrake 1991: 198). Muir here sacralises nature as 'Mother Earth' or 'Mother Nature'.[3] Muir vacillates between nature aestheticized (especially sublimated and incarnated) for nature lovers, nature preserved (especially in the sanctuaries of the modern cathedrals of national parks) for city dwellers and tourists, and nature inhabited (especially enlivened or invigorated by all things, including human visitors to national parks, but not for Muir by Aboriginal human inhabitants or native title holders of national parks).

Cathedrals of the Modern World

In a number of articles published in *The Atlantic Monthly* during the 1890s and later collected in his book, *Our National Parks,* first published in 1901, Muir expressed his ideas and views about national parks (in particular) and nature (in general). Muir also wrote specifically and lovingly of the first two national parks in the United States (and the world), Yellowstone National Park and Yosemite National Park. For Muir, national parks, or more precisely forested and/or mountainous national parks, were seen as fulfilling an important inspirational role as modern cathedrals. Yet forested and/or mountainous national parks are more precisely America's outdoor modern cathedrals distinct, as we will see below, from the indoor modern cathedrals of the cinemas of industrial capitalism and the museums of the nation-state.[4]

Muir, however, goes one step further than simply regarding Yosemite National Park as an outdoor cathedral as he found 'the mighty wilderness of mountains' of the High Sierra not only like 'some Gothic cathedral' but also 'more abundantly spired than Milan's' (1980: 127). The inspiring High Sierran cathedral 'outspired' the smaller, less abundantly spired Christian cathedral. Muir was not alone amongst his conservationist predecessors and his contemporaries in this view of forested and mountainous regions. In 1858 Henry David Thoreau described in his *Journal* 'the quiet and somewhat sombre aisles of a forest cathedral' (1962, *XI*: 353). Yosemite was regarded widely as 'a natural cathedral' in the nineteenth century (see Sears 1989: 122 and 138). Indeed, one of the mountains of Yosemite is named Cathedral Peak, which Muir described as 'a majestic temple [...] adorned with spires and pinnacles in regular cathedral style' (1987: 198).

Yet Yosemite was not a Christian cathedral. For Muir, it was 'one of Nature's cathedrals, hewn from the living rock' (1987: 146) and Cathedral Peak was 'hewn from the living rock' (1987: 198). It was left *in situ* unlike the cathedrals of Europe built of dead stone, the extracted and hewn resource, the transported and erected object. Nature, for Muir, was living agent, not dead matter. No Sierra landscape that Muir saw 'holds anything dead or dull, or any trace of what in manufactories is called rubbish or waste' (1987: 157). Mountainous landscape may have been wasteland in the eyes of his contemporaries, but for Muir it was where 'God himself seems to be always doing his best here, working like a man in a glow of enthusiasm' (1987: 60). God's Promethean, thermodynamic and industrial workshop and home, for Muir, is up in the mountains, not down on the lowlands in the cities, the home of citizens, and certainly not even further down in the netherlands of the swamps, the home of the matrifocal Great Goddess (see Giblett 1996: especially Chapter 6). As Muir refers later to 'Nature's glacial workshops' (1987: 205), God is Nature and Nature God.

Despite, or perhaps because of, being God's best work, mountainous landscape did not fall into the conventional aesthetic category and experience of the picturesque. For William Gilpin in the late eighteenth century, 'the spiry pinnacles of the mountain, and the castle-like arrangement of the rock, give no peculiar pleasure to the picturesque eye' (1794: 43). Similarly, a hundred years later, Muir claimed that 'to artists, few portions of the High Sierra are, strictly speaking, picturesque. The whole massive uplift of the range is one great picture, not clearly divisible into smaller ones' (1980: 104). In other words, the High Sierra with its phallic 'massive uplift' invokes the experience of the sublime as do 'the ineffably chaste and spiritual heights of the Fairweather Range [...] the whole making a picture of icy wildness unspeakably pure and sublime' (Muir 1980: 14).

Muir enacts what Belden Lane calls 'the sublime as the monumental' (1988: 22), or perhaps more precisely, the sublime as the *experience* (the sublime is a *state* of aesthetic sensibility) of the *mountainous* (as distinct from the urban or built) monumental.[5] Again Muir was not alone in the nineteenth century in valourising the mountainous as evocative of the sublime. Indeed, it was a commonplace of nineteenth-century landscape aesthetics, as we saw for Wordsworth in a previous chapter. For Thoreau too, 'sublimity and grandeur [...] belong to mountain scenery' (1980: 44), and for John Ruskin also 'we take our idea of fearfulness and sublimity from the mountains and the sea' (cited by Schama 1995: 513), though he prefers the former to the latter.

Yet Yosemite was 'that sublime Sierra temple' not only because it was mountainous, but also because it was forested. Muir describes how 'the sunbeams streaming through their [the pines'] feathery arches brighten the ground, and you walk beneath the radiant ceiling in devout subdued mood, as if you were in a grand cathedral with mellow light sifting through colored [sic] windows, while the flowery pillared aisles open enchanting vistas in every direction' (1991: 60; see also 226).⁶ For Muir, 'reservations of scenery', as for his compatriot and near contemporary Charles Eliot writing in 1896, were "the cathedrals of the modern world" (cited by Thomas 1984: 269). Or perhaps more precisely, *mountainous forest* reservations (the forerunners of national parks) of 'scenery', the habitual visual aesthetic of the sightseer and tourist, were modern cathedrals.

Yet the cathedral is very much an alien and imported construct imposed on an Aboriginal inhabitation of the land, the Christian, or in Muir's case, his naturalistic Campbellism (but what of his panentheism here?), proselytising the 'pagan' and sublimating the chthonic. Couple the cathedral with the sublime in the monumental mountains and then set it aside in the sanctuary of the national park and the result is a neoromantic sacred sight (not site). In Muir's naturalistic Campbellism, a stern and craggy, patriarchal and mountainous triune God 'brood[s like the Holy Spirit] outspread over the predestined landscape' (1991: 69) of the glacial mountains and valleys instead of a stern and craggy, patriarchal and monumental God brooding spiritlike over predestined saved souls of Calvinism, or over the primordial wetlandscape of the littoral, lacustrine and lagoonine as in the Biblical creation story (for a rereading of Genesis 1:2 in these terms, see Giblett 1996).

By referring to 'the wombs of the ancient glaciers' Muir (1980: 222) displaces the beginnings of the world from the littoral to the glacial, from the world below to the world above. His patriarchal appropriation of maternal functions by birthing metaphors, and his displacement of the primordial landscape from the littoral to the glacial, which does not acknowledge the primordial womb of the wetland, are both crucial for his sublimatory nature aesthetic and religion. In Muir's naturalistic Campbellism, the patriarchal God-function is sublimated into the monumental mountains where God the Father Law gives birth to new life with His own labour, alone in the simulated womb of His glacial workshop. The matrifocal Great Goddess of the swamps is displaced upwards into patriarchally simulated into what Muir calls 'glacier wombs' (1980: 102) and 'the broad white bosoms of the glaciers' (1980: 46). The glacial white bosom is a kind of *tabula rasa*, or in Freud's terms a mystic writing pad, on which Muir could inscribe his writings, and in Freud's terms, a screen on which he could project his phantasies, his daydreams. The whiteness of the bosom serves to smother any trace of the living black waters of the Great Goddess of the swamps, and to sanitize any messiness in parturition.

The forested and/or mountainous national park as modern cathedral is the outdoor extra-urban counterpart to the indoor urban cathedrals of the modern world. These are what David Day calls 'the new stone-built cathedrals of knowledge, the public libraries, art galleries and museums' (1996: 182), and what Paul Virilio calls 'the cinema-cathedrals of the modern state' (1989: 38). Or perhaps more precisely, the cinema-cathedrals of the modern imperialist nation-state in hegemonic alliance with industrial capitalism. As with film, which was for Walter Benjamin 'one of the most advanced machines for the imperialist domination of the masses' (1986: 55), the national park is a machine for the imperialist domination of the earth. 'The empire of nature', as John MacKenzie (1988) calls it, is applicable not just to the nineteenth century in the colonies, but to the capitalist commodification of nature today in national parks, zoos, and other nature theme parks, as well as in nature documentaries, so-called 'natural products' (an oxymoron) and tourism.

Yet the national park and the cinema as modern, imperialist cathedrals performed different quasi-religious functions. The early cinemas, Virilio argues, were regarded as 'deconsecrated sanctuaries in which, as Paul Morand put it, the public sensed the end of the world in an ambience of profanation and black masses' (1989: 31). For Muir, by contrast, Yosemite and Yellowstone National Parks were reconsecrated sanctuaries in which 'the public' could sense the evolutionary, albeit glacial, beginning, and even ongoing recreation of the world in an ambience of reverence and sublime 'white' masses, unlike the mephitic and miasmatic atmosphere of the slimy, living black morasses of wetlands (see Giblett 1996). Yosemite National Park was a paradise for Muir 'that makes even the loss of Eden seem insignificant' (1991: 76). The Park contained parks which were as 'fair as Eden' (Muir 1991: 129), though perhaps Yosemite National Park was more what Roderick Neumann has called in relation to national parks in Africa an 'ersatz Eden' (1995: 155).

Yet, like the cinema with its modern technological simulation of the cathedral's stained-glass windows in which, as Virilio puts it, 'everything visible appears to us in the light' (1989: 38), 'the standard perception of national parks' was, as Alfred Runte describes it, 'as a unique visual experience' (1979: 64) centred on the aesthetically legitimated sense of sight. Like Wordsworth, Muir bemoans the fact that national parks were subjected to what he calls 'the scenery habit' (1991: 2) common amongst his contemporaries. Like Wordsworth too, he was prone to what could be called the sublimatory habit, especially in relation to *mountainous* national parks. The sublimatory habit transcended the common scenery habit and placed the poet and preservationist above his contemporaries as an arbiter of high cultural taste in landscapes.

Yet by functioning as reconsecrated modern cathedrals *forested* national parks could reverse history, or at least hark back to an earlier era, by returning the cathedral to the sacred, pre-Christian, pre-patriarchal grove from which it sprang. As Rupert Sheldrake points out, the cathedral's 'soaring columns and vaults recall sacred groves, and vegetation bursts out everywhere [...] [M]any churches and cathedrals in Europe were built on pre-Christian sacred sites' (1991: 44–45 and 176). The forested national park as cathedral not only re-appropriates the appropriated sacred grove but also could return the sacred place to its pre-architectural, pre-Christian wild(er)ness manifestation, to what Devereux Butcher calls 'temples not built with hands' (1969: 1) (though national parks could contain areas made and worked by Aboriginal hands), unlike 'the great cinema temples' (1989: 31), as Virilio calls them.

Yet, like the cinema temples, Muir found that 'the money-changers were in the temple' (cited by Cohen 1984: 192) of the Yosemite. The forested and mountainous national park as temple needed its modern day Jesus who would drive the moneychangers, the cash-spinners, out. One such Jesus was John Muir who did not need to be reminded that 'great trees and groves used to be venerated as sacred monuments and halls of council and worship' (1991: 209; see also 225,) and 'the hills and groves were God's first temples' (1987: 146). Muir regarded Sequoia forests in particular as 'majestic living temples, the grandest of Gothic cathedrals' (cited by Cohen 1984: 195).

The forested national park as cathedral and temple has meant that, as Sheldrake goes on to suggest, 'a religious experience of the wilderness has endowed many of the American national parks with a transcendental quality. For many who visit them, they are more than recreational areas; they are natural temples or sanctuaries' (1991: 177). John Muir has been ordained as prophet and evangelist of this new religion of naturalistic Campbellism, or simply sanctuarism: a new St John, writer of a new gospel, a new good news about the saving graces of wild(er)ness sanctuary; a new John the Baptist, crying out in and for the wild(er)ness, preparing the way for Aldo Leopold and his saving gospel of a land ethic and a conservation aesthetic; a new St John the Divine, proclaiming the apocalypse of a blighted and benighted urban 'civilization' bereft of wild(er)ness; and a new John Calvin, converting God/Nature dualism into the craggy patriarchal sublime and predestined glaciers of what Muir called 'the stern wilderness' (1991: 173) of the mountains, and of the mountains alone. Muir even saw himself as John the Baptist: 'Heaven knows that John the Baptist was not more eager to get all his fellow sinners into the Jordan than I to baptize mine in the beauty of God's mountains' (cited by Cohen 1984: 259; see also 254). Worster also argues that Muir 'became a kind of frontier evangelist' and 'invented a new kind of frontier religion' (1993: 194–195).

There is some support for these views of Muir in his own writings on national parks. For Muir, the cathedral of the national park can produce a contemplative mood in 'the calmest, stillest scenery' (1991: 31) of its forests, or can render the onlooker 'awe-stricken and silent, in devout, worshipping wonder' in the face of the 'awful uproar' and 'tremendous outburst' of its terrifying, sublime, phallicized geysers (1991: 40–41). For Muir, the forested national park is a public place of community worship, not a private cloister for individual meditation, or more precisely it is a place for 'both solitude and society' (1979: 350). Writing of Yosemite National Park, Muir described how 'nearly all the park is a profound solitude. Yet it is full of charming company, full of God's thoughts, a place of peace and safety amid the most exalted grandeur and eager enthusiastic action, a new song, a place of beginnings abounding in first lessons on life' (1991: 59). The monumental and the mountainous again appropriate the beginnings of life.

Forested national parks are also sacred places for Muir because they are a refuge or sanctuary, like the medieval monastery was for the fugitive. For Muir, Yosemite National Park is 'a place of rest, a refuge from the roar and dust and weary, nervous, wasting work of the lowlands' (1979: 350), unlike the uplifting, sublimating highlands (Muir was, of course, of Scottish descent and in fact was born in Scotland). In an increasingly urbanized world where it seems the only other possible refuge from 'rust and disease' (Muir 1991: 1) is the golf course, but whose membership fees are so prohibitively expensive for most (the golf course is the rich man's private refuge), the forested national park is for Muir 'the poor man's [public] refuge' (1979: 352), but not for him the indigenes' working land. Muir was very much a proponent of the sanctuary idea for national parks that would provide a refuge for native flora and fauna, and for the poor lowlanders, or city dwellers, but not a site of inhabitation and enjoyment of ownership and rights by Aboriginal peoples.

Perhaps the poorest 'man' culturally and spiritually of all in the modern and hypermodern worlds is the tourist, or at least more precisely the modern mass-packaged touristic consumer. For Muir, 'the wildest health and pleasure ground accessible and available to tourists seeking escape from care and dust and early death are the parks and reservations of the West' (1991: 9). National parks can provide the tourist with an escape route from the prison of modern city life provided once s/he gets there s/he slows down. Muir rails that 'nothing can be done well at a speed of forty miles *a day* [sic]. The multitude of mixed, novel impressions rapidly piled on one another make only a dreamy, bewildering, swirling blur, most of which is unrememberable' (1991: 42; my emphasis). If the tourist treats the national park like the city with its flood of impressions, the result will be the same, undistinguished, unremarkable blur of experience.

The tourist also needs to experience the national park alone. For Muir, 'little [...] is to be learned in confused, hurried tourist trips, spending only a poor noisy hour in a branded grove with a guide. You should go looking and listening alone on long walks through the wild forests and groves in all the seasons of the year' (1991: 210). The sublime is a solitary experience. A national park is a cathedral because it takes time to appreciate its vastness, its fastnesses, its nooks and crannies. In Yosemite National Park, for Muir, 'nowhere will you see the majestic operations of nature more clearly revealed beside the frailest, most gentle and peaceful things' (1991: 58). For Muir, Yosemite National Park is not only a means to escape from an early death, but also 'the scenery is wild enough to awaken the dead' (1991: 30). The scenery can even shake the apathetic out of their lethargy. The geysers and hot springs of Yellowstone National Park display 'an exuberance of color [sic] and strange motion and energy calculated to surprise and frighten, charm and shake up the least sensitive out of apathy into newness of life' (Muir 1991: 31). Geysers, for Muir, are terrifying, sublime agents.

Geysers are also masculinized by Muir. The sublime in the masculinist, modern western tradition has been associated inextricably with the masculine virtue of what Terry Eagleton calls 'virile strenuousness' (1990: 54). The sublime is, as Eagleton goes on to argue, 'on the side of enterprise, rivalry and individuation' and is 'the lawless masculine force which violates yet perpetually renews the feminine enclosure of beauty'. For Muir, for example, the 'Big Tree' of the Sequoia shows 'Nature's immortal virility' (1991: 214; see also 228). Similarly geysers for Muir are 'like inverted waterfalls' (1991: 31), but also like the upright mountain in that they are phallic, as Muir shortly leaves his reader in no doubt as he describes the geysers of Yellowstone National Park as 'standing rigid and erect, hissing, throbbing, booming' (1991: 31–32).

Muir generally prefers geysers to waterfalls, both to swamps, and mountains over all three (1991: 33). For Muir, geysers are 'the laboratories and kitchens, in which, amid a thousand retorts and pots, we may see Nature at work as chemist or cook, cunningly compounding an infinite variety of mineral messes' (1991: 4). Nature is here figured ambiguously, even androgynously, as chemist or cook, even alchemist or witch, working in the laboratory and kitchen with thermodynamic technology in 'the hot underworld' as God works in His glacial workshop, the industrial inferno to produce meals (me(t)als?) for modernity. Nature as figured in these terms is not all that far away from the culture of what Muir calls 'these hot, dim, strenuous times' (1991: 2), these modern times in which base matter is sublimated into ethereal commodities using heat (though they are also 'these cold, doubting, questioning, scientific times' [1991: 41] produced by the penetrating light of reason).

God's National Parks

Besides a view of nature sublimated in national parks, Muir also propounded a view of God-the-Father-nature incarnated in mountains, or mountainous scenery, with its dawn lights and alpenglows as a kind of God-the-Son figure. For Muir, 'next to the light of the dawn on the high mountain tops, the alpenglow is the most impressive of all the manifestations of God' (1991: 56). The alpenglow, sublimated above the mountains themselves, could manifest God, and mountains could even be God. When Muir encounters the Fairweather Mountains of Alaska he regards them as God Himself: 'here the mountains themselves were made divine' (1980: 18–19). For Muir, the mountains *were* God.

If the mountains could be God, and God could be incarnated in the alpenglow, the mountaineer could incarnate the mountains as when Muir states 'we are now in the mountains and they are in us' (1987: 15), even to the point of merging with nature in a romantic, oceanic feeling in which Muir could claim that 'you lose consciousness of your own separate existence: you blend with the landscape, and become part and parcel of nature' (1980: 88; see also 1992: 212). Even visitors to mountainous national parks could partake of a sacramental repetition or re-enactment of this incarnation. Muir announced in his 'Preface' to his book on national parks that its aim was 'to show forth the beauty, grandeur, and all-embracing usefulness of our wild *mountain forest* reservations and parks with a view to inciting people to come and enjoy them, and get them into their heart, that so at length their preservation and right use might be made sure' (1991: xvii; my emphases). Muir makes no attempt to disguise the fact that his book is devoted to 'our' *mountain forest* national parks.

Whilst subscribing to some dominant discourses of national parks Muir also flies in the face of others, such as the national parks as useless or worthless lands, the so-called 'worthless lands' thesis (see Runte 1979: 28, 49 and 60), and national parks as nationalist parks in which America saw and commemorated itself as what Perry Miller calls 'nature's nation' (1956: 209; and 1967: 201). Against both discourses Muir advocates a kind of spiritual and sacramental incarnation of nature into the national heart or psyche unlike the material incorporation of nature into and by the gaping maw of the national, capitalist state and industrial technology (see MacCannell 1992: 115). Yet as nature's nation also saw itself as God's nation, national parks were not only God's national parks for Muir but also for the nation at large. Yet the view of national parks in the United States as 'America's secular cathedrals' persists with a previous Secretary of the Interior, Bruce Babbitt (cited in Mitchell 1994: 12), describing them exactly in these terms.

Not only has 'Nature become a secular deity in this post–romantic age' as William Cronon (1996a: 36) puts it, but National Parks are America's secular cathedrals in which this deity is worshipped under the sign of the sublime. Muir's work in particular is caught up, as are national parks in general, in this triangular force field between – even in this American cultural and political triumvirate of – God, nature and nation, with the national park as their point of intersection in what could be called 'God's nation's nature'. The American national park is thus not nature in the raw but nature cooked by culture. Muir repeats what Lawrence Buell calls 'the gesture of putting the nation under the sign of the natural: America as crag, Canada as iceberg, Australia as outback' (Buell 1995: 62).

For Muir, national parks as nature incarnated rather than nature incorporated, will not merely be places out there to 'enjoy' but places to which 'people' (though the question is rasied of *which* people? as is the question of *whose* national parks? in relation to the title of his book – who does 'our' refer to?) belong in a *natural* nationalism and not so much places which belong to the people in *cultural* nationalism. By taking this position Muir sought to reverse the human/nature dualism so endemic to western culture, even subvert the God/nature (including humans) dualism of Calvinism, and replace the democratic ideal with a nature-cratic one ruled by 'the parliament of trees' and the law of Nature rather than the law of God, and supersede cultural nationalism with natural internationalism which would transcend nations and national borders.

Muir also sought to overcome a narrowly utilitarian view of forest reservations, the predecessor of national parks. Against the prevailing view of his time that mountainous landscapes were 'worthless lands' and that forest reservations were only useful for timber, Muir posed what he called 'the use of beauty' (cited by Runte 1979: 62). Of a mountain wild(er)ness experience in general he avowed that:

> [...] the tendency nowadays to wander in wilderness is delightful to see. Thousands of tired, nerve-shaken, over-civilized people are beginning to find out that going to mountains is going home; that wildness is a necessity; and that mountain parks and reservations are useful not only as fountains of timber and irrigating rivers, but as fountains of life. (Muir 1991: 1; see also 217)

Muir equates wilderness with, and reduces it to, mountains. Muir also sees the mountains (and wilderness unlike his settler compatriots) as home.

Like one of the other 'grandfathers' of the American conservation movement in Henry David Thoreau (Tilden called Muir 'the Western Thoreau' [1970: 303]), Muir praised the prophylactic features of wild(er)ness and a wild(er)ness experience. Muir followed the motto of the wilderness wanderer penned by Thoreau: 'in wildness is the preservation of the world' (cited by Hoagland 1987: 48). Yet Thoreau viewed wilderness more broadly than Muir who generally conflates wilderness, mountains and the sublime with their peaks figured as 'colossal spires' of 'massive sublimity' (1991: 61, 70 and 74). This conflation is summed up in Muir's reference to 'a sublime wilderness of mountains' (1991: 70) and to 'the massy sublimity of the mountains' (1991: 141). Muir also refers to 'a sublime wilderness of mountains' (1980: 124) in his essays. By doing so, Muir enacts a masculinist construction of nature and reality in which the glacial, masculine, homely and sublime of the mountains are seen as the origin of life rather than the littoral, feminine, matrifocal (un)homely and slime of the swamp or other wetland.[7]

Yellowstone National Park impressed Muir so much that he regarded climbing its mountains as a sublime experience. Climbing Electric Peak, for Muir, is a means to 'get yourself kindly shaken and shocked. You are sure to be lost in wonder and praise, and every hair of your head will stand up and hum and sing like an enthusiastic congregation' (Muir 1991: 44). Muir, like Walt Whitman, sings the body electric (or more precisely, it sings him) of the individual, masculinized human body in a patriarchal hymn to God the Father Law, not to 'Mother Nature'. The sublime is an individual, not a communal, experience.

For Thoreau and Muir, wild(er)ness, rather than the primitive or the barbarian with their pejorative overtones, was distinct from civilization (Muir 1991: 2). In between the wild(er)ness of mountainous national parks and the civilization of the cities Muir places 'the half wild parks and gardens of towns' (1991: 2), though for him national parks are 'worth infinitely more than all the gardens and parks of town' (1979: 351). Muir, however, sees this care for the parks and gardens of town as encouraging. He even finds encouraging 'the scenery habit in its most artificial forms, mixed with spectacles, silliness, and kodaks' (Muir 1991: 2). Yet the scenery habit is not only mixed with spectacles, silliness and kodaks but also potentially with the sublime and sublimation as both valourize the sense of sight over all other senses. It is perhaps hardly surprising then that Muir would not disparage the scenery habit, but would hope it would lead on in similarly sighted fashion to the sublimatory habit.

If mountainous national parks are a mediating category for Muir, so too are human beings who he describes as 'half animal, half angel' (1991: 4), half slime, half sublime, or 's(ub)lime' in Zoë Sofoulis' parenthetical portmanteau (1988: 12). The angelic is strongly associated for Muir with mountainous wild(er)ness that is 'the dwelling-place of the angels', whereas animals are 'fellow beings, so seldom regarded in civilization' (1991: 56); plants also for that matter will 'soon come to be regarded as brothers' (1979: 350). Animals are even regarded by him as 'brimful of humanity' (Muir 1991: 59) as is 'the whole wilderness [which] seems alive and familiar, full of humanity' (Muir 1987: 238). Muir's assessment of plants, animals and wilderness smacks of anthropocentrism, but it may have been a tactical move to see them at least in human terms and not less than, or alien to, the human.

Or the Great Goddess'?

Yet Muir also propounded a competing view of nature sacralised to that of his naturalistic Campbellism. He concedes that it is not just mountains and forests that are enjoyable and inspirational but all wilderness. Muir stated categorically that 'none of Nature's landscapes are ugly so long as they are wild' (1991: 4). As wildness is a matter of point of view rather than a quality of substance, as I tried to show in a previous chapter, Muir would seem to subscribe to Thoreau's dictum that 'the same object is ugly or beautiful, according to the angle from which you view it' (Thoreau 1962, *VIII*: 275). Indeed, Thoreau maintained later that 'we find only the world we look for' (1962, *IX*: 466), according to the distance from, and the angle at which we view it, as well as our pre-dispositions towards it, as we saw in Chapter 3. The world we look for is the world we find. We cannot find what we do not look for.

Beautiful (because wild) landscapes could include swamps as Muir discovered in his conversion to conservationism, or at least to sanctuarism: '*Calypso borealis* still hides in the arbor vitae swamps of Canada, and away to the southward there a few unspoiled swamps, big ones, where miasma, snakes, alligators, like guardian angels, defend their treasures and keep them as pure as paradise' (1991: 5). Yet rather than separating Muir off as an original figure, this conversion experience in the wilderness makes him fit the pattern of the frontier hero as outlined by Richard Slotkin (1994: 374). According to Wolfe, Muir's encounter with the *Calypso borealis* in a Canadian swamp was one of 'the two supreme moments of his life' (1945: 146–147), the other being his meeting with Emerson, and not his meetings with Roosevelt, the Sierras or sequoias. The swamps referred to as away to the southward were presumably the swamps of Florida, Muir's encounter with which he devotes one chapter of his *A Thousand-Mile Walk to the Gulf* (see Giblett 1996: Chapter 10; and Worster 2008: 93–95).

Muir propounded not only a sublime aesthetics of the mountains, geysers and glaciers, but also a watery and earthy (slimy) experience of the wetlands. Muir looked forward to the day when 'lowlands will be loved more than alps, and lakes and level rivers more than waterfalls' (cited by Runte 1979: 31).[8] That day has far from arrived. Mountains and waterfalls are still a dominant feature of the modern aesthetics of landscape. Yet lowlands for Muir not only included wetlands, but also cities with their 'lowland care and dust and din, where Nature is covered and her voice smothered' (1987: 186). Perhaps he was implying that cities should also be loved more than alps and waterfalls.

Muir's opposition to the narrowly utilitarian point of view of nature and national parks can also be seen in his answer to the rhetorical question 'what are rattlesnakes good for?' Muir replies that they are 'good for themselves' (1991: 25) (as a national park should be looked after 'for its own sake' and 'we need not begrudge them [the rattlesnakes] their share of life' [1991: 43]). Muir's position on rattlesnakes (and alligators) has been seen as the foundation for a biocentric ethic.[9] Muir's anthropocentrism in his aims for his book, and in his attitude to plants and animals in general, and his biocentrism in relation to rattlesnakes in particular, were contradictory positions, but could also be seen as tactical moves depending on the object under discussion and the entrenched attitudes to them either to be extended (in the case of humanism to plants and animals) or reversed (in the case of rattlesnakes).

Yet by converting God into nature and by subscribing to biocentrism rather than to anthropocentrism, Muir was staying within and reproducing their categories. Mountainous, sublimated nature in national parks was still God the Father Law for Muir, though in his pantheon he could also allow for a slimy, desublimated unnamed Palaeolithic Great Goddess in the swamps and a good Neolithic 'Mother Earth' or 'Mother Nature' everywhere. For Muir, 'Nature is a good mother' (1980: 229) as well as a bad father; or more precisely, nature for him is split between the two.

Muir's work on, or more precisely for, mountainous and/or forested national parks marks a shift from an anthropocentric to a biocentric ethic for national park and wild(er)ness areas, though Muir's article on 'The American Forests' for *The Atlantic Monthly* (republished in *Our National Parks*) showed, as Roderick Nash points out, 'Muir's continued ambivalence on the "forestry-or-preservation issue"' (1982: 136). Muir's other articles of the 1890s for *The Atlantic Monthly*, particularly 'The Wild Parks and Forest Reservations of the West' (also republished in *Our National Parks* [see Muir 1991]), are far less ambivalent on this issue and far more committed to the preservation side of the struggle.

Muir saw that the wild(er)ness, and not just mountain wilderness, was already safer than civilization. The implication is that so-called 'civilization', not wild(er)ness, needs to be made safe. Despite the snakes and alligators and other natural predators of the swampy wild(er)ness, Muir thought that 'it is far safer to wander in God's woods than to travel on black highways or to stay at home […] No American wilderness that I know of is so dangerous as a city home "with all the modern improvements". One should go to the woods for safety, if for nothing else' (1991: 21). Perhaps one should not go to swamp for safety, nor to the woods and mountains, though the latter could provide the terrifying and uplifting experience of the sublime, whereas the former could mean a horrifying and down putting immersion in the slimy.

For Muir, one should go to the woods not only for physical safety but also for spiritual succour. In fact, for him, 'what we call parks' would better be called 'places for rest, inspiration, and prayers' (Muir 1991: 23). Wooded national parks for Muir are sacred places in which, as Rupert Sheldrake suggests, 'the spiritual and the physical are experienced together. Sacred places are openings between the heavens and the earth' (1991: 23). Muir certainly saw mountainous and wooded national parks as sacred places in which the spiritual and the physical could be experienced together via a sublime opening between the heavens and the earth. He even saw national parks as sacred places where it would be possible to overcome the dualism between the physical and the spiritual. Indeed, on the one hand, he is largely a Platonist in his reference to 'the truly substantial, spiritual world whose forms flesh and wood, rock and water, air and sunshine, only veil and conceal' and, on the other, a naturalistic Campbellite in his preference for the immanence, or even incarnation, of the spiritual in the physical for 'here [in Yellowstone National Park] is heaven and the dwelling-place of angels […] the terrestrial manifestations of God' (Muir 1991: 55–56).

Muir seems to have sensed no contradiction between these two positions expressed together within a page of each other because for him there was no contradiction between them. Muir saw an exchange and mutuality between the spiritual and the physical exemplified in the forested and/or mountainous national park. He refused the views both of the capitalists, scientists, engineers and technocrats of his time who saw nature as so much raw material and dead matter to be manipulated and exploited, and of the Christians who saw nature as so much clinging and sinful materiality to be sloughed off and transcended. For him, nature was living, divine, dynamic yet it also had its stern and craggy, patriarchal and Campbellite God up in the mountains and its wise, tender, though also stern and matrifocal Great Goddess down in the swamps (see Muir 1987: 142). Nature for Muir was bifurcated, even trifurcated with the third figure of a good Mother Earth or Mother Nature.

Muir subscribed not just to 'the immanence of nature in the divine' as Sheldrake (1991: 197) puts it, but also to the transcendence of the divine in nature. Muir was thus, in Sheldrake's terms, a *panentheist* for whom:

God is not remote and separate from nature, but immanent in it. Yet at the same time, God is the unity that transcends it. In other words, God is not just immanent in nature, as in pantheist philosophies, and not just transcendent, as in deist philosophies, but both immanent and transcendent, a philosophy known as *panentheism*. (1991: 198)

Or should that be Goddess, rather than God? Zimmerman maintains that 'goddess spirituality holds that the divine is both immanent [...] and transcendent' (1994: 254). The divine, for Muir, overarches nature, transcends everything, but is immanent in individual, particular places, and not just in forested and/or mountainous national parks, but also in swamps; the divine is cosmically and locally transcendent and immanent; the whole cosmos and every locality manifests the divine, the divine transcends the local, the divine is in the local, and vice versa. Muir was no mere radical who 'thought globally and acted locally', but a panentheist who thought the divine in the local and enacted the local in the divine.

Writing the Word of Nature

If national parks function as modern cathedrals with their 'sermons in stones' (Muir 1991: 59), then their sacred scriptures are the inscriptions of nature *in* the earth (unlike the writing of the modern, colonial city *on* the earth and unlike the slimy tracery of the Great Goddess, the swamps, the womb of the earth) (see Giblett 1996: especially Chapter 4). Muir advises his readers that 'after this reviving experience [of climbing Electric Peak], you should take a look into a few of the tertiary volumes of the grand geological library of the park [Yellowstone National Park], and see how God writes history' (1991: 45). Muir was the culmination of a nineteenth-century American phenomenon in which, as Perry Miller puts it, 'nature somehow [...] had effectually taken the place of the Bible'

(1956: 211; and 1967: 203). Or more precisely, as nature had taken the place of God for Muir, so the Word of Nature had taken the place of the Word of God. Muir was a self-mythologized literary frontier hero who was, in Richard Slotkin's terms, 'generally disinclined to learn from book culture when the book of nature is free to read before him' (1994: 374). Printing made the word of God available to the vernacular reader, whereas Muir found the book of nature already open ready for him to read freely.

In the modern mountainous wild(er)ness one can see, not how God writes the law in words on tablets of stone as 'He' did in the Judaic wilderness with Moses, but how 'God' writes history in 'words' of stone in 'the divine manuscript' (Muir 1987: 132) of mountainous nature as 'He' does in the law of Muir, the modern day Moses of mountainous national parks. For Muir, here in Yellowstone National Park are 'a wonderful set of volumes lying on their sides – books a million years old, well bound, miles in size, with full-page illustrations […] telling wonderful tales of bygone centuries' (1991: 45). For Muir, the 'natural history', or better national park, or even better still mountainous wild(er)ness writer, 'to get all this ['the wonderful clearness and freshness of the rocky pages'] into words is a hopeless task' (1991: 59). As a result, 'to defrauded town toilers, parks in magazine articles are like pictures of bread to the hungry. I can write only hints to incite good wanderers to come to the feast' (Muir 1991: 59). Rather than the oral sadistic feast of capitalism, the feast Muir had in mind here was more a passover feast, a sacramental communion. Muir as a magazine article writer was the frontier hero of a literary mythology through whom, as Slotkin puts it, 'the deep wisdom of the natural wilderness is transmitted to the sluggish life of the Metropolis' (1994: 374).

One course of the feast, to switch metaphors, would be a richly layered text. In these books of nature 'the post-glacial agents [of air, rain, frost, rivers, earthquakes, avalanches (Muir 1991: 63)] are at work on the grand old palimpsest of the park region, inscribing new characters' (Muir 1991: 49) on the *tabula rasa*, or 'white bosom', of the glaciers rather than tracing stories in the living, black waters of wetlands. The book of nature is not set in stone for all time but is constantly changing with new writings being inscribed over old ones to produce a deeply and richly patterned palimpsest. Muir's own writing on glaciers is one layer of the palimpsest inscribed on its broad white bosom. Glaciers themselves may deserve 'the name of Destroyer […] but we quickly learn that destruction is creation' (Muir 1991: 72) and 'we see that everything in Nature called destruction must be creation' (Muir 1987: 229). That natural (not human) destruction is creation is one of Muir's favourite maxims (see Muir 1987: 238; and 1980: 31 and 53).

Not only glaciers and post-glacial agents write the text of the book of nature, but all inhabitants of the wild(er)ness do, even the swarming insects are 'a cloud of witnesses telling Nature's joy' and the plants are 'singing the old new song of creation'. All creatures have a kind of evangelistic function of spreading the gospel, according to Muir (1991: 52–53), about the religion of nature. Indeed, 'each and all tell the orderly love-beats of Nature's heart', 'the heart of nature, whence we came' (Muir 1980: 46), couched within 'the generous bosom of the woods' (Muir 1992: 155–156), nature's good breast rather than nature's bad breast of the black waters of wetlands.

Similarly, for Muir in terms reminiscent of Gerard Manley Hopkins, the Sierra Nevada mountains in Yosemite National Park are 'pervaded with divine light; every landscape glows like a countenance hallowed in eternal repose; and everyone of its creatures [...] is throbbing and pulsing with the heartbeats of God' (Muir 1991: 57). This creative work of nature is always going on with destructive work: 'Nature is ever at work building and pulling down, creating and destroying, keeping everything whirling and flowing, allowing no rest but in rhythmical motion, chasing everything in endless song out of one beautiful form into another' (Muir 1991: 73). Nature here is always at work, producing not so much a cosmos as a cosmogenesis. Muir's work here is remarkably prescient, even prophetic, of the paradigm shift from modern nature as (dead) machine to postmodern nature as living community, even communion (see Swimme and Berry 1992).

Nature is homely living agent for Muir rather than unhomely dead matter or (un)homely Great Goddess. Going to the woods for Muir (1991: 74) is going home, or 'going to the mountains is like going home' (1980: 118); going to a national park (but not going to a swamp) for him is 'getting in touch with the nerves of Mother Earth' (1991: 2). Nerves communicate with the whole body through electrical impulses, so getting in touch with the nerves of the body electric of Mother Earth meant getting in touch with the fibres that communicate with the whole body of Mother Earth, both inside and outside the national park.

Yet getting in touch with the nerves of Mother Earth meant *not* getting in touch with her whole body. Going *into* the swamp would be getting in touch with the body of Mother Earth. Perhaps it was in going to the mountains, rather than to the national park per se, that Muir got in touch with the sublimated body of Father Law. The mountains could be incarnated in Muir, and Muir in the mountains, so that there was no disconnection between the two and he became 'an inseparable part of it [...] a part of all nature' (1987: 16). For Muir, '[in] the Sierra Cathedral we feel ourselves part of wild Nature, kin to everything' (1987: 243).

If Mother Earth for Muir has nerves she also has a heart, what Muir calls 'the warm, unspoilable heart of the earth' (1991: 4), 'Nature's warm heart' (1991: 180). For Muir, the warm, good breast of 'Mother Earth is ever familiar and the same' (1991: 37), unlike the hot workshops of geysers where Father God Law is ever unfamiliar and different, and unlike the hot netherlands of swamps where the Great Goddess is ever uncanny and (un)homely. 'Nature's sources never fail' (Muir 1991: 42). The good breast of what Muir calls in a letter the 'bosom' of 'sweet kindly Mother Earth' (Badè 1924, *II*: 267) never dries up and the (glacial and/or wetland?) womb generously gives birth demonstrating 'the infinite lavishness and fertility of Nature – inexhaustible abundance' (Muir 1987: 242). Nature, for Muir, is, in short 'a good mother' (1980: 229), though also a bad Father (like his own, about whom we hear so much in the biographies, whilst Muir's 'Mother Earth' is perhaps like his mother about whom his readers hear so little, except for his surrogate mother in Jeanne Carr). This lack of 'a parental tie to anchor him to the Metropolis', or to metropolitan culture more generally, helps to make Muir fit Slotkin's (1994: 374) model of the frontier hero. Muir prefers the warm, living nature of Mother Earth, a nurse maid nature 'always ready to heal every scar' (1991: 268), 'one touch' of whose hand 'makes the whole world kin' (1991: 164), to 'the gray, savage wilderness of crags and peaks', the visage of his mountainous God the Father Law, who 'seems lifeless and bare' (1991: 125).

If Mother Earth has nerves and a heart, then Father Mountain has a face or more precisely a 'divine landscape-countenance' with 'every feature glowing' (Muir 1987: 15 and 115). For Muir, Father God mountain is the body of nature from the neck up, the site of sublimation, intellection and theorisation, the heights of the sublime spires, whereas the Great Goddess and Mother Earth are the body of nature from the neck down, the womb of new life, the organs of nurturing, the depths of the slimy swamps. Muir remarks on how 'the physiognomy and even the complexion of the landscape should still be so divinely fine!' (1991: 55), and 'all the landscape is glowing like a benevolent countenance at rest' (1991: 193), or 'the landscape [is] beaming with consciousness like the face of a god' (1987: 85); the sublimated alpen glow. Muir looks on this face in mountainous and forested national park, the stern, craggy face of God the Father Law and not on the body of the Great Goddess, life-giving and death-dealing.

Notes

1. See Worster (1993: 190–196) for a useful discussion of Muir's more specifically Campbellite upbringing. Worster bemoans the fact that Fox (1981) and Cohen (1984) do not even mention Campbellism and that Turner (1985: 192–193) only treats it in passing. See also Worster (2008: 37–39).
2. According to Worster (1993: 240, n20), the Calvinist doctrine of predestination would have been elitist for the Campbellite Daniel Muir, John's father, though John saw glaciers as predestined. See below.
3. 'Mother Earth' for Muir is not strictly speaking the neolithic earth mother of agriculture and patriarchy, nor is it explicitly the palaeolithic Great Goddess of 'matriarchy'.
4. I discuss cinemas as cathedrals of industrial capitalism in Giblett (2008b: Chapter 5).
5. For mountains as monuments for Muir, see Muir (1980: 35) and for monumentalism as the impetus behind the national park idea, see Runte (1979: 28, 49 and 60).
6. For Yosemite as sublime, see Muir (1991: 67 and 70; 1987: especially Chapter V, 'The Yosemite', where he also repeatedly refers to the Yosemite temple; and 1980: 97). Other forests could also be sublime cathedrals as in Alaska where Muir was 'charmed with the majestic beauty and grandeur of the trees, as well as with the solemn stillness and the beauty of the elastic carpet of golden mosses flecked and barred with the sun-beams that sift through the leafy ceiling' (1980: 48–49).
7. I discuss the s(ub)lime and the wetland as womb of the world in Giblett (1996).
8. I discuss Muir's view of wetlands and swamps in Giblett (1996: Chapter 10).
9. I discuss Muir's encounter with an alligator in Giblett (2009: Chapter 2).

Chapter 8

Sites and Rights of Enjoyment: Nature and Native Title in National Parks

In 1993 the then Western Australian Mines Minister George Cash (Cash by name, cash by nature?) was reported as saying that, as Rudall River (Karlamilyi) National Park in the Pilbara region of north-western Australia has not got a waterfall, it is not a real national park. Cash used this criterion in order to justify the decision of the Liberal-National Party Coalition Government to allow mineral exploration of the Park's infamous Kintyre Uranium deposit. Cash did not acknowledge or respect the fact that the one and a half million hectares of the National Park, the largest in Western Australia (Smith 1979: 112), contains, as the Australian Conservation Foundation (ACF: undated) points out, 'a unique ephemeral river system and representation of almost all ecosystems which occur in the Western Desert'.

The Park is also home to approximately 300 Martu people who live in two communities within its boundaries. The ACF goes on to point out that 'the Martu have also fought against the prospect of mining and exploration on *their land*' (my emphases).[1] The issue of Aboriginal inhabitation and ownership of national parks is raised in relation to Rudall River National Park, but was not taken up by Cash, though it has been by the Aboriginal inhabitants. The Martu people lodged a native title claim over the Park and surrounding areas in 1996. Native title has been recognized for the surrounding areas, but not for the Park. By excluding the Park, the Martu people have not been granted the core of their claim. The Park is the soul of the Martu people. In this chapter, and in the light of the so-called '*Mabo*' decision in Australia that acknowledged native title, and of the Miriuwung-Gajerrong decision by the High Court that ruled that national parks extinguish native title, I will take up this issue of Aboriginal inhabitation and 'ownership' in relation to national parks more generally.

Using the presence of a waterfall as an essential criterion for a national park is part of the modern tradition of aestheticising nature in terms of what Dean MacCannell calls 'outstanding features of the landscape' (1976: 80–81) (including not just a waterfall, but 'a large waterfall'). It is also part of what he goes on to call 'the modern touristic version of nature' which treats it as 'a common source of thrills'. Waterfalls, as Paul Shepard points out, 'have been primary tourist attractions for a thousand years' (1991: 254); national parks, usually with waterfalls, have been primary tourist attractions for a hundred years. Yet national parks are usually more than just tourist attractions. Or more precisely, the touristic functions of national parks are tied up with other colonialist, capitalist and nationalist agendas and only comparatively recently with conservationist ones.

These agendas are worked out in two complementary aspects of modernity: the banal level of everyday life; and the use of modern transportation technologies, such as the railway and the car. Flink argues: 'Our national parks were the product of what Alfred Runte calls a "pragmatic alliance" between upper-class preservationists and western railroads seeking to boost their passenger traffic' (1988:172). The first national parks were monumental landscapes with static tableau set up for a seated spectator in a railway carriage traversing fixed lines through the landscape (across the surface of the earth). The railway passenger looked out side windows at landscapes juxtaposed to the train.

The car changed the relationship of subject to object, but not the pragmatic, if not mercenary, alliance between preservationists and transportationists. The car did more than conservationists to create national parks. Flink goes on to argue that 'Stephen T. Mather, the first director of the National Park Service [established in 1916], recognized that park development was linked intimately to the growth of tourism, so he energetically built a second "pragmatic alliance" [...] between the NPS and automobile interests throughout the country'.[2] The car created a more dynamic set of picturesque or pleasing prospects with various stops for taking in the view. The car driver and passenger looked out front and side windows at sweeping panoramic vistas surrounding the car.

National parks have been produced by and subjected to what Michel Foucault calls 'the discourse of nature' (1970: 157–162). Yet whereas Foucault discusses only one discourse of nature (natural history), I suggested in Chapter 1 that a number of competing discourses of nature operate in a network of power/knowledge relations. The hegemony of one of these conceptualizations and objectifications (or an alliance between several of them) over others has changed historically, though not in a triumphalist progression. Rather they have been caught in a messy political struggle. These conceptualizations and objectifications co-exist in struggle today between politicians and scientists, tour operators and conservationists, policy makers and Aboriginal peoples.

Three competing discourses of nature (with their conceptualizations, objectivizations, enunciative modalities and strategies as Foucault [1972] calls them in *The Archaeology of Knowledge*) outlined in Chapter 1 of *People and Places of Nature and Culture* are deployed around national parks: nature *aestheticized* (especially monumentalized and sublimated in mountains, waterfalls and geysers); nature *preserved* (or at least native fauna and flora and their habitats); and nature *commodified* (whether as natural or cultural resources, raw materials or tourist packages, to be exploited or 'managed' by 'resource managers'). Against these ideas of nature I and others pose a counter language of the earth inhabited, or even better *invigorated* or 'enlivened' by Aboriginal peoples, and native fauna and flora and their ecosytems. Generally, since the invention of national parks, various mercenary and unholy alliances between the three conceptualizations and objectifications of nature have prevailed over the language of the earth and of Aboriginal peoples.

A particular text about national parks will not necessarily adhere or subscribe to one discourse alone but may contain or reproduce several simultaneously, often with one used, albeit disadvantageously, in the service of another. George Cash's pronouncement, for example, utilizes the discourse of nature aestheticized (with his invocation of the waterfall as an essential criterion for a national park applied disadvantageously to Rudall River National Park) in the service of the discourse of nature commodified (as his party and government allowed mineral exploration and mining in national parks, such as Rudall River). Similarly, John Muir's classic, *Our National Parks*, vacillates problematically under the general rubric of nature sanctuarized (as I tried to show in the previous chapter), between nature aestheticized (especially sublimated and incarnated in mountains, forests and geysers), nature preserved in sanctuaries (especially as modern cathedrals) for city dwellers and tourists, and nature inhabited (especially enlivened or invigorated by all living things, including human visitors of settler descent, but excluding Aboriginal inhabitants).

In the three discourses of nature aestheticized, preserved and commodified I will argue that national parks are both national*ist* and national*ized* parks in which 'nature' is colonized, whereas in the language of nature inhabited the possibility of a post-colonialist, post-nationalist park is developed in which 'nature' is decolonized, and even the concept of nature deconstructed. In this chapter I trace (and takes sides in) the struggle between these discourses from the conceptualization of the national park idea, through the legislative establishment of the first national parks in the United States, to the contemporary issues of inhabitation of, and native title in or over, national parks by Aboriginal peoples with reference to Australia in the aftermath of the so-called '*Mabo*' decision.[3] The issues raised here, however, are not only applicable to this context but have a wider pertinence, especially to other settler societies.

What is a National Park?

A number of recent, standard definitions of national parks are couched contradictorily, or perhaps paradoxically, in terms of national parks preserving the nature conservation values of the area in which they are set and promoting the human enjoyment of those values. Yet the appeal to human enjoyment raises the question of which humans? what sort of enjoyment? enjoyment of traditional hunting, gathering and/or fishing rights by Aboriginal peoples? enjoyment of native title? enjoyment of ownership? enjoyment of connection with the country where native title has been deemed to have been extinguished? or enjoyment of touristic spectacles such as waterfalls? These questions have beset the national park idea since its legislative enactment, though perhaps not from its conceptualization, as we shall see below.

Such questions have also come back to haunt it in the Australian context following North American cases where the High Court's so-called '*Mabo*' decision recognized that native title existed at the time of the proclamation of British sovereignty, and that it continues to exist unless otherwise extinguished. Moreover, one of the judges, J. Brennan (cited by Hal Wootten, no date: 323), was of the view that national park status does not necessarily, and may not completely, extinguish native title, and that native title may even continue to exist concurrently.[4] This view, however, has recently been rejected by the High Court of Australia in its decision on Miriuwung–Gajerrong as it ruled that national parks extinguish native title. Yet the recognition of native title by the common law of Australia as announced in the

Mabo decision, and as discussed by Gary Meyers, 'inherently and inescapably recognizes the existence of [...] the rights of Aboriginal peoples in Australia to fish, hunt, and gather food according to their laws and traditions' (1994: 228).[5] Indeed, Meyers argues that these rights 'provide the proof of the *existence* of native title' (1994: 223) as they are 'property rights' (1994: 228).[6] Rights to hunt, fish and gather were enshrined as tests of native title in the Australian *Native Title Act 1993* (§223.[2] Australia 1994: 104). The Martu people have been given these rights in their recently successful native title claim for their land, except in Rudall River National Park.

Definitions of national parks are generally, and probably deliberately, hazy on the point of Aboriginal peoples' rights to, and title in, the land. The United States' National Park Standards, first devised in 1929 and revised in 1968, defines national parks as 'spacious land or National Seashores essentially in their primeval condition and so outstandingly superior in beauty to average examples of their several types as to demand preservation intact and in their entirety for the enjoyment, education and inspiration of all people for all time' (cited by Butcher 1969: 356). Presumably the enjoyment, education and inspiration of all people does not include Aboriginal peoples enjoying their traditional fishing, gathering or hunting rights, nor performing their ceremonies and rituals, nor educating and inspiring non-Aboriginal peoples in their views and experiences of the land, nor being able to enjoy the inspiration afforded to them by their 'sacred sites' or 'sites of significance'.

This definition of national parks in terms of nature aestheticized and preserved also makes no specific reference to the preservation of native fauna and flora. Such an omission was typical of nineteenth-century definitions, but is rather surprising for one stemming (at least in its revised form) from the 1960s. Rather than preservation of native fauna and flora, the fundamental criterion in this definition is the aesthetic experience of landscape or seascape beauty. Yet this emphasis on beauty is highly problematic given the narrow range of objects – usually small, smooth and superficial – which constitute or evoke the aesthetic experience of the beautiful.[7] It is also problematic given the extent to which national parks have included other aesthetic experiences besides the beautiful, such as sublime landscapes like mountains, geysers and waterfalls. I will return to a discussion of definitions of the national park in the last section of this chapter after considering the first national parks and the national park idea.

The First National Parks

The emphasis on enjoyment is fairly typical of most definitions, and its inclusion here harks back to the legislative aims of Yellowstone National Park, considered to be the first national park declared in 1872 (though it was declared precisely as a Public Park [Runte 1977: 73, n.29]), and the first national park to be closed to hunting in 1894 (Leopold 1986: 15). Yet for Alfred Runte, 'in fact, if not in name, Yosemite was the first national park' (1979: 30) and 'the national park *idea* was first realized in 1864' (1979: 47) with the Yosemite Park Bill. Or it was, as Andrew Ross has remarked more recently, 'created by excluding the Miwok Indians' (1994: 92).[8] Similarly, the primary purpose of Yellowstone National Park was, according to the legislation, to be 'a public park or pleasuring-ground for the benefit and enjoyment of the people' (cited by Tilden 1970: 20). This idea, as Michael Cohen remarks, was 'perfectly anthropocentric' (1984: 252). Or perhaps more precisely, it was settler-centric, as reference to 'the people' raises the question of which people? Presumably enjoyment of traditional rights by Aboriginal peoples was ruled out of court, though as we have already seen in the Australian context, these concerns were ruled back in court only to again be ruled out of court by the recent High Court decision that national parks extinguish native title.

Yet the Yellowstone legislation did make an important distinction; Yellowstone National Park was *not*, infers Freeman Tilden, to be 'a private park or pleasuring-ground for the financial [or presumably any other sort of] benefit of the few' (1970: 20), certainly not the few remaining indigenes. The white majority rules, okay? National parks in the United States enshrine ostensibly a democratic ideal, even to the point where national parks for Tilden are 'not merely scenic places in America. They are America' (1970: 305). And they are America because in the nineteenth century America saw itself as what Perry Miller calls 'Nature's nation' (1956: 209; and 1967: 201). This cosy conjunction is fraught with problems for, as Walter Benjamin argues, 'in the parallelogram of forces formed by these two – nature and nation – war is the diagonal' (1999b: 319), not only the Indian wars in America's case, but also the war against nature. According to John Sears, 'from the beginning Americans had sought their identity in their relationship to the land they had settled' (1989: 4). Or perhaps more precisely, as Sears equates Americans with settlers, white Americans fought for their national and cultural identity in this relationship, whereas Amerindigines had already found their identity in the land of which they had been dispossessed. This 'relationship' with the land was thus a troubled one. The national park represented what John MacKenzie calls an extension of 'the concept of separate living spaces' (1988: 265) as a kind of separate bed syndrome in which the estranged partners of nation and nature slept apart, unlike Aboriginal peoples who, in Australia at least and in Meyers' words, 'view themselves as part of the land' (1994: 219).[9] The 'native' slept on the bed of 'nature' and the nation smoothed the pillow of what it saw as a dying race.

National parks are also American in that they were developed out of a sense of cultural nationalism, out of an anxiety to establish a cultural identity for the United States in contradistinction to Europe (see Runte 1977: 65–67). National parks were used to forge and secure this identity through what Alfred Runte calls 'the reliance on nature as proof of national greatness' (1979: 14) by acquiring 'a semblance of antiquity through landscape' (1979: 41), or by developing what Paul Shepard calls 'national tangible evidence of history' (1991: 251). National parks are the product of nationalism as they create a sense of nationhood not only in contradistinction to other nations, but also to other ethnicities, to indigenes and even classes (national parks are largely a middle and lower-middle class phenomenon), and to nature. National parks are national*ist* parks (see Runte 1977: 75).

National parks are also colonialist parks in that they enact the colonisation of nature, and 'the natives' by 'setting aside' areas for the conservation of 'nature', and by the exclusion of the 'natives' from those areas, and their omission from enabling and managing legislation. The development of national parks as colonialist parks can be readily seen in Africa. The establishment of national parks in Africa, Jane Carruthers has argued:

> [...] can be seen as part of the process of the systematic domination of Africans by whites. National parks constitute yet another strand in the consolidation of white interests over black, and in the struggle between black and white over land and labour. The white heritage that national parks commemorated was the sentimental and aesthetic aspects of wildlife. (1989: 189)

The cultural heritage of national parks in the colonies is a white, settler heritage, not an Aboriginal, chthonic heritage.

A similar situation to that in Africa has prevailed in Australia where settlers sought their identity in relation, or more precisely contradistinction, to the bush, especially in the nationalist tradition (as we saw in a previous chapter). National parks, as Tim Rowse puts it bluntly, are 'a contemporary means of colonial expropriation if, as has often been the case, they fail to accommodate the proprietary and other interests of [Australian] Aborigines and [Torres Strait] Islanders' (1993: 106). In response, and instead, Rowse calls on non-Aboriginal Australians to 'regard *their* national parks not just as reserves for species and sites of spectacular enjoyment, but also as Aboriginal-owned sites of cultural experiment – experiments in practical aesthetics' (1993: 126).

Such a practical aesthetics espoused by Rowse would presumably go beyond the aesthetics of sight of spectacular sights like waterfalls to the lived experience of everyday life and to the experience of the other four senses of sites (rather than sights) of enjoyment and significance. Yet, like the experience of beauty, Rowse's reference to aesthetics is problematic given that for Hegel, and in modern western tradition more generally, there is only an aesthetics of two senses (sight and hearing) in three modes (beautiful, picturesque and sublime).[10] National parks should be sites of enjoyment and significance for all five senses, and the whole body, in other modes, not just sights for aesthetic experience for 'rubber necks', Aborindigenes' pejorative slang for tourists.

National parks have involved not only the colonisation of nature and 'the native' but also the cultural nationalism of nature and the monumental. Indeed, cultural nationalism and natural monumentalism went hand in hand in the United States. In his study of nineteenth-century American tourist sites John Sears argues that 'Yosemite matched the beauty of the great monuments of European architecture yet possessed the freshness and wildness of unspoiled American nature' (1989: 122). In the national park, Americans could have their cake and eat it too, have both their culture and nature, their cultural nationalism, natural imperialism and national naturalism all in one and ignore their imperialist naturalism, colonisation of nature and invasion of Amerindigenes' land.

Sites and Rights of Enjoyment: Nature and Native Title in National Parks

Yet American cultural nationalism came with a lot of cultural baggage. The idea of a national park, especially as 'a pleasuring-ground', was constructed, as Paul Shepard (1991: 255; see also Chapter 4 of this book) argues, on the English model of the gentleman's park estate. One of the journals of the Washburn expedition to Yellowstone in 1870 was published under the title of *The **Discovery** of Yellowstone National Park* (my emphasis). Yellowstone National Park, as Shepard (1991: 250; see p. 251 for a discussion of the cultural significance of ruins) goes on to relate, was already 'there' just waiting to be discovered because of its conformity to the English model. To its author, Nathaniel Pitt Langford, according to Shepard, 'the landscape looked anything but wild [...] The natural land forms and vegetation of Yellowstone resembled certain humanized landscapes plus objects that were considered an improvement on wilderness, such as ruins'. Ruins, that declining built feature of the countryside, were much loved of the Romantic poets because, in the words of Malcolm Andrews, 'ruined architecture represents a return to the state of nature' (1989: 45). Ruins represented a regression to the primitive.

Ruins were, as Larser Ziff puts it, 'object lessons in the vanity of human ambition, and the rage for them reinforced both social and political conservatism. With its notable lack of ruins, the American scene was all too clearly an anti-aesthetic one, and, by the same token, a politically progressive one' (1991: 36). To render the American scene aesthetic and conservative, ruins were found in rock formations. Rock formations resembling ruins were the state of nature *par excellence* which threw into relief, as it were, questions about 'man's' relationship to nature. Ruins, Malcolm Andrews argues, 'fascinated the picturesque tourist partly because [...] they raised so many questions about the relationship between man [*sic*] and nature' (1989: 49). Indeed, Larzer Ziff suggests emphatically that 'the fascination with ruins [...] was the corollary of a yearning for a lost wholeness' (1991: 37). This yearning could not be satisfied in the United States with the ruins of buildings – only with the 'ruins' of rock formations.

The resemblance of rock formations to ruins produced the necessary impression of antiquity, and necessary legitimation for American cultural nationalism, for here was, as Paul Shepard puts it, 'an unchartered heritage of castles, fortresses and ramparts already in the American landscape' (1991: 251). America constructed its cultural heritage in natural heritage, or construed its natural heritage as cultural heritage not only in rock formations but also in the *Sequoia gigantea* of California. As Simon Schama puts it, 'The Big Trees were the botanical correlate of America's heroic nationalism' and 'America's own national temple' (1995: 188–189), so 'embodying *both* national magnitude and spiritual redemption' (1995: 193). In geology and botany, and no doubt zoology with the buffalo and the grizzly bear (the 'big trees' were also referred to as 'grizzlies'), and so in the three principal 'kingdoms of nature' (animal, mineral and vegetable), America sought and found its national identity. But its sense of cultural heritage in nature was highly selective and limited to the grandiose and monumental. For Alfred Runte, 'monumentalism, not environmentalism, was the driving impetus behind the 1864 Yosemite Act' (1979: 28). Similarly, Belden Lane concluded that 'the American national measure of landscape is inevitably the monumental' (1988: 22).

Twenty years later Australia caught the same frenzy when, as Tim Bonyhady puts it, 'the mountain ash became a natural substitute for medieval or classical ruins, a time-line into Australia's aboriginal past' (2000: 255) – albeit divested of Aborginal people.

No mention is made in the Yellowstone legislation of the preservation of nature and its conservation values, nor is reference made to Aboriginal people. Yosemite and Yellowstone were, as Alfred Runte argues, 'set aside, first as symbols of national pride and, in time, as areas for public recreation' (1979: 14), and so not for indigenes' recreation and work, and later ranger's work. Work is rendered invisible in the commodity. Like the gentleman's park, the national park reproduces the bourgeois distinctions between work and recreation, labour and leisure, pain and pleasure. Work takes place in the factory and office, whilst recreation is elsewhere, in the country or in 'nature'. As symbols of national pride and areas of public recreation, the early national parks entailed what Shepard calls a process of 'perpetuating something resembling fine English estates' (1991: 267). National parks are another instance of the way in which land has been subjected to, colonized and capitalized by the European landscape aesthetic in the gentleman's park estate. Aboriginal peoples could not be allowed to live on 'fine English estates,' nor would wildlife be preserved – quite the contrary.

Only later were national parks set aside for wildlife preservation as Runte goes on to argue:

> [...] national parks, however spectacular from the standpoint of their topography, actually encompassed only those features considered valueless for lumbering, mining, grazing or agriculture [what has come to be called the 'worthless lands' thesis]. Indeed, throughout the history of the national park idea, the concept of useless scenery has virtually determined which landmarks the nation would protect as well as how it would protect them [...] not until the 1930s would wilderness preservation be recognized as a primary justification for establishing national parks, at least in the eyes of Congress. (1979: 49 and 60)

The inclusion of wildlife preservation came as late as 1934 with the creation of the Everglades National Park in Florida (see Runte 1979: 26). Perhaps it is hardly surprising that the preservation of wildlife should be brought about in relation to that most useless and worthless of areas for lumbering, mining, grazing and agriculture, and to that least aesthetically pleasing of landforms, a wetland.[11]

The National Park Idea

Yet the idea of a national park preserving wildlife *and* Aboriginal peoples inhabiting it goes back over one hundred years prior to the declaration of the Everglades National Park, to George Catlin who, in 1832, conceived the idea of 'a nation's Park, containing man and beast, in all the wild and freshness of their nature's beauty!' (cited by Runte 1979: 26; see also Catlin 1968: 9). Roderick Nash (1970: 728) credits Catlin as giving 'birth' here to the idea of the national park, but it is an idea which is only now beginning to be implemented in the fullness of its implications, including Aboriginal inhabitation, if not ownership.

Some 32 years after Catlin made his proposal, and in the same year as the Yosemite Bill was passed, Henry David Thoreau's posthumously published *Maine Woods* posed the question 'why should not we [...] have our national preserves [...] in which the bear and panther [...] may still exist, and not be "civilized off the face of the earth" – but for inspiration and our own true recreation?' (1988: 212–213). Thoreau combines the emphasis on nature conservation and human enjoyment that one takes for granted today but which was not enshrined in early legislation or in later definitions. Yet Thoreau's call for conservation not only included fauna, but also flora. Five years earlier Thoreau wrote that:

> [...] each town should have a park, or rather a primitive forest, of five hundred or a thousand acres, either in one body or several – where a stick should never be cut for fuel – nor for the navy, nor to make wagons, but stand and decay for higher uses – a common possession forever, for instruction and recreation. (1980: 259; 1962, *XII*: 387; and 2000: 238)

Although presumably Amerindigenes could enjoy this 'common possession' too as day trippers and tourists, Thoreau, unlike Catlin, makes no mention of them specifically, or to them enjoying it for inhabitation, invigoration and celebration.

Catlin gave 'birth' not merely to the idea of the national park, but more precisely to the idea of what Sean Stevens has called the *inhabited* national park, inhabited specifically by its Aboriginal owners (1986: title). The issue of inhabitation of national parks is a contentious one in Australia, not least for the maintenance of Aboriginal cultural identity and for the development of self-determination. The excision of areas within national parks for use by Aboriginal peoples as living areas, for example, was a farsighted recommendation (number 315) and response of the Royal Commission into 'Aboriginal Deaths in Custody'. It addresses the root social and cultural causes of the high incidence of Aboriginal people dying in custody, such as dispossession, rather than just the surface manifestation. This recommendation also involved granting access for Aboriginal people to national parks (and nature reserves) for 'subsistence hunting, fishing and collection of materials for cultural purposes' (Woenne-Green, Johnston, Sultan and Willis, no date: 378).[12]

Writing about national parks in the African colonies, though it is probably applicable to other settler societies, Roderick Neumann has argued that 'national parks were at once symbolic representations of the European vision of Africa [as what he aptly calls an 'ersatz Eden'] and a demonstration of the colonial state's power to control access to land and natural resources' (1995: 155). Elsewhere, in Western Australia for example, the vesting body for national parks has a policy on Aboriginal involvement in national parks and nature conservation which includes a determination to 'negotiate on a case by case basis [...] to resolve such issues as [...] access for hunting, gathering and other cultural activities' (cited by Woenne-Green et. al., no date: 185). Joint management is becoming the norm.

Such colonial control may be implicit in Catlin's conceptualisation of the national park. He contemplated 'a magnificent park' in which not only would natural areas be preserved in 'their pristine beauty and wildness', but also 'where the world could see for ages to come the native Indian in his classic attire' (Caitlin 1968: 9). Although this idea smacks of 'a living museum' of 'noble savagery' which would lock the Amerindigene into some sort of timeless, pre-contact state, at least Catlin did not contemplate *evicting* the indigenes in order to preserve pristine beauty and wildness; a kind of colonialist expropriation of indigenes' land which has beset the national park idea, not from its inception as Catlin attests, but from its legislative enactment. Catlin flew in the face of the frontier drive to destroy Amerindigenes but reproduced the primitivist desire to preserve them. In the 1920s D. H. Lawrence pointed to 'the desire to extirpate the Red Indian. And the contradictory desire to glorify him' (1977: 41). Catlin's idea for a national park posed the latter against the former. National parks have subscribed to, if not been complicit with, the former.

The prevailing idea of the national park has been in terms of a settler ideal of a pre-human, pristine wilderness that would be a justification for and monument to settler dispossession of indigenes by absenting them from the national park itself and from national park legislation. By being reduced to 'nature', as passive and supine, the national park could then be sublimated and commodified and its history of dispossession suppressed. In a famous discussion of the *Blue Guide* Roland Barthes critiqued it on the basis that:

> [...] to select only monuments suppresses at one stroke the reality of the land and that of its people, it accounts for nothing of the present, that is, nothing historical, and as a consequence, the monuments themselves become undecipherable, therefore senseless. (1973: 76)

To set aside monuments in national parks is to do something similar, though monuments do become an empty signifier into which nationalist signifieds are poured, a blank screen onto which collective phantasies are projected.

This suppression, however, comes back as a kind of return of the repressed in discussions of national parks. Intent on continuing to define a national park in terms of what it is not, Freeman Tilden argues further that:

> [...] national parks are *not* merely places of spectacular scenic features and curiosities [...]; national parks are not merely places of physical recreation [...]; national parks are not merely attractions whereby travel facilities are stimulated; railroads, bus lines, and garages made busy; hotels and other accommodations and eating places made profitable; and the hearts of local chambers of commerce made glad [...]; finally, national parks are not in the least degree the special property of those who happen to live near them. (1970: 19–20)

By defining explicitly national parks in the United States by what they are *not* in theory, Tilden concedes implicitly that this is what they are and how they operate in practice, or at least how their 'gateway communities' function as is depicted graphically in a photo by Randy Olson of Pigeon Forge, Tennessee, near the entrance to the Great Smoky Mountains National Park (see Mitchell 1994: 24–25).[13]

National parks are perhaps not so much quintessentially 'America' because they enshrine 'democratic ideals' and cultural nationalism, but because they are subject to the capitalist imperative; national parks are not so much America for what they are in legislative and nationalistic terms but for what they are in late capitalistic and cultural nationalistic, even jingoistic, terms. National parks, as Michael Cohen puts it, are 'a highly organized, centrally planned and directed machine for the purpose of providing recreation' and for 'marketing efficiently an experience for its visitors' (1984: 337). Experience of what is not clear, but that has never stopped a marketer; quite the contrary! The more indeterminate and polysemous the commodity, the greater the marketing challenge and opportunity. National parks are a communication technology; they are not nature, but a pastoro-technical machine for producing meanings and money. Notwithstanding all appearances to the contrary, national parks are industrial landscapes.

What is a National Park Again?

Yet internationally sanctioned definitions of national parks have tried to go against the tide of commodification, especially of natural resource commodification, though the situation is changing with so-called 'multiple use' being permitted. In the 1960s the International Commission on National Parks of the International Union for the Conservation of Nature and Natural Resources enunciated a then basic principle of a national park: it was an area which had been accorded a legal status protecting it from all natural resource exploitation, including specifically mining operations, though not of course from cultural resource exploitation (see Harroy 1968: 22). National parks in some areas of the world, such as in Western Australia, would not qualify under this internationally respected definition as mining operation are allowed in them. This definition also implies preservation of indigenous fauna and flora, though again no mention is made of Aboriginal peoples.

Other definitions are more explicit about preservation. In Australia a former CONCOM (Council of Nature Conservation Ministers of the State, Territory and Federal Governments) defined a national park as:

> [...] a relatively large area set aside for its features of predominantly unspoiled natural landscape, flora and fauna, permanently dedicated for public enjoyment, education and inspiration and protected from all interference other than essential management services, so that its natural attributes are preserved. (cited by Wescott 1993: 15)

This definition of national parks, largely in terms of nature preserved and aestheticized, also does not address the issue of Aboriginal peoples and their rights.

Definitions of national parks in terms of nature conservation and public enjoyment try to have a bet both ways, whilst conveniently overlooking the specific question of what constitutes the public and the more general matter of the rights of Aboriginal peoples. Roderick Nash argues that the United States National Park Service Act of 1916 'tried to sidestep' the issue 'by declaring the parks' mission to be both preserving nature and facilitating public recreation' (1982: 325). Presumably 'the public' did not include Aboriginal peoples, nor did recreation refer to their livelihood. Policy and lawmakers have tended to take the both/and inclusive option of both nature conservation and public enjoyment rather than the either/or exclusive alternative on this issue. Yet rather than sidestepping the issue, and certainly not resolving it, the both/and position recognizes, as Alexander Wilson puts it, that 'nature reserves are cultural artefacts as much as they are natural systems' (1992: 234). But this conclusion again raises the question of whose culture artefacts? It also reduces nature reserves to cultural artefacts abstracted from their particular sites.

National parks are cultural sites, perhaps not so much for what they are, but for what they are not. Historically they were developed during the period of rapid urbanisation, and can only be understood within that context. National parks are a modern urban phenomenon. Of course, national parks are not urban areas, but they are constituted precisely by not being urbanized. They are the counterpoint to, or 'other' of, the city that gives definition and point to the city. They are precisely those places which city dwellers go to from the city to experience what Dean MacCannell calls the 'link of social solidarity with nature', which he goes on to argue is 'integral with modern consciousness and modern social structure' (1976: 81). Stephen Greenblatt has also suggested that 'parks like Yosemite are one of the ways in which the distinction between nature and artifice is constituted in our society' (1989: 9). Rather than culture or nature, national parks are both some sort of hybrid 'culnature', in which nature is in the process of becoming culture through gradual accretion and incorporation, or the place where some sort of steady state, or homeostasis, between the two is ostensibly put on display.

Yet national parks are not homogeneous in themselves. They are usually gradated from their entries with their visitors' centres and picnic grounds to their wilderness backblocks. The idea of clearly demarcating areas of national parks into the touristic foreground and the wilderness backblocks was strongly advocated by Miles Dunphy who has been described by Hall as 'the father of conservation in New South Wales' (Hall 1992: 104) and by Allen Strom as 'the major factor in the development of the national park concept in Australia' (cited by Thompson 1986: 168). Dunphy argued in the 1930s that 'national parks should consist of a true wilderness and roadless core or compact section (not necessarily centrally placed) within an outer protected area open for general motor-tourist use'. Dunphy called the outer area a 'tourist open area', and defined it as 'a stipulated portion of any scenic, tourist, recreation or fauna and flora reserve in which reasonable improvements for the accommodation and comfort of tourists, and all reasonable space for vehicular traffic, will be permitted'. Such an area would conform to the demands for both aesthetic experience of scenes and preservation of fauna and flora.

Sites and Rights of Enjoyment: Nature and Native Title in National Parks

In an essay entitled 'Primitive Areas and Tourist Open Areas' Dunphy called the roadless core a 'primitive area' and defined it as:

[...] an area of primitive wilderness, compact in shape and extensive, so that one may be able to travel on foot in any direction for at least a full day without meeting a road or a highway (American definition). It must preserve its natural characteristics and adjuncts – plant life, wildlife – in every way, and must be roadless but not necessarily trackless. Naturally its purpose must be the preservation of wilderness as it stands. (in Thompson 1986: 183)

Dunphy reduces native flora and fauna to mere adjuncts of 'natural', presumably geographical, characteristics, locks the preservation of primitive wilderness into some sort of timeless past and makes no mention of Aboriginal inhabitation (and their creation of wilderness). The distinction between the two sorts of areas also cedes the foreground as the showcase for the commodified touristic experience of sights, and relegates to the backblocks and background the ecotouristic visiting, even temporary inhabitation, and possibly permanent Aboriginal inhabitation, of sites. Aboriginal inhabitation and interpretation of the land could be foregrounded, and the touristic experience of sights relegated to the dustbin of history as a colonialist anachronism and a blot on the face of the earth.

National parks should be areas set aside for the conservation (rather than preservation) of indigenous flora and fauna and their habitats, for the inhabitation of Aboriginal peoples where native title exists, and for the demonstration of Aboriginal people's connection with the country where title does not exist. But the very act of 'setting aside' is a cultural, human act irrespective of what happens inside national parks. The idea of national parks as 'set aside' was enshrined in the declaration of Yellowstone National Park, which was 'set aside as a public park and pleasuring ground for the enjoyment of the people' (cited by Sheldrake 1991: 68), though not it seems for Aboriginal people to enjoy as they had previously done. According to Runte, the leglisation says 'set apart' (1979: 46). The concepts of 'set apart' and 'set aside' are associated with the biblical sense of 'holy' as Mary Douglas (1966: 8) points out. Certain areas were 'set aside' legally as national parks, and thereby became holy places. As 'nature's nation' was also God's nation, American national parks were also God's national parks. National parks were paradoxically secular sacred places construed along Judaeo-Christian lines rather than 'sacred sites' or 'sites of significance' for Aboriginal peoples. Yet in the aftermath of *Mabo* it was considered that the very colonising and missionary act of 'setting aside' of national parks in Australia may not have extinguished native title over that land (though it has been ruled recently that it does) and may have enabled its preservation (though it has been ruled recently that it doesn't) (Wootten, no date: 310).

Conceptualising national parks as 'set aside' is anthropocentric because it represents power over nature by the very act of 'setting aside', instituting or nationalizing them, or constituting them as holy or sacred places, albeit modernized and sublimated. National parks are not only national*ist* parks but also national*ized* parks; parks taken over from the common ownership of Aboriginal peoples into the public ownership of nation-states. Such nationalization enacted power over Aboriginal peoples, and indigenous flora, fauna and habitats. After the nationalization of Yellowstone in 1872, Dean MacCannell argues that 'the people of the USA developed and put into practice the idea society has the capacity to preserve nature or institutionalize scenery and landmarks' (1976: 81). 'Society', or more precisely the public sphere of the nation-state and the private sphere of civil society (including both corporations and non-government organizations), has thus accorded to itself the power both to destroy *and* preserve nature. Its power has in a sense doubled by adding and arrogating to itself both the power to destroy life through exploitation of resources in an unsustainable way, through destruction of habitat, and through extinction of species; and the power to conserve life by way of preservation of native flora and fauna in the showcases of national parks and nature reserves, like so many pinned butterflies, whichever takes its fancy as an arbitrary and despotic ruler, for whom 'nature' is a mere passive and supine slave to be disposed of or used at will.

The creation of national parks can even be seen not only as a sublimation of the messy settler history of dispossession of indigenes, but also as a massive compensatory device for the guilt experienced as a result of the capitalist destruction of the natural environment. In a paper aptly entitled 'Nature Incorporated' (an oral and digestive metaphor in which 'nature' in the national park is figured as food or nourishment for the gaping, orally sadistic maw of the monstrous national capitalist state, industrial technology and urban citizens to devour and incorporate into themselves and gain sustenance from), Dean MacCannell has argued that:

> [...] the national parks are symptomatic of guilt which accompanies the impulse to destroy nature. We destroy on an unprecedented scale, then, in response to our wrongs, we create parks which re-stage the nature/society opposition now entirely framed by society. The great parks are not nature in any original sense. They are marked-off, interpreted, museumized nature. The park is supposed to be a reminder of what nature would be like *if nature still existed*. As a celebration of nature, the park is the 'good deed' [for the day] of industrial civilization. It also quietly affirms the power of industrial civilization to stage, situate, limit, and control nature. By restricting 'authentic' or 'historic' nature to parks, we assert our right to destroy everything that is not protected by the [US National] Park Act. (1992: 115; my emphasis)

By contrast, wilderness *areas* protected by the US Wilderness Act of 1964 are defined precisely as set apart from modern industry. National parks are industrial products; designated wilderness areas are post-industrial products that hark back to, and even enshrine, the pre-industrial or 'primitive', or at least a progressivist version of it.

Ironically, in 1893, the year prior to the closing of Yosemite to hunting, Theodore Roosevelt had proposed the creation of national hunting parks in *The Wilderness Hunter*. These 'enclaves of preserved wilderness', as Richard Slotkin calls them:

[...] might be the site (for qualified individuals) of a ritual re-enactment of the frontier experience in which the appropriation of the frontier's ideological essence would substitute for the loss of its material reserves of unappropriated wealth. Instead of bagging dinner for the family, hunters in the parks would bring down and carry home an ideological lesson [...] that life and politics are a Darwinian struggle in which superior types not only triumph but are justified in their hegemony. (1992: 56)

The nature reserve with its ideological lessons is a substitute for, and monument to, nature as a reserve of material wealth.

National parks are modern landscapes, arguably the modern, conserved landscape *par excellence* with their waterfalls and mountains, forests and geysers, whereas wilderness areas are postmodern landscapes. The latter bear out Lyotard's contention that 'postmodernism [...] is not modernism at its end but in the nascent state, and this state is constant [...] *Post modern* would have to be understood according to the paradox of the future (*post*) anterior (*modo*)' (1984: 79 and 81). Wilderness areas are paradoxically post-industrial reconstructions of the pre-industrial. National parks, on the other hand, are nature incorporated in the oral-sadistic sense.

Yet despite the fact that, as Alexander Wilson points out, 'parks of all kinds are cultural landscapes' (1992: 223) (though again the question is raised of whose cultural landscape?), 'the myth of the national park in North America' is that of 'an unpeopled sanctuary amid the extensive terrestrial exploitation and settlement that surrounds it' (1992: 235). It seems that in the myth of the North American national park, the consumer and the citizen can have both their biocentric cake and eat their anthropocentric cake too. Yet both the anthropocentrism of natural resource commodity development and mass commodity tourism, and the biocentrism of Deep Ecology and nature preservation, are centrist in that they depend on, and are nostalgic for, a centred subject constituted in and by a discourse of a settled (in two senses) object. Yet national parks could be sites for decentred postmodern subjects produced in and by the languages of Aboriginal interpretation, and the discourses of habitat conservation and scientific identification, etc., not theme parks for nostalgic trips in search of centred subjectivity in which all can experience the joys and knowledges of a culture of nature lived by Aboriginal peoples, enjoying, wherever possible, native title of their sites and lands.

Notes

1. The Martu people's campaign against uranium mining is longstanding (see Lamont 1989: 13). For an extensive discussion of the cultural and natural importance of this area, especially to its Aboriginal inhabitants, see the report by the Western Desert Working Group (1989; see also Walsh 1992: 75–97). For an extensive discussion of the issue of what the editors call, symptomatically, 'resident' peoples, and national parks in what they call, condescendingly, 'developing nations'

(including Canada and Australia!), see West and Brechin 1991. In its concern with 'resource management' and with 'resident' people, this book reduces the whole issue of Aboriginal ownership and native title, and of hunting, fishing and gathering rights, to a euphemistic matter of 'traditional resource use' and 'traditional tenure' now superseded by modern, neo-imperialist 'natural resource management' and ownership. The managerialist discourse of residence, not ownership, with 'resident' peoples as a 'resource' to be managed by 'resource managers', is neo-imperialist.

2. I discusss the car and the railway in Giblett (2008b: Chapters 2 and 6).
3. Native title has been defined in the Australian context as 'the rights and interests of Aboriginal peoples or Torres Strait Islanders in land or waters that are possessed under their traditional law and customs, and that are recognized by the common law' (Department of the Prime Minister and Cabinet 1994: 5). For the latter to be recognized the former has to be established, and the former without the latter has no legal force. Native title entails more than just 'land rights', and not only 'land and sea rights' (as recent *Mabo* style claims in the Arnhem 'land' area of northern Australia attest), but also wetland, riverine and seabed rights. This definition is a summary of that in *Native Title Act 1993* § 223.(1) (Australia 1994: 104).
4. In the light of Brennan's statement, Hal Wootten (no date: 346) has gone on to wonder whether national park status may only constitute an abridgement or regulation of native title anyway rather than an extinguishment. Gary Meyers has commented that 'an exclusive reservation of land for a public purpose, such as national parks, forest reserves, or wildlife conservation areas, [does not] extinguish traditional rights unless Aboriginal use of the land is inconsistent with the objective and purposes of the reservation or dedication' (1994: 225).
5. The *Mabo* decision stated that the Meriam people were entitled to 'possession, occupation, use and enjoyment of the lands of Murray Islands' (cited by Wootten, no date: 315). Yet, as Wootten points out later:

> the prohibition of the taking of indigenous fauna and flora and of lighting fires is a prohibition of the exercize of any rights of hunting or foraging, one of the principal traditional benefits of native title [...] Clearly it is possible to make a strong argument that dedication of land as a national park is, in the absence of provision to the contrary, inconsistent with the continued enjoyment of native title over the land, and hence of an indicative of an intention to extinguish it. (no date: 342)

Nevertheless, Wootten concludes that in Australia native title has not been generally or expressly extinguished in national park legislation (no date: 362). Ergo, native title may still exist in national parks as Brennan stated, though Wootten is at pains to point out on two occasions that the fact that land is in a national park does not create or enhance a *Mabo* claim to native title in the land (no date: 307 and 363). Meyers (1994: 224) asserts that proof of the existence of rights must be made 'by reference to customary and continuing practice'.

6. A recent governmental booklet, however, is not quite so categorical or sanguine: 'native title rights and interests *may not* be incompatible with the holding of other forms of title. For instance, native title rights and interests in a particular case *may encompass* rights of access for cultural purposes and for hunting, gathering and fishing' (Department of the Prime Minister and Cabinet 1994: 6; my emphases). But see the legislation below.
7. I discuss the beautiful in relation to landscape in Giblett (1996: especially Chapter 2).
8. For a discussion of the Miwok-speaking Ahwahneechees of Yosemite, see Runte (1990: 27; and Godfrey 1941: 3). For Michael Cohen also, Yosemite is 'the archetypal National Park' (1984: 314).

Similarly, for Sears, Yosemite was the first national park (1989: 130). For the events leading up to the creation of Yellowstone National Park, see Shepard (1991: 246–257).
9. Meyers provides a brief and convenient account of Australian Aboriginal people's relationship with land on pp. 216–222. See also Chapter 11 of this book.
10. I discuss aesthetics and the senses in Giblett (1996: Chapter 2; and 2009: coda to Chapter 5 and Chapter 9).
11. I extensively discuss aesthetics and wetlands in Giblett (1996: especially Chapter 1).
12. This report contains an extensive and helpful discussion of the inhabitation of national parks in Australia by Aboriginal peoples.
13. Mitchell defines a 'gateway community' as 'the town or village that rises at the gate of a national park to provide the visitor with amusements as well as essential services and to *stake its claim* in that increasingly *lucrative goldfield* called industrial tourism' (35–36; my emphases). The mining metaphors are telling!

Part V

Industrial Land Use

Industrial capitalism produced national parks but it has had a far more direct and devastating impact on the land in resource extraction industries such as mining (the basis for manufacturing) and pastoralism (cattle and sheep ranging). The proponents of both industries often figure them as orally and anally sadistic in consuming good things and excreting bad ones. In psychoanalytic terms, oral and anal sadism are psychopathologies in which oral and anal desires, and fears of an alimental and excremental (eating and excreting) nature, are played out: the desire to consume good things; the desire for fairness and symmetry in an exchange of good things; the desire to get rid of bad things; the fear of being consumed; and the fear of fairness and symmetry being exercized back against one in an exchange of bad things.

These desires and fears are enacted in both the mining and pastoral industries as they consume greedily and gluttonously the good things of the generous earth, excrete ungratefully their bad wastes into it, and then expect the earth to hide them – hardly an equitable exchange! Mining employs monstrous machines to devour the earth and defecate on it, as does pastoralism with domesticated animals. As mining and pastoralism exercize oral and anal sadism against the earth, they are what could be called psycho*geo*pathologies. Chapters 9 and 10 of *People and Places of Nature and Culture* psychoanalyse these investments of desire and capital, yields of pleasure and profit, and relations of power and work in the mining and pastoral industries.

Psychoanalysis arose in the heyday of industrial capitalism and bears the marks of its patriarchal parentage. It diagnosed and attempted to cure psychopathological symptoms manifested in individuals. It was both a product of patriarchal capitalist culture and a palliative for it at the individual and cultural levels, in the private and public spheres. It neglected, or even repressed, the biosphere and other -ospheres and the underlying cultural, historical and ecological causes of psychopathology diagnosed in the previous chapters of *People and Places of Nature and Culture* and in *Postmodern Wetlands* (Giblett 1996). It also had little to say about technology and its relation to psychopathology and psychogeopathology. Freudian psychoanalysis addressed the role of technology in psychopathology, most famously in the Fort/Da game with its attempt to master absence and lack, but nothing to say about the role of technology in the psychogeopathology of orally and anally sadistic and monstrous machines, and their mastery of nature.

Whilst psychoanalysis arose in the heyday of industrial capitalism and is the son of its patriarchal father, it can be used to analyse and engage in a talking cure of its psychogeopathologies, just as it did with its psychopathologies. The limited success of the latter can be partially ascribed to its locating the causes of symptoms within the claustrophobic and sequestered confines of the domestic private sphere of the patriarchal conjugal family rather than in the larger private sphere of civil society, the public sphere of the nation state and their interactions with the bio- and other -ospheres. Psychoanalytic ecology addresses these larger interactions and their psychogeopathologies. The drive here is not only to diagnose the symptoms of psychogeopathology and to engage in a talking cure of them and their causes but also to prevent their manifestation in the first place by promoting eco-mental health through mutuality and sacrality.

Industrial capitalism manifested psychopathological symptoms in association with what Aldo Leopold called 'land pathology' in 'the collective organism of land and society'. Psychogeopathology is the psychological counterpart of land- or geo-pathology. Both always operate together, hence 'psychogeopathology'. Mining and pastoralism are two cases in point of psychogeopathology. Neo-Freudian psychoanalysis is used in the following two chapters to analyse the psychogeopathologies of oral and anal sadism associated with mining and pastoralism. It is also invoked in the final chapter of the book to call for psycho-symbiosis with the earth. These three chapters develop the psychoanalytic ecology begun in *Postmodern Wetlands* (Giblett 1996) in which I drew on Freud's work on the uncanny, sublimation, symptom, mourning and melancholia to diagnose the symptoms, and engage in a talking cure, of the psychogeopathology of the will to fill wetlands. Contitnuing to draw on Freud's work, I developed psychoanalytic ecology further in *Landscapes of Culture and Nature* (Giblett, 2009), particularly in Chapters 2 and 3 on the monstrous uncanny and the uncanny city. In *People and Places of Nature and Culture* I draw on both Melanie Klein's and Karl Abraham's work on oral and anal sadism, and on both Margaret Mahler's and Jessica Benjamin's work on psychological symbiosis in order to promote eco-mental health.

Chapter 9

Eating Earth: Mining and Gluttony

T. Coraghessan Boyle's coruscating novel, *World's End,* relates how:

Depeyster Van Wart, twelfth heir to the Van Wart Manor, the late seventeenth-century country house that lay just outside Peterskill on Van Wart Ridge, where it commanded a sweeping view of the town dump and the rushing, refuse-clogged waters of Van Wart Creek, was a terraphage. That is, he ate dirt [but not just any dirt] [...] what he ate was ancestral dirt, scooped with a garden digger from the cool weatherless caverns beneath the house. Even now, as he sat idly at his ceremonial desk behind the frosted glass door at Depeyster Manufacturing thinking of lunch, the afternoon paper and the acquisition of property, the business envelope in his breast pocket was half-filled with it. From time to time, ruminative, he would wet the tip of his forefinger and dip it furtively into the envelope before bringing it to his lips. Some smoked; others drank, cheated at cards or abused their wives. But Depeyster indulged only this one harmless eccentricity, his sole vice. He was a toddler, no more than two, when he first wandered away from his nurse [...] found the bleached paint-stripped door ajar and pushed his way into the comforting cool depths of the cellar. Silently, he pulled the door to and sat down to his first repast [...] grinding dirt between his milk teeth, shaping it with his tongue, relishing the faint faecal taste of it [...]. He was no child now. Fifty years old [...] smooth and handsome and with an accent rich with the patrician emphases of the Roosevelts, Schuylers, Depeysters and Van Rensselers who'd preceded him, scion of the Van Wart dynasty and nominal head of Depeyster Manufacturing, he was a man in the prime of life, tanned, graceful and athletic [...]. (1987: 33–34)

Terraphagy, or eating dirt, or more precisely eating earth, is here related to infantile development, manufacturing, masculinity and waste disposal. All these aspects can also be related to mining. Mining supplies manufacturing with the raw materials to be produced as products. Terraphagy is also a metaphor for mining as mining consumes minerals from the earth. Moreover, the metaphor is gendered as mining, manufacturing and waste disposal are masculine activities that master feminized nature. Furthermore, the psychodynamics of terraphagy are established in infancy and reinforced, repeated or overturned in adulthood. Relationships to the mother and 'Mother Earth' establish gendered identity and attitudes to mining and manufacturing. The town dump, the refuse-clogged creek and the ecosphere more generally are the sinks for the detritus, excreta and other waste products of manufacturing based on mining. Using Mary Douglas' (1966: 35) terms, mining, manufacturing, mastery and waste-disposal are phases in the process whereby earth becomes dirt. Wanted matter, or matter *in* place, becomes unwanted matter or matter *out* of place: in short, dirt.

Probably the most contentious or curious, or even controversial, of these conjunctions is the tie between infantile development and mining, and more generally between what Verena Conley calls 'the relinquishing of the mother's body' and 'the technological mastery over nature' (1997: 129) of modernity. The connection is hardly novel, though, as it was made half a century before by Melanie Klein, the so-called British Psychoanalyst, though born, unlike Freud, in Vienna, the capital of psychoanalysis. Her work is well-known for its insights into the 'dim and shadowy recesses' (the cave or mine) of early childhood. For Klein, consuming with greed, but without gratitude, is a psychopathology in the young child's, and later the adult's, relation to the mother's body and, by extension I will argue following Zoë Sofoulis, 'Mother Earth'.

Consuming with greed and without gratitude the generosity of Mother Earth results in what Aldo Leopold called 'a land pathology'. For Leopold, one of the 'founding fathers' of the American conservation movement, pathological symptoms have developed in the collective organism of 'land and society'. Soil erosion, for example, was defined in 1939 in *The Rape of the Earth* as 'the modern symptom of maladjustment between human society and its environment' (Jacks and Whyte 1939: 26). These symptoms are pathological as they are what Leopold calls 'self-accelerating rather than self-compensating departures from normal functioning' (1991: 217). Elsewhere, Leopold said that 'I believe that many of the economic forces inside the modern body-politic are pathogenic in respect to harmony with land' (1972: 153).

Mining certainly has been self-accelerating. In 1974 it was calculated that 'the last half-century has seen mankind [*sic*] consume more mineral resources than were used in the whole of previous history' (McDivitt and Manners 1974: 4). Consumption of mineral resources has not abated in the years since this calculation was made, but has increased to the point where it rivals the previous fifty for the dubious distinction of exceeding 'the whole of previous history', and departing even further from the normal functioning of the land. Nor is this increase in consumption equitably distributed as David Suzuki maintains that, 'since 1940, Americans alone have used up as large a share of the Earth's mineral resources as all previous generations of humans put together' (1998: 97).

In this chapter I use the work of Klein, as well as that of Susan Griffin and Carolyn Merchant, and a number of Aboriginal poets such as Oodgeroo and others, to articulate critically the psychodynamics and politics of mining. I also use this work to analyse critically the politics and psychodynamics of the discourses employed by the mining industry and by the mineral disciplines. I argue that they construct the earth as a passive and compliant object to be exploited, and then expect the earth to absorb or hide their wastes in return. I also go on to make some modest proposals for different ways of talking about the earth. I argue for a move away from an emphasis on resource-exploitation, or greed and gluttony, to a relationship of generosity and gratitude, of reciprocity and restoration. Although restoration is a buzzword in environmental and mining circles, it is not often motivated by gratitude and reciprocity, but more by a sense of duty. Instead of seeing the earth as something to exploit, the earth needs to be seen as our equivalent other, not as an inferior object, but at least as our equal in importance with which to have relations of respect and care, even learning to love it.

Mother Earth

Masculinity, manufacturing and modern society are related to the politics of mining, especially to the gender politics of mining. Gender politics relates not only to the politics of relations between the genders but also between gendered entities. Politics is used here in the broad sense of power relations, which are, as the passage from Boyle's novel shows, tied up with investments of desire (as well as capital) in, and yields of pleasure (as well as yields of ore and profits) from, 'ore bodies' (see Trigger 1997: 161–180). These power relations, investments and yields are tied up with the gender and ethnic politics of mining and its relationship with the earth as a gendered entity in both modern and traditional societies. Yet whereas traditional societies revere the earth as Great Mother and so as a living person, modern societies abuse the earth as dead matter.

Carolyn Merchant and Susan Griffin have enunciated the gender politics of mining extensively in terms of the Mother Earth figure. Merchant has argued that:

> [...] for most traditional cultures, minerals and metals ripened in the uterus of the Earth Mother, mines were compared to her vagina, and metallurgy was the human hastening of the birth of the living metal in the artificial womb of the furnace – an abortion of the metal's natural growth cycle before its time. (1980: 3–4; see also 29–41)

As Mircea Eliade puts it, the minerals and metals extracted from 'the womb of the Earth Mother [are] in some way *embryos* [...] [and] their extraction from the bowels of the earth is thus an operation executed before its due time' (1971: 41–42).

One traditional account of mining couched in these terms can be found in Pliny the Elder's *Natural History*. Written in the first century of the common era, Pliny suggests that:

> [...] Earth receives us when we are born and feeds us after birth and always supports us, and, at the very end embraces us in her bosom, sheltering us like a mother especially then, when we have been disowned by the rest of Nature [...] What delights and affronts does she not afford mankind? She is dumped into the sea, or excavated to provide channels. She is tortured at all hours by water, iron, wood, fire, stone and crops, and by far more besides to serve our pleasure rather than our needs. Yet so that what she suffers on her surface, her outermost skin, may seem bearable by comparison, we penetrate her inmost parts, digging into her veins of gold and solver and deposits of copper and lead. We search for gems and certain very small stones by sinking shafts into the depths. We drag out earth's entrails [...] If there were any beings in the nether world, assuredly the tunnelling brought

about by greed and luxury would have dug them up [...] We search for riches deep within the bowels of the earth where the spirits of the dead have their abode, as though the part we walk upon is not sufficiently bountiful and productive [...] But what she has hidden and kept underground – those things that cannot be found immediately – destroy us and drive us to the depths. As a result the mind boggles at thought of the long-term effect of draining the earth's resources and the full impact of greed. How innocent, how happy, indeed how comfortable, life might be if it coveted nothing from anywhere other than the surface of the earth – in brief, nothing except what is immediately available. (1991: 30–31 and 286)

The concept/metaphor of the mineral veins of the body of Mother Earth persisted at least into the sixteenth century as Georgius Agricola (1960: 12, 35, 37 and 107) attests. After colonising the surface of the earth, the depths are colonized by shafting and tunnelling underground. As Walter Benjamin put it, 'everywhere sacrificial shafts were dug in Mother Earth' (1979c: 104; and 1996b: 486).

For traditional cultures, metals are embryos, metallurgy is an abortion and the mine, as Susan Griffin (1978: 118) suggests, is a Caesarean section of Mother Earth, so even though the metals may have reached their term, they are mechanically removed from the earth. Aboriginal critics of mining in Australia have seen it in these terms. Following a tour of mining operations in the Pilbara region of Western Australia, Mudrooroo wrote:

> Nyaninya na-na pala lidiyah.
> Unentire, the earth gapes open;
> The black womb slashed open by
> The grinning tropes of discord.
> He laughs and turns to mining out
> The fruits of her laborious love. (1992: 1)[1]

This produces what the next stanza calls 'the excavated abomination'.

The Nyoongar people of south-western Australia have rejected Mudrooroo's identity as an Aboriginal person. By quoting from his work I do not accept (or deny) his aboriginality. It is not up to me to decide. I do not cite his work in this and subsequent chapters as that of an Aboriginal writer or person, or not. I quote his work as it is invaluable and as his contribution to cross-cultural dialogue and understanding is enormous. In another poem in the same series entitled 'Baby–Man–Talk' Mudrooroo extends the 'trope of discord' to describe mining as a violent abortive intervention:

> The miner cuts through the flesh, drags out the
> Writhing capillaries and empowders the blood,
> Evading any moral issues while a flame flickers
> In the contraction-expansion of the heart pillars,

Gently throbbing out accords, discords, concords. (1992: 2)

As Robert Thayer puts it succinctly and graphically, 'by actually ripping open and consuming parts of the earth, consumptive technology symbolizes a wounding and consumption of the earth's "flesh"' (1994: 123).

Klein on Mining

The work of Melanie Klein can make a valuable contribution to this discussion of mining in three main ways: first, by moving away from simple metaphorics to a recognition that, for the young infant, the body of the mother and Mother Earth are one, and that for indigenes they are (in symbiosis with) the earth. As one Aboriginal poet, W. Les Russell puts it in a poem entitled 'The 'Developers': 'I am this Land and it is mine' (Gilbert 1988: 3). Secondly, by exploring the psychodynamics of the relation between the young child and the mother, and between indigenous and non-Aboriginal people and the earth. And thirdly, by showing the implications both these have for the way in which the earth is treated in later life, primarily in terms of whether one greedily seeks gratification from it/her or gives gratitude back to it/her for its/her generosity.

Zoë Sofoulis has already suggested the pertinence of Klein's work on infantile development to an eco-feminist critique of patriarchal capitalist mining. She has argued that:

> Melanie Klein interpreted exploration, mining, scientific and intellectual research, and artistic production as sublimations of the infantile curiosity about origins ('epistemophilia') which arises before the firm imposition of gender roles, and is associated with infantile sadistic tendencies of oral and excremental character. (Sofia 1989: 7; see also Sofoulis 1984; and nd)[2]

These tendencies are neither necessarily nor essentially ascribed to one gender rather than the other at an early age, though they are ones that typically characterize masculinity later on. Mining and infantile development can be articulated, as Sofia does, around a conceptualisation of Aboriginal relations to the earth, just as B. A. Santamaria does in *The Earth – Our Mother* (nd, ?1945), an early book on land degradation in Australia. Errol West, for instance, describes how 'The Breast of Mother Earth bore me' and how 'All I want is a private dying in the arms of my Mother Earth' (Gilbert 1988: 173).

As there is no firm sense of gender for the young infant, so is there no definite idea of self in relation to other things. Central to Klein's work on early childhood development is the contention that for the young infant there is no differentiation between it and the objects external to it. This contention derives from Freud who, in his London notes of 1938, mimics the child: 'the breast is a part of me, I am the breast' (1975: 299). All objects are initially conflated with one another and equated with the mother, or parts of her, especially her breasts, as she/they are the primary object for the young infant.

Klein extended and developed Freud's contention by suggesting that this object does not necessarily remain unitary; indeed, it can, and does, become split. When the young infant feels frustration at not being fed on demand, or not being fed sufficiently, Klein argues that 'the mother's breast [...] to the child becomes split into a good (gratifying) and bad (frustrating) breast' (1986: 176–177). The good breast is an object of desire, or in Klein's terms envy, for the young infant that s/he regards as completely adequate in fulfilling that desire:

> [...] the first object to be envied is the feeding breast for the infant feels that it possesses everything that he desires and that it has an unlimited flow of milk and love which it keeps for its own gratification. (1986: 213)

For Klein, 'he' seems to be used as a quasi-generic pronoun as the infant is in a state 'prior to the firm imposition of gender roles', to re-use Sofoulis's terms. For this quasi-gendered infant, the feeding, or good, breast is, in Biblical terms, the land flowing with milk and honey – the Promised Land, Australia Felix – whereas the non-feeding, or bad, breast is the dry and barren land – the Wasteland, the desert, the interior of Australia through the eyes of European explorers and settlers (see Falkiner 1992). The construction of the earth as rich and bountiful, especially in mining terms, has recently been employed by the local Chamber of Mines that describes Western Australia as having been 'endowed with rich mineral resources' (1990: 1). Good breast indeed.

For the young infant, though, there is no distinction between the body of the mother and other external objects, so we are not in the realm of the figurative here where the Promised Land and desert are just mere metaphors for the mother's body. No distinction has yet been made between the mother and the external world in general so the child is in a pre-metaphoric stage or state in which the body of the mother and Mother Earth are one. The two topoi are mapped onto each other and the relationship with one becomes the model for the relationship with the other. Not only are the mother's body and the external world mapped onto each other for the young infant, but also the changing and developing relationship between child and his/her mother becomes the model for his/her relationship with the external world. How we human beings treat the earth is modelled on how we treated our mothers.

This oneness and modelling is no more cogently described than by Marie Bonaparte (though interestingly without acknowledging Klein) in her well-known psychoanalytic study of the life and works of Edgar Allen Poe:

> [...] the child at the breast knows nothing of the world: all it knows of it is the breast that gives it milk. This breast is more than something it may claim, it seems part and parcel of its own body. Thus, the mother's proximity, by degrees, develops in the child

its first conceptions of the outside world, for it soon learns to know presence or absence, her yielding or withholding of the breast. Thus, to it, she is the first embodiment of that nature by which it is surrounded, whose every constituent, by degree, attaches itself to the primal figure of the mother. Later, in adult life, nature which both feeds and harshly uses man will, by a sort of regression, come to symbolize the mother upon whom, originally, that nature was modelled but, now, as an immensely magnified, eternal, infinite mother. Thus, the manner in which each of us loves nature, always reflects, more or less, our own mother-complex. (1949: 286)

Yet this relationship not only involves the way 'nature' 'harshly uses man'. It also invariably involves the way modern 'man' harshly uses nature. In psychoanalytic terms, the way modern 'man' harshly uses nature is sadistic, which can be defined, as Freud did, not only as deriving pleasure from the pain of others, but also simply as setting up the subject-object distinction, and instituting a relation of mastery between subject and object. The discourses of nature that construct nature as object and a subject position of power/knowledge against it, and the industries that extract resources from nature and construct it as compliant object, both establish and enact a sadistic, subject-object relationship with nature.

The envy or desire for the good breast gives rise to what Klein calls 'sadistic appropriation and exploration of the mother's body and of the outside world (the mother's body in an extended sense)' (1986: 110), or Mother Earth. For Freud ontogenesis (the beginnings of the individual) recapitulates phylogenesis (the beginnings of the species). The sadistic exploration and appropriation of the body of Mother Earth can be construed in terms of the history of western exploration and colonial appropriation. For the young infant, in Klein's terms, this sadistic exploration and appropriation of the surfaces or the outside of the mother's body, is followed by the sadistic exploration and appropriation of the depths, or the inside of her body:

> [...] in the very first months of the baby's existence it has sadistic impulses directed, not only against its mother's breast, but also against the inside of her body: scooping it out, devouring the contents, destroying it by every means which sadism can suggest. (1986: 116)

Exploration and appropriation of the surfaces of the earth is followed by exploration and appropriation below the surface – landscape by mining, Columbus by Cortez (see Todorov 1984). For Aboriginal poet Errol West in a poem entitled, 'I feel the texture of her complexion with both hand and heart', this process is a cancer:

> [...] you rip out her heart, her spleen and liver –
> mining, digging, drilling, a cancer attacking the essence of my life.
> (Gilbert 1988: 175; and Sabbioni, Schaffer and Smith 1998: 149)

Even standard textbooks on mining and minerals such as *Minerals and Men* [sic!] construct their own discourse in terms similar to those that Klein uses to describe the young infant's relation to his/her mother's body, and Aboriginal poets use to describe mining's relation to Mother Earth, though, of course, uncritically:

> [...] since before the dawn of recorded history, man [sic] has looked to the earth for materials from which to build his shelters and to make his tools and utensils. Over the centuries this gouging and scratching at the surface to find clay, flint, bright stones, or occasional pieces of native copper evolved into a burrowing beneath the surfaces in the broadening search for mineral materials. As history has progressed the need for minerals has increased, and the search has gone on. Indeed, the passage of time has seen the use of an ever-increasing array of mineral raw materials, in ever-expanding quantities, for a multitude of purposes – materials which man recovers from the ends and depths of the earth. (McDivitt and Manners 1974: 3)

Early mining is here figured in the sadistic terms of gouging and scratching at the surface of the earth. Later, industrial capitalist mining is figured as 'burrowing' beneath the surface like a mole and 'recovering' what would otherwise be 'lost' in the 'depths' of Mother Earth. Elsewhere, mining is figured as 'winning' and 'bringing to fruition' 'the potential riches that lie buried' (see Trigger 1997: 165 and 167). More 'environmentally friendly' metaphors are needed than these for mining, such as eating gratefully at the table of Mother Earth and appreciating sensually the goods she generously gives rather than greedily gorging on ore bodies and resource commodities.

For Klein, the sadistic impulse of the young infant to appropriate the good things in the depths of his mother's body is described as 'oral-sadistic impulses to rob the mother's body of its good contents' (1986: 177). Discourses of mining have also seen mining as stealing the good contents of the earth. This is no more graphically illustrated than on the cover of a booklet produced by the Australian Mining Industry Council entitled *Mining ... and the Environment* (Hore-Lacy 1976). Note the order of priority (why not *The Environment and Mining*?) and the ellipses indicating deferral and delay as if the environment were an afterthought. The cover depicts the good contents of the earth in an image of sparkling and shiny goodies at the bottom of a deep, penetrating shaft. Mining is figured in the illustration as a penetration of the surface of the earth through a discrete, and discreet, hole that leaves untouched the surrounds. Much mining, however, does not in fact take place through this confined penetration but by scratching and gouging the surface of the earth through 'strip mining', or in the words of Aboriginal poet Elizabeth Brown, in a poem entitled 'Spiritual Land', 'Hunger for money, stripped the land/mined the Earth' (Gilbert 1988: 184). This can readily be seen as a kind of phallic fantasy of mining/rape, of 'shafting' the earth in two senses.

For Klein, this sadistic impulse of the young infant to rob the mother of her good contents is coupled to and followed by a sadistic impulse to expel the bad things of his own body into her. Klein refers to these as the young infant's 'anal-sadistic impulses to put his excrements into her' (1986: 177). In environmental terms, the good contents of Mother Earth are robbed, 'recovered' or 'reclaimed' (see Trigger 1997: 170) by mining, and the bad excrements of consumption are put back into the earth by 'sanitary land-fill'. This process is no more powerfully, and protestingly, put than in the words of Aboriginal poet Oodgeroo Noonuccal:

> The miner rapes
> The heart of earth
> With his violent spade.
> Stealing, bottling her black blood
> For the sake of greedy trade.
> On his metal throne of destruction,
> He labours away with a will,
> Piling the mountainous minerals high
> With giant tool and iron drill.
>
> In his greedy lust for power,
> He destroys old nature's will.
> For the sake of the filthy dollar,
> He dirties the nest he builds. (Gilbert 1988: 101)

The throne here is ambiguously the seat of regal power and the toilet pan in the waste closet. Whereas soil erosion 'rapes' the surface of the earth, mining 'rapes' its depths. Mineral raw-materials are extracted, processed, munched over, transformed into energy and commodities which are bought and sold, consumed and used, ingested and digested, excreted and discarded into 'sanitary land-fills' and elsewhere in the earth-household, including the atmosphere. Mining scoops out the earth and creates hollow places; sanitary landfill finds hollow places in the earth and fills them up. Invariably these hollow places have been wetlands. An all too familiar scene in Australia and the United States has been of what was once a wetland, but is now a wasteland full of rusting car-bodies, bald tyres, superseded whitegoods and sundry other household rubbish; the detritus of capitalist production and consumption.[3]

These oral-sadistic and anal-sadistic impulses arise for Klein (1986: 183) not only out of a desire to sadistically hurt or harm the mother and to derive pleasure from that, but also out of a desire to master and own her. In drawing this distinction between the *oral*-sadistic impulses to 'suck dry, bite up, scoop out and rob the mother's body of its good contents' and the *anal*-sadistic impulses to 'expel dangerous substances (excrements) out of the self and into the mother', Klein goes on to argue that these dangerous substances and bad parts of the self are:

[…] meant not only to injure but also to control and to take possession of the object. In so far as the mother comes to contain the bad part of the self, she is not felt to be a separate individual but is felt to be the bad self. Much of the hatred against parts of the self is now directed towards the mother. (1986: 183)

In environmental terms, insofar as Mother Earth comes to contain excrement, she is not felt to be a separate entity, but is felt to be the bad self. Much of the hatred against parts of the self is now directed towards Mother Earth. Insofar as wetlands come to contain rubbish and other excrement, they are not felt to be separate entities. They become environmental 'dunny holes' into which waste is dumped or flows (see McComb and Lake 1990: 12). Much of the hatred against parts of the self is now directed towards wetlands.

For Klein, oral-sadistic impulses can be seen as greed and anal-sadistic impulses as envy. She defines greed as:

[…] an impetuous and insatiable craving, exceeding what the subject needs and what the object can and wishes to give. At the unconscious level, greed aims primarily at completely scooping out, sucking dry and devouring the breast, that is to say, its aim is destructive introjection; whereas envy not only aims at robbing in this way, but also at putting badness, primarily bad excrements and bad parts of the self, into the mother – first of all into her breast – in order to spoil and destroy her; in the deepest sense this means destroying her creativeness. This process I have defined […] as a destructive aspect of projective identification. (Klein 1986: 212–213)

Greed is voracious and destructive mining, and envy both this and shitting on the earth and attempting to destroy its creativeness. Besides Oodgeroo's protestation about mining as a greedy trade and the miner's greedy lust for power, other Aboriginal poets, such as W. Les Russell have also protested that 'the Company kills with greedy mirth' (Gilbert 1988: 3). Unlike Michael Douglas' yuppie entrepreneur Gordon Gecko in Oliver Stone's film *Wall Street* for whom 'greed is good', for Klein greed is gluttony, or more precisely, cannibalistic and destructive gluttony, as it is for the Aboriginal people of Australia.

Minerals and Men unapologetically constructs its own discourse in similar oral-sadistic terms – albeit unwittingly and uncritically:

[…] the world's appetite for minerals is great, and is steadily increasing […] This gargantuan appetite for raw materials, and the questionable ability of the earth to continue satisfying it, provides the starting point for any consideration of minerals. The possible exhaustion of useful mineral supplies has long been a matter of concern for thinking man. (McDivitt and Manners 1974: 4)

Here, greed is writ large in all its oral sadism, particularly in the use of the adjective 'gargantuan' (see also Trigger 1997: 166). Drawing on Chapters 7 and 44 of Rabelais'

Gargantua, Mikhail Bakhtin has traced how the word 'gargantua' 'in Spanish [...] means the throat. The Provencal tongue has the word "gargantuan" meaning a glutton' (Bakhtin 1968: 459–60). He goes on to argue that 'gargantua' 'symbolize[s] the gullet, not as a neutral anatomical term but as an abusive-laudatory image: gluttony, swallowing, devouring, banqueting. This is the gaping mouth, the grave-womb, swallowing and generating' (ibid.). Fears about birth and the mother's body are displaced into images of oral gluttony.

Although the gargantuan gluttonous like Rabelais' Gargantua consume vast quantities, they do not necessarily become obese as a result of their gluttony. The gluttonous swallow dead objects external to themselves, whereas for Baudrillard the obese may be thought of as having 'swallowed their own dead bodies while still alive' (1990: 32). The gluttonous do not show any sign of their gluttony with their bodies, whereas the obese show with the expansiveness of their own bodies the sign of their auto-necrophagy.

Envy for the creativeness of the mother's body and of Mother Earth is ultimately envy of the mother's ability to produce children (womb envy) and milk (breast envy), and of the earth to produce life and raw materials. The young infant is unable to create anything new; all s/he does is transform food into excrement as an eating/shitting factory. For Klein, 'excessive envy of the breast is likely to extend to all feminine attributes, in particular to the woman's capacity to bear children. At bottom, envy is directed against creativeness' (1986: 219). Industrial capitalism does not create, nor bring into being out of nothing (*ex nihilo*, like God). Rather, it transmutes prior existing matter, reshaping raw materials into 'commodities' and commodities into consumer 'goods', sublimating solid matter into gaseous air. Arguably there are no economic modes of production, only modes of transmutation. There is, however, a biological mode of production and it is the reproduction of humans by women.

The envy of the breast, this desire for the creativeness of the mother's body, gives rise to what Klein calls 'the femininity complex' in males, in which 'the vagina and the breasts, the fountain of milk [...] are coveted as organs of receptivity and bounty', or what could simply be called 'womb envy' (1986: 74). These involve firm gender roles in which the boy/son may develop a complex about the creativeness of his mother's body and of Mother Earth, and continues to direct envy, greed and sadism towards it/her, whereas in Kleinian terms the girl/daughter may convey gratitude toward it/her.

In terms of mining as it is currently construed, the rich and bountiful insides of the earth are coveted as 'organs' which receive and create. This covetousness, one of the seven deadly sins in medieval Christianity and sometimes seen as the basis for all the others, gives rise to technologies of 'production', to simulated organs, 'Bachelor Machines for Bachelor Births',[4] which receive raw materials and transmute them into consumer goods.

In these terms, envy evades obesity that Baudrillard describes as 'a foetal obesity, primal and placental: as if they were pregnant with their own bodies but could not be delivered of them' (1990: 27). Unlike the gluttonous, who swallow objects besides themselves and envy the creativity of the mother's body and the fecundity of Mother Earth, the obese swallow themselves and become, as it were, pregnant with, but unable to be delivered of, themselves. The gluttonous envy motherhood, whereas the obese take it over into themselves.

Gluttonous envy of the creativeness of the mother's body is associated for Klein with the formation of the super ego – the internalized principle of the Law of the Father. Klein argues that 'the internalization of an injured and therefore dreaded breast on the one hand, and of a satisfying and helpful breast on the other, is the core of the super ego' (1986: 50–51). It is the core of the super ego because it involves a turning away from the mother and her body and a turning towards the father and the Law. This is effected through a splitting in not only the mother's body into the good and bad breast, but also in the infant him/herself. Klein argues that 'the ego is incapable of splitting the object – internal and external – without a corresponding splitting taking place within the ego' (1986: 181). The ego is split between the super ego, the internalization of the Law of the Father, and the id, the site of repressed desire for the creativeness of the mother's body.

In this process of internalisation, of gluttony and obesity, the ego gives birth to itself as a split ego. Indeed, it gives birth to itself as an infantile ego, which it remains, as Norman O. Brown argues:

> [...] through the institutionalisation of the super ego the parents [including the mother insofar as she is complicit with the Law of the Father] are internalized, and man finally succeeds in becoming father of himself, but at the cost of *becoming his own child and keeping his ego infantile*. (cited by Eagleton 1990: 272; my emphases)

Klein located the formation of the super ego far earlier than Freud did in the period when the young infant desires to scoop out and devour the contents of his or her mother's body. In this process, the young infant demonstrates envy for the creativeness of his/her mother's body and is able to give birth to him/herself as an ego but at the price of keeping that ego infantile. Thus, by implication and analogy, the desire to scoop out and devour the good contents of Mother Earth is, in Kleinian terms, infantile.

As this ego is infantile it is not strictly precise to describe the system that it founds as 'patriarchal capitalism'. Although it is certainly male-dominated, it is not dominated by the fathers, but by the sons. Klaus Theweleit, in his suggestive and sweeping two volume study of *Male Fantasies* (1989), prefers the term 'filiarchal', the rule of the sons. Gayle Rubin has proposed that the term patriarchy be reserved for Old Testament families of the pastoral nomad type in which the father did rule (1975: 168). All post-pastoralist social arrangements (such as agricultural and capitalist ones) would be by implication filiarchal. Yet, as I have tried to show using Klein's work, it is not just sons per se who rule industrial capitalism, but infantile sons, so if it were not such a mouthful and so hard to swallow, it would be more precise to talk about infantile filiarchal capitalism instead of patriarchal capitalism. In this system, infantile sons sadistically devour the contents of Mother Earth and sadistically excrete their waste into it/her not realising, or more precisely, repressing, the realisation that the earth sustains their very life and being, that its resources are not inexhaustible, that she is not an indulgent and forgiving Mother who will allow herself to be abused indefinitely, and that there are limits to her resources and to her ability to absorb and hide his excrements, all too obvious in these days of widespread air, land and water pollution.

In a critical inversion of the terms and in a critique of industrial capitalism, Émile Zola figured the mine as an oral-sadistic monster. In *Germinal,* first published in 1885, instead of the miner eating the earth, the mine eats miners. The mine pit is figured as 'evil-looking, a voracious beast crouching ready to devour the world' (Zola 1954: 21) that soon 'gulped down men in mouthfuls' (Zola 1954: 39). The mine, not the miner, is a greedy, oral sadistic monster like the steam saws that ate up the forests, the steam dredgers that ate up wetlands and the steam trains that ate up the bush as we saw in a previous chapter. The pit is figured later as a greedy and gluttonous mouth: 'the cages slid up and down stealthily like beasts of the night, and went on swallowing men as though the pit were a mouth gulping them down' (Zola 1954: 44).

The mine consumes 'men' (though also children) and mining is figured as 'burrowing' beneath the surface, as it is in *Minerals and Men*: 'the greedy pit had swallowed its daily ration of men; nearly seven hundred of them were now toiling in this immense ant-hill, burrowing in the earth, riddling it with holes like old, worm-eaten wood' (Zola 1954: 49). Burrowing begins with shafting, and in Zola's *Germinal* the shaft is figured in oral-sadistic terms as eating 'men' (though the 'men' include young girls and boys): 'the shaft went on with its meal for half an hour, gulping men down more or less greedily according to the depth of the level they were bound for; but it never stopped, for the hunger of this gigantic maw could swallow up a whole people' (1954: 40). Yet it is a maw created and produced by 'men'. It is the greedy, oral-sadistic monster of industrial capitalism with its greedy, oral-sadistic machines.

Similar sentiments were voiced earlier in Australia. On his visit to Australia in 1871 Anthony Trollope described how a quartz-crushing machine 'goes on day and night eating up the rock which is dragged forth [kicking and screaming, or mute and inarticulate?] from the bowels of the earth', and how 'the noisy monster continued his voracious meals without cessation' (1987, I: 61; see also II: 213). Like the steam trains that ate up the bush, the steam dredgers that devoured wetlands, the steam saws that chewed up forests, the mines that eat up men, women and children and the miners that consume the earth, the crushing machine is an oral-sadistic monster that eats up rock.

These monsters were the brain-child of monstrous parents as D. H. Lawrence put it: 'the idea, the IDEA, that fixed gorgon monster, and the IDEAL, that great stationery engine, these two gods-of-the-machine have been busy destroying all *natural* reciprocity and *natural circuits,* for centuries' (1977: 124). The copulation, or articulation, of these two monsters/machines created the oral sadistic machines of industrial capitalism that devoured everything and produced the wasteland of trench warfare that Benjamin saw:

> [...] it should be said as bitterly as possible: in the face of 'this landscape of total mobilisation', the German feeling for nature has had an undreamed-of upsurge. The pioneers of peace, who settle nature in so sensuous a manner, were evacuated from these

landscapes, and as far as anyone could see over the edge of the trench, the surroundings had become the terrain of German Idealism; every shell crater had become a problem; every wire entanglement an antinomy; every barb a definition; every explosion a thesis; by day, the sky was the cosmic interior of the steel helmet, and at night, the moral law above. Etching the landscape with flaming banners and trenches, technology wanted to recreate the heroic features of German idealism. It went astray. What it considered heroic were the features of Hippocrates, the features of death. Deeply imbued with its own depravity, technology gave shape to the apocalyptic face of nature and reduced nature to silence – even though this technology had the power to give nature its voice. (1999b: 318–319)[5]

Industrial technology reduced nature to the mined moonscape, the town dump and the refuse-clogged creek, the landscape of the trench war that modern industrial 'man' has declared and fought against nature.

Towards Gratitude for Generosity

Rather than enviously and sadistically devouring the good contents of the earth, gratitude should be given in response to the generosity of the earth. Unlike envy that has a desire only for gratification, gratitude has a desire for complementarity and mutuality that may give rise to love. Klein argues that:

> [...] a full gratification at the breast means that the infant feels he has received from his loved object a unique gift, which he wants to keep. This is the basis of gratitude. Gratitude includes belief in good objects and trust in them. It includes also the ability to assimilate the loved object – not only as a source of food – and to love it without envy interfering. The more often this gift is fully accepted, the more often the feeling of enjoyment and gratitude – implying the wish to return pleasure – is experienced. Gratitude is closely bound up with generosity. (1986: 215–216)

Presumably, on the other hand, by implication, envy is closely bound up with possessiveness and parsimony. In terms of mining, this would require not just some sort of 'landcare ethic', certainly not as an externally imposed code, but learning to be grateful to the earth and loving it. Many mining companies are good corporate citizens. They have programs of environmental rehabilitation and restoration of their own sites, or programs promoting land care and bush regeneration, or programs nurturing cross-cultural understanding of indigenous culture, but how many have programs promoting gratitude and generosity to the earth amongst its employees, its customers and the consumers of commodities made from its raw materials?

Along similar lines in the 1920s, Walter Benjamin warned that:

> In accepting what we receive so abundantly from nature we should guard against a gesture of avarice. For we are able to make Mother Earth no gift of our own. It is therefore fitting to show respect in taking, by returning a part of all we receive before laying hands on our share. This respect is expressed in the ancient custom of the libation. (1979c: 60; and 1996b: 455)

How many mining companies make annual libations or perform rituals to express gratitude to the earth for its generosity in giving ore, jobs, profits to mining companies and dividends to shareholders? How many mining companies have an annual barbeque or picnic on World Environment Day or on Mother's Day (Earth Mother's Day?) at which, say, 'a slab of tinnies' (Australian slang for a carton of 24 or 30 aluminium cans of beer) is buried to give back a token of what has been taken from the earth? A block of concrete commemorating the event with a suitable inscription on it expressing gratitude for generosity placed over the buried booty would also help to prevent theft by the greedy and ungrateful. This may sound like a trivial and tokenistic gesture when a grand political strategy is required, but its pragmatic and tactical reciprocity at the level of everyday life may help to develop mutuality with the earth.[6] It is at this popular cultural level that conservationism and green politics need to engage with industrial workers, their families and friends.

Without such acts of libation the consequences of greed and gluttony are disastrous. Benjamin went on to forewarn that:

> If society has so degenerated through necessity and greed that it can now receive the gifts of nature only rapaciously, that it snatches the fruit unripe from the trees in order to sell it most profitably, and is compelled to empty each dish in its determination to have enough, the earth will be impoverished and the land yield bad harvests. (1979c: 60; and 1996b: 455)

Taking the good things of the earth sadistically without returning a portion in gratitude results in bad things being given back in return.

Rather than discoursing about the earth as a passive and compliant object, a new way of talking about mining is needed that will recognize and respect the earth as an active, equal and different agent and subject, and then interact accordingly in complementarity and dialogue with it. Instead of seeing the earth as something out there to exploit by mining, mining needs to see the earth as its equivalent other, not its inferior object, but at least its equal in importance with which to have relations of respect and care, and even learn to love it/her. After all, the earth is our mother beyond mere metaphor. She can live without us, but we human beings cannot live without her.

Notes

1. I am grateful to Mudrooroo and Hugh Webb for making this 'report' available to me.
2. I am grateful to Zoë for making copies of her work available to me. Sofia is a *nom de plume*.
3. For a graphic representation of such scenes see the photographs by Wayne Lawler in McComb and Lake (1990: 225) and by Joseph Muench in Niering (1966: 164–165).
4. For metaphors of fertility and pregnancy in mining, see Trigger (1997: 173).
5. I discuss the landscapes of world warfare in Giblett (2009: Chapters 4 and 5).
6. For the distinction between strategy and tactic, see de Certeau (1984: xix–xx). I discuss de Certeau's distinction in Giblett (2008a: 115–117).

Chapter 10

Kings in Kimberley Watercourses and Wetlands: Sadism and Pastoralism

Mary Durack's *Kings in Grass Castles* (hereafter *Kings* for short) is a classic of Western Australian settler literature. First published in 1959, it is also a bestseller having gone through eighteen printings up to 1991 and is still in print. Besides selling well, it seems to be well-read, or at least well-borrowed, as 35 copies are circulating in the public library system in Western Australia.[1] Generically, *Kings* is a family chronicle (Durack 1966: 13 and 17) of the founding in the 1880s of a Western Australian pastoral dynasty in the northernmost Kimberley region of the state by its patriarch, Durack's grand-father, Patrick 'Patsy' Durack. Accordingly, it is a myth of origins of the self-proclaimed royal family of the east Kimberley who may have only been 'kings in grass castles' of a 'cattle kingdom' (Durack 1966: 399), but who were kings initially of a kingdom of 'one and a half million acres [...] on either side of the Ord River' (Durack 1966: 231), and eventually emperors, as Durack modestly boasts, of 'a sizeable pastoral empire of six to seven million acres or roughly ten thousand square miles' (1966: 379). As it is also an epic (Durack 1966: 20, 232 and 262), *Kings* has an epic hero in the person of Patrick's brother, Michael 'Stumpy' Durack, who makes the obligatory descent into the underworld of the east Kimberley and emerges triumphant with his masculine identity secured and the dynastic aspirations of his family vindicated.

Furthermore, *Kings* is a quest narrative in search of the Golden Fleece (or more precisely, 'the golden Kimberley savannah lands' (Durack 1966: 225), 'pastoral paradise' (Durack 1966: 207, also 'a cattleman's paradise' [208]) and 'Promised Land' (Durack 1966: 221) of the Ord River. In this combined Biblical and classical journey Michael ('Stumpy') Durack doubles as both Jason and part Moses. He finds the Golden Fleece of the east Kimberley and returns with the news to Queensland. Although he does not personally lead the chosen few on the 'big trek' (Durack 1966: 231) to the Promised Land of the east Kimberley in Western Australia, through the wilderness of outback Queensland and the Northern Territory (the role of leader of the trek is later taken by his nephew and the author's father, 'Long' Michael, or 'Miguel' Durack), 'Stumpy' Michael does get to enter the Promised Land unlike his Old Testament prototype.

For good measure, a 'boys' own' (in a number of senses) imperialist adventure story of 'the conquest of this new country' to 'make a pastoral [*sic*] empire' (Durack 1966: 210) is thrown in, not to mention the occasional episode from 'some Davy Crockett serial in Australian setting' (Durack 1966: 356). Finally, *Kings* combines elements of the naturalist's attention to the details of flora and fauna, the romantic's love of the beautiful, the picturesque and the sublime, and last, but not least, the pastoralist's view of the land with an eye out for waterfowl, or 'game', and good cattle country whilst the other eye is kept on the weather.

Yet these elements, and the discourses, the institutionalized 'ways of seeing, saying, and doing', from which they arise, do not co-exist in blissful harmony. Rather there is a constant struggle for hegemony between them that enacts a powerful class and gender politics. In patriarchy, the romantic and the naturalist have been assigned to, and associated with, the female/feminine and the pastoralist to and with the male/masculine. *Kings* is no exception to this general rule. What is exceptional about it, though, is the way these elements are combined in a single text, even in a single sentence. No doubt this combination of discourses is related to its generic hybridity and, in fact, is probably even constitutive of it.

The gender, and generic, (and gender and genre are closely related as Jacques Derrida [1980], Cate Poynton [1985: especially 21] and Terry Threadgold [1988: especially 64] have argued) politics of the natural environment is most evident when it comes to the descriptions of water-bodies, especially rivers, or 'watercourses', as Durack prefers, in *Kings*. In this chapter I trace the struggle between the discourses of naturalism, pastoralism and romanticism in the representation of what could be called the wetlandscape. I also explore what could be called the eco-gender and eco-generic (also in the sense of 'genus') politics of this struggle and its psychodynamics using the work of Karl Abraham in order to show how, in the driest continent on earth, it is not just any water which is valuable for settlers, but preferably water which flows permanently and is readily accessible.

The body of patriarchal capitalism desires a constant stream of good things to consume in order to produce goods, but it also thereby produces bads. Patriarchal pastoralists are driven by corporeal demands, both their own and those of their cattle and sheep, but these have been culturally constructed in orally and anally sadistic terms in whose reproduction they collude. These terms contrast strongly with those of Aboriginal peoples for whom there is what Mudrooroo calls 'a loving oneness of people and earth' (1979: 70), as we shall see in the conclusion to this chapter and in the next chapter. The demands of the body are not free from acculturation; the body is not an ideologically neutral zone (see Giblett 2008a).

Nor is the body of the earth. Water is a good and bad thing. It is a highly ambivalent substance for settlers as Durack points out when she refers to 'death-dealing, life-giving water' (1966: 252). Living water is the life-blood of the body of the living earth (see Giblett 2008a: Chapter 11; and 2009: Chapter 11); polluted water is the death-poison for the corpse of the earth. From the pastoralist point of view, flowing and masculinized rivers are generally preferred over still and feminized wetlands, whereas from the romantic and naturalist perspective the reverse largely applies, with the notable exception of slimy bogs and sloughs. An eco-gender politics and taxonomy of the landscape, or more precisely wetlandscape, operates just as much, and as powerfully, as taxonomies of flora and fauna with their own eco-generic politics. In the conclusion to the chapter I will offer, by way of a reading of Randolph Stow's *To the Islands* and 'Colin Johnson's' (now Mudrooroo) *Long Live Sandawara*, views of the Kimberley wetlandscape which contrast with those in *Kings* and make some modest proposals for an alternative, or oppositional, way of talking about it.

Politics of Water

In *Kings*, water is preferably of a certain type in a branching and descending set of distinctions and scale of preferences dividing into finer and finer detail, until ultimately the taxonomy is resolved into a simple binary opposition. For a start, waters which are clean, shiny and contained are preferred over those which are dirty, slimy and extensive: or in other words, billabongs rather than bogs or sloughs; rivers or 'watercourses' which flow in prescribed channels rather than swamps which are stagnant without definite boundaries; rivers which are permanent, not temporary; permanent rivers which are accessible to stock (and so orally satisfying) and not inaccessible at the bottom of steep gorges (and so orally sadistic); all of which boils down ultimately to the privileging of the Ord River over all non-Ord waters and the binary opposition between the two. I have attempted to lay out these distinctions spatially in a chart (see Figure 4). A distinctive pastoralist and patriarchal political and economic agenda for the natural environment is pursued in *Kings*, which ultimately wins out over the naturalist's and romantic's view, though both these are arguably as patriarchal as the pastoralist as I try to indicate are all aspects of the patriarchal paradigm (as outlined in Figure 2, Chapter 1).

In *Kings*, the worst water of all, the lowest of the low, is muddy, slimy water, though 'a well of stagnant water' (Durack 1966: 90) is better than nothing when you're dying of thirst. The physical needs of the body assert themselves occasionally over aesthetic desires and the pleasures of the eye. Generally, however, slimy water is treated, not merely with disdain, but with horror.[2] It is also morally opprobrious: it is 'bad water thick with green slime' (Durack 1966: 104). When 'Stumpy' Michael first lands in Cambridge Gulf, he and his men have to 'plough through the reeking mud' in which they 'floundered and sank' (Durack 1966: 217). Descriptions of cattle droving in *Kings* abound in references to the 'slimy mud' (Durack 1966: 248), 'sticky mud' (Durack 1966: 257) and even to 'the evil slime' (Durack 1966: 248) of bogs and sloughs (Durack 1966: 301). This dirty, slimy water mixed with earth is beyond the pale and denigrated in odious comparison to the clear, flowing water of rivers.[3]

Stagnant, swampy water is not much better, though, than dirty, slimy water. It is subject to the utilitarian view, especially for cattle, and found to be wanting: 'the vast tracts of useless, rough range, claypan and cadjibut swamp [...] lay between the good grazing areas' (Durack 1966: 355; see also 263). The 'good grazing areas' are ones 'fed' by rivers, though not just any old river. A contrast can be made between Durack's romantic view of rivers in her native Queensland and those in the Kimberley. Writing of 'the watercourse' on the Cooper Plains near Thylungra in a chapter entitled 'A Land Loved By Birds', Durack describes how 'through the ragged arches of bordering coolibah and wild oranges the water shone polished bright in the setting sun' (1966: 110). The brightly shining billabong with definite borders is the epitome of the beautiful in Durack's nature aesthetic.[4]

This romantic view of an aestheticized landscape (that operates in a sterile antinomy with the pastoralist and patriarchal view and so is locked into the same logic) gives way quickly to the naturalist's desire to identify and classify the birds disturbed by the coming of 'the travellers' (though the relationship of the settlers to the land was not as fleeting as this euphemistic appellation might suggest): 'parrots and water fowl of all kind, wild geese, plumed duck, spoonbill, avocets. Flocks of teal wheeled noisily with egrets, ibises, herons and pigmy geese, while pelicans, heavily rising, flapped off in the wake of low-flying brolgas' (Durack 1966: 110). These birds can all be classified as waterbirds (with the exception of the parrots).

Aesthetic delight in wheeling waterbirds persists throughout the book. Indeed, wheeling waterbirds ascending into the heights, though also to some extent acrobatic, brightly coloured bush birds (mainly parrots or budgerigars), produce the state of the sublime in Durack's nature aesthetic. Yet this production of the sublime sits uneasily with the status of the waterbird's class or sub-family of 'game' when she describes how 'game was plentiful, magpie geese, whistling duck, Burdekin duck went wheeling and calling in dense clouds over the lush wet-weather landscape' (Durack 1966: 260). This is one sentence which combines the romantic's natural aesthetic, especially the sublime, the naturalist's observation of individual bird species, with the pastoralist's eye on his dinner and the weather. But in the process of the sublime-producing wheeling waterbirds rising above the lush wet-weather landscape, the waterbirds are abstracted from the landscape and reduced to agents of aesthetic or culinary – in the case of 'game' – satisfaction, whilst the landscape becomes objectified as background for the wheeling waterbirds, rather than being seen as their habitat, let alone as an ecosystem. Even the term 'game' smacks of what Tim Bonyhady calls 'class oppression under England's draconian old laws' (2000: 351). Objectifying land as landscape and classifying edible animals as 'game' reproduces class oppression.

The waterbirds and the landscape are not only differentiated in terms of their status as agents and objects, but also in terms of the aesthetic and other responses they evoke. Whereas the waterbirds produce a sublime pleasure bordering on pain, and the satisfaction of hunger in the case of 'game', the land arouses a horrifying desire: 'here now was the lush, tropical north that returning drovers spoke of with mixed repugnance and fascination' (Durack 1966: 260). The doubling of repugnance and fascination is a precise definition of the Freudian concept of the uncanny which, Zoë Sofoulis (1988) argues, is the obverse of the sublime.[5] Fascination and repugnance were ambivalent feelings found by Freud to be aroused in men by the sight of female genitalia.[6] The uncanny wet-weather wetlandscape is the womb of the tropics from which new life springs.

The combination of the sublime and uncanny here is an aesthetic of both visual pleasure and oral surfeit, of waterbirds ascending in formless profusion, and of cloying taste to the point of profligate excess.[7] 'Lush' can refer to the tender and juicy, orally satisfying qualities of luxuriant grass. It also has connotations of sexual attractiveness and excessive drinking. Generally, the overall image created is that of a blowsy, slightly tipsy, middle-aged outback mother who is both sexually fascinating and physically repugnant to the randy drovers.

Lush pasture, in general, is the object of desire and the end of the quest in *Kings*, but in the wet season the pasture is too lush, provoking repugnance and fascination rather than giving satisfaction. The ideal pasture, satisfying both orally and aesthetically, is that which 'sprang sweet and succulent on the *parched* plains' (Durack 1966: 105; my emphasis), almost a contradiction in terms and nearly an impossible object. When it grows lush on the *drenched* plains in 'the wet', however, it is an object of fascination and repugnance.

The description of sublime-producing, wheeling waterbirds culminates later with the billabong where 'thousands of wild whistling duck rose from among the reeds and lilies, and wheeled away, in serpent coils against the sunset sky' (Durack 1966: 288). This is probably the only positive description of a wetland in the book and it is hardly surprising that it is of that archetypal and quintessential Anglo-Celtic Australian wetland – the billabong – mythologized in 'Waltzing Matilda'. Yet the discourses of the aesthetic and the naturalist, especially the sublime, are not allowed to persist for too long over that of the utilitarian and pastoralist, especially the culinary, for on the next page the whistling ducks have reverted to 'game' with Uncle John shooting them and boasting of bringing down twenty-four with one shot.

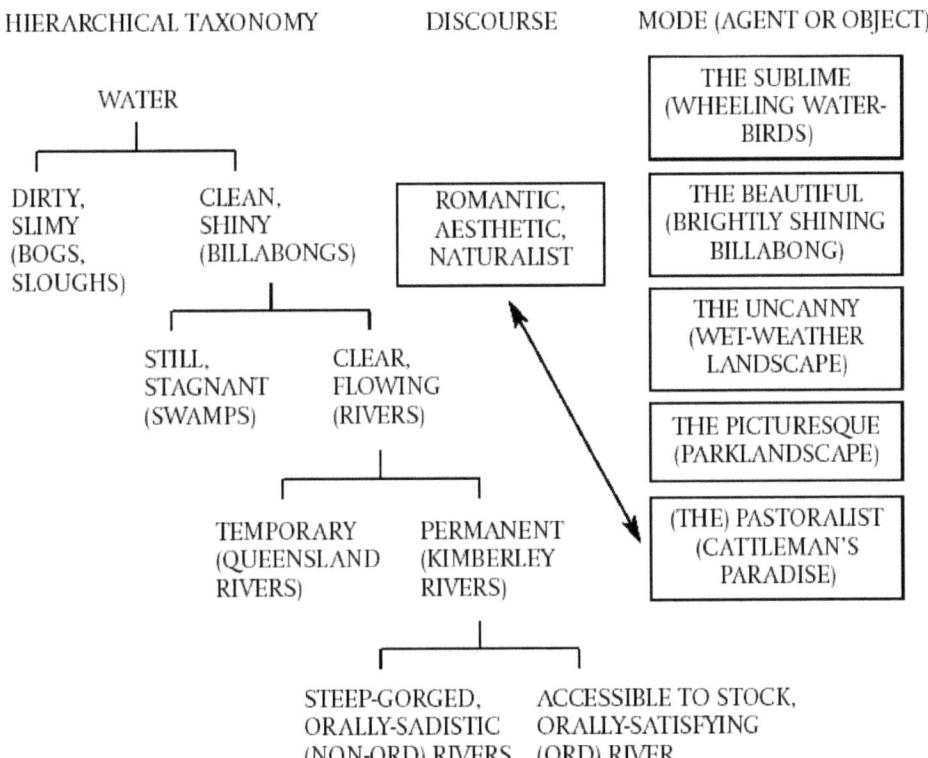

Figure 4: The Structural Process of *Kings in Grass Castles*.

Note: The 'Hierarchical Taxonomy' column of this chart plots the narrative trajectory and aquatic politics of *Kings* and should be read from top to bottom. The 'Discourse' and 'Mode' columns plot the narrational trajectory and representational politics of *Kings* and can be read from top to bottom and in conjunction with the 'Hierarchical Taxonomy' column (billabongs are beautiful, bogs and sloughs are uncanny). Each pivotal moment in the narrative, each significant site in the story corresponds with a bifurcation in the hierarchical taxonomy and with a shift in mode. Each mode is couched in an appropriate discourse; each discourse is instantiated in an apposite mode. The sublime, the beautiful and the picturesque modes in the romantic, aesthetic and naturalist discourses are in tension with, and eventually subsumed beneath, pastoralist discourse. The uncanny is an aberrant, anti-romantic and counter aesthetic mode that threatens to inundate and undermine both the pastoralist and romantic discourses, and to return the subject to primeval and placental slime, to the abject.

A similar description of a beautiful, brightly shining billabong with sublime-producing, wheeling waterbirds as well, and thus what would be the pinnacle of aesthetic delight for Durack, can be found in her novel *Keep Him My Country*: 'the billabong shone like bright enamel under a sunset sky, reflecting the wheeling birds, pale lilies and dark bordering trees' (1983: 100). A beautiful billabong, though, can always revert to a slimy bog, and the sublime-producing, wheeling waterbirds be replaced by swarming and sadistic predatory bush birds as occurs later in *Keep Him My Country*: 'after two light seasons the big billabong had dwindled to a fetid, shallow pool in a crazy pavement of dried mud rimmed with grey coolibahs and streaky paper barks. The water birds had flown but the crows and hawks swarmed about the worm-raddled carcasses of perished stock and tormented the living animals imprisoned in the bog' (Durack 1983: 206: see also 254). Crows and hawks are more like insects than birds. Indeed, they are implicitly not living things and they are certainly not edible, or at least they should not be eaten in accordance with the Biblical injunction of Mosaic law that 'every swarming thing that swarms upon the earth is an abomination; it shall not be eaten' (Leviticus 11: 41).

Swarming creatures, Mary Douglas has commented, are:

> Both those that teem in the waters and those that swarm on the ground. Whether we call it teeming, trailing, creeping or swarming, it is an interminable form of movement [...] 'swarming', which is not a mode of propulsion proper to any particular element, cuts across the basic classification. Swarming things are neither fish, nor flesh, nor fowl. Eels and worms inhabit water, though not as fish; reptiles go on dry land, though not as quadrupeds; some insects fly, though not as birds. There is no order in them [...] As fish belong in the sea so worms belong in the realm of the grave with death and chaos. (1966: 56)

For Durack, swarming bush birds are neither game to be shot nor fowl to be eaten; for her, some birds fly (and torment like insects), but do not wheel as waterbirds. The only living and edible things in this half-dead land seem to be waterbirds and cattle; a carnivorous diet.

This settler view can be contrasted with that of a visitor, Isaac Steinberg, the Jewish Territorialist, who visited the east Kimberley in 1939 to assess its suitability for a Jewish settlement. According to Gettler, he had expected to find 'the dead country, the wilted Nature, the arid waste land' (1993: 75). Instead, he found 'the very opposite: a country that was alive, a Nature that breathed and teemed, a land peopled with all sorts of creatures'. Steinberg, though, is like Durack, as we shall see later, when he occasionally comes across 'grass so fragrant and cheerful that I could have fancied himself on some exquisitely cultivated English estate' (Steinberg 1948: 19).

In both *Kings in Grass Castles* and *Keep Him My Country* waterbirds are constantly privileged over all other birds, especially predatory bush birds, mainly on the basis that waterbirds in general produce the state of the sublime when wheeling, and that 'game' presumably are orally satisfying when eaten (though there are no descriptions of the process of eating and the taste of 'game' in the book), whereas bush birds are sadistic when swarming and frustrate orally as they are inedible. Durack's taxonomy of birds is based on both aesthetic and culinary criteria with predatory bush birds being sadistic and inedible, wheeling birds producing the sublime, and 'game' being edible.

Generally the number of waterbird species, and indeed the presence of the waterbirds themselves, is merely indexical of 'good land'. In *Kings* the settlers are described as 'ardent naturalists' (Durack 1966: 116), not so much because they could identify and classify waterbirds and appreciate their colours, flight and song, but because they had learned 'to read significance in the habits and antics of birds' (Durack 1966: 117). Birds are reduced to agents of the sublime when wheeling, or to mere signifiers, indeed indices, in a semiotic chain in which they either signify 'good land' in the case of waterbirds, or 'bad season', as we shall see in a moment in the case of bush birds. The romantic's and naturalist's view of waterbirds and the land gives way immediately to the pastoralist's in which 'a land loved by birds must be good land' (Durack 1966: 110). Waterbirds are abstracted from their habitat and reduced to indices of good land in pastoralist terms, or if wheeling to agents of the sublime in aesthetic terms. 'Good land' is 'the pastures of a grazier's dream' (Durack 1966: 109–110), a wish-fulfilling wet daydream no doubt. The land is good, not for the birds themselves, but for cattle, where goodness is equated with and reduced to the ability of the land to sustain or 'run' a certain number or 'head' of cattle per acre.

Birds in general had their pastoralist uses. The presence of waterbirds indicated good land, on the one hand as we have just seen, and the antics of bush birds pointed to bad seasons on the other:

> [...] the blacks predicted there would be no rain that season for the chattering hordes of budgerigars that so delighted the eye with acrobatic displays, now darkening the sun like a storm cloud, now turning in a conjuror's vanishing trick on the knife edges of a million wings, were congregating too thickly about the remaining waterholes. (Durack 1966: 119)

This sentence is another which combines the romantic's natural aesthetic, especially the sublime, and the naturalist's observation of individual bird species, particularly their behaviour, with the pastoralist's eye on the weather. It is also one of the few positive representations of bush birds in the book.

Good land is land that could feed cattle and a bad season is a season that will not be able to feed cattle, whereas bad land is cruel and sadistic which cannot feed cattle. This distinction between good land as orally satisfying, a bad season as orally depriving and bad land as orally sadistic operates in the contrast between Queensland and Kimberley rivers: 'unlike the sprawling Queensland rivers that spread far and wide after the rains to disappear sometimes completely when the floods had run their course, the larger of these Kimberley streams had bitten deep, tortuous channels in the plains and worn towering gorges through the ranges' (Durack 1966: 220). The evanescence of Queensland rivers is unfavourable, but at least their easy-going, leisurely sprawl is in some ways preferable to the incisive oral-sadism of the larger Kimberley rivers with their sharp teeth and deep throats ('gorge' is both throat and ravine).

Oral Sadism

Durack anthropomorphizes the gorge rivers in the Kimberley (and the Kimberley more generally by referring to it as 'Kimberley', ironically the name of the author's brother, one of the dedicatees of the book) by displacing onto them (by way of metaphor) the oral-sadistic qualities of tortuous biting, or more precisely, projecting on to them the fear of being bitten back by Mother Earth after having bitten into her so savagely by pastoralism. The desire for and the fear of symmetry, fairness and reciprocity are important factors here. Indeed for Karl Abraham 'the craving for symmetry and "fairness" [...] is often represented in the anal character' (1966a: 185), especially the *anal*-sadistic whereby good things done to others are expected in return, whereas arguably the fear of symmetry and fairness being exercized back against oneself characterizes the *oral*-sadistic whereby bad things done to others are feared in return.

The fear of being eaten by the mother after eating her characterizes the oral-sadistic stage interposed between what Freud calls the 'primitive oral organisation – the fear of being eaten up [...] by the father' and the 'anal-sadistic phase – the wish to be eaten by the father' (1984: 419). The oral sadism enacted in *Kings* is not necessarily symptomatic of any psychopathology on Durack's part personally (and I am not implying, suggesting or diagnosing any), but it is symptomatic of what could be called a cultural psychogeopathology, in which there is no hard and fast divide between the normal and the pathological, but more of a continuum between them. In Jacques Derrida's terms, I am 'putting the text on the couch' (1977: 96), analysing, in Pierre Macherey's words, 'the unconscious of the work (not of the author)' (1978: 92), and getting it to speak its repressed by free association though, for Kristeva, 'the text has no unconscious' (1984: 160–161). This 'talking cure', though, is not designed to make the symptom disappear (as Freud believed it would for the analyst) from the text or from culture, but to speak the cultural symptom which figures the (Western Australian) environment in psychopathological terms.[8] In the conclusion to this chapter, I offer some alternative, or oppositional, ways to the psychogeopathological way of talking about the Kimberley (and Western Australian) wetlandscape.

Kings can be read as a symptom of a cultural pscyho*geo*pathology as it includes and represents what Aldo Leopold calls 'a land pathology' in the 'collective organism of land and society' (1992: 217). As Leopold goes on to point out, and as we saw with mining in the previous chapter, a pathology is indicated by 'self-accelerating rather than self-compensating departures from normal functioning'. *Kings* is, amongst other things, a history of pastoralism in Australia which plots the self-acceleration of the industry in the 50 years from *circa* 1850 to 1900, and the consequent departure of 'vast tracts' of land from their normal, Aboriginal functioning over the previous 50,000 years at least, 1,000 times longer.

The growth of the Australian pastoral industry constitutes land pathology, if there ever were one, that manifests itself in the cultural symptom of the textual trope, such as metaphor. The trope is the symptom that manifests the cultural repressed through displacement and sublimation. If, as that ostensibly arch anti-Freudian Vladimir Nabokov suggests, 'tropes are the dreams of speech' (1971: 328), and if, as Freud maintains, 'the interpretation of dreams is the royal road to the unconscious activities of the mind' (1976: 769), then the interpretation of tropes is therefore the royal road to the unconscious activities of speech. By reversing the processes of displacement and sublimation, the unconscious conditions of possibility of the trope can be analysed and its cultural psychogeopathology allayed, and even an alternative, or oppositional, means of meaning-making created, or at least intimated.

In Abraham's psychoanalytic terms, the love of observing nature in *Kings*, such as is exemplified in bird watching, would be seen as the sublimation of repressed desires for oral satisfaction. He suggests that:

> [...] the displacement of the infantile pleasure in sucking to the intellectual sphere is of great practical significance. Curiosity and the pleasure in observing receive important reinforcements from this source, and this not only in childhood, but also during the subject's whole life. In persons with a special inclination for observing Nature, and for many branches of scientific investigation, psychoanalysis shows a close connection between those impulses and repressed oral desires. (Abraham 1966b: 162–163)

Observing masters objects at a distance and reduces them to passivity, whereas oral satisfaction, unlike oral sadism, entails immediacy and generosity between self and other. Indeed, for Abraham,

> [...] the act of sucking is one of incorporation, but one which does not put an end to the existence of the object. The child is not yet able to distinguish between its own self and the external object. There is yet no differentiation made between the sucking child and the suckling breast. (1965: 450)

Abraham distinguishes the earlier orally satisfying stage of the overall oral phase from the later orally sadistic stage in which 'the individual incorporates the object and so destroys it' (1965: 451). The reciprocal and mutual relationship between self and other has been taken over and superseded by the masterly and sadistic distinction between subject and object. These processes can be seen to operate in pastoralism that separates itself from the external object of the land, incorporates it orally by sheep and cattle grazing on it, and so generally destroys it. By and large, pastoralism does not operate in an environmentally sustainable way.

Pastoralism separates itself off from the land in *Kings* and sets up a sadistic subject-object relationship with it. Visual observation is dominant over oral satisfaction, the eyes over the mouth, the sense of sight over the sense of taste. Some early settlers demonstrated 'a taste for the land' (Durack 1966: 207), but they are considered naive to do so and the infantile, orally fixated cattle 'nuzzled and sucked' (Durack 1966: 248), like breast-feeding babies, slimy water when nothing else was available. But what else could be expected of 'dumb animals'?! The Duracks, though, distinguish themselves from the other early settlers, and from cattle of course, by ostensibly eschewing such infantile oral pleasures and avowing adult visual pleasures.

Kings abounds in references to watching, observing, inspecting, surveying, taking 'a bird's eye view' (Durack 1966: 243), not as an identification, or even empathy with the bird, but as an appropriation of the bird's point of view in order to 'look down' (Durack 1966: 227) on and master the land from above. These sublimations of the oral into the visual mark a shift from oral-sadism to anal-sadism, from the fear of being eaten by (the) mother (earth), to what Abraham calls 'the subject's pleasure in looking at his [sic] own possessions' (1966a: 180). It also marks a shift from the realm of the mother to that of the father, from the left-hand to the right-hand paradigm of Figure 2, Chapter 1.

The inspection of the land in *Kings* often has patriarchal romantic and reproductive connotations when, for example, 'the Kimberley district looked promising [...] but [...] there was a tendency with surveyor-explorers to fall in love on sight with country they discovered if it was in any way fertile' (Durack 1966: 207). The reproductive metaphor is carried through into references to 'vast open plains heavy with pasture' (Durack 1966: 208), like the patriarchal stereotype of a woman 'heavy with child', though early reports of the land's 'fertility and abundance' had deceived many naive early settlers for 'this was after all a hard land [...] a remote and lonely land of long, dry winters and wet tropical summers' (Durack 1966: 229). The bad, hard land is figured as a kind of dried-up spinster aunt, rather than as fecund mother earth.[9] However, the Durack pastoralist empire on both sides of the Ord was 'a vast fertile tract of river frontage' (Durack 1966: 356). The Duracks may have only been 'kings in grass castles', but they were kings of the king of Kimberley watercourses. There is more than a modicum of sadism implicitly exercized here against those who were less fortunate and well-off than the Duracks.

The pastoral conquest of the country is not only seen in sadistic terms, but also in masculinist sexual terms, as 'the opening up of new and untried country' (Durack 1966: 355) with its 'virgin pastures' (Durack 1966: 20) when 'Stumpy' Durack 'surveys the lay of the land'

(Durack 1966: 222): 'far below stretched the golden Kimberley savannah lands, cut through by green ribbons of timbered gullies and creeks' (Durack 1966: 225). The settler view of the land as 'virgin' territory ready for deflowering by phallic heroes is a cliché of explorer's journals (see Strang 1997: 25–126). The good, soft land is figured, and fantasized, as a passively supine female body laid open to, and decorated for, the penetrating gaze of the epic hero as it was for the romantic poet William Wordsworth. To cap it off, inevitably there is the obligatory reference to the 'whiteman's penetration in this lonely land' (Durack 1966: 227; see also 103), with its obvious overtones of rape.

The desire to taste and ingest Mother Earth is literally one that it is quickly repressed in western childhood, and this desire and its repression is merely symptomatic of a larger desire to know her intimately, to feed on her as one fed on the breast of one's mother or its substitute. This desire is displaced and sublimated into the love of looking, or scopophilia, with the emphasis shifting from immediacy to distance, from the sense of taste to that of sight, from reciprocity to sadism. The naturalist's desire to observe (and to identify and classify, and so to master) is then as equally masculine and sadistic as the pastoralist's desire to possess (and to own as a king of the king of Kimberley watercourses and to rule albeit from 'grass castles').

This repression of oral desire is borne out by the fact that streams in the Kimberley are contrasted between 'expanses of dry bed [which] alternated with deep green reaches where waters were held between high banks, creviced by centuries of wind and water, luxuriant with trees, creepers and trailing palms' (Durack 1966: 220). The narrow, deep-throated, orally-sadistic gorge rivers and the old, dry dug/bed of the bad breast contrasts with the deep and wide expanse of the good breast, the Ord River; 'twenty chain width of water reaching out of sight' (Durack 1966: 226), graphically illustrated in the photograph of Plate XXXVIII of the hardback edition (only) of *Kings in Grass Castles*.

The land by the Ord River is the land flowing with milk and honey, the land where, in Abraham's terms, the orally fixated or dissatisfied 'expect the mother's breast to flow for them eternally' (1966b: 157) and so obtain oral satisfaction. Queensland rivers and the other Kimberley rivers continually frustrated this expectation. The promised land of riverine water feeding lush pasture that, in turns, feeds cattle is where the good breast of Mother Earth flows eternally. The pastoralist discourse wins out over the discourses of romanticism and naturalism, the male/masculine over the female/feminine. Such is the completeness of this victory here that *Sons in the Saddle*, the sequel to *Kings*, has hardly a trace of the discourses of romanticism and naturalism.

The course of the other, non-Ord streams in the Kimberley is generally marked as tortuous. The Durack River is no exception in *Kings*: 'the river swung north, south and west on a tortuous route through plain and range, cutting through dense pandanus thickets and tattered cadjibuts, cascading over rocky falls and into still reaches of pale blue lotus where jabiru and ibis preened and fished' (Durack 1966: 221). The still reaches of placid and feeding maternity are contrasted with the sadistic knifing of the river cruelly twisting through gorges.

Rather than the gorges, Durack's great-uncle and his expedition were 'cheered [but not overjoyed] by the sight of open plains and abundant grasses – a wonderland of pasture and fine trees' with its 'even spread of golden grass' giving the impression of 'park land, artistically planned, a reserve of wild life [...] an artist's paradise of scenery in the grand manner (1966: 220–221). The romantic's appreciation for a picturesque, English-style gentleman's parklandscape competes with, and here triumphs temporarily over, the cattleman's eye for good pasture; the pastoral wins out momentarily over the pastoralist.

The land itself, though, is generally reduced to the site of a quest, specifically an interior quest in two senses: a quest for 'manhood'; and a quest for the Ord River. Both quests are undertaken by journeying into 'the Kimberley hinterland' (Durack 1966: 86; also 'the lonely hinterland' [Durack 1966: 307]) beginning at 'the mouth of the Ord River' (Durack 1966: 217–219) [10], or at what was supposed was its 'mouth', and proceeding inside it only to find other, orally sadistic rivers instead, as well as 'impenetrable gorges' (Durack 1966: 301). It seems as if, despite the colonisation of 'vast tracts' of the surface of Mother Earth, especially of the good breast of the Ord River and despite his desire to penetrate further, the 'whiteman's penetration in this lonely land' was only into the mouth of the Ord and not down its throat. This double quest involves the obligatory descent into the underworld as part of the epic hero's journey through which he must negotiate his way successfully in order to achieve 'manhood' and the goal of his quest.

Psychodynamically, the underworld into which the epic hero descends is the female body (in general) and female sexuality (in particular) both figured in terms of bodies of water. This journey into the interior, or hinterland, of Mother Earth via her mouth is a regal, oral insemination by the king pastoralists of 'the queen of Australian rivers' (Durack 1966: 209) out of which union a patrilineal pastoral empire is born. The patriarch was later able to boast about '"this country that I brought to life"' (Durack 1966: 274). The patriarch views the creation of new life as a parthenogenesis that typically overlooks the role of (the) mother (earth) and the labour of women (in a number of senses) in reproducing life. One of the ways in which *Kings* is a boys' own story is that women, especially Aboriginal women, and their labour, are largely absent from it.[11]

The attainment of the object of the quest is repeatedly deferred by not finding the right mouth to begin with. In fact, the epic hero was not even in the area known as the 'false mouths' of the Ord on the east side of Cambridge Gulf. The epic hero has an inverted notion of female anatomy and a strange concept of sexual reproduction because he confuses the vagina with the mouth. No doubt this inversion and confusion revolves around the *vagina dentate*, and no doubt this is related to seeing the tortuous gorges as orally sadistic.

The oral-sadistic fear of symmetry and reciprocity being exercized back by the mother against the self produces the fear that the mother's vagina/uterus, which gave life, and the mother's mouth, which must give pleasure to her like the infant's, gives pleasure to it by taking sustenance, will coalesce into the *vagina dentate*, which would take life and pleasure back from the infant, or the infantile epic hero. This fear gives rise to the desire for oral penetration and insemination such is both the extent, and distance, to which the orally dissatisfied displace sexuality and the kind of pre-emptive 'I'll do you before you do me' *modus operandi* employed by them. This displacement of sexuality to the oral even has narcissistic and incestuous overtones when one of the river mouths entered in *Kings* turns out mistakenly to be the Durack, but this River 'too was not the Ord' (Durack 1966: 222). The Durack is constituted as not being the Ord, a very serious liability indeed and the ultimate binary opposition in Durack's taxonomy of waters (see Figure 4).

Finally, in *Kings*, 'a river [...] gave every promise of being the Ord at last' (Durack 1966: 222–223). The phallic pastoralists fantasize that they are 'on a promise'. The promise is fulfilled, for this is the 'Promised Land,' the title of Durack's twenty-first chapter and the fulfilment of Patsy's vision that 'the Kimberley district looked promising' (1966: 207). This district is the land flowing with milk and honey; the good breast of mother earth, from which the questing pastoralist looking for (a) good feed for his cattle can receive oral satisfaction, unlike the orally sadistic tortuous gorge rivers/*vagina dentata* which threaten to eat him up, and the dry beds/dugs of the bad breast from which he can get no satisfaction.

In this quest, the pastoralist's view of the country ultimately wins out over the romantic's and the naturalist's, the sadistic over the satisfying, the anal over the oral, the masculine over the maternal (though all the former and all the latter terms are not synonymous as I have already suggested). In finding the Ord River, 'here was the pioneer landseeker's [not the romantic's nor the naturalist's] dream-come-true' (Durack 1966: 226); a wet dream in a number of senses. In contrast with Dorothea MacKellar's 'land of droughts and flooding rains', the Ord River country is 'this new promised land of neither drought nor flood' (Durack 1966: 232).

The attainment of the object of the quest marks a further shift from the oral satisfaction (of lush pastures), through the oral sadism (of the gorge rivers; the oral desires repressed by repugnance for lush pastures in the wet season and displaced into observation; the oral dissatisfaction of the dry bed), through the anal sadism of the love of looking into the anal sadism of ownership and possession. For Abraham, 'an inordinate desire to possess [...] belong[s] to the clinical phenomena of the anal character [...] built up on the ruins of an oral erotism whose development has miscarried' (1966b: 156). This development has miscarried (an entirely appropriate metaphor) because the object of desire (lush pasture) is found (in the wet-season) to be fascinating and repugnant, whereas previously (in the dry season) the object of desire was satisfying.

Durack writes in *Kings* about how her grandfather read about the Kimberley and thought that this was 'the country he most desired – a land of splendid rivers, fine pastures and reliable rainfall' (1966: 207), and she later quotes with approval how her great-uncle found "'the country everything that could be desired, suitable for all kinds of stock'" (1966: 226). The desirability of the country is equated with, and reduced to, its suitability for stock. This desire finds satisfaction in what Abraham calls 'the pleasure in acquiring desired objects' (a bigger station on the accessible, permanent Ord River), rather than 'the pleasure in holding fast to existing possessions' (1966b: 157) (a smaller station in Queensland near disappearing, temporary rivers). Patriarch Patsy says of the Ord River country "'it's not a property [...] it's a Principality'" (Durack 1966: 232) with its king and queen (though Grandmother Mary Durack, the author's namesake, does not rate much of a mention), princes and princesses (including 'the author' [see the photograph facing p. 209], a princess of the principality and of princessly prose).

In 'marked contrast' to the evanescent, temporary rivers of Queensland, the Ord River was 'the land of permanent water, regular rainfall and abundant pasture' (Durack 1966: 233). Ironically, by a cruel twist of fate (or perhaps poetic justice), Argyle Downs Station is now even more so than ever 'a land of permanent water' as it lies beneath the waters of the artificial Lake Argyle; Argyle Downs Station is no longer temporarily 'an inland sea' (Durack 1966: 252) during floods, but permanently beneath one. Perhaps the ultimate irony (or eponymous poetic justice) is that Kimberley Durack seems to have been one of the first to propose the scheme of damming the Ord (Durack 1966: 400). In later life Mary Durack appears to have had second thoughts about the damming, though, and to have become ambivalent about it to the point of penning a poem entitled 'Lament for the Drowned Country' (1986: 65–68).

'A Loving Oneness of People and Earth'

The politics of Durack's views about Kimberley rivers and wetlands can be contrasted with those in the work of two other Western Australian writers: Randolph Stow's novel *To The Islands*, first published in 1958, the year before *Kings*, and the novel *Long Live Sandawara* by 'Colin Johnson' (now Mudrooroo), first published in 1979, twenty years after *Kings*. Unlike *Kings*, which involves a quest for the promised pastoral land, *To The Islands* centres around the desire for a quiet death. On his journey from the interior to the exterior, Stephen Heriot, the dying missionary, encounters 'a clear pool with a few lilies' (Stow 1962: 170). At first he is concerned, like Durack, to identify the species of waterbirds there. He then sees the pool and its waterbirds in romanticized terms with an eye, like Durack, for the aesthetic forms of dance:

> 'Look at the birds', Heriot said. 'Brolgas'. He pointed to where, not far from them, a great flock of grey-blue birds was gathered, and three or four of them were dancing, measured and graceful, with a flowing interplay of wide wing and thin leg. 'They're happy', said Heriot. (Stow 1962: 170)

Unlike Durack though, Heriot anthropomorphizes the waterbirds in glowing, romantic terms, rather than seeing the wetlandscape in sadistic, psychogeopathological ones.

Moving closer to the pool, Heriot observes more with the eye of the amateur ornithologist and aesthetic naturalist the antics of the waterbirds:

> They came to the edge of the pool, and with a great splash and a clap of wings the ducks fled from their coming, and circled above, and above the disturbed waterhole, brown ducks and black ones, and the small delicate teal in a high outcry of whistling. (Stow 1962: 171)

Heriot's observation of nature is, like that in Durack's book (and in Wordsworth's *Guide*), a sublimation of oral desire. This sublimation can be seen in the contrast between Heriot's romanticized natural aesthetic and the attitude of his Aboriginal companion, Justin, who sees the pool both as source of food and object of love. After Justin shoots a goose – an act which initially appals Heriot – he remarks that, "'you love the things you kill, but you never regret killing them'" (Stow 1962: 172), whereas white people kill the things they love and regret doing so.

The difference between the oral-sadistic fear of being eaten by the land, along with the anal-sadistic desire to possess the land in *Kings* and the oral desire in *To the Islands* to use and love the wetland, is characteristic of what Abraham calls:

> [...] the differences in the inclination to share one's possessions with others. Generosity is frequently found as an oral-character trait. In this the orally gratified person is identifying himself [and presumably herself as well] with the bounteous mother. (1996b: 161)

Unlike the anal sadistic craving for, and the oral-sadistic fear of, fairness and symmetry, the orally satisfied values mutual reciprocity and generosity.[12] This conclusion may smack of romanticized 'noble savagery' when it is applied to Justin and indigenes more generally, but it certainly is indicative of a different kind of relationship, oral and otherwise, with the Western Australian (wet)landscape than that enacted in *Kings*, and may be indicative of a broader cultural difference in ways of living in the natural environment, of a different corporeal politics.

These differences come out strongly in *Long Live Sandawara* in which Noorak describes how:

> [...] his first ancestors passed across this land, leaving it intact but known. Each tree, each bush, each animal, the waterholes and soaks were named and formed into a loving oneness of people and earth. No one raped and no one pillaged; love formed the bond and the Law held firm each and every particle until [...] – (Mudrooroo 1979: 70)

– the unmentionable and unthinkable happened. The white man came, the invaders (Mudrooroo 1979: 75), with their cattle 'like an army', the invading infantry of the cavalry cattlemen, which bawl like children and pollute the waterholes (Mudrooroo 1979: 76), killing living water. Wetlands, for Aboriginal people, however, are bonded into a loving unity between them and the earth, not mythologized into beautiful billabongs, nor psychgeopathologized into useless swamps, nor sublimated into wheeling waterbirds, nor polluted by trampling cattle into slimy bogs or sloughs.

Nor later in the novel are gorge rivers orally sadistic – quite the contrary:

> [...] the Lennard river has churned [not bitten] the wild Wandjina gorge right through the Napier range. In the wet season, the Wandjina spirits send floods to pour in torrents

between the cliff faces. In the dry season, the water retreats into the sky and the deep Wandjina pool lies peacefully between the steep limestone breasts of the mountain range. (Mudrooroo 1979: 112)

The loving, nourishing and orally satisfying oneness of Aboriginal people, with their bountiful gorge rivers, waterholes and soaks is worlds away, and cultures apart, both from the aestheticisations, observations and orally sublimated distantiations of romantic naturalism, with its beautiful billabongs and sublime waterbirds, and from the cruel, lonely and orally dissatisfied mastery of sadistic pastoralism, with its slimy bogs or sloughs, useless swamps, tortuous gorge rivers and plentiful plains rivers, such as the Ord River, where the Duracks were once kings in their grass castles of the king of Kimberley watercourses.

Notes

1. State Library Service of Western Australia cataloguing data.
2. I discus the 'horror of the slimy' and its relation to the sublime in Giblett (1996: especially Chapter 2).
3. I discuss the cross-cultural colour-coding of water in Giblett (2009: Chapter 11).
4. For Edmund Burke (1958: 114), the beautiful has, or is associated with, a smooth and polished surface.
5. I discuss the uncanny as the obverse of the sublime in Giblett (1996: Chapter 2).
6. And described in his essay on the uncanny. See Giblett (1996: Chapter 2).
7. Kant (1952: 90) associated the formless with the sublime.
8. I discuss Freud's theory of symptom in relation to cities and wetlands in Giblett (1996: especially Chapter 3).
9. For further discussion, see Giblett (1996).
10. I discuss the mistaken view of anatomy that places the 'mouth' of a river at what is in fact the opposite end of the alimentary canal or digestive tract in Giblett (2008a: Chapter 11; and 2009: Chapter 11).
11. Aboriginal women in the Kununurra area in the 1990s still complained about the harsh treatment they received as domestic slaves at the hands of the Duracks (Hugh Webb, personal communication).
12. For lack of 'balanced reciprocity' in pastoralist use of Aboriginal Country, see Strang (1997: 113).

Part VI

Land Symbiotics

Opposed to the discourses of nature and resisting their hegemony were (and are) the politics and practices of environmentalism and earthly mutuality, bioregionalism and sustainability, sacrality and symbiosis exemplified today in Australian Aboriginal Country. Here, there is no landscape to be culturally constructed or greedily consumed, no discourse to produce an object and a subject, but a loving union of people and place, culture and country. Aboriginal Country is not a construction, so it cannot be deconstructed. It is not a discourse, an institutionalized way of seeing, saying and doing, but a symbiosis, an intimate and intuitive way of being. Aboriginal Country is outside history (white chronological history); it is (in) prehistory, it is (in) the Dreaming; it is not in the past, but in the past, present and future, the now, the 'nowtime'. It precedes and refuses the colonisation of time. It is what could be called a 'natural cultural landscape' to oppose the 'cultured natural landscapes' of the gentleman's park and enclave estate, national park, wilderness, mining, pastoralism, the bush, and the city.

Aboriginal Country is a cultural landscape in the sense that it is land made with human hands, though it is also made by ancestral beings. It is a human landscape, not an inhuman one. It is not a natural landscape in the sense that it is not made with human hands; a *terra nullius*. It is not a landscape in the sense that it is only the surface of the land, as it is also the depths. The Aboriginal person, according to Galarrwuy Yunupingu, 'treats that land as not only the surface, it is the very bone of the land' (cited by Mulligan and Hill 2001: 241). It is not a landscape in the sense that it is only the dryland, as it is also the land under the water, the wetland, the seabed and riverbeds, the rivers and seas. It is a cultural landscape in the sense that it is the land on which Australian cities and towns were built. Aboriginal Country runs up against the limits of white terminology. A cultural landscape that is not a cultural construction seems like a contradiction in terms, an evident impossibility, whereas it is a manifest reality.

Running up against the limits of terminology and negotiating the bounds of categories is one way to engage in dialogue over cultural difference in terms other than cultural apartheid. Rather than a binary opposition between black and white, political solidarity has been forged, and is maintained between, activists for Aboriginal land rights, social justice and earthly mutuality. Rather than a binary opposition between black and white, political opposition to patriarchal industrial capitalism cuts across the colonial and neo-colonial category of 'race'. Rather than setting up or perpetuating a binary opposition between black and white, *People and Places of Nature and Culture* supports that political opposition and solidarity – and takes that side in the struggle for Aboriginal land rights, social justice and earthly mutuality.

People and Places of Nature and Culture concludes with a call for a land symbiotics that acknowledges the ways in which we human beings are dependent on the ecosphere, and that changes for the better the ways we impact on it and inter-relate with it. The final chapter draws on Raymond Williams' work on ecology and on his concept of livelihood, neglected in both cultural studies and environmental studies. It also draws critically on the American idea of bioregion. It then turns to the concept of symbiosis, both Lynn Margulis' concept of biological symbiosis and Margaret Mahler's and Jessica Benjamin's concept of psychological symbiosis. It goes on to argue for bio- and psycho-symbiosis in a local place and global space – the earth household of the ecosphere. Rather than consuming the earth as dead matter, all human beings need to live with the earth as living being. The very final section of *People and Places of Nature and Culture* is devoted to celebrating the living earth.

Chapter 11

'We are the Land Ourselves'[1]: Aboriginal Country is a Cultural Landscape

The Australian landscape was crucial for the formation of Australian nationalism, and Anglo-Celtic Australian culture more generally, and still is for its maintenance. Australia sought its national identity in, and even against, the bush. The bush forms the backdrop for, and even figures as a character in, nationalist novels and films, as we saw in a previous chapter. Contemporary Anglo-Celtic Australian culture continues to turn to the landscape as a source of meaning and as a site ripe for semiotic exploitation.

Yet Roslynn Haynes has argued that the emphasis over the past century has shifted from the bush to the desert as 'the nation's most widely publicized landscape' (1998: 87). It is also now corporate capitalism's most widely publicized landscape in Australia. The nation and corporations agree about which Australian landscape should be publicized. Haynes goes on to argue that this shift started to take place a century ago, as 'already by the 1890s the desert had succeeded the bush as the actual frontier' (1998: 144). Celebration of the bush as the frontier was nostalgic even in the 1890s. The bush frontier had been closed and superseded by the desert frontier. The frontier had shifted to the desert, as had the defining landscape of Australian nationalism. By the 1990s the desert had succeeded the bush as the defining landscape of Australian nationalism and the primary site ripe for semiotic exploitation.

The desert has been brought within the semiotic fold but it has not been 'tamed', as recent travellers in it have found to their peril. The 'red centre', or desert, has been used to market everything from four-wheel drive vehicles to a well-known black-coloured soft drink. It is marketed in tourist advertisements and brochures, especially as eco-tourist destinations and experiences. For Haynes, tourism is 'the new above-ground goldmine of the desert' (1998: 263). Or perhaps more precisely, the desert is the new above-ground goldmine for tourism. From the desert, profits come. The bush has been relegated nostalgically to the past as the landscape of nation-formation or federation, whilst the desert has become the contemporary frontier both in space and time, and as the landscape of neo-nationalism and corporate capitalism. The desert is the frontier of the future; the bush is the bygone frontier. The desert is the frontier for agriculture (albeit irrigated), pastoralism and mining.

Country is Culture, Culture is Country

Yet the desert is not only the only 'untamed' land left in Australia according to Anglo-Celtic mythology, but also home for many Aboriginal people. The desert is not an unpeopled landscape – a *terra nullius* – which Anglo-Celts can colonize, capitalize and industrialize heedlessly through irrigated agriculture, pastoralism or mining. Nor is it an empty screen – a *tabula rasa* – onto which they can project willy-nilly their phantasies of technological mastery, touristic leisure or New Age spirituality, or their fears of entrapment in the 'dead heart' of the 'red centre'. It is a peopled landscape, peopled not only by humans but also by non-humans. The desert and the bush are Aboriginal Country. The Australian landscape is thus not a unitary and homogeneous entity nor is it an ahistorical and immutable object. There is no quintessential Australian landscape except in nationalist mythology, but a number of Australian landscapes. They are sites of contestation, not least over the very concept of landscape itself deriving from the European aesthetic tradition.

There are a number of problems with the category of landscape as we have seen. Not least amongst them is that the general category of landscape includes both 'natural' landscapes (supposedly not made with human hands) and 'cultural' landscapes (made with human hands, the signs of which are visible and decipherable). This distinction has flowed through into the distinction between city and country. In modern European culture the city has been regarded as a cultural landscape and the country as a natural landscape. Yet the country is just as much cultural as it is natural, especially when the country is agri-cultural. The city is 'natural' as well as 'cultural' as it is located in a biological region, and its residents depend on air, water and food supplied largely by that region.

The distinction between cultural and natural landscapes boils down to a question of whose cultural landscape is being talked about? And even down to whose culture is boss? Whose culture gets to decide what is a cultural landscape and what is a natural landscape? The city is the cultural landscape par excellence (see Giblett 2009: Chapter 3). In a two-term system, the country is the natural landscape par excellence, but it is also a cultural landscape.

No doubt the distinction between the country and the city is as old as the city itself and is constitutive of it. Without the country there would be no city. The city needs the country to define itself against; the city defends itself against the country. Yet the distinction between the two becomes marked in and with modernity; indeed, it would not be going too far to suggest that the marked distinction between the two is modernity. Modernity sets up a certain sort of distinction and relationship between the city and the country (the bush or the desert) with the modern city dependent, if not parasitical, on the country, or at least on a certain sort of country – agricultural, pastoral, mining and, ultimately, Aboriginal Country. There is thus no single, homogeneous country but a number of competing countries with agricultural, pastoral and mining country (or the bush and the desert) mapped, and inscribed in some places, over Aboriginal Country. These countries have arisen out of different cultural ways. European country is a cultural construction, a way of seeing, saying and doing, a discourse; Aboriginal Country is 'not a construction but a way of being, a way of feeling', as Hugh Webb (1996: 74) puts it.

Before I go on to discuss Aboriginal Country in detail I need to make a caveat and a disclaimer for cultural and political reasons. First, the disclaimer: I am not an Aboriginal person so I cannot and do not speak with cultural authority on this topic. Nor do I speak on behalf of Aboriginal people. I am merely a white fella who is trying to engage in cultural dialogue, to understand as much as I can about Aboriginal culture and country, and to convey that to others. I am trying to avoid the cultural apartheid that would ghettoize Aboriginal culture and country in a unique cultural experience that white people cannot possibly understand. Without dialogue and understanding both sides are doomed to playing out an antagonistic conflict of mutual incomprehensibility. My approach is to assemble a number of statements from key informants and to minimise commentary and interpretation. The aim, as in a previous collection with which I was involved, is 'to allow Aboriginal voices to speak their understandings of Country, which is far more than territory, or landscape' (see Giblett and Webb 1996: 5).

Secondly, the caveat: there is no singular and homogeneous 'Aboriginal Country' nor, on the other hand, is there is a disparate, pluralistic and heterogenous collection of countries with nothing in common. Rather, 'Aboriginal Country' is a common way of being. Within that commonality there is a rich variety of different ways of relating to and understanding country. Two instances will suffice to substantiate this claim. As stated in the film *Exile and the Kingdom*, the Aboriginal people of the Roebourne area of the Pilbara region of Western Australia do not have, or refer to, the Dreaming or 'Dreamtime' (a white cliché about Aboriginal culture), but have and refer to the time and state 'when the world was soft'.

The Aboriginal people of south-western Australia do not have or refer to the 'Rainbow Serpent' supposedly common to all Aboriginal cultures in Australia. Rather, living water for them is embodied in the Waugal. According to Mudrooroo, the Waugal is black and, for him, the idea of a 'Rainbow Serpent' supposedly common to all Australian Aboriginal cultures is an anthropologist's invention (1996a: 33; and 36–37).[2] Within this variety there is a core of commonality around the role and status of Country. It is not an object that can be owned privately, but is a living being that gives and takes life and that should be accorded respect and care. In referring to Aboriginal Country I do so to invoke this commonality. I do not do so to subsume vital variety beneath gross generality, nor to reduce rich difference to bland sameness.

Besides agricultural, pastoral and mining country in Australia, besides the bush and the desert, there is this other country – Aboriginal Country. Or more precisely, Australia is Aboriginal Country. It is this country first and foremost before it became in places, and while it still remains in places, agricultural, pastoral, mining and urban country. Aboriginal Country is the country of the culture that has, in the words of Jennifer Sabbioni, 'the longest continuous cultural history in the world' (1998: xx) and the country of 'the first environmentalists in the world' (1998: xxi). Using Emmanuel Levinas's terms, Aboriginal Country is what Deborah Rose defines simply and eloquently as 'a nourishing terrain' (Rose 1996). The terrain nourishes Aboriginal people, other inhabitants and itself.

As a nourishing terrain, Aboriginal Country is not a consuming terrain for orally sadistic agriculture, mining, pastoralism and cities to devour greedily and gluttonously, nor for anally sadistic industrial production and consumption to excrete its wastes into. Aboriginal peoples certainly had an impact on the natural environment, but their cultures and country were sustainable in the very long term, for more than 40,000 years in fact, whereas European culture and Australian country are in serious trouble in less than 250. Rose goes on to elaborate how Aboriginal 'country is a place that gives and receives life: [...] country is a living entity [...] country is home' (1996: 7). On this view the city is not home; the city is unhome. The city is the place of the unhomely, the homeless, the lost souls, the dead. City is necropolis, *polis* is necropolis, the dead landscape, the dead surface of private property as Jacques Derrida (1981: 331) puts it. Agricultural, pastoral, mining and city country are terrains that receive life but they do not give life. Indeed, they take life and give back death. They are not nourishing terrains but deadening wastelands.

Aboriginal Country, by contrast, is not unhome, not uncanny (though it is a womb that gives life, and a tomb that receives the dead and also recreates life), not wilderness. Aboriginal Country not only takes in (and can refer to the same piece of land as) agricultural, pastoral and mining country, but also is what early explorers and settlers and present-day conservationists call 'wilderness'; non-agricultural, non-pastoral, non-mining, non-urban country. Wilderness is what is left over, the remains of the day after the cake of the country is divided up, the spoils left after 'their greed stole our sacred land' in the words of Kevin Gilbert (Sabbioni, Schaffer and Smith 1998: 35).

However, as Deborah Rose puts it bluntly, 'in Australia, there is no wilderness [...] wilderness is actually home' (1988: 384 and 385[3]). Unlike the settler for whom wilderness is not home (as we saw in a previous chapter) and whose God-given task is to carve out a home in the wilds, for Aboriginal peoples home *is* the wilds; it is not *in* the wilds. As Marcia Langton says emphatically, 'there is no wilderness, but there are cultural landscapes' (1998: 18). There are no non-cultural landscapes. A non-cultural landscape is an oxymoron, a contradiction in terms, an evident impossibility. Cultural landscapes are not just urban landscapes, or townscapes. Aboriginal Country is a cultural landscape (see also Low 2002: 45).

Aboriginal Country is not only a cultural landscape and the country outside the city, but also the city, the land or country where the cities and the suburbs now stand, the alien European cultural landscape imposed on the land. Aboriginal Country is the country not only of Aboriginal people who live in the country, but also for those who live in the city and the towns. It is important to recognize that 'even in the absence of physical access to sites, people maintain strong spiritual associations with land, hold the same responsibilities for that country, and retain detailed information about it' (McKeown 1994: 40). This connection has legal implications as 'the legal system may not be able to recognize the very real experience of land Aboriginal people feel even when in European terms they have not visited it for generations' (McKeown 1994: 41).

Native title as such, and at present, does not recognize this experience as it only recognizes hunting, gathering, fishing and ceremonial activities or 'traditional practices' as valid criteria for the establishment of native title. Yet the entire country (dryland as well as wetlands, rivers and seas – the land under the water as we shall see) was, and still is, Aboriginal Country that precedes and refuses the modern European distinction between the city and the country, culture and nature, cultural and natural landscapes. Australian cities and suburbs were

'We are the Land Ourselves': Aboriginal Country is a Cultural Landscape

built on Aboriginal Country; not only Aboriginal in the sense that the land was owned and worked by Aboriginal peoples, but also the original land itself.

Aboriginal people are thus often not only in contestation over agricultural, pastoral and mining country, but also over European conceptions of land as landscape and over the philosophy of land and property. For Mick Dodson, 'culture transforms land and environment into landscape, and into "country" [...] Culture is what enables us to conceive of land and environment in terms that are different to conventional European notions [...] "landscape" and "environment" are human constructs' (cited by Langton 1998: 7). Conventional European notions conceive of landscape and environment as nature and not as human constructs, not as culture. Yet the concept of nature denies, represses and occludes precisely the ways in which landscape and environment are human constructs, are cultural. All of Australia is Aboriginal Country but parts of it, such as agricultural, pastoral and mining country and the cities and the suburbs, are also European landscapes laid over and constructed on top of Aboriginal Country. The crucial distinction is not between culture and nature, nor between city and country, but between the cultures of first, or worked, nature and second, or worked-over, even third, overworked, nature as discussed in Chapter 1.

This distinction comes out strongly when considering land and water, dryland and wetland. For Aboriginal people there is not one law for the land and another for the sea. Nor is there strictly a law for land and sea, but land and sea are part of the same law. As Deborah Rose points out, 'land and sea are all part of the same law' (1996: 13). There is not the law of the sea separate and distinct from law of the land. For Ginytjirrang Mala, 'land rights stop, under your law, where the sea meet up with the land', whereas Aboriginal Country is 'our land and sea country' (cited by Rose 1996: 13). Aboriginal Country is not only dryland, but also wetland, the land under the water. Hugh Webb describes how, 'on reading the Seaman Report [*The Aboriginal Land Inquiry*], one senses a strong element of surprise that, as part of the Inquiry about "Land", Aboriginal spokespeople emphasized the importance of "Water"' (1996: 67). 'Land rights' are also water rights; land without water is dead land. 'Native Title' is just as much about title to sea, river and wetlands as it is to drylands. As Mick Dodson puts it succinctly, 'Native title is not just in relation to land' (in McKeown 1994: 43). As part of his Ten Point Wik Plan to amend Native Title legislation, the former Prime Minister, John Howard, deliberately excluded water from native title and ceded title to it back to the States. This was a cruel and telling blow to reconciliation.

Aboriginal Country is not a landscape for, as Rose puts it, '"landscape" signals a distance between the place, feature or monument and the person or society which considers its existence' (1996: 10). Writing of Aboriginal poetry Mudrooroo argues that:

> [...] the primordial split between man [sic] and nature as found in European poetry [and elsewhere in European culture for that matter] and which is a referent [sic] to the dualism implicit in European thought, is absent [...] The Aborigine is placed firmly in the landscape, or on the landscape, and buildings and cities are intrusive elements into a pristine oneness, the loss of which is regretted. (1990: 100)

Built heritage is colonial history, the inscription of the history of the colonisation of Aboriginal peoples and their lands on the land itself. Mudrooroo thus refers to the 'smudge of putrefaction termed Perth' (1996b: 147), the capital city of Western Australia and the foundation settlement in the colony.⁴ Colonial art records and reproduces colonial history, and the colonisation of the land.

For Aboriginal peoples, history and art are not separate. Galarrwuy Yunupingu referred to 'the land as art' (cited by Mudrooroo 1995: 206). Unlike the European landscape aesthetic, Kay Schaffer and Sidonie Smith argue that for Aboriginal people 'landscape is not merely an "object" for representation but a space in which art, spirituality, nature, and land ultimately interconnect' (Sabbioni 1998: xlv). As Hugh Webb puts it:

> [...] there is no emotional or intellectual need to stand *outside of* the land (wet or dry) to see it as something to be regarded aesthetically, something to be developed, something to be tamed. For lands are the sites – in some senses the 'meanings' – of very important cultural stories. (Giblett and Webb 1996: 5)

For Sally Morgan writing in *My Place*, 'the swamp behind our place had become an important place for me. It was now part of me, part of what I was as a person' (1996: 105).

Culture and country are not distinct as culture is traced in and on the country rather than written in the city. The city writes on the earth, not with mutual benefit to the country, but monumentally and parasitically to the exclusive benefit of the city. Mudrooroo describes how 'once we inscribed ourselves on our bodies, on our land; now we were inscribed into books, made the subject of a discourse' (1995: v). Or perhaps more precisely, made the *object* of a discourse whose subject was the explorer, settler, administrator, anthropologist, etc, and not Aboriginal people. They were not the subjects of the discourse about them. Colonial writing on Aborigines, literally on their bodies (whips, chains, diseases, flour, etc.) and metaphorically on paper in books (anthropology, letters, journals, etc.), attempted to inscribe European law on them as it had been inscribed on their land in survey lines, railway lines, telegraph lines and the lots and streets of the grid-plan town.

Aboriginal writing took place on their own bodies (paint, cicatrices, etc.) and on the land (song and story lines), and not on paper with pens using an alphabet (and so was not considered to be proper writing). For David Mowaljarlai, 'these stories are not written down, but they are written on the land, into nature [...] they are there for everyone to see – not just to read about [...] everything is written into the country' (1993: 82 and 194). Song lines and story lines are written *into* the country not *onto* it like the lines of the grid-plan settler's town, the railway line and the telegraph line, the 'singing line' that colonized 'songlines' (see Thomson 1999; Giblett 1996: Chapter 3; 2008b: Chapters 2 and 3).

Aboriginal people certainly made their mark on country, but only in performing ceremonies such as dancing, singing or storytelling or in hunting or gathering food. Galarrwuy Yunupingu relates how, when he was 16 years old, he went fishing with his Dad:

'We are the Land Ourselves': Aboriginal Country is a Cultural Landscape

As I walked along behind I was dragging my spear on the beach which was leaving a long line behind me. He told me to stop doing that. He continued telling me that that if I made a mark, or dig, with no reason at all, I've been hurting the bones of the traditional people of that land. We must only dig and mark marks on the ground then we perform or gather food. (cited by Mulligan and Hill 2001: 224)

Aboriginal writing on the land (and on the body) did not take place on a separate object of private property. Rather than land belonging to people, Mudrooroo states that 'indigenous people [...] belong to the earth' (1995: 4), and that 'indigenous' 'simply means originating in or from a country' (1995: 7). Rather than 'indigenous people', Aboriginal people have recently opted for this term to refer to themselves. The earth does not belong to Aboriginal people; there is no private property but there is ownership or 'native title'. Mudrooroo goes on to argue that 'land to us Aborigines is not a possession in material terms, as the white man looks upon the land, but a responsibility held in sacred trust. "We do not say the land belongs to us, but we belong to the land"' (1995: 200), and 'we are part of it' (1995: 202). 'Country' is a key term of Aboriginal English, now used, as Jay Arthur points out, 'all over Aboriginal Australia to name the place where a person belongs' (cited by Bonyhady and Griffiths 2002: 3).

By referring to a place belonging to a person or group of Aboriginal people, the concept of 'native title' is thus a crude and cruel cultural travesty of the relationship between Aboriginal people and ('their') land, or perhaps more precisely between the land and its people. An anthropologist writing half a century ago in a chapter called 'The Land and the Aborigines' got closer (though it took him three editions to do so): 'from one point of view, the members who belong to the local group by birth, own their subdivision of the tribal territory. But it is truer to say that the country owns them and that they cannot remain away from it indefinitely and still live' (Elkin 1954: 47). In the words of Aboriginal poet W. Les Russell, 'I am this Land and it is mine' (Gilbert 1988: 3).

This intimate relationship between people and land is related to an intimate relationship between people, land and language. Aboriginal languages of Australia were not imposed onto an alien landscape; they did not objectify the land; they were not a discourse, an institutionalized way of seeing, saying and doing, that produced an object (the land, landscape) and a position for a subject (property-owner, unlike the *polis*, or an artist or poet as in European landscape aesthetics of the sublime, the picturesque [the pleasing prospect of the gentleman's park estate] and the beautiful). Rather, as Mudrooroo puts it, Aboriginal languages were 'developed in the environments of Australia to give it a voice and to sing its praises' (1995: 65). They also brought the land to life. For instance, the Yolgnu people of northern Australia 'continue to sing the world into existence as an everyday activity' (Watson 1989: 6). Singing the land and signing the land is different from singing the line (railway and telegraph) and signing the line (alphabetic writing). The languages gave the land a voice and life that it did not have before, though it was not dead or meaningless.

These languages spoke the land but the land was not meaningless before this as there were, as Mudrooroo puts it, 'signs [...] to be found in the environment' (1995: 95). In the words of two anthropologists (though it took them a revised edition to get to it) and in a chapter entitled 'Relationship with the Land', 'all the land was (and is) full of signs' (Berndt 1981: 137). The land is composed of 'found objects' or signs that are not disconnected from their 'referents'. Rather than a sign representing an object (as in European rationalist languages), an object is its sign; instead of living in capitalist modernity where signs are disconnected from their object, signs are their objects. Anthropologist Nancy Williams argues that:

> Aboriginal people regard the environment as sentient and as communicating with them [...] Distinguishing 'natural' from 'cultural' or 'social' in conceptualising the environment, and indeed defining environmental resources, becomes problematic in understanding Aboriginal perceptions. Each individual's identity is based on relationships to particular land (and sea [...])'. (cited by Langton 1998: 27) [5]

Instead of a sign, like marks on a map referring to land, the land is a map. If the land is a map, why would one ever want or need a map of it? Or want or need to map it? And as the land *is* a map, it can never lay at ones feet *like* a map as it did for explorers. As Herb Wharton puts it, 'the land was charted, mapped and known' (Sabbioni, Schaffer and Smith 1998: 99) through song and story, so why would anybody want to survey it by theodolite and map it by cartography? Or how could anyone liken it to a map? As David Mowaljarlai puts it, 'everything under Creation is represented in the soil and in the stars' (1993: 5). Indeed, the stars are mapped in the soil, or in the rock. This mapping is shown graphically in the film *Exile and the Kingdom* where the stars are represented in markings on rock. The land is a map of the cosmos, of space and time, the earth a map of the heavens, and vice versa. Why would one ever want or need to draw a map of the stars when they are already mapped in the land and vice versa?

Rather than being bereft of meaning or replete with money – with shares and sales, investments and profits – for Aboriginal people, as Mudrooroo puts it, 'the land is dense with meaning – with song and story' (1995: 205). Hugh Webb relates how 'story is people, history, belief, spirituality – the whole understandable through lines of story. The story-lines hold the whole cosmology together' (1996: 69). The singing lines of telegraphy held colonialism together and wrote it on the land. Their descendants, the vectors of telecommunications, hold global capitalism together and write it in the ecosphere. Song and story lines write Aboriginal history into the land. As Deborah Rose puts it, 'there is no place without a history; there is no place that has not been imaginatively grasped through song, dance and design, no place where traditional owners cannot see the imprint of sacred creation' (1996: 18). A story by Archie Weller exemplifies this sense of story being read in the sacred creation of a place and how the white walking dead man from the necropolis wrote his secular story over the sacred story of creation (cited by Webb 1996: 64).

Rather than writing their history on the land as the zombies do, Aboriginal peoples find their history already written in the land (so why would they ever want or need to write it down on paper?). A group of Aboriginal people wrote in the 1980s that, 'Aboriginal history is written – in the land around us!' (cited by Mudrooroo 1995: 197), whilst another group wrote similarly in the 1990s that, 'our tribal law is written in the country' (Ieramugadu Group 1995: 18). The land is Aboriginal history writing; the Country, law writing. For Aboriginal peoples, land is not only their history but also family and family land. Consequently, Mudrooroo goes on to argue, 'a feeling for the land' and 'an idea of a community' (1995: 13) are bound together to such an extent that 'our network of kinship was inscribed on the land, on the environment, on the skies' (1995: 20), not on tablets of stone nor on paper in books.

Community or 'kinship' is not just a matter of family, or even human, kinship. As Rose points out, 'the relationship between people and their country' (or perhaps more precisely, between a country and its people) is 'a kinship relationship with 'obligations of [mutual] nurturance' (1996: 49). The terrain nourishes and the terrain must be nourished in order for it to go on nourishing. People and land, humans and non-humans are kin because they descend from common ancestors. Marcia Langton describes how, 'in the Aboriginal cosmology, humans and non-humans are related in special ways, as if they were kin, through their common descent from the ancestral beings' (1998: 14). Aboriginal history is family, is land, and land is family, is history: 'our general philosophy [is that] everything – human beings, animals, plants and inanimate objects including the stars in the sky – is seen as forming one vast universal family', according to Mudrooroo (1995: 23), enduring in time (past, present and future) and extensive in space (here and there). Everything is united in what Rose calls 'the unified field of Dreaming ecology' (1996: 49). Aboriginal people were arguably not only the first environmentalists in the world, but also the first ecologists to theorize the earth-household and practice earth-home economics.

There is no ownership of the land by Aboriginal people but ownership of the people by the land. There was property, but no private property; no *polis*, no *oikos*, but 'a loving oneness of people and earth' as we saw in the previous chapter; an earth-household. There was no 'wilderness' though settlers thought that there was. As Deborah Rose argues:

> [...] the egocentric quality of standard European and American-derived concepts of wilderness [...] all involve the peculiar notion that if one cannot see traces or signs of one's own culture in the land, then the land must be 'natural' or empty of culture [...] Not seeing the signs of ownership and property to which they were accustomed, many settlers assumed there was no ownership and property. (1996: 17)

The irony, though, is that some explorers and settlers did find, or thought that they had found, some signs of their own culture in the land as they found land in Australia that was, or more precisely that they saw as, a gentleman's park (as we saw in a previous chapter).

The Dreaming

The intimacy of people (families), land, story and song, etc, is part of what is meant by the Dreaming. For Jennifer Sabbioni, 'the Dreaming determines the system of values, beliefs, behaviours, and relationships that draw human beings, the natural world, landscape and the spirit world into one interconnected entity' (1998: xxi). Yet this oneness is not an interconnected lifeless entity like a network or a web, but a living organism like, or as, a body. As Mudrooroo puts it, 'the earth is a vast dreaming organism, the environment is a community or family arranged in kinship patterns across her skin' (1995: 54). The earth is not dead, rationalist matter, nor is it a vast deadening machine, nor is the environment background, geographical context, a source of raw materials and industrial commodities. David Tacey relates how:

> [...] in Aboriginal cosmology, landscape is a living field of spirits and metaphysical forces [...] Landscape is mytho-spiritual field [...] For contemporary Western consciousness, landscape is barren, empty, unalive [...] landscape is seen as a dead objective background [...] If the landscape is felt to possess a certain character or mood, then this is said to be created by the perceiving subject and *projected* upon the land [...] Nature is at best a dead background to our human endeavours, at worst a surreal or nightmare projection from our own heads. (1995: 148–150)

Nature and landscape are screens against which Europeans projected fears and phantasies, as we saw in Chapter 3. Psyche and landscape are vertical screens set up against each other, whether it is the vertical landscape of the sublime or the vertical landscape painting of it, or the picturesque landscape (painting or scene). The former projects against the latter and landscape becomes, as Chris Wallace-Crabbe puts it, 'a back formation from art to life' (1992: 160). The tourist tries to find the picturesque scenes that they have seen in paintings and photographs, to experience first-hand and viscerally what they have only hitherto experienced second-hand, visually and virtually. Yet the latter is the template and frame for the former.

Aboriginal people do not construct the land in this way, and do not make this distinction between 'art' and 'life'. Life is art, and art life. As Roslynn Haynes puts it, 'Aborigines look [...] down at the ground as though looking down through it to the powerful spirits dwelling within it [...] European art viewed landscape as a vertical slice' (1998: 89 and 282), even when it is a depiction of horizontal land such as a desert. The desert is the contemporary Australian sublime, or at least what Rudolf Otto called 'the sublime in the horizontal' (cited by Brown 1992: 32; see also Haynes 1998: 4) as distinct from the sublime in the vertical of the mountains and mountainous seas. Both are reproduced in the vertical plane of the picture – the screen – onto which the sublime, the picturesque or the beautiful are projected with all their attendant fears and phantasies.

'We are the Land Ourselves': Aboriginal Country is a Cultural Landscape

In the European landscape tradition, the vertical surface of the painting is set up between the painter and viewer and the horizontal surface of the earth. The European landscape painting mediates the earth. In the Aboriginal cultural tradition, the surface of the earth and the surface of the painter's body are continuous. Aboriginal land painting is immediate to the earth. Aboriginal painters generally paint sitting on the ground with the painting lying on the ground before them. They do not paint standing at an easel with the painting propped up in front of them.[6] Mudrooroo describes how the Papunya painters 'regarded the surface of the earth as a skin similar to their own' (1995: 165). Errol West puts it succinctly: 'feel the earth; you touch my flesh' (Sabbioni, Schaffer and Smith 1998: 115)! To inscribe the surface of one (with settlement, city, farm, mine, whip or chain) was to inscribe the surface of the other. Mudrooroo argues that for Aboriginal peoples, 'life came from and through the land and is manifested in the land. The land is not an inanimate thing: it is alive' (1995: 165).

Interconnection not only embraces the living but also the not living. For Aboriginal peoples, Mudrooroo argues that 'our spirituality is a oneness and an interconnectedness with all that lives and breathes, even with all that does not live or breathe' (1995: 33). Yet perhaps there is nothing that does not live or breathe. Not only is the land alive but also everything is. Rose argues that 'for many Aboriginal people, everything in the world is alive' (1996: 23). Or in David Mowaljarlai's terms, Yorro Yorro is 'everything standing up alive' and 'Yorro Yorro is continual creation and renewal of nature in all its forms' (1993: 133). There is no dead matter. All matter is alive. Death is a part of life. Death and life are interconnected, as are the natural and the spiritual. For Silas Roberts, the first Chairman of the Northern Lands Council, 'our connection to all things natural is spiritual' (cited by Rose 1996: 26).

Spirituality is not divorced from the natural. For Aboriginal people, as Elkin puts it, 'their own territory [...] is the home of their own spirits and the source of life of the natural species on which they depend for sustenance' (1954: 28). Spirituality is not divorced from sustenance and everyday life; people and land are married. The land is a source of food and of spirituality. It is not merely material. For Eddie Kneebone, 'Aboriginal spirituality is the belief that all objects are living and share the same soul or spirit that Aboriginals share. Therefore, all Aborigines have a kinship with the environment' (cited by Mudrooroo 1995: 34–35). Mudrooroo argues later that 'this spirituality is preoccupied with the relationship of the earth, nature and people in the sense that the earth is accepted as a member of our family' (1995: 47). What white Australian family would accept the earth as a member of its family? What white Australian household would regard the earth as a member of its household? For Aboriginal peoples, the earth-household is a member of their family household and vice versa.

The Dreaming has been regarded as the 'Dreamtime' and relegated to the past. Yet the sense of interconnection between people and land not only embraces the living and the non-living, but also the present and the past. Marcia Langton argues that 'the past pervades the present in the Aboriginal domain' (1998: 10). Or as the poet Oodgeroo of the Noonuccal Tribe, puts it:

> The past is still so much a part of us
> Still about us, still within us […]
> Let no one say the past is dead.
> The past is all about us and within us.
>   (Sabbioni, Schaffer and Smith 1998: 22 and 256)

People and land, past and present, the spiritual and material, are intimately connected in the Dreaming. And the future, as Neville Morlumbun puts it: 'the Dreaming was not thought of only in the past, but was a significant part of present and future' (1980: 15). By constituting the land as *terra nullius* or as gentleman's park, explorers and settlers colonized past Aboriginal land practices and colonized the land into the future. Not only was space and the land colonized, but also time, the past and future.

Yet the colonisation of space and time cannot erase the traces of Aboriginal people from the land. For poet Lionel Fogarty in a poem entitled 'Fellow Being':

> The aboriginal is the bread of man's rich land.
> We are the rocks of ages and purpling skies.
> Look at every scenery in bush you will see an aboriginal face,
> Body and spirit.
> We are music […]
>
> An Aboriginal is nature's soil […]
> We are the gods of men in this land […]
> The earth above us is our spirituals […]
> The sea, hills and lakes are in our hearts and minds.
>   (Sabbioni, Schaffer and Smith 1998: 187–188)

The sea, hills and lakes are not out there in the landscape. The land and the people have evolved together. Marcia Langton concludes that 'the intimate relationships and interdependence of Aboriginal people with their non-human domains' has been characterized by Posey as 'co-evolution' (Langton 1998: 75). Co-evolution is mutually beneficial symbiosis, not parasitism.

Land is Body

For Aboriginal people, society and environment are not separate categories, and the individual person and society (and environment) are not separate from each other. Rather, they are united in what Mudrooroo describes as 'the unity of the people with nature and all living creatures and life forms' (1995: 201). Elkin argues that 'the different aspects of Aboriginal life are almost inextricably intertwined' (1954: 48). They can only be extricated to the extent that they can be translated into European terms of people, landscape, past, present, future, material, spiritual, natural, cultural and country. Mudrooroo relates how the Nyungar people of south-western Australia 'saw their society as being arranged like a huge human body' (1995: 23). David Mowaljarlai, in north-western Australia saw Australia as 'Bandaiyan – *Corpus Australis*', with Cape York and Arnhem Land the lungs, Uluru the navel and the Great Australian Bight the 'pubic section' (1993:190). The map of Australia is remapped as a map of the human body.[7] The land is a map of the body; the land is a map not only of the cosmos but also of the corpus. European cartography is deconstructed and decolonized by being corporealized, by being made body.

In Mowaljarlai's map the line from the Gulf of Carpentaria to the Great Australian Bight would be the spine. For Gallarrwuy Yunupingu, 'The land [is] my backbone […] My land is my foundation […] Without land I am nothing' (cited by Sabbioni: xxviii; and Rose 1996: 40). The land is the spinal column on which the body is constructed. As Mudrooroo puts it, 'for the Indigenous person, life and land are intimately connected, and if the land is harmed so is the person' (1995: 126), and so is the family presumably. Land is health, and health land. Mudrooroo goes on to point out that 'over the last two hundred years so much of the land of Australia has suffered, so many of our sacred sites have been desecrated, that the health of Indigenous people is in as bad a way as the land. If the Indigenous people are to regain their health, their countries must regain their health' (ibid.). Yet the concept of 'sacred site' localizes the sacred, whereas 'the whole land was [and is] sacred' (Berndt 1981: 137).

Land health is connected with human health: if one is not healthy, neither is the other. This is not just making a case for environmental health, about keeping the environment healthy in order to keep humans healthy, but keeping 'the collective organism of land and society', as Aldo Leopold put it, healthy. It is not about land-care in a narrow sense but about land health. It is about promoting and communicating land health and not just diagnosing and curing what Leopold called 'land pathology'. Land-care is land and human health. Mudrooroo argues that 'tending and caring for the land is tending and caring for not only humans but all that lives, and when the land is exploited and ruined, so are the humans, the flora and fauna' (1995: 126). Later, he goes on to argue that 'the denial of cultural and spiritual heritage and lack of recognition of relationship to the land are the root cause of loss of identity, loss of health, and subsequent degradation' (Mudrooroo 1995: 197). The solution is simple and unequivocal if non-Aboriginal people just listen to Aboriginal people: 'we want our land back' (McKeown 1994: 126 and 181). The same desire can also be heard if, in the title of a recent exhibition of Aboriginal art (and life), all people 'listen to the land' (Davis 1998: 4–5). The land wants its people back. The land is crying. Aboriginal people want their land back. The people are crying.

Notes

1. (Mowaljarlai 1994: 60).
2. See also Mudrooroo (1994: 2, 141 and 173) on 'Akurra Serpent', 'Rainbow Snake' and 'Wagyal'. The 'Rainbow Serpent' and 'Wagyal' are discussed further in Giblett (1996: 198–201).
3. This article is a much more heartfelt and impassioned expression than her more bureaucratically balanced, but still extremely rich and useful report, *Nourishing Terrains* (Rose 1996).
4. For the early colonial history and landscapes of Perth, see Giblett (1996: 55–76).
5. For Aboriginal Country as 'sentient country', see also Strang (1997: 252–258).
6. An interesting Australian artist in this regard is the expatriate Briton, John Wolseley, who sometimes buries his works so that the land can mark them. See Grishin (1998: especially 125).
7. Bandaiyan is illustrated in Mowaljarlai (1993: 194, more elaborately on 205; and 1992: 183), and reproduced in Giblett (2008a: 190; and 2009: 185).

Chapter 12

Home is Here: Livelihood, Bioregion and Symbiosis

To just plain live on earth and to revalue the meaning and inhabitation of nature, humans need new ways of thinking and acting, new ways of seeing, saying and doing, new ways of being. The three concepts of bioregion, livelihood and symbiosis have figured prominently in recent discussions about the relationship between humans and habitat. A *bioregion* is a geomorphological and biological region – the watershed, the valley, the plain, the wetland, the aquifer, etc. where or on which humans live and work, and which sustains our life. Raymond Williams' concept of *livelihood* implies both our work and our physical surrounds; their environmental supports and effects. *Symbiosis* is both a biological and a psychological term, what could be called bio-symbiosis and psycho-symbiosis. Lynn Margulis used the term to convey biological mutuality as distinct from parasitism. Margaret Mahler applied the term to child-mother relationships covering a continuum from the 'normal' to the psychotic, and for phases of childhood development from union with the mother to separation and individuation. In this chapter I develop a connection between all three by arguing that a bioregion always sustains our livelihood in relationship with the living earth. This relationship is situated on a continuum between mutually beneficial and 'normal' biological and psychological symbiosis and mutuality at one end, and parasitical and psychotic mastery at the other. I conclude the chapter and the book by advocating the former, and calling for mutuality with the living earth.

Livelihood

During the 1980s Raymond Williams, the 'father' of both cultural studies and ecocriticism, developed the concept of 'livelihood' in the essays and books he published in the last years of his life. It is noteworthy, though, that livelihood and ecology drop from view in one of Williams' posthumously published collections, *The Politics of Modernism* (1989a), though not from the other, *Resources of Hope* (1989b). This absence is curious as both terms and topics figured prominently in Williams' work of the 1980s as we shall see below. Equally curious is the fact that he discusses the future of cultural studies and the uses of cultural theory in essays of these titles in *The Politics of Modernism* without mentioning ecology. Surely one of the futures of cultural studies lies in ecology and 'the environment'; surely one of the uses of cultural theory is to apply it to ecological and environmental issues.

Although the contribution of Williams to the formation of cultural studies is acknowledged in the standard histories, even to the point of being seen as one of its 'founding fathers', the ecological and environmental aspects of his work are ignored (see, for example, Turner 1990), whereas he should be acknowledged as one of the 'founding fathers' of ecocriticism as well. Willliams' *The Country and the City* (1973) is the foundational text of ecocriticism. Cultural studies, with the notable exception of Williams and some more recent instances, such as Alexander Wilson, Tom Jagtenberg and David McKie, has suffered just as much from the 'two cultures' divide between the humanities and the sciences and from the culture/nature binary and hierarchy as the sciences. The green Williams is one way of crossing the great divide, deconstructing the binary and decolonising the hierarchies of culture over nature, of science as the master discourse of nature, and of the discourse of technology over the humanities.

In his study of Williams' life and work Fred Inglis only mentions the green Williams once and largely dismisses this aspect of his work in his 'Prologue' when he condescendingly quotes Williams' eldest daughter in passing as claiming him, 'not quite unexpectedly, for green politics, for ecology; for Gaia' (1995: 14). In terms of Williams' work over at least the last sixteen years of his life, it was entirely apposite and appropriate for her to do so as we will see below. The intellectual and political sons (including myself) and the biological daughter struggle over the legacy of the father to claim it for ecology, or socialism, or cultural studies, or communication studies, or all four. That his work is engaged in all these fields is its major strength and indicative of his enormous and still pertinent contribution (to all four).[1]

Developing his earlier work on the country and the city, and acknowledging that the distinction he drew between them was too stark and that they are, in fact, 'indissolubly linked', Williams (1984: 209) developed and used the concept of livelihood as a term that mediates both. Livelihood takes place in both the country and the city. The livelihood of the inhabitants of both are dependent, and impact upon, the livelihoods of inhabitants of the other. Livelihood also deconstructs the culture/nature binary and hierarchy of culture over nature. It is both cultural and natural. Livelihood decolonizes the oppression of the natural environment. Livelihood implies both one's work and one's physical surrounds, their environmental supports and effects, as well as something like the American concept of a bioregion; one's geomorphological and biological region – the watershed, the valley, the plain, the wetland, the aquifer, etc. – where, or on which, one lives and works and which sustains one's life, the lives of indigenes before one (and still does so now in places, not to forget the resource regions exploited elsewhere), and the life of other species of fauna as well as flora on which one impacts environmentally.

Ecology, for Williams, was not the ecology of a small minority of nature lovers or accredited experts as critiqued by Felix Guattari. Williams extended ecology into what Guattari called (as we saw in Chapter 2) a third, generalized ecology that 'questions the whole of subjectivity and capitalist power formations', an ecology that I am also calling a postmodern, political ecology. For Williams:

> [...] what is now known as the ecological argument should not be reduced to its important minor forms; the dangerously rising scale of industrial and chemical pollution; the

destruction of some natural habitats and species. The case of the argument is very much harder [...] What is really at issue is a version of the earth and its life forms as extractable and consumable wealth. What is seen is not the sources and resources of many forms of life but eveything, including people, as available raw material, to be appropriated and transformed. Against this, the ecological argument has shown, in case after case, and then as a different way of seeing the whole, that a complex physical, and its intricated and interacting biological process, cannot for long be treated in such ways, without grave and unforeseen kinds of damage. (1985: 214–215; see also 1989b: 210–226)

For Williams, the only way to mount a revolution against the capitalist conquest and mastery of nature is to produce 'a new social and natural order' via the concept and practice of 'livelihood'. Williams warns that:

[...] the deepest problems we have now to understand and resolve are in [the] real relations of nature and livelihood [...] [T]he central change we have to make is in the received and dominant concept of the earth and its life forms as raw material for generalized production [...] [In order to do so] it is important to avoid a crude contrast between 'nature' and production', and to seek the practical terms of the idea which would supersede both: the idea of 'livelihood', within, and yet active within, a better understood physical world and all truly necessary physical processes. Both industrial and agrarian capitalism have overridden this idea of livelihood, putting generalized production and profit above it. (1984: 219; see also 1985: 266–267)

The country is not the last bastion of nature against exploitation by capitalism, nor the final refuge of nature in flight from capitalism, but its happy hunting (and gathering, and farming) ground in agrarian and industrial capitalism. Industrial capitalism was, and still is, just as active in and with the country as it was, and is, in and with the city.

'Livelihood', for Williams, is a concept and practice which cuts across the rural/country (though these cannot be simply equated as Williams argues), the capital/city, and nature/culture distinctions and divisions. Livelihood deconstructs the culture/nature binary by showing how the relationship between them is hierarchical, with the former privileged over the latter. Culture is valourized over nature in culturalism and nature is denied and repressed; nature is exploited and oppressed in and by capitalism and nation-states. The valourization of nature in naturalism is merely the flip side and reactionary mirror image of culturalism. For the distinction to be made between culture and nature, and the relationship between them to be established, a third party and term has to be excluded. The excluded third between culture and nature is livelihood. Livelihood is both cultural and natural. There is no livelihood that is not both cultural and natural. Livelihood is cultural and natural.

Livelihood decolonizes the distinction between culture and nature, and the unsustainable exploitation of the country by the city, and of nature by capitalism. Capitalism is intimately tied up with 'capital-ism'; the fixation on and privileging of the capital city, whether it be of the nation, state or province, over the margins, outskirts and outlying regions. Livelihood empowers the country to resist its exploitation and oppression by the city through creating a sense of place and a viable local economy based on local produce and local markets.

Furthermore, livelihood unites city and country in common dependence and impact on a bioregion. Livelihood takes place in a particular bioregion. Country and city are part of a bioregion. Neither country nor city can survive without their bioregion. Both are dependent, if not parasitic, on it. Agrarian capitalism is parasitic on the country, and industrial capitalism based in the city is parasitic on the country. Agriculture for Michel Serres is that 'old primary parasitism [that] is eliminated by parasites of a superior level, accustomed to noise, the parasites of the megalopolis' (1982: 167). The city parasites the country and the country parasites the bioregion. The city is doubly parasitic on its bioregion.

Bioregion

The concept of bioregion was developed in the 1970s. In less Graeco-Latinate terms and more plain Anglo-Saxon one's, Kirkpatrick Sale suggests that bioregion literally means 'life-territory' (1985: 43; see also Sale 2001). Even plainer and simpler is 'home land' rather than 'homeland'. The disjunction between the two words signifies uncoupling the conjunction between nationalistic attachment to, and sentiment evoked by, the father- or mother-land. Elaborating on these basic definitions Thomas Berry has defined a bioregion as 'an identifiable geographical area of interacting life systems that is relatively self-sustaining in the ever-renewing processes of nature' (1988: 166; see also 86). The bioregion is simply home-habitat.

Extending the concept much further to consider human habitation become problematic. Sale goes on to define a bioregion in more detail as:

> [...] any part of the earth's surface whose rough boundaries are determined by natural characteristics rather than human dictates, distinguishable from other areas by particular attributes of flora, fauna, water, climate, soils, and landforms, and by the human settlements and cultures those attributes have given rise to. (1985: 55)

Sale's definition of a bioregion raises a number of questions such as: which humans and whose dictates would determine the rough boundaries of a bioregion? The fact that Sale can distinguish between boundaries determined by 'human dictates' and by 'natural characteristics' presupposes humans already distanced from their bioregion and perhaps implies modern humans and their dictates. Boundaries between Australian Aboriginal language and cultural groups are by no accident bioregional boundaries. Sale implicitly includes the role and work of indigenous peoples who have not only been given rise to by the bioregion (which smacks of biological determinism), but have actually shaped and produced the bioregion.

Without explicitly including the perceptions of and uses by indigenous inhabitants, the concept of bioregion can smack of a new doctrine of *terra nullius* with new settlers as new explorers and colonizers. It can be seen as some sort of attempt to get back to a bedrock of biological reality outside indigenous work of the land that writes out the impact of indigenous inhabitants in shaping and producing a bioregion. Williams' concept of livelihood is more inclusive in this respect as it deconstructs the capitalist culture/nature binary opposition and decolonizes the European human being/enviroment, city/country dualisms. It situates humans within the context and the supports which sustain their (our) life.

Bioregion is associated with a 'bioregionalism' movement whose threefold aims are, as Jim Dodge lists them: 'a decentralized, self-determined mode of social organization; a culture predicated upon biological integrities and acting in respectful accord [with them]; and a society which honors and abets the spiritual development of its members' (1990: 10). Bioregionalism as a political philosophy has been critiqued on the basis that it is only a viable economic option for those 'new settlers' who have the financial and other resources to leave the city and relocate in a smaller rural community. Bioregionalism is also part of a much larger social phenomenon whose practitioners may not conceptualize or articulate what they are doing in those terms. Urban baby boomer professionals undergoing a midlife crisis and seeking a seachange brought about by their disenchantment and disillusionment with the alienating city and with its and their 'lifestyle' ('rat race'), leave it on a journey of self-discovery to find authenticity, community and themselves in the country.

To this extent bioregionalism is nostalgic and utopian (utopia as nostalgia), even reactionary as Andrew Ross has warned:

> [...] in enshrining the principles of small-scale economies, decentralization, and face-to-face democracy of eco-anarchist thinking, bioregionalism looks back to a low density, rural-tribal past when communities 'coincided' geographically with bioregions defined by watersheds, or microclimates, or biomes [...] Above all, bioregionalism embodies, as a political and cultural policy, fundamentalist strains of biological determinism that run unevenly throughout mainstream environmentalist thought. (1994: 11)

In its ideas of bioregions giving rise to cultures and settlements in which the latter are merely products of the former (autochthonous) rather than being in a dialectic, or better dialogic, or even better mutually beneficial, relationship with its bioregion, bioregionalism is biologically deterministic. Nevertheless, all urban dwellers live in a bioregion anyway, irrespective of whether or not they subscribe to bioregionalism as a political philosophy and respond to their midlife crisis by leaving the city to find solace in the country; even Andrew Ross lives in a bioregion; even New York is in a bioregion (see Sanderson 2009).

The shift from bioregion to bioregionalism, from an acknowledgement of the bio- and geo-features of one's region to a fully-fledged political philosophy, is fraught with danger. Yet the baby of the bioregion does not need to be thrown out with the bathwater of bioregionalism. The value of bioregion lies not only in making connections with a larger sense of place in which one lives and on which one depends, but also in reconstruing a sense of community from a narrow, stultifying human community to a broader and richer sense of community of all beings, what I am calling a bioregional home-habitat. For Berry, 'the bioregion is the domestic setting of the community' (1988: 166). The bioregion is the communal home – home land.

Perhaps the writer to have most precisely and passionately expressed this sense of the bioregion as home-habitat is Henry David Thoreau. In his *Journal* he wrote how:

> Here I am at home. In the bare and bleached crust of the earth I recognize my friend [...] the constant endeavour should be to get nearer and nearer *here* [...] A man dwells in his native valley like a corolla in its calyx, like an acorn in its cup. *Here*, of course, is all that you love, all that you expect, all that you are. Here is your bride elect, as close to you as she can be got. Here is all the best and all the worst you can imagine. (Thoreau 1962, *XI*: 275)

Home is here. It is not there. Life is here; it is not elsewhere. Home here is the bioregion. It is not the narrow confines of one's quarter acre, or fifth of an acre, suburban block, or one's townhouse and its pocket-handkerchief garden, or one's apartment and its balcony. One's bioregion is home; home is the bioregion.

A similar sense of the bioregion as home has been enunciated more recently by Charles Frazier in his novel *Cold Mountain*. As with the bioregionalists, a bioregional quiz assesses knowledge of the physical features of the bioregion (Frazier 1997: 106). Bioregionalists formulated a remarkably similar set of questions that assess the level of one's knowledge of one's bioregion (see Charles, Dodge, Milliman and Stockley 1990: 29–30). This kind of knowledge and this sense of place, produces a desire *not* to travel in the inhabitants of this bioregion, just as Thoreau's sense of 'home is here' did in him (Frazier 1997: 192; and Thoreau 1962, *VIII*: 204). Travel is only desired in order to return home after a forced displacement, such as the central character experiences returning home from the Civil War. Home is first reached, not when Inman sees his house or property, but his home land (Frazier 1997: 281). Home is gained when he can names the features of his home land and speak the language of the place. Rather than naming the place and giving names to features of it, the place is already named (Frazier 1997: 307).

Home land is a conjunction of land mass and water flows, a dynamic process, not a static product. Elyne Mitchell, a pioneer Australian conservationist, argued that, 'catchment and drainage areas are [...] a natural unit of life, a region unified by the water flowing through it – by the conformation of the land' (1946: 76). Mitchell's work is curiously absent from two major histories of Australian conservation (see Hutton and Connors 1999; and Mulligan and Hill 2001). Her book was published three years prior to Aldo Leopold's *A Sand County Almanac*. It takes a remarkably similar approach to similar topics. Mitchell deserves a similar esteemed place in Australia as a mother of post-war Australian conservation as Leopold enjoys as a father of post-war American conservation.[2]

Along similar lines to Mitchell, and 50 years later, the bioregion has been defined by Charlene Spretnak as:

> [...] the land masses of earth are organized into bioregions delineated by watersheds (drainage areas) of the river systems or other natural demarcations. Everyone lives in a bioregion and in the earth's commons [...] The health of communities and nations is dependent on the health of the bioregions. (1997: 104)

The boundaries of the bioregion are mapped on the earth's surface by the curving lines of water flows. They are not mapped in the straight lines of national and state borders but cut across them. No one can escape their bioregion and the commons of land, air and water in which everyone lives and on which everyone depends. The bioregion is the community of living beings and non-living things.

For Sale, 'the community is the single basic building block of the ecological world' (1985: 62). He defines it as 'a self-sufficient and self-perpetuating collection of different species that have adapted as a whole to the conditions of their habitat' (ibid.). Indigenous inhabitants of a bioregion living in a hunting-gathering culture would exemplify this sort of community. For indigenous communities, the bioregion is their home. The bioregion is the domestic setting of the indigenous community. Non-indigenous residents, especially city-dwellers, are usually locked into a community/individual divide. For them, the home is the domestic setting of the individual, the bioregion is the background, the noise, the resource, the setting, not the home of the community. Bioregionalism seeks to change the order of priorities between city and country; to see and live in the bioregion as home. The concept of bioregion could extend the boundaries of home beyond the limits of one's piece of land to the edges of the geomorphic and vegetative region in which one lives, and in which indigenous inhabitants lived before one (the settler).

Bioregionalism acknowledges and respects boundaries not made with human hands. In a couple of places John McPhee tells the story of:

> [...] a journey that tends to mock the idea of a nation, of a political state, as an unnatural subdivision of the globe, as a metaphor of the human ego, sketched on paper and framed in straight lines and in riparian boundaries beween unalterable coasts. The United States: really a quartering of a continent, a drawer in North America. Georgia. A state? Really a core sample of a continent, a plug in the melon, a piece of North America [...] a terrain crisscrossed with geological boundaries, mammalian boundaries, amphibian boundaries: the limits of the world of the river frogs, the extent of the Nugget Formation, the range of the mountain cougar. (1976: 285; and 1981: 15)

The concept of bioregion could even extend the boundaries of home not only outwards from the house and the garden, but also inwards to include humans and the body. As David Suzuki points out:

[...] boundaries cannot be drawn between us and air, water, or soil – in fact, we are, quite literally, air, water, soil, and sunlight [...] Whatever we do to the air, water, soil, energy, and biodiversity, we also do to ourselves because there is no separation [...] the way we act towards the environment is the way we act towards ourselves. (1998: 59)

A new environmental golden rule: do unto the environment as you would be done to for you are your environment. After all, humans are predominantly water and humans do grow intestinal flora. In Suzuki's later book with McConnell (1997) the ways in which humans are our environment are discussed more extensively.

Bioregion extends the boundaries of home outwards and inwards. Yet they are not usually extended far enough outwards to include all that humans make home, or call home, or need for home. Human settlements and cultures have increasingly extended their boundaries beyond the earth's surface to take in more of the earth's depths in mining, and more of the earth's heights beyond the mountains and the atmosphere, into the electronmagnetosphere and orbital extra-terrestrial space by way of communication technologies such as radio, television and telecommunication satellites. After the surface of the earth was colonized, the depths and heights are being increasingly colonized. These regions have not yet become regarded or cared for as home, though cyborgs live in them and depend on them. These regions are not only part of the earth-household but also part of the ecoregion. 'Ecoregion' is the more apposite term today to include not only the bioregion on the earth's surface and heights in the atmosphere in which all beings live and on which they depend, but also the regions of the earth's depths and heights, the -ospheres, in which cyborgs and symbionts live and on which they depend, including other bioregions from which they 'source' goods in trade (see Haraway 1995: xi–xx; and Giblett 2008a: Chapter 9).

Symbiosis

Biologically, humans are a community. Indeed, as Theodore Roszak argues, citing Lynn Margulis, 'all organisms are "metabolically complex communities of a multitude of tightly organized beings"' (Roszak 1992: 154). For her, Roszak goes on to relate, 'from the symbiotic point of view, there are no "individuals" – except perhaps the bacteria. All beings are "intrinsically communities"' (1992: 155). For nearly 40 years Margulis has been the most cogent proponent of the notion of symbiosis, 'the term coined by the German botanist Anton deBary in 1873' (1998: 33), and taken up by Eugene Warming (1909: 83–95) in the early twentieth century. Margulis defines symbiosis as 'the living together of two or more organisms in close association. To exclude the many kinds of parasitic relationships known in nature, the term is often restricted to associations that are of mutual advantage to the partners' (1971: 49; see also 1981: 161).

Symbiosis is also one of the key concepts of bioregionalism. One of the features of the bioregional paradigm, for Sale, particularly as it relates to 'society', and presumably in relation to the natural environment, is symbiosis, or, as he defines it, 'biological interaction' (1985: 50) and 'mutual dependence as the means of survival' (1985: 112). Symbiosis in biological terms operates primarily at a microbiological, interspecies level, though it has wider macrobiological pertinence between animals and plants. Sale extends its range even further and uses it as a model for 'a successful human society' (1985: 113), which would operate symbiotically at the macrobiological or bioregional level, particularly when it comes to cities. Yet Sale is using symbiosis in the restricted or narrow sense of mutual benefit as all animal species (including humans) are always already in symbiosis in a broader sense with the natural environment to greater or lesser extent, with greater or lesser mutual dependency and benefit. Human beings are, whether we like it or not, in symbiosis with the oxygen-producing plants of this planet. Every breath of air we breathe re-affirms this symbiosis. As Margulis puts it, 'we are symbionts on a symbiotic planet' (1998: 5).

Parasitism can be, and has been, a model for a 'successful' human society, which survives, however parasitically, to the detriment of other species, habitats, ecosystems and biomes. Sale wants symbiosis to be a model (even a realizable utopian model) for a human society which is mutually 'successful' or sustainable with its bioregion. Rather than being a model for, or a metaphor of, a successful or better human society, symbiosis is the current state of play as humans are organisms, are biological creatures. Mutualism may be a useful model for a better human society, though all appeals to nature for a model of society are at best fraught with danger as nature is a cultural construct, and at worst imbued with class politics, for nature is an object of capitalist exploitation. Appeals to nature are sent to a court whose only recourse for further appeals is to refer the case on to the higher court of culture where the case is argued (and won or lost) on cultural grounds.

A mutualistic theory of human society is all very well in theory, but when it comes to putting it into practice it is another matter, especially in relation to that most parasitic of beasts or even monsters – the city. It is easy to be long on generalities and short on specifics on how the city might live mutually and not parasitically in symbiosis with its bioregion. It is easy to diagnose the parasitic ills of the city, but much harder to get the city to take its mutualistic medicine. Cities, Sale argues:

> [...] particularly modern industrial cities, are like colonizers, grand suction systems drawing their life from everywhere in the surrounding nation, indeed the surrounding world [...] The contemporary high-rise city, in short, is an environmental parasite as it extracts its lifeblood from elsewhere and an environmental pathogen as it sends back its wastes. (1985: 65)

It is difficult to see how such cities might cease to be parasites on their bioregion and live mutually with it. Smaller scale, decentralized communities may be able to do so.

The modern city is founded and continues to depend on a parasitic relationship with its bioregion. Despite the parasitism of the modern city, it is still in a symbiotic relationship with its bioregion and with the earth. Perhaps, as Sale suggests, it is in a pathologically symbiotic rather than healthily symbiotic relation with the world. In Margaret Mahler's terms, it is in psychotic symbiosis rather than 'normal' symbiosis. For Mahler, '"growing up" entails a gradual growing away from the normal state of human symbiosis, of "one-ness" with the mother' (1972: 333). Similarly, modernity entails a gradual growing away from the 'normal' or traditional state of human symbiosis, of 'one-ness' with the earth. Modernity is thus a pathology, a land pathology and a psychopathology, a psychogeopathology. Indigenous people's oneness with the earth is the norm from which modern people have deviated pathologically, both physiopathologically and psychopathologically.[3]

Mahler could be described as a neo-Freudian psychoanalyst whose work on what she calls 'the symbiosis theory of the development of the human being' (1968: 6) spans over three decades, beginning in the 1950s. In this theory there are basically three phases of personality development: the normal autistic; the normal symbiotic; and the separation-individuation phases. These phases refer primarily to 'the development of object relationship', especially with the mother, and corresponding roughly to Freud's oral, anal and phallic stages.

Mahler's theory begins from the foundation of what she calls 'that vital and basic need of the human young in his [sic] early months of life: symbiosis with a mother or mother substitute' (1968: 2). For Mahler, Pine and Bergman, normal symbiosis is the phase in which 'the infant behaves and functions as though he [sic] and his mother were an omnipotent system – a dual unity within one common boundary' (1975: 44; see also Mahler 1968: 8), just as the bioregion normally is the dual unity of indigenous humans with the earth within one common boundary.

The autistic child, for Mahler, develops a psychotic defense against the lack of this need. The psychotic symbiotic child is thus, in the terms of Mahler, Pine and Bergman, 'unable to use the mother as a real external object as a basis for developing a stable sense of separateness from, and relatedness to, the world of reality' (1975: 12). Similarly, the psychotic city-dweller is generally unable to see the earth as separate, and is unable to relate to her other than as Mother Nature in the packaged commodities of nature documentaries, national parks, processed food, tourist destinations, and so on.

For Mahler and Furer, this lack of separation in 'symbiotic child psychosis' involves 'a regression to the stage of object relationship that exists before self and other representation have been distinguished' (1966: 559). In other words, symbiotic psychosis entails a regression to the symbiotic state of early infancy, even to the parasitic, or perhaps more precisely, intrauterine state, in which the infant is unable to distinguish between self and (m)other. Following Helene Deutsch, Mahler argues that, 'the intrauterine, parasite-host relationship within the mother organism must be replaced in the postnatal period by the infant's being enveloped, as it were, in the extrauterine matrix of the mother's nursing care, a kind of *social symbiosis*' (Mahler 1952: 286). Mahler (1968: 34) repeated the same view 16 years later. Yet it is arguable whether the intrauterine relationship is strictly parasitic as the foetus does not gain considerably at the mother's expense. It is perhaps more precisely inquilistic (see below) as the uterus shares the body of the mother usually without significant disadvantage to the mother in the short-term, but often in the long run with a prolapse and the need for surgical intervention, including a hysterectomy.

Just as the symbiotic psychotic infant is unable to distinguish between self and (m)other, so the symbiotic psychotic city-dweller is unable to distinguish between self and the earth. This regression is thus, Mahler and Furer argue, 'an archaic defence mechanism, a restitutive attempt that, by way of the delusion of oneness with the "mothering principle", serves the function of survival' (1966: 560). This delusion of oneness entails delusional feelings of omnipotence, so for Mahler, within this sense of oneness, lie the seeds of its own destruction. Later she goes on to argue with Pine and Bergman that, 'the essential feature of symbiosis is hallucinatory or delusional somatopsychic *omnipotent* fusion with the representation of the mother and, in particular, the delusion of a common boundary between two physically separate individuals' (Mahler, Pine and Bergman 1975: 45; see also Mahler 1968: 9).[4] The psychotic city dweller has a delusional oneness with the mothering principle of nature, and a delusional omnipotence over it/her, through the produced and packaged commodities of the hypermarket shelf and the electronic media, which serve the function of survival (and to that extent is 'successful'), but not the function of living symbiotically, sustainably and spiritually with the earth.

The symbiotic psychotic, Mahler and Furer go on to argue, does not cling to the mother per se, but to 'a hypercathected, yet at the same time divitalized and deanimated concrete symbol which he [sic] substitutes for her – a psychotic transitional object to which he constantly resorts in stereotyped fashion' (1966: 560), what she also calls 'a "psychotic fetish"'. The living body of the earth, nurturing and horrifying, life-giving and death-dealing, becomes the dead matter of Mother Nature, an industrial resource to be extracted and exploited, a commodity to be bought and sold, produced and consumed, a bauble to be fetishized by modern communication and information technologies in advertising, documentaries and tourism.

The modalities of this relationship between subject and object give rise to what Mahler calls 'the brittle ego of the "symbiotic psychotic child"', who experiences the world as 'hostile and threatening because it has to be met as a separate being' (1953: 292). The response of the symbiotic psychotic, the fragile, hard-edged ego of the city dweller to this world is to phantasize it precisely as *not* a separate being. So much for the symbiotic psychotic. What of the normal symbiotic?

The normal symbiotic child in Mahler's sense would presumably be the isolated individualist who is constituted as subject insofar as the earth is constituted as object. These terms need to be reconstrued critically in postmodern ecological terms. The 'normal' symbiotic city dweller (if such a thing is possible), or the normal symbiotic bioregion dweller, would use the bioregion as a real external subject in her own right, as Great Goddess, for developing a stable sense of inter-subjective interaction and mutual aid with her. The normal symbiotic has developed from and cannot return to the symbiosis of early infancy.

In theorisng the normal symbiotic phase of early infancy, Mahler is quite explicit that 'the term symbiosis is borrowed from biology, where it is used to refer to a close functional association of two organisms to their mutual advantage' (1968: 7). Yet, if there is mutual advantage in the symbiosis of early infancy, it is not equal as the infant requires the mother or mother substitute to survive biologically, whereas the mother does not require the infant for her to survive biologically. In biological terms, the relationship is strictly commensal: benefit to one, no harm to the other. Infantile and childhood development can be seen to go through two distinct symbiotic phases: first, an intrauterine period of inquilinism where, in the words of a dictionary of biology, 'one party shares the nest or home of the other without significant disadvantage to the "owner"' in contrast to parasitism 'where one party gains considerably at the other's expense'; secondly, a postnatal period of commensalism 'where one party gains some benefit [...] while the other suffers no serious disadvantage' (Abercrombie, Hickman, Johnson and Thain 1990: 542–543). A third stage of mutuality, where both parties benefit and neither suffers, would perhaps ideally be achieved and maintained in later childhood and adulthood with the proviso mentioned earlier of a possible prolapse and/or hysterectomy.

Yet rather than using the term symbiosis in a strict biological sense, Mahler, Pine and Bergman go on to argue that:

> [...] the term *symbiosis* in this context is a metaphor. Unlike the biological concept of symbiosis, it does not describe what actually happens in a mutually beneficial relationship between two *separate* individuals of different species. It describes that state of undifferentiation, of fusion with mother, in which the 'I' is not yet differentiated from the 'not-I', and which inside and outside are only gradually coming to be sensed as different. (1975: 44; see also Mahler 1968: 9)

Yet symbiosis in the normal symbiotic relationship could describe what actually happens in a mutually beneficial relationship between two separate individuals, or more precisely, communities of different species living in a bioregion. Symbiosis would no longer be a mere 'metaphor', or a heuristic device or explanatory trope for something else, but a lived relationship. Rather than being in a state of fusion with the earth, humans in bioregional symbiosis would experience themselves as members of a community interacting in mutual benefit with other species within a common bioregion, indeed, with the whole earth, and with the whole earth considered as a living organism.

Mahler's work has been critiqued for this dubious premise of an undifferentiated, symbiotic union between mother and child (see Klein 1980). In the 1980s Daniel Stern contended bluntly that 'infants never experience a period of total self/other undifferentiation' (1985: 10). Analogously, the indigene is never totally undifferentiated from or completely symbiotic with the earth. In the loving union of people and earth, Aboriginal people are not subsumed beneath, or swallowed up by, or completely identified with, the earth to the point of losing their own separate identity. People and earth are subjects in their own right, just as the mother is a subject in her own right. Jessica Benjamin picked up and developed Stern's position and argued that:

> [...] the other whom the self meets is also a self, a subject in his or her own right [...] that other subject is different and yet alike [...] the idea of intersubjectivity reorients the conception of the psychic world from a subject's relations to its object toward a subject meeting another subject. (1990: 20; see also Plumwood 1993: 154–160)

The earth whom the self meets is also a self, a subject in its or her own right.

Although the earth is a subject like the self, the earth is not the same as the self. The earth is different and yet alike. Jessica Benjamin argues that:

> [...] sameness and difference exist simultaneously in mutual recognition [...] self and other are not merged [...] the externality of the other makes one feel one is truly being 'fed', getting nourishment from the outside, rather than supplying everything for oneself. (1990: 47)

In mutual recognition, the earth is different from, and the same as, people. Aboriginal people and the earth are not merged into an oceanic feeling of complete undifferentiation or loss of mutually distinct identity. The externality and recognition of the earth makes one feel one is truly being fed by nourishing terrains rather than fed by consuming land, by eating earth.

The idea of intersubjectivity reorients the conception of the psychic world away from a subject's relations to its object, toward a subject meeting another subject. The earth is another subject as Jessica Benjamin puts it in relation to the mother:

> The idea of mutual recognition is crucial to the intersubjective view [...] the mother is a subject in her own right [just as the earth is, or should be, a subject in her own right] [...] She is external reality [the earth is external reality] – but she is rarely regarded as another subject. (1990: 23)

The earth is rarely regarded as another subject despite its generosity, despite our lack of gratitude towards it and despite the lack of reciprocity in our relationship with it/her. Yet, as Serres puts it, 'the parasitic relation is intersubjective' (1982: 8). The parasitic city and the parasitic modern city-zen constitutes itself as subject and its host, the earth, as subject. The psychotic city dweller, by constrast, has a hypercathected and delusional sense of oneness with the earth that denies it/her subjectivity. Despite this difference, the flow of goods between the earth and the psychotic and parasitic city dweller is one way as is the flow of bads back.

A similar imbalance pertains in the relationship between the child and its parents. Jessica Benjamin argues that 'mutuality [...] persists in spite of the tremendous inequality of the parent-child relationship' (1990: 14). Mutuality persists in spite of the tremendous inequality of the earth-indigene, and the even greater inequality of the earth/modern city-dweller relationship. Modern mastery has tried to supersede traditional mutuality and to reverse the tremendous inequality of the earth–indigene relationship. Despite the inequality of the modern-earth relationship, the former is still in symbiosis with the latter.

All people are parasites on the earth to a greater or lesser extent. Serres argues that:

> [...] man [*sic*] is the universal parasite, everything and everyone around him is a hospitable space. Plants and animals are always his hosts; man is always necessarily their guest. Always taking, never giving. He bends the logic of exhange and of giving in his favour when he is dealing with nature as a whole. When he is dealing with his kind, he continues to do so; he wants to be the parasite of man as well. (1982: 24)

Human beings are always the guest of the earth, other animals and plants the host. But there is a world of difference between the oral and anal sadism of mining and pastoralism and the mutual recognition and symbiosis of Aboriginal people and the earth; between the mediated relationship and interaction of the former and the immediacy of the other.

There is also a difference between indigenes and what Serres calls astronauts who live 'off-ground' in the extra-terrestrial world of cities: 'we have all become astronauts, completely deterritorialized [...] Astronaut humanity is floating in space like a fetus in amniotic fluid, tied to the placenta of Mother Earth by all the nutritive passages' (1995: 120 and 122). Astronaut humanity is floating in the womb of the biosphere tied to the earth mothership at the mouth and the anus, and bathing in the amniotic fluid of the atmosphere and the electomagnetosphere inside the skin of oribital extra-terrestrial space (see the cover photograph of *People and Places of Nature and Culture*). Astronaut humanity is not standing with two feet planted firmly on, and rooted in, the ground, drawing nourishment from it and its goods and giving back gratitude and respect. Astronaut humanity ingests good things from the ecosphere, digests them and then excretes bad things back into it. According to Milton Klein, Mahler's concept of symbiosis is based on 'the image of an unsevered umbilical cord' (1980: 91). All humanity has 'an unsevered umbilical cord' attaching it symbiotically to the earth, but astronaut humanity is attached parasitically to the earth sucking out nutrients and giving back wastes, and not giving back gratitude and care.

Astronaut humanity is a parasite who, as Lawrence Schehr puts it in his 'Translator's Introduction' to Serres' *The Parasite*, 'takes without giving and weakens without killling. The parasite is also a guest, who exchanges his talk, praise and flattery for food' (Serres 1982: x). The city and the citizen is a parasite which takes from the earth without giving back anything except rubbish and weakens the earth without killling it – yet – for that would be to kill itself. The parasite cannot live without the host; the host can live without the parasite. The city and the citizen at home or abroad is also a guest who exchanges his praise and flattery of the earth for sustenance. Perhaps more precisely, a parasite is what Serres calls 'an abusive guest' (1982: 8). For Serres, 'everything begins with what I call abuse value. The first economic relation is of abuse' (1982: 168). Relations of use and use value are pre-economic, or certainly pre-capitalist. The agricultural, manufacturing, mining, and pastoralist industries are instances of industrial capitalist land *ab*use. Serres goes on to argue later that 'the parasite routinely confuses use and abuse. The parasite would destroy the host without realizing it' (1995: 36). And him or herself in the process.

Without mutual recognition humans cease to exist and the earth ceases to exist too. Jessica Benjamin argues that:

> [...] if we fully negate the other, that is, if we assume complete control over him [or her] and destroy his [or her] identity and will, then we have negated ourselves as well. For then there is no one there to recognize us, no one there for us to desire. (1990: 39)

If humans fully negate the earth, that is, if humans assume complete control over her and destroy her identity and will, then humans have negated ourselves as well. For then there is no one there to recognize us, no one there for us to desire. As Serres puts it, 'former parasites have to become symbionts [...] This is history's bifurcation: either death or symbiosis' (1995: 34). The choice is simple: either no future of death or a future of symbiosis. Margulis concurs that 'without "the other" we do not survive' (1998: 111).

Mutual recognition is not a moral stricture, something that humans should do or have to do out of a sense of moral obligation. Rather it is a fact of life, or perhaps more precisely a fact for life, as without it humans are dead meat. Jessica Benjamin insists that 'mutual recognition cannot be achieved through obedience, through identification with the other's power, or through repression. It requires, finally, contact with the other' (1990: 40). Mutual recognition between people and earth cannot be achieved through obedience to environmental laws or to the figure of the Great Goddess, nor through identification with the Great Mother's power, nor through repression of desire.

Nor even through a natural contract along the lines proposed by Serres that 'we must add to the exclusively social contract a natural contract of symbiosis and reciprocity' (1995: 38). Mutual recognition between people and earth requires contact (rather than contract) with the other, with the earth in mutual reciprocity and symbiosis. Not only seeing the earth, but also tasting (and not just eating) the earth, listening, smelling and touching it – or her. To the social and natural contracts, the natural contact of symbiosis and reciprocity needs to be added.

That contact can not only be sensual, but also erotic. Rather than an undifferentiated relationship with the mother, Jessica Benjamin suggests that the best model for mutual recognition is erotic union:

> [I]n erotic union we can experience that form of mutual recognition in which both partners lose themselves in each other without loss of self; they lose self-consciousness without loss of awareness. Thus, early experiences of mutual recognition already prefigure the dynamics of erotic life. (1990: 29)

The loving oneness of Aboriginal people and earth is an erotic union in which both partners lose themselves in each other without loss of self; losing self-consciousness without loss of awareness. This loving oneness and the dynamics of erotic life may prefigure mutual recognition between modern people and earth. Dreaming ecology is erotic ecology. The bioregional dweller is a nature lover who knows intimately his or her home habitat, in what could be called an erotic ecology involving intimacy, pleasurable play, sensual appreciation through all the senses and their creative expression in many media (see Giblett, 2009: Chapter 9). S/he is also a third ecologist who gains their livelihood sustainably from, and with, the living earth.

Living Earth

Symbiosis is a fact of evolution: no evolution without symbiosis. Symbiosis is a factor in evolution: species evolve through symbiosis with other species. It is also a factor in bioregions and bioregionalism. Darwin's theory of evolution by natural selection was not possible without bioregions and symbiosis. This theory was a Copernican revolution in biology that ranks alongside the Marxian revolution in political economy and the Freudian revolution in psychology. All three decentred human subjectivity. Louis Althusser acknowledged the pivotal role of Freud and Marx, whilst overlooking Darwin. He argued that:

> Not in vain did Freud sometimes compare the critical reception of his discovery with the upheavals of the Copernican revolution. Since Copernicus, we have known that the earth is not the 'centre' of the universe. Since Marx, we have known that the human subject, the economic, political or philosophical ego is not the 'centre' of history – [...] that history has no centre [...] In turn, Freud has discovered for us that the real subject, the individual in his real essence, has not the form of the ego, centred on the 'ego', on 'consciousness' or on 'existence' – [...] that the human subject is de-centred, constituted by a structure which has no 'centre' either, except in the imaginary misrecognition of the 'ego', that is, in the ideological formations in which it 'recognizes' itself. (Althusser 1984: 170–171)

Principally, the subject misrecognizes itself in its narcissistic reflection in the fetishized commodity in which the consuming subject recentres itself (or more precisely finds itself recentred) as the addressee of (or is recentred by) every advertisement, every mass-produced message.

To Freud and Marx as the decenterers of psychic and productive human subjectivity, Darwin needs to be added as the decenterer of embodied and biological human subjectivity. Since Darwin 'Man' no longer occupies, as William Godfrey-Smith puts it, 'a *biologically* privileged position' (1979: 317; my emphasis). 'Man', however, continues to occupy a culturally privileged position in the production of commodities from raw materials supplied by the earth, in the consumption of fetishized commodities manufactured from those materials, and in the expulsion of pollutants and wastes back into the earth-household.

Yet while Freud, Marx and Darwin were decentring the subject psychologically, productively and biologically, Ford and Wanamaker were recentring the subject in consumption in a counter-Copernican revolution. Since Wanamaker, the leading founder of the American department store, the consuming subject has been reinstituted as the centre of his or her own consumptive world (see Leach 1993). Since Ford, the inventor not only of the assembly line and mass production, but also of mass consumption, the subject consuming the commodities of industrial technology (especially the car) is the centre of the history of modernity (however alienated the individual producer may be). The consumer is the centred subject of every commodity, the addressee of every shop window display, every advertisement, every fashion catwalk, every cinema, every film, every television set and show, every computer monitor. The consuming subject is a desiring subject whose desires are repressed and sublimated in, and by, semiosis and consumption. Desire, for Deleuze and Guattari, 'lacks a fixed subject; there is no fixed subject unless there is repression' (1977: 26). And its counterpart sublimation I would add.

Besides the Copernican revolution in subjectivity brought about by Marx, Freud and Darwin, a Copernican revolution in ecology was wrought by Haeckel, Kropotkin and Swallow that saw the embodied subject as not only a biological being with no special privileges, but also as the member of a community of living beings and non-living things with responsibilities. Since Leopold, the embodied subject is, or should be, a member of a biological community, not the owner of land as property or a consumer of commodities as fetishes. Humans should not only be part of a cultural community, but also good citizens of a natural community. Leopold's 'land ethic simply enlarges the boundaries of the community to include soils, waters, plants, and animals, or collectively: the land [...] a land ethic changes the role of *Homo sapiens* from conqueror of the land community to plain member and citizen of it' (1949: 204).

The land ethic also changes the relationship to the land from mastery to mutuality, and the role of the land from commodity to community. William Godfrey-Smith comments that 'land in Leopold's view is not a commodity which belongs to us, but a community to which we belong' (1979: 314), where a community is construed as 'a collection of individuals who engage in cooperative behaviour to their mutual benefit' (1979: 317). Whereas the counter-Copernican revolution in capitalist consumption has triumphed, the Copernican revolution in land community has not yet had its day.

Darwin decentred the embodied subject as biological being, but his theory of 'the survival of the fittest' and 'the struggle for existence' was centred in the urban and industrial capitalist 'jungle' rather than in the tropical rainforest. In a letter to Engels, Marx critiqued Darwin for, in the words of Keith Thomas:

> [...] representing the natural world of the animal kingdom as one of free competition and for seeing among the beasts and plants his own English society, 'with its division of labour, competition, opening up of new markets, 'inventions' and the Malthusian "struggle for existence"'. (Thomas 1984: 90)

Yet 'free competition' is never a level playing field on which all players are treated equally and the game is played fairly, just as 'free trade' is not fair trade. There are 'winners and losers', and violence, as Walter Benjamin argued in 1921, is the only other means besides natural selection for Darwin by which winners win and losers lose. Darwin's biology for Benjamin, 'in a thoroughly dogmatic manner, regards violence as the only original means, besides natural selection, appropriate to all the vital ends of nature' (1979a: 133; and 1996a: 237). Violence becomes the *sine qua non* of nature, but the violence Darwin saw in nature was cultural, or to be more preceise, the violence of modern industrial capitalism projected onto nature. Darwin, for Theodore Roszak, 'read the ethos of industrial capitalism into the jungle' (1992: 155). The jungle was then used to support the ideology of industrial capitalism. Nature confirmed culture, as it did in landscape aesthetics and the gentleman's park estate.

The Social Darwinists took the law of the jungle and applied it to industrial capitalism and the urban jungle, but Darwin had already taken the law of industrial capitalism and the urban jungle and applied it to the tropical rainforest. Biologists such as Tim Low who use the Social Darwinian law in which 'winners prosper and losers disappear' (2002: especially 112, 115 and 122) to describe the way in which some species survive in human modified environments whilst others become extinct close the circle. But late in the day Low, at the end of his book, charges that 'one of the worst eco-crimes we commit is helping winners displace losers' (2002: 280). The trope returns full circle to consume its own tail (tale) like the uroborous. Industrial capitalism was an urban jungle of the 'survival of the fittest' that Darwin read into the rainforest. The urban and extra-urban jungle in which 'winners prosper and losers disppear' reads Darwinism onto industrial capitalism.

Certainly there is competition in nature but there is also cooperation. Nature can be 'red in tooth and claw' as it was for Tennyson, though this projects the sadistic (especially oral sadistic) features of industrial capitalism and the urban 'jungle' on to nature. All those orally sadistic monsters (including dinosaurs) of Hollywood films and American and British television are projections of industrial capitalist oral sadism and its monstrous machines that are used to justify, and designed to deflect attention away from, the latter. Nature is not only 'red in tooth and claw' but also green in leaf and branch.

Cooperation is as much a part of nature as competition, if not more so. For Peter Kropotkin, 'mutual aid is as much a law of animal life as mutual struggle, but [...] as a factor of evolution, it most probably has a far greater importance' (1989: 6). Tim Flannery has concurred that:

> [...] evolution in Australia is not driven solely by nature 'red in tooth and claw'. Here, a more gentle force – that of coadaptation – is important [...] It is cooperation rather than competition which has been selected for in many Australian environments. (1994: 15 and 84)

For Kropotkin, 'the war of each against all is not *the* law of nature [...] Life is struggle; and in that struggle the fittest survive' (1989: 30 and 60), but the fittest (the survivors) are those who are the most cooperative, not the most competitive. The Hobbesian war of each against all was a projection of Hobbes' royalist reaction to the terrors of the English Civil War onto the state of nature in order to justify and legitimate restoration of the monarchy. The law of nature is each with all, for each is all.

The most mutually symbiotic survive. Symbiosis strictly considered only occurs between living things; living things in order to live require other living things. As William Trager puts, 'no organism lives alone' (1970: 1). No 'man', or woman, or child, or plant, or animal, is an island, as John Donne said. Yet for an organism to live, it not only requires other organisms, but also the life-supporting habitats or bioregions in which those other organisms live, and so in which it lives. Those bioregions for all species, however microscopic, are made up of intricately interweaving and interconnecting exchanges of matter which sustain life. So intertwined are these relationships that it is ultimately impossible to separate out an organism from its habitat. In a sense, an organism is, or is the product and producer of, its habitat. This habitat, this bioregion, is living and bioregions live with other bioregions in a living whole, breathing in air, rooted in earth, drinking water.

This idea of earth as living organism, rather than as dead matter, is by no means new. R. G. Collingwood (1945: 31 and 95) found it in the Ancient Greeks, as we saw in the first chapter of *People and Places of Nature and Culture*, so we have returned full circle to where we began. It is there too in the work of P. D. Ouspensky in his key words of 'animated nature', 'a living earth' and '"dead-nature" lives' as 'some gigantic [though not gargantuan or monstrous] organism' (1951: 178–191). The work of V. I. Vernadsky (1945: 1–12), the inventor of the concept of the biosphere, is credited by Jeremy Rifkin with being 'the first modern acknowledgment of earth as a living organism' (1991: 258). It may be more precise to see Vernadsky as the first *post*modern acknowledgment, and Thoreau as the first modern acknowledgement. For Thoreau, nearly a hundred years before Vernadsky, 'the earth is all alive' (1962, *VI*: 121). For us, too, today, humans need to (re-learn to) live with the earth as living being.

The earth as living is in the poetry of Walt Whitman (1982: 363–368[5]) too, especially in 'The Song of the Rolling Earth', with much else besides that resonates with *People and Places of Nature and Culture*, so it is its epilogue (and its epigraph):

The earth does not withhold, it is generous enough,
The truths of the earth continually wait, they are not so conceal'd either,
They are calm, subtle, untransmissible by print,
They are imbued through all things conveying themselves willingly [...]

The earth does not argue,
Is not pathetic, has no arrangements,
Does not scream, haste, persuade, threaten, promise,
Makes no discriminations, has no conceivable failures,
Closes nothing, refuses nothing, shuts none out,
Of all the powers, objects, states, it notifies, shuts none out.

The earth does not exhibit itself nor refuse to exhibit itself [...]
To her children the words of the eloquent dumb great mother never fail [...]

I swear the earth shall surely be complete to him or her who shall be complete,
The earth remains jagged and broken only to him or her who remains jagged and broken.
I swear there is no greatness or power that does not emulate those of the earth,
There can be no theory of any account unless it corroborate the theory of the earth,
No politics, song, religion, behavior [sic], or what not, is of account, unless it compare
    with the amplitude of the earth,
Unless it face the exactness, vitality, impartiality, rectitude of the earth.

I swear I begin to see love with sweeter spasms than that which responds love,
It is that which contains itself, which never invites and never refuses.

I swear I begin to see little or nothing in audible words,
All merges toward the presentation of the unspoken meanings of the earth,
Toward him who sings the songs of the body and of the truths of the earth,
Toward him who makes the dictionaries of words that print cannot touch
[...] the words of the earth.

Notes

1. I discuss Williams' work on communications and its technologies in Giblett (2008b).
2. I discuss Mitchell's work on soil conservation in Giblett (2008a: 175–177).
3. I discuss the possibility of the sustaitnable city (and make some proposals for it) in Giblett (2009: Chapter 3).
4. The word 'physically' is added to the later version.
5. This poem is (strangely and inexplicably) not included in *The Portable Whitman* (1945). Perhaps its editor, Mark Van Doren, did not appreciate Whitman's green politics of earthly mutuality.

References

Abercrombie, M., Hickman, M., Johnson, M. and Thain, M. (1990), 'Symbiosis', in *The New Penguin Dictionary of Biology*, Eighth Edition, London: Penguin, pp. 542–543.
Abraham, K. (1965), 'The Process of Introjection in Melancholia: Two Stages of the Oral Phase in the Libido', in *Selected Papers* (trans. D. Bryan and A. Strachey), London: Hogarth, pp. 442–453.
—— (1966a), 'Contributions to the Theory of the Anal Character (1921)', in B. Lewin (ed.), *On Character and Libido Development: Six Essays* (trans. D. Bryan and A. Strachey), New York: Basic Books, pp. 165–187.
—— (1966b), 'The Influence of Oral Erotism on Character Formation (1924)', in B. Lewin (ed.), *On Character and Libido Development: Six Essays* (trans. D. Bryan and A. Strachey), New York: Basic Books, pp. 151–164.
Adorno, T. (1984), 'The Beauty of Nature', in G. Adorno and R. Tiedemann (eds.), *Aesthetic Theory* (trans. C. Lenhardt), London: Routledge and Kegan Paul, pp. 91–115.
—— and Horkheimer, M. (1972), *Dialectic of Enlightenment*, New York: Herder and Herder.
Agricola, G. (1960), *De re Mettalica* (trans. H. Hoover and L. Hoover), New York: Dover.
Alford, C. (1985), *Science and the Revenge of Nature: Marcuse and Habermas*, Tampa/Gainesville: University Presses of Florida.
Althusser, L. (1984), *Essays on Ideology* (trans. B. Brewster), London: Verso.
Andrews, M. (1989), *The Search for the Picturesque: Landscape Aesthetics and Tourism in Britain, 1760–1800*, Aldershot: Scolar Press.
Appleton, J. (1975), *The Experience of Landscape*, New York: John Wiley and Sons.
Arendt, H. (1958), *The Human Condition*, Chicago: University of Chicago Press.
Arnold, D. (1996), *The Problem of Nature: Environment, Culture and European Expansion*, Oxford: Blackwell.
Athanisiou, T. (1996), *Divided Planet: The Ecology of Rich and Poor*, Boston: Little, Brown.
Australia (1994), *Native Title: Native Title Act 1993: Legislation with Commentary by the Attorney-General's Legal Practice*, Canberra: Australian Government Publishing Service.
Australian Conservation Foundation (ACF) (no date), 'Exploration and Mining in National Parks', *Western Australian Campaign Update*.
Badè, W. (1924), *The Life and Letters of John Muir, Volumes I and II*, Boston: Houghton Mifflin.
Baker, K. (1992), 'Women and the Public Sphere', in 'Defining the Public Sphere In Eighteenth-Century France: Variations on a Theme by Habermas', in C. Calhoun (ed.), *Habermas and the Public Sphere*, Cambridge, Massachusetts: The MIT Press, pp. 198–208.
Bakhtin, M. (1968), *Rabelais and His World* (trans. H. Iswolsky), Cambridge, Massachusetts: Massachusetts Institute of Technology.

Barnes, J. (1986), '"Through Clear Australian Eyes": Landscape and Identity in Australian Writing', in P. Eaden and F. Mares (eds.), *Mapped But Not Known: The Australian Landscape of the Imagination...*, Kent Town: Wakefield Press, pp. 86–104.

Barrell, J. (1972), *The Idea of Landscape and the Sense of Place 1730-1840: An Approach to the Poetry of John Clare*, Cambridge: Cambridge University Press.

Barthes, R. (1973), *Mythologies* (trans. A. Lavers), London: Granada.

Baudrillard, J. (1990), *Fatal Strategies: Crystal Revenge* (trans. P. Beitchman and W. Niesluchowski), New York and London: Semiotext(e) and Pluto.

Baynton, B. (1995), *Bush Studies*, Pymble, NSW: Angus and Robertson. First published 1902.

Beauvoir, S. de (1972), *The Second Sex* (trans. H. Parshley), Harmondsworth: Penguin.

Bender, B. (1993), 'Introduction: Landscape – Meaning and Action', in B. Bender (ed.), *Landscape: Politics and Perspectives*, Oxford: Berg, pp. 1–17.

Benjamin, J. (1990), *The Bonds of Love: Psychoanalysis, Feminism, and the Problem of Domination*, London: Virago.

Benjamin, W. (1979a), 'Critique of Violence', in *One Way Street and Other Writings* (trans. E. Jephcott and K. Shorter), London: New Left Books, pp. 132–154.

—— (1979b), 'Moscow', in *One Way Street and Other Writings* (trans. E. Jephcott and K. Shorter), London: New Left Books, pp. 177–208.

—— (1979c), 'One Way Street', in *One Way Street and Other Writings* (trans. E. Jephcott and K. Shorter), London: New Left Books, pp. 45–104.

—— (1986), *Moscow Diary*, G. Smith (ed.), (trans. R. Sieburth), Cambridge, Massachusetts: Harvard University Press.

—— (1996a), 'Critique of Violence', in *Selected Writings: Volume 1, 1913-1926*, Cambridge, Massachusetts: Belknap Press of Harvard University Press, pp. 236–252.

—— (1996b), 'One Way Street', in *Selected Writings: Volume 1, 1913-1926*, Cambridge, Massachusetts: Belknap Press of Harvard University Press, pp. 444–488.

—— (1999a), 'Moscow', in *Selected Writings: Volume 2, 1927-1934*, Cambridge, Massachusetts: Belknap Press of Harvard University Press, pp. 22–46.

—— (1999b), 'Theories of German Fascism', in *Selected Writings: Volume 2, 1927-1934*, Cambridge, Massachusetts: Belknap Press of Harvard University Press, pp. 312–321.

Bennett, A. (1910), *Clayhanger*, London: Eyre Methuen.

Bennett, T. (1998), *Culture: A Reformer's Science*, St Leonards, NSW: Allen and Unwin.

Berman, M. (1983), *All That Is Solid Melts Into Air: The Experience of Modernity*, London: Verso.

Bermingham, A. (1986), *Landscape and Ideology: The English Rustic Tradition 1740-1860*, Berkeley: University of California Press.

Berndt, R. and Berndt, C. (1981), *The World of the First Australians*, Revised Edition, Sydney: Lansdowne.

Berry, T. (1988), *The Dream of the Earth*, San Francisco: Sierra Club Books.

Berry, W. (1987), 'Two Economies', in *Home Economics: Fourteen Essays*, San Francisco: North Point, pp. 54–75.

Blainey, G. (1983), *A Land Half Won*, Revised Edition, Chippendale, NSW: Pan Macmillan.

Bolton, G. (1992), *Spoils and Spoilers: A History of Australians Shaping Their Environment*, Second Edition, North Sydney: Allen and Unwin.

Bonaparte, M. (1949), *The Life and Works of Edgar Allan Poe: A Psycho-Analytic Interpretation* (trans. J. Rodker), London: Imago.

Bonyhady, T. (1985), *Images in Opposition: Australian Landscape Painting 1801-1890*, Melbourne: Oxford University Press.

References

—— (2000), *The Colonial Earth*, Melbourne: Miegunyah Press/Melbourne University Press.

—— and Griffiths, T. (2002), 'Landscape and Language', in T. Bonyhady and T. Griffiths (eds.), *Words for Country: Landscape and Language in Australia*, Sydney: University of New South Wales Press, pp. 1–13.

Bookchin, M. (1991), *The Ecology of Freedom: The Emergence and Dissolution of Hierarchy*, Revised Edition, Montreal: Black Rose.

Boyle, T. (1987), *World's End*, New York: Viking Penguin.

Brady, V. (1998), *South of my Days: A Biography of Judith Wright*, Pymble, NSW: Angus and Robertson.

Briggs, R. (1977), *Fungus the Bogeyman*, London: Hamish Hamilton.

Brooks, P. (1980), *Speaking for Nature: How Literary Naturalists from Henry Thoreau to Rachel Carson Have Shaped America*, San Francisco: Sierra Club Books.

Brown, C. (1992), 'The Language of the Landscape: An Interview', *Faith and Freedom*, 1: 2, pp. 30–36.

Buber, M. (1970), *I and Thou*, Third Edition (trans. W. Kaufmann), Edinburgh: T. and T. Clark.

Buell, L. (1995), *The Environmental Imagination: Thoreau, Nature Writing, and the Formation of American Culture*, Cambridge, Massachusetts: Harvard University Press.

Burke, E. (1958), *A Philosophical Enquiry into the Origin of our Ideas of the Sublime and the Beautiful*, J. Boulton (ed.), London: Routledge and Kegan Paul. First published 1757.

Burn, I. (1980), 'Beating About the Bush: The Landscapes of the Heidelberg School', in A. Bradley and T. Smith (eds.), *Australian Art and Architecture: Essays Presented to Bernard Smith*, Melbourne: Oxford University Press, pp. 83–98.

—— (1992), 'The Landscape Question', in *The Lie of the Land*, Clayton, Victoria: National Centre for Australian Studies at Monash University, p. 26.

Butcher, D. (1969), *Exploring Our National Parks and Monuments*, Sixth Edition, Revised, Boston: Houghton Mifflin.

Carroll, J. (1982), 'National Identity', in J. Carroll (ed.), *Intruders in the Bush: The Australian Quest for Identity*, Melbourne: Oxford University Press, pp. 209–225.

Carruthers, J. (1989), 'Creating a National Park, 1910 to 1926', *Journal of Southern African Studies*, 15: 2, pp. 188–216.

Carter, P. (1989), *The Road to Botany Bay: An Exploration of Landscape and History*, Chicago: University of Chicago Press.

Catlin, G. (1968), 'An Artist Proposes a National Park', in R. Nash (ed.), *The American Environment: Readings in the History of Conservation*, Reading, Massachusetts: Addison-Wesley, pp. 5–9.

Certeau, M. de (1986), 'The Arts of Dying: Celibatory Machines', in *Heterologies: Discourse on the Other* (trans. B. Massumi), Manchester: Manchester University Press, pp. 156–167.

—— (1984), *The Practice of Everyday Life* (trans. S. Rendall), Berkeley: University of California Press.

The Chamber of Mines and Energy of Western Australia (Inc.) (1990), *Land Access for Mineral Exploration: The Way Ahead*, Perth, Western Australia: The Chamber of Mines and Energy of Western Australia (Inc.).

Charles, L., Dodge, J., Milliman, L. and Stockley, V. (1990), 'Where You At? – A Bioregional Quiz', in V. Andruss et. al. (eds.), *Home! A Bioregional Reader*, Philadelphia: New Society, pp. 29–30.

Cicero (1972), *The Nature of the Gods* (trans. H. McGregor), London: Penguin.

Clarke, M. (1993a), 'Preface to Adam Lindsay Gordon's *Sea Spray and Smoke Drift*', in M. Ackland (ed.), *The Penguin Book of Nineteenth-Century Australian Literature*, Ringwood, Victoria: Penguin, pp. 43–46.

—— (1993b), 'Pretty Dick', in M. Ackland (ed.), *The Penguin Book of Nineteenth-Century Australian Literature*, Ringwood, Victoria: Penguin, pp. 50–61.
Clarke, R. (1973), *Ellen Swallow: The Woman who Founded Ecology*, Chicago: Follett.
Clunies-Ross, B. (1986), 'Landscape and the Australian Imagination', in P. Eaden and F. Mares (eds.), *Mapped But Not Known: The Australian Landscape of the Imagination...*, Kent Town: Wakefield Press, pp. 224–243.
Coetzee, J. (1974), 'The Narrative of Jacobus Coetzee', in *Dusklands*, Johannesburg: Ravan, pp. 55–134.
—— (1988a), 'The Picturesque, the Sublime and the South African Landscape', in *White Writing: On the Culture of Letters in South Africa*, New Haven: Yale University Press, pp. 36–62.
—— (1988b), 'Reading the South African Landscape', in *White Writing: On the Culture of Letters in South Africa*, New Haven: Yale University Press, pp. 163–177.
Cohen, M. (1984), *The Pathless Way: John Muir and American Wilderness*, Madison: University of Wisconsin Press.
Collingwood, R. (1945), *The Idea of Nature*, London: Oxford University Press.
Conley, V. (1993), 'Eco-Subjects', in V. Conley (ed.), *Rethinking Technologies*, Minneapolis: University of Minnesota Press, pp. 77–91.
—— (1997), *Ecopolitics: The Environment in Poststructuralist Thought*, London and New York: Routledge.
Cosgrove, D. (1993), 'Landscapes and Myths, Gods and Humans', in B. Bender (ed.), *Landscape: Politics and Perspectives*, Oxford: Berg, pp. 281–305.
Cronon, W. (1996a), 'Introduction: In Search of Nature', in W. Cronon (ed.), *Uncommon Ground: Rethinking the Human Place in Nature*, New York: W. W. Norton, pp. 23–66.
—— (1996b), 'The Trouble with Wilderness: or, Getting Back to the Wrong Nature', in W. Cronon (ed.), *Uncommon Ground: Rethinking the Human Place in Nature*, New York: W. W. Norton, pp. 69–90.
Crosby, A. (1986), *Ecological Imperialism: The Biological Expansion of Europe, 900-1900*, Cambridge: Cambridge University Press.
Daly, H. and Cobb, J. (1994), *For the Common Good: Redirecting the Economy Toward Community, the Environment, and a Sustainable Future*, Second Edition, Boston: Beacon Press.
Davis, A. (1998), 'Listen to the Land', *Artworks*, 8, pp. 4–5.
Day, D. (1996), *Claiming a Continent: A History of Australia*, Pymble, NSW: Angus and Robertson.
Deleuze, G. and Guattari, F. (1977), *Anti-Oedipus: Capitalism and Schizophrenia* (trans. R. Hurley, M. Seem and H. Lane), New York: Viking.
Department of the Prime Minister and Cabinet (1994), *The Native Title Act 1993: What it Does and How it Works*, Canberra: Australian Government Publishing Service.
Dermody, S. and Jacka, E. (1988), *The Screening of Australia, Volume 2 – Anatomy of a National Cinema*, Sydney: Currency.
Derrida, J. (1977), 'Fors: The Anglish Words of Nicolas Abraham and Maria Torok', *The Georgia Review*, 31: 1, pp. 64–116.
—— (1980), 'La loi du genre/ The Law of Genre', *Glyph*, 7, pp. 176–232.
—— (1981), *Dissemination* (trans. B. Johnson), London: Athlone.
Dodge, J. (1990), 'Living by Life: Some Bioregional Theory and Practice', in V. Andruss et. al. (eds.), *Home! A Bioregional Reader*, Philadelphia: New Society, pp. 5–12.
Douglas, M. (1966), *Purity and Danger: An Analysis of the Concepts of Pollution and Taboo*, London: Routledge.
Durack, M. (1966), *Kings In Grass Castles*, Moorebank, NSW: Corgi. First published 1959.
—— (1983), *Keep Him my Country*, Moorebank, NSW: Corgi. First published 1955.

—— (1986), 'Lament for the Drowned Country', in S. Hampton and K. Llewellyn (eds.), *The Penguin Book of Australian Women Poets*, Ringwood, Victoria: Penguin, pp. 65–68.
Eagleton, T. (1990), *The Ideology of the Aesthetic*, Oxford: Basil Blackwell.
Eccleston, R. (2002), 'Where the Buffalo Roam', *The Weekend Australian Magazine*, 20–21 July, pp. 22–25.
Editors (1996), 'Denying the Global a Home', *The Ecologist*, 26: 4, pp. 123–124.
Eldershaw, F. (1952), 'The Landscape Writers', *Meanjin*, 11, pp. 215–228.
Eldershaw, M. Barnard (1939), *My Australia*, London: Jarrolds.
Eley, G. (1992), 'Gender and the Public Sphere', in 'Nations, Publics, and Political Cultures: Placing Habermas in the Nineteenth Century', in C. Calhoun (ed.), *Habermas and the Public Sphere*, Cambridge, Massachusetts: The MIT Press, pp. 307–319.
Eliade, M. (1971), *The Forge and the Crucible* (trans. S. Corrin), New York: Harper and Row.
Elkin, A. (1954), *The Australian Aborigines: How to Understand Them*, Third Edition, Sydney: Angus and Robertson.
Elliott, B. (ed.) (1979), *The Jindyworobaks*, St. Lucia: University of Queensland Press.
Falkiner, S. (1992), *Wilderness: The Writer's Landscape*, East Roseville, NSW: Simon and Schuster.
Finch, R. and Elder, J. (eds.) (1990), *The Norton Book of Nature Writing*, New York: W. W. Norton.
Flannery, T. (1994), *The Future Eaters: An Ecological History of the Australasian Lands and People*, Chatswood, NSW: Reed.
—— (1997), 'The fate of empire in low- and high-energy ecosystems', in T. Griffiths and L. Robin (eds.), *Ecology and Empire: Environmental History of Settler Societies*, Melbourne: Melbourne University Press, pp. 46–59.
—— (ed.) (1998), *The Explorers*, Melbourne: Text.
Flichy, P. (1995), *The Dynamics of Modern Communication: The Shaping and Impact of New Communication Technologies* (trans. L. Libbrecht), London: Sage.
Flink, J. (1988), *The Automobile Age*, Cambridge, Massachusetts: The MIT Press.
Foucault, M. (1970), *The Order of Things: An Archaeology of the Human Sciences*, London: Tavistock.
—— (1972), *The Archaeology of Knowledge* (trans. A. Sheridan Smith), London: Tavistock.
—— (1977), *Discipline and Punish: The Birth of the Prison* (trans. A. Sheridan), Harmondsworth: Penguin.
—— (1981), *History of Sexuality, Volume 1: An Introduction* (trans. R. Hurley), Harmondsworth: Penguin.
Fowler, A. (ed.) (1994), *The Country House Poem: A Cabinet of Seventeenth-Century Estate Poems and Related Items*, Edinburgh: Edinburgh University Press.
Fox, S. (1981), *John Muir and his Legacy: The American Conservation Movement*, Boston: Little, Brown.
Fraser, N. (1992), 'The Public Sphere: Alternative Histories, Competing Conceptions', in 'Rethinking the Public Sphere: A Contribution to the Critique of Actually Existing Democracy', in C. Calhoun (ed.), *Habermas and the Public Sphere*, Cambridge, Massachusetts: The MIT Press, pp. 112–118.
Frazier, C. (1997), *Cold Mountain*, London: Sceptre.
Freud, S. (1975), 'Findings, Ideas, Problems', in *Standard Edition of the Complete Psychological Works of Sigmund Freud, Volume XXIII*, London: Hogarth, pp. 299–300. First published 1938.
—— (1976), *The Interpretation of Dreams*, Pelican Freud Library, 4, Harmondsworth: Penguin. First published 1900.
—— (1984), 'The Economic Problem of Masochism', in *On Metapsychology: The Theory of Psychoanalysis*, Pelican Freud Library, 11, Harmondsworth: Penguin, pp. 413–426. First published 1924.

Frodeman, R. (1992), 'Radical Environmentalism and the Political Roots of Postmodernism: Differences that Make a Difference', *Environmental Ethics*, 14: 4, pp. 307–319.
Funk, R. (1959), 'The Wilderness', *Journal of Biblical Literature*, 78, pp. 205–214.
Gettler, L. (1993), *An Unpromised Land*, South Fremantle: Fremantle Arts Centre Press.
Giblett, R. (1996), *Postmodern Wetlands: Culture, History, Ecology*, Edinburgh: Edinburgh University Press.
—— (1997), 'Going Green', *Continuum*, 11: 2, pp. 128–139.
—— (2008a), *The Body of Nature and Culture*, Houndmills: Palgrave Macmillan.
—— (2008b), *Sublime Communication Technologies*, Houndmills: Palgrave Macmillan.
—— (2009), *Landscapes of Culture and Nature*, Houndmills: Palgrave Macmillan.
—— (forthcoming), *Black Swan Lake*.
—— and Webb, H. (1996), 'Living Water or Useless Swamps?', in R. Giblett and H. Webb (eds.), *Western Australian Wetlands: The Kimberley and South-West*, Perth, Western Australia: Black Swan Press/Wetlands Conservation Society, pp. 1–9.
Gibson, R. (1993), 'Camera Natura: Landscape in Australian Feature Films', in J. Frow and M. Morris (eds.), *Australian Cultural Studies: A Reader*, St Leonards, NSW: Allen and Unwin, pp. 209–221.
Gilbert, K. (ed.) (1988), *Inside Black Australia: An Anthology of Aboriginal Poetry*, Ringwood, Victoria: Penguin.
Gilpin, W. (1794), *Three Essays: on Picturesque Beauty; on Picturesque Travel; and on Sketching Landscape...*, Second Edition, London: A. Blamire.
Gimbutas, M. (1982), *The Goddesses and Gods of Old Europe 6500–3500BC: Myths and Cult Images*, Berkeley: University of California Press.
—— (1989), *The Language of the Goddess: Unearthing the Hidden Symbols of Western Civilization*, San Francisco: Harper and Row.
—— (1991), *The Civilization of the Goddess: The World of Old Europe*, San Francisco: Harper.
Godfrey, E. (1941), *Yosemite Indians*, Yosemite Natural History Association.
Godfrey-Smith, W. (1979), 'The Value of Wilderness', *Environmental Ethics*, 1, pp. 309–319.
Gottlieb, R. (1993), *Forcing the Spring: The Transformation of the American Environmental Movement*, Washington, D.C.: Island Press.
Greenblatt, S. (1989), 'Towards a Poetics of Culture', in H. Veeser (ed.), *The New Historicism*, New York: Routledge, pp. 1–14.
Griffin, S. (1978), *Woman and Nature: The Roaring Inside Her*, New York: Harper and Row.
Griffiths, T. (1996), *Hunters and Collectors: The Antiquarian Imagination in Australia*, Cambridge: Cambridge University Press.
—— (1997), 'Ecology and Empire: Towards an Australian history of the world', in T. Griffiths and L. Robin (eds.), *Ecology and Empire: Environmental History of Settler Societies*, Melbourne: Melbourne University Press, pp. 1–16.
—— (2002), '"The Outside Country"', in T. Griffiths and T. Bonyhady (eds.), *Words for Country: Landscape and Language in Australia*, Sydney: University of New South Wales Press, pp. 222–244.
Grishin, S. (1998), *John Wolseley: Land Marks*, North Ryde: Craftsman House.
Grove, R. (1995), *Green Imperialism: Colonial Expansion, Tropical Island Edens and the Origins of Environmentalism*, Cambridge: Cambridge University Press.
Guattari, F. (1989), 'The Three Ecologies', *New Formations*, 8, pp. 131–147.
—— (1995), *Chaosmosis: An Ethico-Aesthetic Paradigm* (trans. P. Bains and J. Pefanis), Sydney: Power.
Habermas, J. (1989), *The Structural Transformation of the Public Sphere: An Inquiry into a Category of Bourgeois Society* (trans. T. Burger) Cambridge: Polity Press.

References

Haggard, H. Rider (1989), *King Solomon's Mines*, Oxford: Oxford University Press. First published 1885.

Hall, C. (1992), *Wasteland to World Heritage: Preserving Australia's Wilderness*, Carlton: Melbourne University Press.

Haraway, D. (1978), 'Animal sociology and a natural economy of the body politic, Part one: A political physiology of dominance', *Signs*, 4: 1, pp. 21–36.

—— (1992), 'The Promises of Monsters: A Regenerative Politics for Inappropriate/d Others', in L. Grossberg, C. Nelson and P. Treichler (eds.), *Cultural Studies*, New York: Routledge, pp. 295–337.

—— (1995), 'Cyborgs and Symbionts: Living Together in the New World Order', in C. Gray (ed.), *The Cyborg Handbook*, London: Routledge, pp. xi–xx.

Harroy, J-P. (1968), 'The Development of the National Park Movement', in J. Nelson and R. Scace (eds.), *The Canadian National Parks, Today and Tomorrow*, Proceedings of a Conference Organized by the National and Provincial Parks Association of Canada and the University of Calgary, Calgary, Alberta, 9–15 October, Volume One, pp. 17–34.

Haynes, R. (1998), *Seeking the Centre: The Australian Desert in Literature, Art and Film*, Cambridge: Cambridge University Press.

Hegel, G. (2004), *Introductory Lectures on Aesthetics*, M. Inwood (ed.), (trans. B. Bosanquet.), London: Penguin.

Herman, E. and McChesney, R. (1997), *The Global Media: The New Missionaries of Corporate Capitalism*, London: Cassell.

Hirsch, E. (1995), 'Landscape: Between Place and Space', in E. Hirsch and M. O'Hanlon (eds.), *The Anthropology of Landscape*, Oxford: Clarendon Press, pp. 1–30.

—— and O'Hanlon, M. (eds.) (1995), *The Anthropology of Landscape*, Oxford: Clarendon Press.

Hirst, P. and Woolley, P. (1982), *Social Relations and Human Attributes*, London: Tavistock.

Hoagland, E. (1987), 'In Praise of John Muir', in D. Halpern (ed.), *On Nature: Nature, Landscape, and Natural History*, San Francisco: North Point Press, pp. 45–58.

Hore-Lacy, I. (1976), *Mining... and the Environment*, Australian Mining Industry Council.

Horigan, S. (1988), *Nature and Culture in Western Discourses*, London: Routledge.

Hügel, Baron C. von (1994), *New Holland Journal, November 1833–October 1834* (trans. and ed. D. Clark), Melbourne: Melbourne University Press.

Hunt, J. (1992), 'Sense and Sensibility in the Landscape Designs of Humphry Repton', in *Gardens and the Picturesque: Studies in the History of Landscape Architecture*, Cambridge, Massachusetts: The MIT Press, pp. 139–168.

Hutchinson, G. (1970), 'The Biosphere', in *The Biosphere: A Scientific American Book,* San Francisco: W. H. Freeman, pp. 3–11.

Hutton, D. and Connors, L. (1999), *A History of the Australian Environment Movement*, Cambridge: Cambridge University Press.

Ieramugadu Group (1995), *Know the Song, Know the Country: The Ngarda-ngali Story of Culture and History in the Roebourne District*, Roebourne: Ieramugadu Group.

Inglis, F. (1995), *Raymond Williams*, London: Routledge.

Irigaray, L. (1985), *Speculum of the Other Woman* (trans. G. Gill), Ithaca, New York: Cornell University Press.

Jacks, G. and Whyte, R. (1939), *The Rape of the Earth: A World Survey of Soil Erosion*, London: Faber and Faber.

Jacobs, M. (1989), 'Green Blues in Europe', *Australian Society*, August, pp. 32–33.

Jagtenberg, T. and McKie, D. (1997), *Eco-Impacts and the Greening of Postmodernity: New Maps for Communication Studies, Cultural Studies and Sociology*, Thousand Oaks: Sage.

Johns, E., Sayers, A. and Kornhauser, E. with Ellis, A. (1998), *New Worlds from Old: 19th Century Australian and American Landscapes*, Canberra: National Gallery of Australia; and Hartford, Connecticut: Wadsworth Atheneum.
Kant, I. (1952), *Critique of Judgement* (trans. J. Meredith), Oxford: Clarendon Press.
Klein, Melanie (1986), *The Selected Melanie Klein*, J. Mitchell (ed.), Harmondsworth: Penguin.
Klein, Milton (1980), 'On Mahler's Autistic and Symbiotic Phases: An Exposition and Evaluation', *Psychoanalysis and Contemporary Thought*, 4: 1, pp. 69–105.
Kolodny, A. (1975), *The Lay of the Land: Metaphor as Experience and History in American Life and Letters*, Chapel Hill: University of North Carolina Press.
—— (1984), *The Land Before Her: Fantasy and Experience of the American Frontiers 1630–1860*, Chapel Hill: University of North Carolina Press.
Kornhauser, E. (1998), '"All Nature here is new to Art": Painting the American Landscape 1800–1900', in *New Worlds from Old: 19th Century Australian and American Landscape*, Canberra: National Gallery of Australia; and Hartford, Connecticut: Wadsworth Atheneum, pp. 71–91.
Kristeva, J. (1982), *Powers of Horror: An Essay on Abjection* (trans. L. Roudiez), New York: Columbia University Press.
—— (1984), *Revolution in Poetic Language* (trans. M. Waller), New York: Columbia University Press.
—— (1995), *New Maladies of the Soul* (trans. R. Guberman), New York: Columbia University Press.
Kropotkin, P. (1989), *Mutual Aid: A Factor in Evolution*, Montreal: Black Rose Books. First published 1902.
Lamont, P. (1989), 'Rudall River: Danger in the Dust', *Habitat*, 17: 3, p. 13.
Landes, J. (1995), 'The Public and the Private Sphere: A Feminist Reconsideration', in J. Meehan (ed.), *Feminists Read Habermas: Gendering the Subject of Discourse*, New York: Routledge, pp. 91–116.
Landor, E. (1998), *The Bushman: Life in a New Country*, Twickenham: Tiger. First published 1847.
Lane, B. (1988), *Landscapes of the Sacred: Geography and Narrative in American Spirituality*, Mahwah, New Jersey: Paulist Press.
Langton, M. (1998), *Burning Questions: Emerging Environmental Issues for Indigenous Peoples in Northern Australia*, Darwin: Centre for Indigenous Natural and Cultural Resource Management, Northern Territory University.
Lawrence, D. H. (1950), *Kangaroo*, Harmondsworth: Penguin. First published 1923.
—— (1977), *Studies in Classic American Literature*, Harmondsworth: Penguin. First published 1923.
Lawson, H. (1976), *Portable Australian Authors: Henry Lawson*, B. Kiernan (ed.), St. Lucia: University of Queensland Press.
Leach, W. (1993), *Land of Desire: Merchants, Power and the Rise of a New American Culture*, New York: Random House.
Leopold, A. (1949), *A Sand County Almanac and Sketches Here and There*, New York: Oxford University Press.
—— (1972), *Round River: From the Journals of Aldo Leopold*, L. Leopold (ed.), Oxford: Oxford University Press.
—— (1986), *Game Management*, Madison: University of Wisconsin Press. First published 1933.
—— (1991), 'Land Pathology (1935)', in S. Flader and J. Callicott (eds.), *The River of the Mother of God and Other Essays*, Madison: University of Wisconsin Press, pp. 212–217.
Lesslie, R. and Maslen, M. (1995), *National Wilderness Inventory Australia: Handbook of Procedures, Content, and Usage*, Second Edition, Canberra: Australian Heritage Commission.
Lévi-Strauss, C. (1974), *Tristes Tropiques* (trans. J. and D. Weightman), New York: Atheneum.
Lindsay, J. (1970), *Picnic at Hanging Rock*, Harmondsworth: Penguin.
—— (1987), *The Secret of Hanging Rock*, North Ryde, NSW: Angus and Robertson.

Lines, W. (1991), *Taming the Great South Land: A History of the Conquest of Nature in Australia*, North Sydney: Allen and Unwin.
Linn, R. (1999), *Battling the Land: 200 Years of Rural Australia*, St Leonards, NSW: Allen and Unwin.
Lloyd, G. (1992), 'Greek Antiquity: The Invention of Nature', in J. Torrance (ed.), *The Concept of Nature: The Herbert Spencer Lectures*, Oxford: Clarendon Press, pp. 1–24.
Low, T. (1999), *Feral Future*, Ringwood, Victoria: Penguin.
—— (2002), *The New Nature*, Camberwell: Penguin.
Lyotard, J-F. (1993), '*Oikos*', in *Political Writings* (trans. B. Readings and K. Paul), Minneapolis: University of Minnesota Press, pp. 96–107.
—— (1984), *The Postmodern Condition: A Report on Knowledge* (trans. G. Bennington and B. Massumi), Manchester: Manchester University Press.
Mabey, R. (ed.) (1995), *The Oxford Book of Nature Writing*, Oxford: Oxford University Press.
MacCannell, D. (1976), *The Tourist: A New Theory of the Leisure Class*, London: Macmillan.
—— (1992), 'Nature Incorporated', in *Empty Meeting Grounds: The Tourist Papers*, London: Routledge, pp. 114–117.
Macherey, P. (1978), *A Theory of Literary Production* (trans. G. Wall), London: Routledge and Kegan Paul.
MacKenzie, J. (1988), *The Empire of Nature: Hunting, Conservation and British Imperialism*, Manchester: Manchester University Press.
Mahler, M. (1952), 'On Child Psychosis and Schizophrenia: Autistic and Symbiotic Infantile Psychoses', *The Psychoanalytic Study of the Child*, 7, pp. 286–305.
—— (1968), *On Human Symbiosis and the Vicissitudes of Individuation, Volume 1: Infantile Psychosis*, New York: International Universities Press.
—— (1972), 'On the First Three Sub-Phases of the Separation-Individuation Process', *International Journal of Psychoanalysis*, 53, pp. 333–338.
—— and Furer, M. (1966), 'Development of Symbiosis, Symbiotic Psychosis, and the Nature of Separation Anxiety...', *International Journal of Psychoanalysis*, 47, pp. 559–560.
——, Pine, F. and Bergman, A. (1975), *The Psychological Birth of the Human Infant: Symbiosis and Individuation*, New York: Basic Books.
Margulis, L. (1971), 'Symbiosis and Evolution', *Scientific American*, 225, pp. 49–57.
—— (1981), *Symbiosis in Cell Evolution: Life and its Environment on the Early Earth*, San Francisco: W. H. Freeman.
—— (1998), *Symbiotic Planet: A New Look at Evolution*, New York: Basic Books.
McCarthy, T. (1984), *The Critical Theory of Jürgen Habermas*, Cambridge: Polity Press.
McComb, A. and Lake, S. (1990), *Australian Wetlands*, North Ryde, NSW: Angus and Robertson.
McDivitt, J. and Manners, G. (1974), *Minerals and Men: An Exploration of Minerals and Metals, Including Some of the Major Problems That Are Posed*, Revised and Enlarged Edition, Baltimore: The Johns Hopkins University Press.
McKeown, F. (ed.) (1994), *Native Title: An Opportunity for Understanding*, Perth, Western Australia: National Native Title Tribunal.
McKibben, B. (1990), *The End of Nature*, London: Penguin.
McPhee, J. (1976), 'Travels in Georgia', in W. Howarth (ed.), *The John McPhee Reader*, New York: Farrar, Straus and Giroux, pp. 267–308.
—— (1981), *Basin and Range*, New York: Farrar, Straus and Giroux.
Merchant, C. (1980), *The Death of Nature: Women, Ecology and the Scientific Revolution*, San Francisco: Harper and Row.
—— (1992), *Radical Ecology: The Search for a Liveable World*, London: Routledge.

Meyers, G. (1994), 'Aboriginal Rights to the "Profits of the Land": The Inclusion of Traditional Fishing and Hunting Rights in the Content of Native Title', in G. Meyers and R. Bartlett (eds.), *Native Title Legislation in Australia*, Perth, Western Australia: The Centre for Commercial and Resources Law, University of Western Australia and Murdoch University, pp. 213-230.

Miller, P. (1956), 'Nature and the National Ego', in *Errand Into the Wilderness*, Cambridge, Massachusetts: Belknap Press of Harvard University Press, pp. 204-216.

—— (1967), 'The Romantic Dilemma in American Nationalism and the Concept of Nature', in *Nature's Nation*, Cambridge, Massachusetts: Belknap Press of Harvard University Press, pp. 197-207.

Mitchell, E. (1946), *Soil and Civilization*, Sydney: Angus and Robertson.

Mitchell, J. (1994), 'Our National Parks', *National Geographic*, 186: 4, pp. 2-55.

Moorehead, A. (1966), *The Fatal Impact: An Account of the Invasion of the South Pacific 1767-1840*, London: Hamish Hamilton.

Morgan, S. (1996), 'The Swamp Behind Our Place', in H. Webb and R. Giblett (eds.), *Western Australian Wetlands: The Kimberley and South-West*, Perth, Western Australia: Black Swan Press/Wetlands Conservation Society, p. 105.

Morlumbun, N. (1980), 'In the Beginning', in *Visions of Mowanjum: Aboriginal Writings from the Kimberley*, Adelaide: Rigby, pp. 10-16.

Morris, W. (1914), 'Art and the Beauty of Earth', in *Collected Works, Volume XXII*, London: Longmans Green, pp. 155-174.

Mowaljarlai, D. (1992), 'Wayrrull – Aboriginal Traditional Responsibility in Cultural Resource Management in the Northwest Kimberley of Western Australia', in J. Birckhead, T. de Lacy and L. Smith (eds.), *Aboriginal Involvement in Parks and Protected Areas*, Canberra: Aboriginal Studies Press, pp. 179-189.

—— (1993), *Yorro Yorro: Everything Standing Up Alive: Spirit of the Kimberley*, Broome: Magabala.

—— (1994), 'Ngarinyin Cosmology', in F. McKeown (ed.), *Native Title: An Opportunity for Understanding*, Perth, Western Australia: National Native Title Tribunal, pp. 59-60.

Mudrooroo/Johnson, C. (1979), *Long Live Sandawara*, Melbourne: Quartet.

Mudrooroo (1990), *Writing From the Fringe: A Study of Modern Aboriginal Literature*, Melbourne: Hyland House.

—— (1992), 'Digging the Mining Tour', in *North West Academic Staff Seminar: Commentary for a Tour of Pilbara Mining Operations by Academic Staff from the Perth University Campuses...*, 9-11 July, pp. 1-12.

—— (1994), *Aboriginal Mythology*, London: Harper Collins.

—— (1995), *Us Mob: History, Culture, Struggle: An Introduction to Indigenous Australia*, Pymble, NSW: Angus and Robertson.

—— (1996a), 'A Snake Story of the Nyoongah People: A Children's Tale', in H. Webb and R. Giblett (eds.), *Western Australian Wetlands: The Kimberley and South-West*, Perth, Western Australia: Black Swan Press/Wetlands Conservation Society, pp. 33 and 36-37.

—— (1996b), 'Sunlight Spreadeagles Perth in Blackness: A Bicentennial Gift Poem (Extracts)', in H. Webb and R. Giblett (eds.), *Western Australian Wetlands: The Kimberley and South-West*, Perth, Western Australia: Black Swan Press/Wetlands Conservation Society, p. 147.

Muir, J. (1979), 'Thoughts Upon National Parks', in L. Wolfe (ed.), *John of the Mountains: The Unpublished Journals of John Muir*, Madison: University of Wisconsin Press, pp. 350-354.

—— (1980), *Wilderness Essays*, F. Buske (ed.), Salt Lake City: Peregrine Smith.

—— (1987), *My First Summer in the Sierras*, New York: Penguin. First published 1911.

—— (1991), *Our National Parks*, San Francisco: Sierra Club Books. First published 1901.

—— (1992), *A Thousand-Mile Walk to the Gulf*, New York: Penguin. First published 1916.

Mulligan, M. and Hill, S. (2001), *Ecological Pioneers: A Social History of Australian Ecological Thought and Action*, Cambridge: Cambridge University Press.
Murray, J. (1995), *The Sierra Club Nature Writing Handbook: A Creative Guide*, San Francisco: Sierra Club Books.
Nabokov, V. (1971), *Ada, or Ardor: A Family Chronicle*, Harmondsworth: Penguin.
Nash, R. (1970), 'The American Invention of National Parks', *American Quarterly*, 22, pp. 726–735.
—— (1982), *Wilderness and the American Mind*, Third Edition, New Haven: Yale University Press.
Neumann, R. (1995), 'Ways of Seeing Africa: Colonial Recasting of African Society and Landscape in Serengeti National Park', *Ecumene*, 2, pp. 149–169.
Niering, W. (1966), *The Life of the Marsh: The North American Wetlands*, New York: McGraw Hill.
Oelschlaeger, M. (1991), *The Idea of Wilderness: From Prehistory to the Age of Ecology*, New Haven: Yale University Press.
Opie, J. (1986), 'The Environment and the Frontier', in R. Nichols (ed.), *American Frontier and Western Issues: A Historiographical Review*, Westport, Connecticut: Greenwood, pp. 7–25.
O'Regan, T. (1996), *Australian National Cinema*, London: Routledge.
Ortner, S. (1974), 'Is female to male as nature is to culture?', in M. Rosaldo and L. Lamphere (eds.), *Woman, Culture and Society*, Stanford: Stanford University Press, pp. 67–87.
Ouspensky, P. (1951), *Tertium Organum: The Third Canon of Thought: A Key to the Enigmas of the World*, Third Edition (trans. N. Bessaraboff and C. Bragdon), New York: Alfred A. Knopf.
Pliny the Elder (1991), *Natural History: A Selection* (trans. J. Healy), Harmondsworth: Penguin.
Plumwood, V. (1993), *Feminism and the Mastery of Nature*, London: Routledge.
Poynton, C. (1985), *Language and Gender: Making the Difference*, Geelong: Deakin University Press.
Pratt, M. (1992), *Imperial Eyes: Travel Writing and Transculturation*, London: Routledge.
Prichard, K. (1980), *Working Bullocks*, London: Angus and Robertson. First published 1926.
Pyne, S. (1997), *Vestal Fire: An Environmental History, Told through Fire, of Europe and Europe's Encounter with the World*, Seattle: University of Washington Press.
Repton, H. (1980), *Observations on the Theory and Practice of Landscape Gardening...*, Facsimile Edition, London: Phaidon. First published 1803.
Reynolds, H. (1982), *The Other Side of the Frontier: Aboriginal Resistance to the European Invasion of Australia*, Ringwood, Victoria: Penguin.
—— (1987), *Frontier: Aborigines, Settlers and Land*, Sydney: Allen and Unwin.
Rifkin, J. (1991), *Biosphere Politics: A New Consciousness for a New Century*, New York: Crown.
Robinson, J. (1980), 'Introduction', in Humphry Repton, *Observations on the Theory and Practice of Landscape Gardening...*, Facsimile Edition, London: Phaidon, unpaginated.
Rose, D. (1988), 'Exploring an Aboriginal Land Ethic', *Meanjin*, 47: 3, pp. 378–387.
—— (1996), *Nourishing Terrains: Australian Aboriginal Views of Landscape and Wilderness*, Canberra: Australian Heritage Commission.
Ross, A. (1994), *The Chicago Gangster Theory of Life: Nature's Debt to Society*, London: Verso.
Roszak, T. (1992), *The Voice of the Earth*, London: Bantam.
Rowse, T. (1993), *After Mabo: Interpreting Native Traditions*, Melbourne: Melbourne University Press.
—— (1996), 'Rationing the Inexplicable', in S. Morton and D. Mulvaney (eds.), *Exploring Central Australia: Society, the Environment and the 1894 Horn Expedition*, Chipping Norton, NSW: Surrey Beatty, pp. 104–113.
Rubin, G. (1975), 'The Traffic in Women: Notes on the "Political Economy" of Sex', in R. Reiter (ed.), *Toward an Anthropology of Women*, New York: Monthly Review Press, pp. 157–210.

Runte, A. (1977), 'The National Park Idea: Origins and Paradox of the American Experience', *Journal of Forest History*, 21: 1, pp. 64–75.
—— (1979), *National Parks: The American Experience*, Lincoln: University of Nebraska Press.
—— (1990), *Yosemite: The Embattled Wilderness*, Lincoln: University of Nebraska Press.
Ryan, S. (1996), *The Cartographic Eye: How Explorers Saw Australia*, Cambridge: Cambridge University Press.
Sabbioni, J., Schaffer, K. and Smith, S. (eds.) (1998), *Indigenous Australian Voices: A Reader*, New Brunswick, New Jersey: Rutgers University Press.
Sachs, W. (1992), *For Love of the Automobile: Looking Back in the History of Our Desires* (trans. D. Reneau), Berkeley: University of California Press.
Sale, K. (1985), *Dwellers in the Land: The Bioregional Vision*, San Francisco: Sierra Club Books.
—— (2001), 'There's No Place Like Home', *The Ecologist*, 31: 2, pp. 40–43.
Sanderson, E. (2009), *Mannahatta: A Natural History of New York City*, New York: Abrams.
Santamaria, B. (nd, ?1945), *The Earth – Our Mother*, Melbourne: Araluen.
Schaffer, K. (1988), *Women and the Bush: Forces of Desire in the Australian Cultural Tradition*, Cambridge: Cambridge University Press.
Schama, S. (1995), *Landscape and Memory*, London: HarperCollins.
Schiebinger, L. (1993), *Nature's Body: Sexual Politics and the Making of Modern Science*, London: Pandora.
Sears, J. (1989), *Sacred Places: American Tourist Attractions in the Nineteenth Century*, New York: Oxford University Press.
Seddon, G. (1997), *Landprints: Reflections on Place and Landscape*, Cambridge: Cambridge University Press.
Serres, M. (1982), *The Parasite* (trans. L. Schehr), Baltimore: The Johns Hopkins University Press.
—— (1995), *The Natural Contract* (trans. E. MacArthur and W. Paulson), Ann Arbor: University of Michigan Press.
Sheldrake, R. (1991), *The Rebirth of Nature: The Greening of Science and God*, New York: Bantam.
Shepard, P. (1991), *Man in the Landscape: A Historic View of the Esthetics of Nature*, College Station: Texas A&M University Press. First published 1967.
Sjöö, M. and Mor, B. (1991), *The Great Cosmic Mother: Rediscovering the Religion of the Earth*, San Francisco: Harper.
Slotkin, R. (1973), *Regeneration Through Violence: The Mythology of the American Frontier 1600–1860*, Hanover: Wesleyan University Press.
—— (1992), *Gunfighter Nation: The Myth of the Frontier in Twentieth-Century America*, New York: HarperCollins.
—— (1994), *The Fatal Environment: The Myth of the Frontier in the Age of Industrialization 1800–1890*, New York: HarperCollins.
Smith, B. (1985), *European Vision and the South Pacific*, Second Edition, New Haven: Yale University Press.
Smith, F. (1979), 'National Parks Western Australia', *Australia's One Hundred Years of National Parks*, Reprint from *Parks and Wildlife*, 2: 3–4, pp. 108–112.
Smith, H. (1950), *Virgin Land: The American West as Symbol and Myth*, Cambridge, Massachusetts: Harvard University Press.
Sofia, Z. (1989), 'The Hyperreal and the Overworked: A Philosophical View of Metro Mania', *Praxis M*, 24/*Arx 1989 Journal: Metro Mania*, pp. 5–10.
Sofoulis, Z. (1983), 'Alien Pre-Oedipus: Penis Breast, Cannibaleyes', Qualifying Essay, History of Consciousness, Santa Cruz, University of California.

—— (1984), 'Exterminating Fetuses: Abortion, Disarmament, and the Sexo-Semiotics of Extraterrestrialism', *Diacritics*, 14: 2, pp. 47–59.

—— (1988), *Through the Lumen: Frankenstein and the Optics of Re-Origination*, Ph.D. Thesis, History of Consciousness, Santa Cruz, University of California.

Soper, K. (1995), *What is Nature? Culture, Politics and the Non-Human*, Oxford: Blackwell.

Spearitt, P. and Stephen, A. (1992), 'The Selling of the Land', *The Australian Magazine*, 22–23 February, pp. 26–30.

Spretnak, C. (1997), *The Resurgence of the Real: Body, Nature and Place in a Hypermodern World*, Reading, Massachusetts: Addison-Wesley.

Steinberg, I. (1948), *Australia– The Unpromised Land: In Search of A Home*, London: Gollancz.

Steiner, U. (2010), *Walter Benjamin: An Introduction to his Work and Thought* (trans. M. Winkler), Chicago: University of Chicago Press.

Stern, D. (1985), *The Interpersonal World of the Infant: A View from Psychoanalysis and Developmental Psychology*, New York: Basic Books.

Stevens, S. (1986), 'Inhabited National Parks: Indigenous Peoples in Protected Landscapes', *East Kimberley Impact Assessment Project*, East Kimberley, Working Paper No.10.

Stewart, F. (1995). *A Natural History of Nature Writing*, Washington D.C.: Island Press.

Stow, R. (1958), *To the Islands*, Ringwood, Victoria: Penguin.

Strang, V. (1997), *Uncommon Ground: Cultural Landscapes and Environmental Values*, Oxford: Berg.

Suzuki, D. (1998), *Earth Time*, St Leonards, NSW: Allen and Unwin.

—— with McConnell, A. (1997), *The Sacred Balance: Rediscovering our Place in Nature*, St Leonards, NSW: Allen and Unwin.

Swimme, B. and Berry, T. (1992), *The Universe Story: From the Primordial Flaring Forth to the Ecozoic Era – A Celebration of the Unfolding of the Cosmos*, San Francisco: Harper.

Tacey, D. (1995), *Edge of the Sacred: Transformation in Australia*, North Blackburn, Victoria: HarperCollins.

Thayer, R. (1994), *Gray World, Green Heart: Technology, Nature and the Human Landscape*, New York: John Wiley.

Theweleit, K. (1987), *Male Fantasies, Volume I: Women, Floods, Bodies, History* (trans. S. Conway), Cambridge: Polity Press.

—— (1989), *Male Fantasies, Volume II: Male Bodies: Psychoanalyzing the White Terror* (trans. C. Turner and E. Carter), Cambridge: Polity Press.

Thomas, K. (1984), *Man and the Natural World: Changing Attitudes in England 1500–1800*, Harmondsworth: Penguin.

Thompson, J. (1995), *The Media and Modernity: A Social Theory of the Media*, Cambridge: Polity Press.

Thompson, P. (ed.) (1986), *Miles Dunphy: Selected Writings*, Sydney: Ballagirin.

Thomson, A. (1999), *The Singing Line*, London: Chatto and Windus.

Thoreau, H. (1962), *The Journal of Henry D. Thoreau, Volumes I – XIV*, B. Torrey and F. Allen (eds.), New York: Dover.

—— (1980), *Natural History Essays*, Salt Lake City: Gibbs Smith.

—— (1982), *The Portable Thoreau*, C. Bode (ed.), New York: Penguin.

—— (1988), *The Maine Woods*, New York: Penguin. First published 1864.

—— (1998), *A Week on the Concord and Merrimack Rivers*, New York: Penguin. First published 1849.

—— (2000), *Wild Fruits: Thoreau's Rediscovered Last Manuscript*, B. Dean (ed.), New York: Norton.

Threadgold, T. (1988), 'Language and Gender', *Australian Feminist Studies*, 6, pp. 41–70.

Tilden, F. (1970), *The National Parks*, Revised and Enlarged Edition, New York: Alfred A. Knopf.
Todorov, T. (1984), *The Conquest of America: The Question of the Other* (trans. R. Howard), New York: Harper and Row.
Trager, W. (1970), *Symbiosis*, New York: Van Nostrand Reinhold.
Trigger, D. (1997), 'Mining, Landscape and the Culture of Development Ideology in Australia', *Ecumene*, 4: 2, pp. 161–180.
Trollope, A. (1987), *Australia, Volumes I and II*, Gloucester: Alan Sutton. First published 1873.
Turner, F. (1985), *Rediscovering America: John Muir in his Time and Ours*, New York: Viking.
Turner, F. (1961), 'The Significance of the Frontier in American History', in *Frontier and Section: Selected Essays of Frederick Jackson Turner*, Englewood Cliffs: Prentice-Hall, pp. 37–62.
Turner, G. (1990), *British Cultural Studies: An Introduction*, London: Unwin Hyman.
Vernadsky, W. (1945), 'The Biosphere and the Noösphere', *American Scientist*, 33, pp. 1–12.
Virilio, P. (1989), *War and Cinema: The Logistics of Perception* (trans. P. Camiller), London: Verso.
—— (1998), *Open Sky* (trans. J. Rose), London: Verso.
—— (2009), *Grey Ecology* (trans. D. Burk), New York: Atropos.
Wallace-Crabbe, C. (1992), 'Escaping Landscape', in J Carroll (ed.), *Intruders in the Bush: The Australian Quest for Identity*, Second Edition, Melbourne: Oxford University Press, pp. 157–180.
Walsh, F. (1992), 'The Relevance of Some Aspects of Aboriginal Subsistence Activities to the Management of National Parks: With Reference to Martu People of the Western Desert', in J. Birckhead, T. de Lacy and L. Smith (eds.), *Aboriginal Involvement in Parks and Protected Areas*, Canberra: Aboriginal Studies Press, pp. 75–97.
Wark, M. (1994), 'Third Nature', *Cultural Studies*, 8: 1, pp. 115–132.
Warming, E. (1909), *Oecology of Plants: An Introduction to the Study of Plant Communities*, Oxford: Clarendon Press.
Watson, H. (1989), *Singing the Land, Signing the Land: A Portfolio of Exhibits*, Geelong: Deakin University Press.
Webb, H. (1996), 'Aboriginal Country: Not a Construction, a Way of Being', in H. Webb and R. Giblett (eds.), *Western Australian Wetlands: The Kimberley and South-West*, Perth, Western Australia: Black Swan Press/Wetlands Conservation Society, pp. 61–75.
Wescott, G. (1993), 'Loving Our Parks to Death? A Cautionary Tale', *Habitat*, 21: 1, pp. 13–19.
West, P. and Brechin, S. (eds.) (1991), *Resident Peoples and National Parks: Social Dilemmas and Strategies in International Conservation*, Tucson: University of Arizona Press.
Western Desert Working Group (1989), *The Significance of the Karlamilyi Region to the Martujarra of the Western Desert*, Prepared for the Department of Conservation and Land Management on Behalf of the Western Desert Puntukurnuparna Aboriginal Corporation.
White, G. (1987), *The Natural History of Selborne*, R. Mabey (ed.), London: Penguin. First published 1788–1799.
White, R. (1981), *Inventing Australia: Images and Identity 1688–1980*, Sydney: George Allen and Unwin.
Whitebook, J. (1979), 'The Problem of Nature in Habermas', *Telos*, 40, pp. 41–69.
Whitman, W. (1945), *The Portable Walt Whitman*, M. Van Doren (ed.), New York: Penguin.
—— (1982), *Complete Poetry and Collected Prose*, New York: Library of America.
Wilding, M. (1986), '"Weird Melancholy": Inner and Outer Landscapes in Marcus Clarke's Stories', in P. Eaden and F. Mares (eds.), *Mapped But Not Known: The Australian Landscape of the Imagination...*, Kent Town: Wakefield, pp. 128–145.
Williams, D. (1996), 'Mapping the Imaginary: Ross Gibson's *Camera Natura*, with *Camera Natura*: Shooting Script by Ross Gibson and John Cruthers', *The Moving Image*, 4, pp. 4–105.

Williams, R. (1972), 'Ideas of Nature', in J. Benthall (ed.), *Ecology, the Shaping Enquiry*, London: Longman, pp. 146–164.
—— (1973), *The Country and the City*, London: Chatto and Windus.
—— (1976), 'Culture' and 'Nature', in *Keywords: A Vocabulary of Culture and Society*, Glasgow: Fontana, pp. 76–82 and 184–189.
—— (1984), 'Between Country and City', in R. Mabey (ed.), *Second Nature*, London: Cape, pp. 209–219.
—— (1985), *Towards 2000*, Harmondsworth: Penguin.
—— (1989a), *The Politics of Modernism: Against the New Conformists*, T. Pinkney (ed.), London: Verso.
—— (1989b), 'Socialism and Ecology (1982)', in R. Gable (ed.), *Resources of Hope: Culture, Democracy, Socialism*, London: Verso, pp. 210–226.
Wilson, A. (1992), *The Culture of Nature: North American Landscape From Disney to the Exxon Valdez*, Cambridge, Massachusetts: Blackwell.
Woenne-Green, S., Johnston, R., Sultan, R. and Willis, A. (no date), *Competing Interests: Aboriginal Participation in National Parks and Conservation Reserves in Australia, A Summary*, Fitzroy: Australian Conservation Foundation.
Wolfe, L. (1945), *Son of the Wilderness*, New York: Alfred A. Knopf.
Woodring, C. (1989), *Nature into Art: Cultural Transformations in Nineteenth-Century Britain*, Cambridge, Massachusetts: Harvard University Press.
Wootten, H. (no date), 'The Mabo Decision and National Parks', in S. Woenne-Green, R. Johnston, R. Sultan and A. Willis, *Competing Interests: Aboriginal Participation in National Parks and Conservation Reserves in Australia, A Summary*, Fitzroy: Australian Conservation Foundation, unpaginated.
Wordsworth, W. (1906), *Guide to the Lakes: Fifth Edition (1835)*, Oxford: Oxford University Press.
—— (1972), *The Prelude: A Parallel Text*, J. Maxwell (ed.), London: Penguin.
Worster, D. (1993), *The Wealth of Nature: Environmental History and the Ecological Imagination*, New York: Oxford University Press.
—— (2008), *A Passion for Nature: The Life of John Muir*, Oxford: Oxford University Press.
Wright, J. (1991), 'Australian Wilderness and Wasteland', in *Born of the Conquerors: Selected Essays*, Canberra: Aboriginal Studies Press, pp. 143–150.
Ziff, L. (1991), *Writing in the New Nation: Prose, Print and Politics in the United States*, New Haven: Yale University Press.
Zimmerman, M. (1994), *Contesting Earth's Future: Radical Ecology and Postmodernity*, Berkeley: University of California Press.
Zola, É. (1954), *Germinal* (trans. L. Tancock), London: Penguin.

Index

Aboriginal Country 10, 12, 16, 91-94, 219-236
Abraham, K. 180, 202, 208-211, 213, 215
Adorno, T. 63, 72-73, 75
   and M. Horkheimer 29
Althusser, L. 254
Andrews, M. 74, 86, 165
Appleton, J. 108
Arendt, H. 43-45
Athanisiou, T. 49
Austen, J. 82-91
Australian
   bush 11, 12, 97, 124-134, 223-224
   desert 223-224, 232
   frontier 105-107, 108, 110-111,
   gentleman's park 60, 91-94
   landscape 97, 119-126, 132-134, 223-224
   mateship 11, 126-129
   sublime 232
   wilderness 97, 101-103, 226

Bachelor Machines for Bachelor Births 69, 76n2, 127, 193
Bakhtin, M. 38n3, 193
Barnard Eldershaw, M. 124, 127, 129, 133
Barrell, J. 68, 82, 85, 90, 91
Barnes, J. 120, 125
Barthes, R. 74, 168,
Baudrillard, J. 193
Beauvoir, S. de 29
Bender, B. 67
Benjamin, J. 180, 220, 250-251, 253
Benjamin, W. 38n27, 38n28, 144, 163, 186, 196-197, 256
Bennett, A. 86
Bennett, T. 109

Bermingham, A. 66
Berry, T. 242, 244
Berry, W. 51
bioregion 10, 11, 220, 239-250, 257
Bonaparte, M. 188-189
Bonyhady, T. 64, 92, 130, 204
Bookchin, M. 142
Brady, V. 67
Briggs, R. 65-66
Brontë, C. 34-37
Brown, C. 232
Brown, E. 190
Brown, N. 194
Buber, M. 38 n13, 38n14
Buell, L. 149
Bulletin School 97, 132
Burke, E. 112, 216n4
Burn, I. 129-130, 131-132

Carroll, J. 121, 134,
Carruthers, J. 164
Carter, P. 38n23, 105, 108,
Catlin, G. 141, 166-168
Certeau, M. de 16, 38n25, 52, 75, 76n2, 198n6,
Cicero 15, 21-22
Clarke, M. 125, 132-134
Clunies–Ross, B. 120
Coetzee, J. 67, 76, 104-105, 116n3
Cohen, M. 163, 169, 175n8
Collingwood, R. 24-25, 257
Collins, T. 123-125, 128
Conley, V. 51, 52, 54, 55, 184,
conservation counter–aesthetics 10, 59, 64, 72-76,
Cook, J. 22, 92

Cosgrove, D. 67.
Cronon, W. 109, 149
Crosby, A. 50

Darwin, C. 254-256
Deleuze, G and F. Guattari 255
Derrida, J. 16, 43, 54, 202, 208, 226
Dodson, M. 227
Douglas, M. 171, 183-184, 206
Dunphy, M. 170-171
Durack, M. 201-216

Eagleton, T. 147
ecology
  generalized 53, 240
  grey 52
  home 56n3
  participatory, postmodern, political 10, 11, 16, 17, 27, 41, 45-46, 47, 50, 52-55, 141, 240
  psychoanalytic 11, 179-216
  third 53-54
  third term of 54-55
ecosphere 10, 16, 17, 44-47, 220, 230, 252
Eldershaw, F. 127-128

filiarchal 32, 37n6, 194
Flannery, T. 110-111, 128, 256
Flink, J. 159-160
Foucault, M. 15, 24-26, 27, 160
Fraser, N. 48-49
Frazier, C. 244
Freud, S. 64-65, 106, 133, 144. 179, 180, 187, 189, 194, 205, 208. 209, 216n8, 248, 254
Frodeman, R. 52

Gibson, R. 119-121, 124, 141n1
Gilbert, K. 226,
Gilpin, W. 71. 75-76, 143
Gimbutas, M. 30
Godfrey-Smith, W. 102, 254-255
Gottlieb, R. 109
Griffiths, T. 27, 92-93, 106-108, 110
Griffin, S. 185-186
Guattari, F. 53

Habermas, J. 41-51
Haggard, R. 106

Haraway, D. 28-29, 49, 246
Haynes, R. 223, 232
Heidelberg School 97, 121, 124, 127, 131-132, 134
Hirsch, E. 67-68
Hunt, J. 87-88
Hutton, D. and L. Connors 244

Irigaray, L. 29

Jagtenberg, T. and D. McKie 51, 54-55, 240

Klein, M. 180, 184, 187-194, 196
Kristeva, J. 10, 133, 208
Kropotkin, P. 255, 256

landscape 9, 11, 22, 25, 26, 59-60, 63, 67-68, 74, 76, 89-91, 224-228, 232-234
landscape writing 26-27, 65, 69
Lane, B. 143, 165
Langton, M. 226, 231, 233, 234
Lawrence, D. 106, 122-123, 134, 168, 195
Lawson, H. 114, 125, 127, 130-134
Leopold, A. 51, 72-73, 111, 114, 146, 180, 184, 209, 244, 255
Lévi-Strauss, C. 74-75
Lindsay, J. 121-122
livelihood 220, 239-243
Low, T. 23, 37n1, 256,
Lyotard, J-F. 43-44, 173

Macarthur, E. 92
Macarthur, J. 106
MacCannell, D. 75, 159, 170, 172
Macherey, P. 208
MacKenzie, J. 50, 145, 163
Mahler, M. 180, 220, 239, 248-252
Margulis, L. 220, 239, 246-247, 253
Marshall, B. 101
Marx, K. 101, 254-255
McKibben, B. 24,
McPhee, J. 245
Merchant, C. 24, 49, 185
Meyers, G. 162-163, 174n4, 174n9
Miller, P. 148, 153-154, 163
Mitchell, E. 244-245, 258n2
Moorehead, A. 79, 91

Morgan, S. 228
Morris, W. 76
Mowaljarlai, D. 228, 230, 233, 235, 236n1, 236n7
Mudrooroo 186, 202, 214-216, 225, 227-235, 236n2
Muir, J. 109, 137, 141-156, 156n1-3, n4-6, n8-9
Mulligan, M. and S. Hill 107, 133, 244

Nabokov, V. 94n1, 209
Nash, R. 107, 152, 166-167, 170
nature/s, 10, 12, 15, 17, 21-22, 24-25, 28-29, 31, 41-43, 50-53, 83-84, 91
   aesthetics of, 9-10, 26, 43, 50, 59-60, 63-73, 75-76, 91, 159-160, 203-204
   birth of, 24
   conquest/colonisation/empire of, 9, 16, 49-50, 55, 145, 161, 164
   culture/s of, 10, 15, 21-23, 25, 31, 33-34, 37, 41, 73
   death of, 24-27, 30, 43, 91
   decolonisation of, 16-17, 50, 53-55
   discourse/s of, 9, 12, 15, 24-29, 43, 53, 59, 83, 91, 112, 160, 189
   feminisation/gendered construction of, 11, 15-16, 27, 29-37, 41-42, 44, 49-50, 109, 121, 183
   history of, 23-24
   rebirth of, 24, 27
   writing 26-27, 37n3, 73
Neumann, R. 145, 167

Oelschlaeger, M. 10, 30, 107,
Oodgeroo 184, 191, 233-234,
O'Regan, T. 120
–ospheres 17, 41-42, 44, 47, 55
Ouspensky, P. 257

pastoro–technical idyll 16, 60, 69, 81, 169
Pliny the Elder 185
Prichard, K. 128, 134
Pyne, S. 107

Repton, H. 84, 87-88
Reynolds, H. 105-106
Rose, D. 92, 107, 225-227, 230-231, 233, 236n3
Ross, A. 28, 108, 163, 243
Roszak, T. 246, 256

Rowse, T. 128, 164
Rubin, G. 194
Runte, A. 145, 159-160, 162-163, 165-166, 171
Ryan, S. 84, 93

Sabbioni, J. 225, 228, 232
Sachs, W. 68
sacrality 10, 16, 31, 34, 219
Sale, K. 242, 245-247
sanctuarism 9-10, 16, 31, 34, 141, 146
Schaffer, K. 134n3, 228
Schama, S. 165
Sears, J. 74, 143, 163-164, 175n8
Seddon, G. 24, 93, 126
Serres, M. 31, 51-53, 55, 242, 251-253
Sheldrake, R. 24, 142, 145-146, 152-153
Shepard, P. 159, 163, 165-166, 175n8
Slotkin, R. 109, 151, 154-155, 172-173
Smith, H. 75
Sofia/Sofoulis, Z. 7, 31, 64, 150, 184, 187, 198n2, 204
Spretnak, C. 245
Stern, D. 250
Stevens, S. 167
Stow, R. 214-215
Suzuki, D. 184, 245-246
Swallow, E. 38n31, 56n3
symbiosis, bio– and psycho– 11, 12, 32, 47, 50, 52, 53, 180, 187, 219-220, 234, 239, 246-254

Tacey, D. 133-134, 232
Thayer, R. 187
Theweleit, K. 194
Thompson, J. 41-42, 45-46, 48
Thoreau, H. 26-27, 73, 108, 111-115, 116n10, 143, 149-151, 167, 244, 257
Tilden, F. 141, 149, 163, 168
Trollope, A. 97, 124-126, 129, 195
Turner, F. 103, 111
Turner, G. 240

Vernadsky, V. 257
Virilio, P. 52, 54, 144-145

Wallace–Crabbe, C. 232
Wark, McK. 22-23
Webb, H. 224, 227-228, 230

West, E. 187, 189, 233
Wharton, H. 93, 230
White, G. 26
White, R. 130, 132
Whitman, W. 150, 257-258
Wilding, M. 132
Williams, R. ii, 21, 34, 65-67, 83-86, 90-91, 220, 239-242, 243, 258n1
Williams, N. 230
Wilson, A. ii, 15, 21, 170, 173, 240

Wordsworth, W. 26-27, 65, 68-71, 74, 76, 80-82, 89
Worster, D. 141, 146, 151, 156n1, 156n2
Wright, J. 67, 92

Yunupingu, G. 219, 228, 235

Ziff, L. 165
Zimmerman, M. 142, 153
Zola, É. 195